# THE ROAD TO UNFREEDOM

# THE ROAD

## TO

# UNFREEDOM

RUSSIA, EUROPE, AMERICA

TIMOTHY SNYDER

TIM
DUGGAN
BOOKS

NEW YORK

Copyright © 2018 by Timothy Snyder

All rights reserved.

Published in the United States by Tim Duggan Books,
an imprint of the Crown Publishing Group, a division of
Penguin Random House LLC, New York.
crownpublishing.com

TIM DUGGAN BOOKS and the Crown colophon are trademarks
of Penguin Random House LLC.

Library of Congress Cataloging-in-Publication Data is available upon request.

Hardcover ISBN 978-0-525-57446-0
Ebook ISBN 978-0-525-57448-4
International Edition ISBN 978-0-525-57540-5

PRINTED IN THE UNITED STATES OF AMERICA

*Jacket design by Christopher Brand*
*Maps by Beehive Mapping*

Page 32: (left) photo of Vladimir Ilyich Lenin c. 1917: Universal History Archive/
Getty Images; (right) photo of Ivan Alexandrovich Ilyin c. 1920: Fine Art Images/
Heritage Images/Getty Images

Page 149: image of two flags: Konstantinks/Getty Images

Page 159: Paul Celan, Mohn und Gedächtnis © 1952, Deutsche Verlags-Anstalt,
München, in der Verlagsgruppe Random House GmbH

10 9 8 7 6 5 4 3 2 1

First Edition

*For the reporters, the heroes of our time*

# CONTENTS

# PROLOGUE (2010)

**M**y son was born in Vienna. It was a difficult delivery, and the first concern of the Austrian obstetrician and the Polish midwife was the baby. He breathed, his mother held him for a moment, and then she was wheeled to an operating room. The midwife, Ewa, handed him to me. My son and I were a bit lost in what happened next, but we stuck together. He was looking upward with unfocused violet eyes as the surgeons ran past us at a dead sprint, footfalls and snaps of masks, a blur of green scrubs.

The next day all seemed well. The nurses instructed me to depart the ward at the normal time, five o'clock in the afternoon, leaving mother and child in their care until the morning. I could now, a little belatedly, send out a birth announcement by email. Some friends read the good news at the same moment that they learned of a catastrophe that took the lives of others. One friend, a fellow scholar whom I had met in Vienna in a different century, had rushed to board an airplane in Warsaw. My message went out at the speed of light, but it never caught up to him.

———

**THE YEAR 2010** was a time of reflection. A financial crisis two years before had eliminated much of the world's wealth, and a halting recovery was favoring the rich. An African American was president of the United States. The great adventure of Europe in the 2000s, the enlargement of the European Union to the east, seemed complete. A decade into the twenty-first century, two decades away from the end of communism in Europe, seven decades after the beginning of the Second World War, 2010 seemed like a year for reckonings.

I was working on one that year with a historian in his time of dying. I admired Tony Judt most for his history of Europe, *Postwar*, published in 2005. It recounted the improbable success of the European Union in assembling imperial fragments into the world's largest economy and most important zone of democracy. The book had concluded with a meditation on the memory of the Holocaust of the Jews of Europe. In the twenty-first century, he suggested, procedures and money would not be enough: political decency would require a history of horror.

In 2008, Tony had fallen ill with amyotrophic lateral sclerosis (ALS), a degenerative neurological disorder. He was certain to die, trapped in a body that would not serve his mind. After Tony lost the use of his hands, we began recording conversations on themes from the twentieth century. We were both worried, as we spoke in 2009, by the American assumptions that capitalism was unalterable and democracy inevitable. Tony had written of the irresponsible intellectuals who aided totalitarianism in the twentieth century. He was now concerned about a new irresponsibility in the twenty-first: a total rejection of ideas that flattened discussion, disabled policy, and normalized inequality.

As he and I spoke, I was writing a history of the political mass murders committed by Nazi Germany and the Soviet Union in the Europe of the 1930s and 1940s. It began with people and their homes, in particular the Jews, Belarusians, Ukrainians, Russians,

2

Balts, and Poles who had experienced both regimes in the places where Nazi and Soviet power overlapped. Although the book's chapters were grim—planned starvations, death pits, gas chambers—its premise was optimistic: the causes of mass murder could be ascertained, the words of the dead recalled. The truth could be told, and lessons could be learned.

A chapter of that book was devoted to a turning point of the twentieth century: the Nazi-Soviet alliance that began the Second World War in Europe. In September 1939, Nazi Germany and the Soviet Union both invaded Poland, each with the goal of destroying the Polish state and the Polish political class. In April 1940, the Soviet secret police murdered 21,892 Polish prisoners of war, most of them educated reserve officers. The men (and one woman) were shot in the back of the head at five killing sites, one of them the Katyn Forest, near Smolensk in the Russian republic of the Soviet Union. For Poles, the Katyn massacre came to stand for Soviet repression generally.

After the Second World War, Poland was a communist regime and a Soviet satellite, so Katyn could not be discussed. Only after the dissolution of the Soviet Union in 1991 could historians clarify what had happened. Soviet documents left no doubt that the mass murder had been deliberate policy, personally approved by Joseph Stalin. Since the end of the Soviet Union, the new Russian Federation had been struggling to address the legacy of Stalinist terror. On February 3, 2010, as I was finishing my book, the Russian prime minister made a surprising proposal to his Polish counterpart: a joint commemoration of Katyn that April, on the seventieth anniversary of the crime. At midnight on the first of April, the day my son was due to be born, I sent my book to the publisher. On the seventh of April a Polish governmental delegation, led by the Polish prime minister, arrived in Russia. The next day my wife gave birth.

Two days after that, a second Polish delegation set out for Russia. It included the Polish president and his wife, commanders of the Polish armed forces, parliamentary deputies, civic activists, priests, and family members of those murdered at Katyn in 1940. One of its members was my friend Tomek Merta, an admired political theorist—and the vice minister of culture responsible for commemoration. Early in the morning of Saturday, April 10, 2010, Tomek boarded an airplane. It crashed at 8:41 a.m., short of a landing strip at the Russian military airfield at Smolensk. There were no survivors. In a maternity ward in Vienna a cell phone rang, and a new mother shouted in Polish across the room.

The next evening, I read the responses to my birth announcement. One friend was concerned that I understand the tragedy amidst my own joy: "So that you don't find yourself in a difficult situation, I have to tell you that Tomek Merta was killed." Another friend, whose name was on the passenger list, wrote to say that he had changed his mind and stayed home. His wife was due to give birth a few weeks later.

He signed off: "Henceforth everything will be different."


IN AUSTRIAN maternity wards, mothers stay for four days, so that nurses can teach about feeding, bathing, and care. This is long enough for families to become acquainted, for parents to learn what languages they share, for conversations to begin. The following day in the maternity ward the talk in Polish was of conspiracy. Rumors had taken shape: the Russians had shot down the airplane; the Polish government had been in on the plot to kill the Polish president, who was of a different party than the prime minister. A new Polish mother asked me what I thought. I said that this was all very unlikely.

The day after that, my family was allowed to go home. With the baby sleeping in a basket, I wrote two articles about Tomek: one an obituary in Polish, the other an account of the disaster in English that concluded with a hopeful word about Russia. A Polish president had lost his life hastening to commemorate a crime committed on Russian soil. I expressed the hope that the Russian prime minister, Vladimir Putin, would use the occasion to consider the history of Stalinism more broadly. Perhaps that was a reasonable appeal amidst grief in April 2010; as a prediction, it could not have been more wrong.

Henceforth everything was different. Putin, who had already served two terms as president before becoming prime minister, announced in September 2011 that he wanted to be president again. His party did poorly in parliamentary elections that December, but was granted a majority in parliament regardless. Putin became president again in May 2012 after another election that seemed flawed. He then saw to it that discussions of the Soviet past, such as the one he himself had initiated about Katyn, would be treated as criminal offenses. In Poland, the Smolensk catastrophe united society for a day, and then polarized it for years. The obsession with the disaster of April 2010 grew with time, crowding out the Katyn massacre that its victims had meant to commemorate, indeed crowding out all historical episodes of Polish suffering. Poland and Russia had ceased to reflect on history. Times were changing. Or perhaps our sense of time was changing.

The European Union fell under a shadow. Our Vienna maternity ward, where inexpensive insurance covered everything, was a reminder of the success of the European project. It exemplified services that were taken for granted in much of Europe but were unthinkable in the United States. The same might be said of the quick and reliable subway that brought me to the hospital: normal in Europe, unattainable in America. In 2013, Russia turned against the European Union, condemning it as decadent and hostile. Its success might encourage Russians to think that former empires could become prosperous democracies, and so its existence was suddenly at risk.

As Russia's neighbor Ukraine drew closer to the European Union, Russia invaded the country and annexed some of its territory in 2014. By 2015, Russia had extended an extraordinary campaign of cyberwarfare beyond Ukraine to Europe and the United States, with the assistance of numerous Europeans and Americans. In 2016, the British voted to leave the European Union, as Moscow had long advocated, and Americans elected Donald Trump as their president, an outcome Russians had worked to achieve. Among other shortcomings, this new U.S. president could not reflect upon history: he was unable to commemorate the Holocaust when the occasion arose, nor condemn Nazis in his own country.

The twentieth century was well and truly over, its lessons unlearned. A new form of politics was emerging in Russia, Europe, and America, a new unfreedom to suit a new time.

I WROTE those two articles about the Smolensk disaster after years of thinking about the politics of life and death, on a night when the membrane between them seemed thin. "Your happiness amidst unhappiness," one of my friends had written, and the first seemed as undeserved as the second. Endings and beginnings were too close, or seemed to be in the wrong order, death before life, dying before living; time was out of joint.

On or about April 2010, human character changed. When I wrote the birth announcement of my first child, I had to go to my office and use a computer; smartphones were not yet widespread. I expected replies over the course of days or weeks, not at once. By the time my daughter was born two years later, this had all changed: to own a smartphone was the norm, and responses were either immediate or not forthcoming. Having two children is quite different than having one; and yet I think that, for all of us, time in the early 2010s became more fragmented and elusive.

The machines that were meant to create time were consuming it instead. As we lost our ability to concentrate and recall, everything seemed new. After Tony's death, in August 2010, I toured to discuss the book we had written together, which he had entitled *Thinking the Twentieth Century*. I realized as I traveled around the United States that its subject had been forgotten all too well. In hotel rooms, I watched Russian television toy with the traumatic American history of race, suggesting that Barack Obama had been born in Africa.

It struck me as odd that the American entertainer Donald Trump picked up the theme not long thereafter.

Americans and Europeans were guided through the new century by a tale about "the end of history," by what I will call the *politics of inevitability,* a sense that the future is just more of the present, that the laws of progress are known, that there are no alternatives, and therefore nothing really to be done. In the American capitalist version of this story, nature brought the market, which brought democracy, which brought happiness. In the European version, history brought the nation, which learned from war that peace was good, and hence chose integration and prosperity.

Before the collapse of the Soviet Union in 1991, communism had its own politics of inevitability: nature permits technology; technology brings social change; social change causes revolution; revolution enacts utopia. When this turned out not to be true, the European and American politicians of inevitability were triumphant. Europeans busied themselves completing the creation of the European Union in 1992. Americans reasoned that the failure of the communist story confirmed the truth of the capitalist one. Americans and Europeans kept telling themselves their tales of inevitability for a quarter century after the end of communism, and so raised a millennial generation without history.

The American politics of inevitability, like all such stories, resisted facts. The fates of Russia, Ukraine, and Belarus after 1991 showed well enough that the fall of one system did not create a blank slate on which nature generated markets and markets generated rights. Iraq in 2003 might have confirmed this lesson, had the initiators of America's illegal war reflected upon its disastrous consequences. The financial crisis of 2008 and the deregulation of campaign contributions in the United States in 2010 magnified the influence of the wealthy and reduced that of voters. As economic inequality grew, time horizons shrank, and fewer Americans believed that the future held a better version of the present. Lacking a functional state that assured basic social goods taken for granted elsewhere—education, pensions, health care, transport, parental leave, vacations—Americans could be overwhelmed by each day, and lose a sense of the future.

The collapse of the politics of inevitability ushers in another experience of time: *the politics of eternity.* Whereas inevitability promises a better future for everyone, eternity places one nation at the center of a cyclical story of victimhood. Time is no longer a line into the future, but a circle that endlessly returns the same threats from the past. Within inevitability, no one is responsible because we all know that the details will sort themselves out for the better; within eternity, no one is responsible because we all know that the enemy is coming no matter what we do. Eternity politicians spread the conviction that government cannot aid society as a whole, but can only guard against threats. Progress gives way to doom.

In power, eternity politicians manufacture crisis and manipulate the resultant emotion. To distract from their inability or unwillingness to reform, eternity politicians instruct their citizens to experience elation and outrage at short intervals, drowning the future in the present. In foreign policy, eternity politicians belittle and undo the achievements of countries that might seem like models to their own citizens. Using technology to transmit political fiction, both at home and abroad, eternity politicians deny truth and seek to reduce life to spectacle and feeling.

PERHAPS MORE was happening in the 2010s than we grasped. Perhaps the tumbling succession of moments between the Smolensk crash and the Trump presidency was an era of transformation that we failed to experience as such. Perhaps we are slipping from one sense of time to another because we do not see how history makes us, and how we make history.

Inevitability and eternity translate facts into narratives. Those swayed by inevitability see every fact as a blip that does not alter the overall story of progress; those who shift to eternity classify every new event as just one more instance of a timeless threat. Each masquerades as history; each does away with history. Inevitability politicians teach that the specifics of the past are irrelevant, since anything that happens is just grist for the mill of progress. Eternity politicians leap from one moment to another, over decades or centuries, to build a myth of innocence and danger. They imagine cycles of threat in the past, creating an imagined pattern that they realize in the present by producing artificial crises and daily drama.

Inevitability and eternity have specific propaganda styles. Inevitability politicians spin facts into a web of well-being. Eternity politicians suppress facts in order to dismiss the reality that people are freer and richer in other countries, and the idea that reforms could be formulated on the basis of knowledge. In the 2010s, much of what was happening was the deliberate creation of political fiction, outsized stories that commanded attention and colonized the space needed for contemplation. Yet whatever impression propaganda makes at the time, it is not history's final verdict. There is a difference between memory, the impressions we are given; and history, the connections that we work to make—if we wish.

This book is an attempt to win back the present for historical time, and thus to win back historical time for politics. This means trying to understand one set of interconnected events in our own contemporary world history, from Russia to the United States, at a time when factuality itself was put into question. Russia's invasion of Ukraine in 2014 was a reality test for the European Union and the United States. Many Europeans and Americans found it easier to follow Russia's propaganda phantoms than to defend a legal order. Europeans and Americans wasted time by asking whether an invasion had taken place, whether Ukraine was a country, and whether it had somehow deserved to be invaded. This revealed a capacious vulnerability that Russia soon exploited within the European Union and the United States.

History as a discipline began as a confrontation with war propaganda. In the first history book, *The Peloponnesian Wars,* Thucydides was careful to make a distinction between leaders' accounts of their actions and the real reasons for their decisions. In our time, as rising inequality elevates political fiction, investigative journalism becomes the more precious. Its renaissance began during the Russian invasion of Ukraine, as courageous reporters filed stories from dangerous locations. In Russia and Ukraine, journalistic initiatives clustered around the problems of kleptocracy and corruption, and then reporters trained in these subjects covered the war.

WHAT HAS already happened in Russia is what might happen in America and Europe: the stabilization of massive inequality, the displacement of policy by propaganda, the shift from the politics of inevitability to the politics of eternity. Russian leaders could invite Europeans and Americans to eternity because Russia got there first. They understood American and European weaknesses, which they had first seen and exploited at home.

For many Europeans and Americans, events in the 2010s—the rise of antidemocratic politics, the Russian turn against Europe and invasion of Ukraine, the Brexit referendum, the Trump election— came as a surprise. Americans tend to react to surprise in two ways: either by imagining that the unexpected event is not really happening, or by claiming that it is totally new and hence not amenable to historical understanding. Either all will somehow be well, or all is so ill that nothing can be done. The first response is a defense mechanism of the politics of inevitability. The second is the creaking sound that inevitability makes just before it breaks and gives way to eternity. The politics of inevitability first erodes civic responsibility, and then collapses into the politics of eternity when it meets a serious challenge. Americans reacted in these ways when Russia's candidate became president of the United States.

In the 1990s and in the 2000s, influence flowed from west to east, in the transplant of economic and political models, the spread of the English language, and the enlargement of the European Union and the North Atlantic Treaty Organization (NATO). Meanwhile, unregulated spaces of American and European capitalism summoned wealthy Russians into a realm without an east-west geography, that of offshore bank accounts, shell companies, and anonymous deals, where wealth stolen from the Russian people was laundered clean. Partly for this reason, in the 2010s influence flowed from east to west, as the offshore exception became the rule, as Russian political fiction penetrated beyond Russia. In *The Peloponnesian Wars*, Thucydides defined "oligarchy" as *rule by the few*, and opposed it to "democracy." For Aristotle "oligarchy" meant *rule by the wealthy few*; the word in this sense was revived in the Russian language in the 1990s, and then, with good reason, in English in the 2010s.

Concepts and practices moved from east to west. An example is the word "fake," as in "fake news." This sounds like an American invention, and Donald Trump claimed it as his own; but the term was used in Russia and Ukraine long before it began its career in the United States. It meant creating a fictional text that posed as a piece of journalism, both to spread confusion about a particular event and to discredit journalism as such. Eternity politicians first spread fake news themselves, then claim that all news is fake, and finally that only their spectacles are real. The Russian campaign to fill the international public sphere with fiction began in Ukraine in 2014, and then spread to the United States in 2015, where it helped to elect a president in 2016. The techniques were everywhere the same, although they grew more sophisticated over time.

Russia in the 2010s was a kleptocratic regime that sought to export the politics of eternity: to demolish factuality, to preserve inequality, and to accelerate similar tendencies in Europe and the United States. This is well seen from Ukraine, where Russia fought a regular war while it amplified campaigns to undo the European Union and the United States. The advisor of the first pro-Russian American presidential candidate had been the advisor of the last pro-Russian Ukrainian president. Russian tactics that failed in Ukraine succeeded in the United States. Russian and Ukrainian oligarchs hid their money in a way that sustained the career of an American presidential candidate. This is all one history, the history of our moment and our choices.

CAN HISTORY be so contemporary? We think of the Peloponnesian Wars as ancient history, since the Athenians fought the Spartans more than two thousand years ago. Yet their historian Thucydides was describing events that he experienced. He included discussions of the past insofar as this was necessary to clarify the stakes in the present. This work humbly follows that approach.

*The Road to Unfreedom* delves into Russian, Ukrainian, European, and American history as necessary to define the political problems of the present, and to dispel some of the myths that enshroud them. It draws on primary sources from the countries concerned, and seeks patterns and concepts that can help us make sense of our own time. The languages of the sources—Russian, Ukrainian, Polish, German, French, and English—are tools of scholarship but also fonts of experience. I read and watched media from Russia, Ukraine, Europe, and the United States during these years, traveled to many of the places concerned, and could sometimes compare accounts of events with my own experiences or those of people I knew. Each chapter focuses upon a particular event and a particular year—the return of totalitarian thought (2011); the collapse of democratic politics in Russia (2012); the Russian assault upon the European Union (2013); the revolution in Ukraine and the subsequent Russian invasion (2014); the spread of political fiction in Russia, Europe, and America (2015); and the election of Donald Trump (2016).

By suggesting that political foundations cannot really change, the politics of inevitability spread uncertainty as to what those foundations really are. If we think the future is an automatic extension of good political order, we need not ask what that order is, why it is good, how it is sustained, and how it might be improved. History is and must be political thought, in the sense that it opens an aperture between inevitability and eternity, preventing us from drifting from the one to the other, helping us see the moment when we might make a difference.

As we emerge from inevitability and contend with eternity, a history of disintegration can be a guide to repair. Erosion reveals what resists, what can be reinforced, what can be reconstructed, and what must be reconceived. Because understanding is empowerment, this book's chapter titles are framed as alternatives: Individualism or Totalitarianism; Succession or Failure; Integration or Empire; Novelty or Eternity; Truth or Lies; Equality or Oligarchy. Thus individuality, endurance, cooperation, novelty, honesty, and justice figure as political virtues. These qualities are not mere platitudes or preferences, but facts of history, no less than material forces might be. Virtues are inseparable from the institutions they inspire and nourish.

An institution might cultivate certain ideas of the good, and it also depends upon them. If institutions are to flourish, they need virtues; if virtues are to be cultivated, they need institutions. The moral question of what is good and evil in public life can never be separated from the historical investigation of structure. It is the politics of inevitability and eternity that make virtues seem irrelevant or even laughable: inevitability by promising that the good is what already exists and must predictably expand, eternity by assuring that the evil is always external and that we are forever its innocent victims.

If we wish to have a better account of good and evil, we will have to resuscitate history.

## CHAPTER ONE

# INDIVIDUALISM OR TOTALITARIANISM (2011)

With law our land shall rise, but it will perish with lawlessness.
—*NJAL'S SAGA,* C. 1280

He who can make an exception is sovereign.
—CARL SCHMITT, 1922

The politics of inevitability is the idea that there are no ideas. Those in its thrall deny that ideas matter, proving only that they are in the grip of a powerful one. The cliché of the politics of inevitability is that "there are no alternatives." To accept this is to deny individual responsibility for seeing history and making change. Life becomes a sleepwalk to a premarked grave in a prepurchased plot.

Eternity arises from inevitability like a ghost from a corpse. The capitalist version of the politics of inevitability, the market as a substitute for policy, generates economic inequality that undermines belief in progress. As social mobility halts, inevitability gives way to eternity, and democracy gives way to oligarchy. An oligarch spinning a tale of an innocent past, perhaps with the help of fascist ideas, offers fake protection to people with real pain. Faith that technology serves freedom opens the way to his spectacle. As distraction replaces concentration, the future dissolves in the frustrations of the present, and eternity becomes daily life. The oligarch crosses into real politics from a world of fiction, and governs by invoking myth and manufacturing crisis. In the 2010s, one such person, Vladimir Putin, escorted another, Donald Trump, from fiction to power.

Russia reached the politics of eternity first, and Russian leaders protected themselves and their wealth by exporting it. The oligarch-in-chief, Vladimir Putin, chose the fascist philosopher Ivan Ilyin as a guide. The poet Czesław Miłosz wrote in 1953 that "only in the middle of the twentieth century did the inhabitants of many European countries come to understand, usually by way of suffering, that complex and difficult philosophy books have a direct influence on their fate." Some of the philosophy books that matter today were written by Ilyin, who died the year after Miłosz wrote those lines. Ivan Ilyin's revival by official Russia in the 1990s and 2000s has given his work a second life as the fascism adapted to make oligarchy possible, as the specific ideas that have helped leaders shift from inevitability to eternity.

The fascism of the 1920s and 1930s, Ilyin's era, had three core features: it celebrated will and violence over reason and law; it proposed a leader with a mystical connection to his people; and it characterized globalization as a conspiracy rather than as a set of problems. Revived today in conditions of inequality as a politics of eternity, fascism serves oligarchs as a catalyst for transitions away from public discussion and towards political fiction; away from meaningful voting and towards fake democracy; away from the rule of law and towards personalist regimes.

History always continues, and alternatives always present themselves. Ilyin represents one of these. He is not the only fascist thinker to have been revived in our century, but he is the most important. He is a guide on the darkening road to unfreedom, which leads from inevitability to eternity. Learning of his ideas and influence, we can look down the road, seeking light and exits. This means thinking historically: asking how ideas from the past can matter in the present, comparing Ilyin's era of globalization to our own, realizing that then as now the possibilities were real and more than two. The natural successor of the veil of inevitability is the shroud of eternity, but there are alternatives that must be found before the shroud drops. If we accept eternity, we sacrifice individuality, and will no longer see possibility. Eternity is another idea that says that there are no ideas.

When the Soviet Union collapsed in 1991, American politicians of inevitability proclaimed the end of history, while some Russians sought new authorities in an imperial past. When founded in 1922, the Soviet Union inherited most of the territory of the Russian Empire. The tsar's domain had been the largest in the world, stretching west to east from the middle of Europe to the shores of the Pacific, and north to south from the Arctic to Central Asia. Though largely a country of peasants and nomads, Russia's middle classes and intellectuals considered, as the twentieth century began, how an empire ruled by an autocrat might become more modern and more just.

Ivan Ilyin, born to a noble family in 1883, was typical of his generation as a young man. In the early 1900s, he wanted Russia to become a state governed by laws. After the disaster of the First World War and the experience of the Bolshevik Revolution of 1917, Ilyin became a counterrevolutionary, an advocate of violent methods against revolution, and with time the author of a Christian fascism meant to overcome Bolshevism. In 1922, a few months before the Soviet Union was founded, he was exiled from his homeland. Writing in Berlin, he offered a program to the opponents of the new Soviet Union, known as the Whites. These were men who had fought against the Bolsheviks' Red Army in the long and bloody Russian Civil War, and then made their way, like Ilyin, into political emigration in Europe. Ilyin later formulated his writings as guidance for Russian leaders who would come to power after the end of the Soviet Union. He died in 1954.

After a new Russian Federation emerged from the defunct Soviet Union in 1991, Ilyin's short book *Our Tasks* began to circulate in new Russian editions, his collected works were published, and his ideas gained powerful supporters. He had died forgotten in Switzerland; Putin organized a reburial in Moscow in 2005. Ilyin's personal papers had found their way to Michigan State University; Putin sent an emissary to reclaim them in 2006. By then Putin was citing Ilyin in his annual presidential addresses to the general assembly of the Russian parliament. These were important speeches, composed by Putin himself. In the 2010s, Putin relied upon Ilyin's authority to explain why Russia had to undermine the European Union and invade Ukraine. When asked to name a historian, Putin cited Ilyin as his authority on the past.

The Russian political class followed Putin's example. His propaganda master Vladislav Surkov adapted Ilyin's ideas to the world of modern media. Surkov orchestrated Putin's rise to power and oversaw the consolidation of media that ensured Putin's seemingly eternal rule. Dmitry Medvedev, the formal head of Putin's political party, recommended Ilyin to Russian youth. Ilyin's name was on the lips of the leaders of the fake opposition parties, the communists and (far-Right) Liberal Democrats, who played a part in creating the simulacrum of democracy that Ilyin had recommended. Ilyin was cited by the head of the constitutional court, even as his idea that law meant love for a leader ascended. He was mentioned by Russia's regional governors as Russia became the centralized state that he had advocated. In early 2014, members of Russia's ruling party and all of Russia's civil servants received a collection of Ilyin's political publications from the Kremlin. In 2017, Russian television commemorated the hundredth anniversary of the Bolshevik Revolution with a film that presented Ilyin as a moral authority.

Ilyin was a politician of eternity. His thought held sway as the capitalist version of the politics of inevitability collapsed in the Russia of the 1990s and 2000s. As Russia became an organized kleptocracy in the 2010s, as domestic inequality reached stupefying proportions, Ilyin's influence peaked. The Russian assault on the European Union and the United States revealed, by targeting them, certain political virtues that Ilyin the philosopher ignored or despised: individualism, succession, integration, novelty, truth, equality.

ILYIN FIRST proposed his ideas to Russians a century ago, after the Russian Revolution. And yet he has become a philosopher for our time. No thinker of the twentieth century has been rehabilitated in such grand style in the twenty-first, nor enjoyed such influence on world politics. If this went unnoticed it was because we are in the thrall of inevitability: we believe that ideas do not matter. To think historically is to accept that the unfamiliar might be significant, and to work to make the unfamiliar the familiar.

Our politics of inevitability echo those of Ilyin's years. Like the period from the late 1980s to the early 2010s, so the period from the late 1880s to the early 1910s was one of globalization. The conventional wisdom of both eras held that export-led growth would bring enlightened politics and end fanaticism. This optimism broke during the First World War and the revolutions and counterrevolutions that followed. Ilyin was himself an early example of this trend. A youthful supporter of the rule of law, he shifted to the extreme Right while admiring tactics he had observed on the extreme Left. The former leftist Benito Mussolini led his fascists in the March on Rome soon after Ilyin was expelled from Russia; the philosopher saw in the Duce hope for a corrupted world.

Ilyin regarded fascism as the politics of the world to come. In exile in the 1920s, he was troubled that Italians had arrived at fascism before Russians. He consoled himself with the idea that the Russian Whites were the inspiration for Mussolini's coup: "the White movement as such is deeper and broader than [Italian] fascism." The depth and breadth, Ilyin explained, came from an embrace of the sort of Christianity that demanded the blood sacrifice of God's enemies. Believing in the 1920s that Russia's White exiles could still win power, Ilyin addressed them as "my White brothers, fascists."

Ilyin was similarly impressed by Adolf Hitler. Although he visited Italy and vacationed in Switzerland, Ilyin's home between 1922 and 1938 was Berlin, where he worked for a government-sponsored scholarly institute. Ilyin's mother was German, he undertook psychoanalysis with Sigmund Freud in German, he studied German philosophy, and he wrote in German as well and as often as he did in Russian. In his day job he edited and wrote critical studies of Soviet politics (*A World at the Abyss* in German and *The Poison of Bolshevism* in Russian, for example, just in the year 1931). Ilyin saw Hitler as a defender of civilization from Bolshevism: the Führer, he wrote, had "performed an enormous service for all of Europe" by preventing further revolutions on the Russian model. Ilyin noted with approval that Hitler's antisemitism was derivative of the ideology of Russian Whites. He bemoaned that "Europe does not understand the National Socialist movement." Nazism was above all a "Spirit" of which Russians must partake.

In 1938, Ilyin left Germany for Switzerland, where he lived until his death in 1954. He was supported financially in Switzerland by the wife of a German-American businessman, and also earned some money by giving public lectures in German. The essence of these lectures, as a Swiss scholar noted, was that Russia should be understood not as present communist danger but as future Christian salvation. According to Ilyin, communism had been inflicted upon innocent Russia by the decadent West. One day Russia would liberate itself and others with the help of Christian fascism. A Swiss reviewer characterized his books as "national in the sense of opposing the entire West."

Ilyin's political views did not change as the Second World War began. His contacts in Switzerland were men of the far Right: Rudolf Grob believed that Switzerland should imitate Nazi Germany; Theophil Spoerri belonged to a group that banned Jews and Masons; Albert Riedweg was a right-wing lawyer whose brother Franz was the most prominent Swiss citizen in the Nazi extermination apparatus. Franz Riedweg married the daughter of the German minister of war and joined the Nazi SS. He took part in the German invasions of Poland, France, and the Soviet Union, the last of which Ilyin saw as a trial of Bolshevism in which Nazis might liberate Russians.

When the Soviet Union won the war and extended its empire westward in 1945, Ilyin began to write for future generations of Russians. He characterized his work as shining a small lantern in a great darkness. With that small flame, Russian leaders of the 2010s have begun a conflagration.

**ILYIN WAS** consistent. His first major work of philosophy, in Russian (1916), was also his last major work of philosophy, in its edited German translation (1946).

The one good in the universe, Ilyin maintained, had been God's totality before creation. When God created the world, he shattered the single and total Truth that was himself. Ilyin divided the world into the "categorical," the lost realm of that single perfect concept; and the "historical," human life with its facts and passions. For him, the tragedy of existence was that facts could not be reassembled into God's totality, nor passions into God's purpose. The Romanian thinker E. M. Cioran, himself once an advocate of Christian fascism, explained the concept: before history, God is perfect and eternal; once he begins history, God seems "frenetic, committing error upon error." As Ilyin put it: "When God sank into empirical existence he was deprived of his harmonious unity, logical reason, and organizational purpose."

For Ilyin, our human world of facts and passions is senseless. Ilyin found it immoral that a fact might be grasped in its historical setting: "the world of empirical existence cannot be theologically justified." Passions are evil. God erred in his creation by releasing "the evil nature of the sensual." God yielded to a "romantic" impulse by making beings, ourselves, who are moved by sex. And so "the romantic content of the world overcomes the rational form of thought, and thought cedes its place to unthinking purpose," physical love. God left us amidst "spiritual and moral relativism."

By condemning God, Ilyin empowered philosophy, or at least one philosopher: himself. He preserved the vision of a divine "totality" that existed before the creation of the world, but left it to himself to reveal how it might be regained. Having removed God from the scene, Ilyin himself could issue judgments about what is and what ought to be. There is a Godly world and it must be somehow redeemed, and this sacred work will fall to men who understand their predicament—thanks to Ilyin and his books.

The vision was a totalitarian one. We should long for a condition in which we think and feel as one, which means not to think and feel at all. We must cease to exist as individual human beings. "Evil begins," Ilyin wrote, "where the person begins." Our very individuality only proves that the world is flawed: "the empirical fragmentation of human existence is an incorrect, a transitory, and a metaphysically untrue condition of the world." Ilyin despised the middle classes, whose civil society and private life, he thought, kept the world broken and God at bay. To belong to a layer of society that offered individuals social advancement was to be the worst kind of human being: "this estate constitutes the very lowest level of social existence."

LIKE ALL immorality, eternity politics begins by making an exception for itself. All else in creation might be evil, but I and my group are good, because I am myself and my group is mine. Others might be confused and bewitched by the facts and passions of history, but my nation and myself have maintained a prehistorical innocence. Since the only good is this invisible quality that resides in us, the only policy is one that safeguards our innocence, regardless of the costs. Those who accept eternity politics do not expect to live longer, happier, or more fruitful lives. They accept suffering as a mark of righteousness if they think that guilty others are suffering more. Life is nasty, brutish, and short; the pleasure of life is that it can be made nastier, more brutish, and shorter for others.

Ilyin made an exception for Russia and for Russians. The Russian innocence he proclaimed was not observable in the world. It was Ilyin's act of faith directed at his own people: salvation required seeing Russia as it was not. Since the facts of the world are just the corrupt detritus of God's failed creation, true seeing was the contemplation of the invisible. Corneliu Codreanu, the founder of a kindred Romanian fascism, saw the Archangel Michael in prison and recorded his vision in a few lines. Although Ilyin dressed up his idea of contemplation in several books, it really was no more than that: he saw his own nation as righteous, and the purity of that vision was more important than anything Russians actually did. The nation, "pure and objective," was what the philosopher saw when he blinded himself.

Innocence took a specific biological form. What Ilyin saw was a virginal Russian body. Like fascists and other authoritarians of his day, Ilyin insisted that his nation was a creature, "an organism of nature and the soul," an animal in Eden without original sin. Who belonged within the Russian organism was not for the individual to decide, since cells do not decide whether they belong to a body. Russian culture, Ilyin wrote, automatically brought "fraternal union" wherever Russian power extended. Ilyin wrote of "Ukrainians" in quotation marks, because he denied their separate existence beyond the Russian organism. To speak of Ukraine was to be a mortal enemy of Russia. Ilyin took for granted that a post-Soviet Russia would include Ukraine.

Ilyin thought that Soviet power concentrated all of the Satanic energy of factuality and passion in one place. And yet he argued that the triumph of communism showed that Russia was more rather than less innocent. Communism, he maintained, was a seduction by foreigners and deracinated Russians whom Ilyin called "Tarzans." They lusted to violate immaculate Russia precisely because it was guileless and defenseless. In 1917, Russians had simply been too good to resist the cargo of sin arriving from the West. Despite the depredations of Soviet leaders, Russians retained an imperceptible goodness. Unlike Europe and America, which accepted facts and passions as life, Russia retained an underlying "Spirit" that recalled God's totality. "The nation is not God," wrote Ilyin, "but the strength of its soul is from God."

When God created the world, Russia had somehow escaped

history and remained in eternity. Ilyin's homeland, he thought, was therefore free from the forward flow of time and the accumulation of accident and choice that he found so intolerable. Russia instead experienced repeating cycles of threat and defense. Everything that happened must be an attack from the outside world on Russian innocence, or a justified Russian response to such a threat. In such a scheme it was easy for Ilyin, who knew little of actual Russian history, to grasp centuries in simple phrases. What a historian might see as the spread of power from Moscow across northern Asia and half of Europe was for Ilyin nothing more than "self-defense." According to Ilyin, every single battle ever fought by Russians was defensive. Russia was always the victim of a "continental blockade" by Europe. As Ilyin saw matters, "the Russian nation, since its full conversion to Christianity, can count nearly one thousand years of historical suffering." Russia does no wrong; wrong can only be done to Russia. Facts do not matter and responsibility vanishes.

**BEFORE THE** Bolshevik Revolution, Ilyin was a student of law and a believer in progress. After 1917, everything seemed possible and all permitted. Lawlessness from the far Left, Ilyin thought, would have to be exceeded by a still greater lawlessness from the far Right. In his mature work, Ilyin thus portrayed Russian lawlessness as patriotic virtue. "The fact of the matter," he wrote, "is that fascism is a redemptive excess of patriotic arbitrariness." The Russian word *proizvol*, arbitrariness, has always been the bête noire of Russian reformers. In portraying *proizvol* as patriotic, Ilyin was turning against legal reform and announcing that politics must instead follow the caprice of a single ruler.

Ilyin's use of the Russian word for "redemptive," *spasitelnii*, released a profound religious meaning into politics. Like other fascists, such as Adolf Hitler in *Mein Kampf*, he turned Christian ideas of sacrifice and redemption towards new purposes. Hitler claimed that he would redeem the world for a distant God by ridding it of Jews.

"And so I believe that I am acting as the almighty creator would want," wrote Hitler. "Insofar as I restrain the Jew, I am doing the work of the Lord." The Russian word *spasitelnii* would usually be applied, by an Orthodox Christian, to the deliverance of believers by Christ's sacrifice on Calvary. What Ilyin meant was that Russia needed a redeemer who would make the "chivalrous sacrifice" of shedding the blood of others to take power. A fascist coup was an "act of salvation," the first step towards the return of totality to the universe.

The men who redeemed God's flawed world had to ignore what God said about love. Jesus instructed his disciples that, after loving God, the most important law was to love one's neighbor. In the parable of the Good Samaritan, Jesus refers to Leviticus 19:33–34: "And if a stranger sojourn with thee in your land, ye shall not vex him. *But* the stranger that dwelleth with you shall be unto you as one born among you, and thou shalt love him as thyself; for ye were strangers in the land of Egypt: I *am* the LORD your God." For Ilyin there were no neighbors. Individuality is corrupt and transient, and the only meaningful connection is the lost divine totality. So long as the world is fractured, loving God means a constant struggle "against the enemies of divine order on earth." To do anything but to join this war was to enact evil: "He who opposes the chivalrous struggle against the devil is himself the devil." Faith meant war: "May your prayer be a sword and your sword be a prayer!"

Because the world was sinful and God was absent, his champion must emerge from some uncorrupted realm beyond history. "Power," Ilyin imagined, "comes all by itself to the strong man." A man would appear from nowhere, and Russians would recognize their redeemer: "We will accept our freedom and our laws from the Russian patriot who leads Russia to salvation." Emerging from fiction, the redeemer disregards the facts of the world and creates a myth around himself. By taking on the burden of Russians' passions, he channels "the evil nature of the sensual" into a grand unity. The leader will be "sufficiently manly," like Mussolini. He "hardens himself in just and manly service. He is inspired by the spirit of totality rather than by a particular personal or party motivation. He stands alone and goes alone because he sees the future of politics and knows what must be done." Russians will kneel before "the living organ of Russia, the instrument of self-redemption."

The redeemer suppresses factuality, directs passion, and generates myth by ordering a violent attack upon a chosen enemy. A fascist scorns any politics rooted in society (its preferences, its interests, its visions of the future, the rights of its members, and so on). Fascism begins not with an assessment of what is within, but from a rejection of what is without. The outside world is the literary source material for an enemy image composed by a dictator. Following the Nazi legal theorist Carl Schmitt, Ilyin defined politics as "the art of identifying and neutralizing the enemy." Ilyin thus began his article "On Russian Nationalism" with the simple claim that "National Russia has enemies." The flawed world had to oppose Russia because Russia was the only source of divine totality.

The redeemer had the obligation to make war and the right to choose which one. Ilyin believed that war was justified when "the spiritual attainments of the nation are threatened," which they always will be until individuality is brought to an end. To make war against the enemies of God was to express innocence. Making war (not love) was the proper release of passion, because it did not endanger but protected the virginity of the national body. In the 1930s, Romanian fascists sang of "iron-clad breasts and lily-white souls." By guiding others to bloodshed, Russia's redeemer would draw all of Russia's sexual energy to himself, and guide its release. War was the only "excess" that Ilyin endorsed, a mystical communion of virginal organism and otherworldly redeemer. True "passion" was fascist violence, the rising sword that was also a kneeling prayer.

"EVERYTHING BEGINS in mystique and ends in politics," as the poet Charles Péguy reminds us. Ilyin's thought began with a contemplation of God, sex, and truth in 1916, and ended a century later as the orthodoxy of the Kremlin and the justification for war against Ukraine, the European Union, and the United States.

Destruction is always easier than creation. Ilyin found it difficult to specify the institutional form a redeemed Russia would take—and his unsolved problems haunt Russia's leaders today. The chief of these is the durability of the Russian state. Legal institutions that permit the succession of power allow citizens to envision a future where leaders change but states remain. Fascism, however, is about a sacred and eternal connection between the redeemer and his people. A fascist presents institutions and laws as the corrupt barriers between leader and folk that must be circumvented or destroyed.

Ilyin tried to design a Russian political system, but in his sketches could never get beyond this conundrum. He attempted to solve the problem semantically by treating the personality of the redeemer as an institution. The redeemer should be regarded as "leader" (*gosudar*'), "head of state," "democratic dictator," and "national dictator," an assemblage of titles that recalled the fascist leaders of the 1920s and 1930s. The redeemer would be responsible for all executive, legislative, and judiciary functions, and command the armed forces. Russia would be a centralized state with no federal units. Russia should not be a one-party state as the fascist regimes of the 1930s had been. That was one party too many. Russia should be a zero-party state, redeemed only by a man. Parties should exist, according to Ilyin, only to help ritualize elections.

Allowing Russians to vote in free elections, thought Ilyin, was like allowing embryos to choose their species. Voting with a secret ballot allowed citizens to think of themselves as individuals, and thereby confirmed the evil character of the world. "The principle of democracy is the irresponsible human atom," and so individuality must be overcome by political habits that excite and sustain Russians' collective love for their redeemer. Thus "we must reject the mechanical and arithmetical understanding of politics" as well as "blind faith in the number of votes and its political significance." Voting should unite the nation in a gesture of subjugation. Elections should be public, and ballots signed.

Ilyin imagined society as a corporate structure, where every person and every group would hold a defined place. There would be no distinction between the state and the population, but rather "the organic-spiritual unity of the government with the people, and the people with the government." The redeemer would stand alone at the heights, and the middle classes would lie crushed at the bottom, under the weight of everyone else. In normal parlance, middle classes are in the middle because people rise (and fall) through them. Placing the middle classes at the bottom was to assert the righteousness of inequality. Social mobility was excluded from the outset.

An idea that Ilyin intended as fascist thus permits and justifies oligarchy, rule by the wealthy few—as in Russia in the 2010s. If the purpose of the state is to preserve the wealth of the redeemer and his friends, then the rule of law is impossible. Without the rule of law, it is difficult to earn the money that will allow for better lives. Without social advancement, no story of the future seems plausible. The weakness of state policy is then recast as the mystical connection of a leader with his people. Rather than governing, the leader produces crisis and spectacle. Law ceases to signify neutral norms that allow social advance, and comes to mean subordination to the status quo: the right to watch, the duty to be entertained.

Ilyin used the word "law," but he did not endorse the rule of law. By "law" he meant the relationship between the caprice of the redeemer and the obedience of everyone else. Again, a fascist idea proved to be convenient for an emerging oligarchy. The loving duty of the Russian masses was to translate the redeemer's every whim into a sense of legal obligation on their part. The obligation, of course, was not reciprocal. Russians had a "special arrangement of the soul" that allowed them to suppress their own reason and accept "the law in our hearts." By this Ilyin understood the suppression of individual reason in favor of national submission. With the redeemer in command of such a system, Russia would exhibit "the metaphysical identity of all people of the same nation."

The Russian nation, summoned to instant war against spiritual threats, was a creature rendered divine by its submission to an arbitrary leader who emerged from fiction. The redeemer would take upon himself the burden of dissolving all facts and passions, thereby rendering senseless any aspiration of any individual Russian to see or feel or change the world. Each Russian's place in the corporate structure would be fixed like a cell in a body, and each Russian would experience this immobility as freedom. Unified by their redeemer, their sins washed away in the blood of others, Russians would welcome God back to his creation. Christian fascist totalitarianism is an invitation to God to return to the world and help Russia bring an end to history everywhere.

Ilyin placed a human being in the role of the true Christ, required to break the laws of love in the name of God. In doing so, he blurred the line between what is human and what is not, and between what is possible and what is not. The fantasy of an eternally innocent Russia includes the fantasy of an eternally innocent redeemer, who does no wrong and therefore will not die. Ilyin could not answer the question of who might succeed the redeemer, since doing so would make of the redeemer a human subject to aging and death, no less part of the flawed universe than the rest of us. Ilyin had no earthly idea, in other words, of how a Russian state could endure.

The very dread of what comes next generates a sense of threat that can be projected upon others as foreign policy. Totalitarianism is its own true enemy, and that is the secret it keeps from itself by attacking others.


IN THE 2010s, Ilyin's ideas served post-Soviet billionaires, and post-Soviet billionaires served them. Putin and his friends and allies accumulated vast wealth beyond the law, and then remade the state to preserve their own gains. Having achieved this, Russian leaders had to define politics as being rather than doing. An ideology such as Ilyin's purports to explain why certain men have wealth and power in terms other than greed and ambition. What robber would not prefer to be called a redeemer?

To men raised in the Soviet Union in the 1970s, Ilyin's ideas were comfortable for a second reason. To the Russian kleptocrats of that generation, the men in power in the 2010s, his entire style of thinking was familiar. Although Ilyin opposed Soviet power, the shape of his argument was eerily similar to that of the Marxism, Leninism, and Stalinism in which all Soviet citizens were educated. Although Russian kleptocrats are by no means philosophers, the instruction of their youth led them surprisingly close to the justifications they would need in their maturity. Ilyin and the Marxism he opposed shared a philosophical origin and language: that of Hegelianism.

G. W. F. Hegel's ambition was to resolve the difference between what is and what should be. His claim was that something called Spirit, a unity of all thoughts and minds, was emerging over time, through the conflicts that defined epochs. Hegel's was an appealing way of seeing our fractious world, since it suggested that catastrophe was an indication of progress. History was a "slaughter bench," but the bloodshed had a purpose. This idea allowed philosophers to pose as prophets, seers of hidden patterns that would resolve themselves into a better world, judges of who had to suffer now so that all would benefit later. If Spirit was the only good, than any means that History chose for its realization was also good.

Karl Marx was critical of Hegel's idea of Spirit. He and other Left Hegelians claimed that Hegel had smuggled God into his system under the heading of Spirit. The absolute good, suggested Marx, was not God but humanity's lost essence. History was a struggle, but its sense was man's overcoming of circumstance to regain his own nature. The emergence of technology, argued Marx, allowed some men to dominate others, forming social classes. Under capitalism, the bourgeoisie controlled the means of production, oppressing the mass of workers. This very oppression instructed workers about the character of history and made them revolutionaries. The proletariat would overthrow the bourgeoisie, seize the means of production, and thereby restore man to himself. Once there was no property, thought Marx, human beings would live in happy cooperation.

Ilyin was a Right Hegelian. In a typically sharp phrase, he wrote that Marx never got out of the "waiting room" of Hegelian philosophy. Ilyin nevertheless agreed that by "Spirit" Hegel meant God. Like Marx, Ilyin thought that history had begun with an original sin that doomed humanity to suffering. It was perpetrated not by man upon man through property, as the Marxists thought, but by God upon man through the creation of the world. Rather than killing God, as the Left Hegelians had done, Ilyin left him wounded and lonely. Life was poor and chaotic, as the Marxists thought, but not because of technology and class conflict. People suffered because God's creation was irresolvably conflictual. Facts and passions could not be aligned through revolution, only through redemption. The only totality was God's, which a chosen nation would restore thanks to a miracle performed by a redeemer.

Vladimir Lenin (1870–1924) was the most important Marxist, since he led a revolution in the name of the philosophy. As an activist of a small and illegal party in the Russian Empire, Lenin believed that a disciplined elite had the right to push history forward. If the only good in the world was the restoration of man to his essence, then it was reasonable for those who understood the process to hasten it. This reasoning enabled the Bolshevik Revolution of 1917. The Soviet Union was ruled by a small group of people who claimed legitimacy from this specific politics of inevitability. Lenin and Ilyin did not know each other, but were uncannily close: Lenin's patronymic was "Ilyich" and he used "Ilyin" as a pen name; the real Ilyin read and reviewed some of that work. When Ilyin was arrested by the Bolshevik secret police, the Cheka, Lenin intervened on his behalf in order to express his admiration of Ilyin's philosophy.

Ilyin despised Lenin's revolution, but he endorsed its violence

Lenin              Ilyin

and its voluntarism. Like Lenin, he thought that Russia needed a philosophical elite (himself) to define ends and means. Like the Marxist socialist utopia, Ilyin's "divine totality" required violent revolution—or rather violent counterrevolution. Other Russian philosophers saw the resemblance. Nikolai Berdyaev found in Ilyin's work "the nightmare of evil good." Reviewing a book that Ilyin published in 1925, Berdyaev wrote that "a Cheka in the name of God is more horrifying than a Cheka in the name of the devil." His judgment was prophetic: "The Bolsheviks would have no fundamental problem accepting Ivan Ilyin's book. They consider themselves the bearers of absolute good and oppose those whom they regard as evil with force."

As Ilyin aged in Germany and Switzerland, his positions tracked those of Lenin's successors. After Lenin died in 1924, Joseph Stalin consolidated power. Ilyin shared Stalinist judgments about the contagious perversity of Western culture down to the smallest detail. He believed, for instance, that jazz was a deliberate plot to reduce European listeners to mindless dancers incapable of normal sexual intercourse. The communist party newspaper *Pravda* offered a strikingly similar description of the experience of listening to African American music: "some centaur must be conducting with his gigantic phallus." Though Ilyin wrote books chronicling terror under Stalin, his attitude to the law was essentially similar to that of its perpetrators. Andrei Vyshynskii, the notorious prosecutor at the show trials, believed that "formal law is subordinate to the law of the revolution." This was precisely Ilyin's attitude with respect to his planned counterrevolution.

Although Ilyin had initially hoped that the Second World War would destroy Stalin's Soviet Union, in its aftermath he presented Russia much as Stalin did. Stalin called the USSR the homeland of socialism. If the Soviet Union were destroyed, went his argument, communism would have no future, and humanity's only hope would be lost. Thus any action to defend the Soviet Union was justified. Ilyin saw Russia as a homeland of God to be preserved at all costs, since it was the only territory from which divine totality could be restored. After the war, Stalin gave priority to the Russian nation (as opposed to Ukraine, Belarus, Central Asia, the Caucasus, the dozens of peoples of the Soviet Union). Russia, Stalin claimed, had saved the world from fascism. Ilyin's view was that Russia would save the world not *from* but *with* fascism. In both cases the only receptacle of absolute good was Russia, and the permanent enemy the decadent West.

Soviet communism was a politics of inevitability that yielded to a politics of eternity. Over the decades, the idea of Russia as a beacon for the world gave way to the image of Russia as a victim of mindless hostility. In the beginning Bolshevism was not a state but a revolution, the hope that others around the world would follow the Russian example. Then it was a state with a task: to build socialism by imitating capitalism and then overcoming it. Stalinism was a vision of the future that justified millions of deaths by starvation and another million or so by execution in the 1930s. The Second World War changed the story. Stalin and his supporters and successors all claimed after 1945 that the self-inflicted carnage of the 1930s had been necessary to defeat the Germans in the 1940s. If the 1930s were about the 1940s, then they were not about a distant future of socialism. The aftermath of the Second World War was the beginning of the end of the Soviet politics of inevitability, and thus the opening gesture towards a Russian politics of eternity.

Stalin's economic policy, forced industrialization funded by collectivized agriculture, created social mobility for two generations but not for three. In the 1950s and 1960s, Soviet leaders agreed not to kill one another, which removed dynamism from politics. In the 1970s, Leonid Brezhnev took a logical step towards a politics of eternity, portraying the Second World War as the apogee of Soviet history. Soviet citizens were instructed to look not forward but backward, to the triumph of their parents or grandparents in the Second World War. The West was no longer the enemy because it represented a capitalism that would be surpassed; the West was the enemy because the Soviet Union had been invaded from the west in 1941. Soviet citizens born in the 1960s and 1970s were raised in a cult of the past that defined the West as a perpetual threat. The last decades of Soviet communism prepared Soviet citizens for Ilyin's view of the world.

The oligarchy that emerged in the Russian Federation after 1991 had a great deal to do with the centralization of production under communism, the ideas of Russian economists thereafter, and the greed of Russia's leaders. American conventional wisdom contributed to the disaster by suggesting that markets would create institutions, rather than stressing that institutions were needed for markets.

In the twenty-first century, it proved easier to blame the West than to take stock of Russian choices. The Russian leaders who did the blaming in the 2010s were the very individuals who stole the national wealth. Those who proclaimed Ilyin's ideas from the heights of the Russian state were the beneficiaries rather than the victims of capitalism's career in Russia. The men of Putin's entourage ensured that the rule of law had no chance in Russia, since they themselves created and profited from a state monopoly on corruption. Ilyin's ideas sanctified radical inequality at home, changed the subject of politics from reform to innocence, while defining the West as a permanent source of a spiritual threat.

No Russian state could be built on Ilyin's concepts. But they did help robbers to present themselves as redeemers. They enabled new leaders to choose enemies and thus create fictional problems that could not be solved, such as the permanent hostility of a decadent West. The notion that Europe and America were eternal foes because they envied pristine Russian culture was pure fiction that generated real policy: the attempt to destroy the attainments abroad that Russia's leaders could not manage at home.

The politics of eternity cannot make Putin or any other man immortal. But it can make other ideas unthinkable. And that is what eternity means: the same thing over and over again, a tedium exciting to believers because of the illusion that it is particularly theirs. Of course, this sense of "us and them," or, as fascists prefer, "friends and enemies," is the least specific human experience of them all; to live within it is to sacrifice individuality.

The only thing that stands between inevitability and eternity is history, as considered and lived by individuals. If we grasp eternity and inevitability as ideas within our own history, we might see what has happened to us and what we might do about it. We understand totalitarianism as a threat to institutions, but also to selves.

In the fury of their assault, Ilyin's ideas clarify individualism as a political virtue, the one that enables all the others. Are we individuals who see that there are many good things, and that politics involves responsible consideration and choice rather than a vision of totality? Do we see that there are other individuals in the world who might be at work on the same project? Do we understand that being an individual requires a constant consideration of endless factuality, a constant selection among many irreducible passions?

The virtue of individualism becomes visible in the throes of our moment, but it will abide only if we see history and ourselves within it, and accept our share of responsibility.

## CHAPTER TWO

# SUCCESSION OR FAILURE (2012)

History has proven that all dictatorships, all authoritarian forms of government, are transient. Only democratic systems are intransient.
—VLADIMIR PUTIN, 1999

Ilyin's conception of the innocent nation disguised the effort required to make a durable state. To propose that a Russian redeemer would enchant the world was to dodge the question of how he would establish political institutions. In discrediting democratic elections in 2011 and 2012, Vladimir Putin took on the mantle of the heroic redeemer and placed his country on the horns of Ilyin's dilemma. No one can change Russia for the better so long as he lives, and no one in Russia knows what will happen when he dies.

The fascists of Ilyin's time fantasized away the problem of endurance. In 1940, the Romanian fascist Alexandru Randa proclaimed that fascist leaders "transform the nation into a permanent force, into a 'corpus mysticus' freed from borders." The redeemer's charisma removes the nation from history. Adolf Hitler claimed that all that mattered was the struggle of the race, and that the elimination of Jews would restore nature's eternal balance. His Thousand-Year Reich lasted twelve years, and he committed suicide. A state does not endure because a leader mystifies a generation. The problem of political endurance cannot be solved by people who think only of the present. Leaders must think beyond themselves and their clans, to imagine how other people might succeed them in the future.

Functional states produce a sense of continuity for their citizens. If states sustain themselves, citizens can imagine change without fearing catastrophe. The mechanism that ensures that a state outlasts a leader is called the principle of succession. A common one is democracy. The meaning of each election is the promise of the next one. Since each citizen is fallible, democracy transforms cumulative mistakes into a collective belief in the future. History goes on.

THE SOVIET Union that expelled Ilyin and educated Putin had a troubled relationship with time. It lacked a succession principle and lasted only sixty-nine years. The Bolsheviks were not concerned about succession because they believed that they were beginning a global revolution, not creating a state. The Russian Revolution of 1917 was for the world, a stroke of lightning to set civilization aflame, to start history anew. When this prophecy failed, the Bolsheviks had no choice but to establish a state on the territories they controlled, a new regime, which they called the Soviet Union.

In the Soviet Union, as founded in 1922, power lay with the communist party. The party claimed legitimacy not from legal principle or continuity with the past, but from the glory of the revolution and bright promise of the future. In principle, all authority lay with the working class. Workers were represented by the party, the party by its central committee, the central committee by its politburo, and the politburo usually by a single leading man, Lenin and later Stalin. Marxism-Leninism was a politics of inevitability: the course of events was known in advance, socialism would displace capitalism, and party leaders knew the details and made the plans. The initial state was purpose-built to accelerate time, to replicate the industry that capitalism had created elsewhere. Once the Soviet Union had the factories and the cities, it could undo the principle of property, socialist harmony would result, and the state could fade away.

Although the USSR's state-controlled agriculture and planned economy did generate a modern infrastructure, workers never gained power and the state never vanished. Because no principle of succession was ever established, the death of each leader threatened the system as a whole. After Lenin's death in 1924, it took Stalin about six years to defeat his rivals, several of whom were killed. He presided over the dramatic modernization of the First Five-Year Plan of 1928–1933, which built cities and factories at the price of the starvation of millions and the exile of millions more to concentration camps. Stalin was also the chief author of the Great Terror of 1937–1938, in which 682,691 Soviet citizens were shot, and of a smaller terror of 1939–1941, when Soviet borders were extended westward during the Soviet alliance with Nazi Germany. Among other episodes of mass killing and deportation, this smaller terror involved the murder of 21,892 Polish citizens at Katyn and other sites in 1940.

Stalin was surprised when he was betrayed by his ally Hitler in 1941, but after the victory of the Red Army in 1945 he portrayed himself as the savior of the socialist project and the Russian nation. After the Second World War, the Soviet Union was able to establish an outer empire of replicate regimes on or near its western frontier: Poland, Romania, Hungary, Czechoslovakia, Bulgaria. It also reincorporated Estonia, Latvia, and Lithuania, the three Baltic states it initially annexed thanks to Stalin's alliance with Hitler.

After Stalin's death in 1953, only one candidate for power was killed, and by the end of the 1950s Nikita Khrushchev seemed to have consolidated power. Khrushchev, however, was superseded in 1964 by Leonid Brezhnev. It was Brezhnev who proved to be Stalin's most important successor, because he redefined the Soviet attitude to time: he buried the Marxist politics of inevitability, and replaced it with a Soviet politics of eternity.

The Bolshevik Revolution had been about youth, about a new

start to be made after capitalism. This image depended, at home and especially abroad, on the blood purges that allowed new men and women to rise through the party ranks. When these ceased in the 1960s, Soviet leaders aged along with the Soviet state. Rather than of a victory of communism to come, Brezhnev spoke in the 1970s of "really existing socialism." Once Soviet citizens expected no improvements from the future, nostalgia had to fill the vacuum left by utopia. Brezhnev replaced the promise of future perfection with a cult of Stalin and his leadership in the Second World War. The story of revolution was about the inevitable future; the memory of war was about the eternal past. This past had to be one of immaculate victimhood: it was taboo, indeed illegal, to mention that Stalin had begun the war as Hitler's ally. For a politics of inevitability to become a politics of eternity, the facts of history had to be sacrificed.

The myth of the October Revolution promised everything; the myth of the Great Fatherland War promised nothing. The October Revolution foresaw an imaginary world in which all men would be brothers. To commemorate the Great Fatherland War was to evoke an eternal return of fascists from the West who would always seek to destroy the Soviet Union, or perhaps simply Russia. A politics of radical hope gave way to a politics of bottomless fear (which justified extraordinary expenditures on conventional and nuclear armaments). The great military parades of the Red Army on Red Square in Moscow were meant to demonstrate that the Soviet Union could not be changed. The men who ruled Russia in the 2010s were educated in this spirit.

The same held for the actual deployment of the Red Army: it was to preserve the status quo in Europe. In the 1960s, some Czechoslovak communists believed that communism could be renewed. When the Soviet Union and its Warsaw Pact allies invaded Czechoslovakia to overthrow reform communists in 1968, Brezhnev spoke of "fraternal assistance." According to the Brezhnev Doctrine, Soviet armies would halt any development in communist Europe that Moscow deemed threatening. The post-invasion regime in Czechoslovakia spoke of "normalization," which nicely caught the spirit of the moment. What was, was normal. To say otherwise in Brezhnev's Soviet Union was to be condemned to an insane asylum.

Brezhnev died in 1982. After two short interludes of rule by dying men, Mikhail Gorbachev came to power in 1985. Gorbachev believed that communism could be reformed and a better future promised. His main opponent was the party itself, in particular the ossified lobbies accustomed to the status quo. So Gorbachev tried to build new institutions to gain control over the party. He encouraged the communist leaders of the Soviet satellites in eastern Europe to do the same. Polish communists, facing economic crisis and political opposition, took him at his word, scheduled partially free elections in 1989, and lost. This led to the creation of a non-communist Polish government and copycat revolutions throughout eastern Europe.

Within the Soviet Union, Gorbachev faced a similar challenge. The Soviet state, when constructed in 1922, had taken the form of a federation of national republics: Russia, Ukraine, Belarus, and so forth. To reform the state, as Gorbachev wished, meant enlivening the federal units. Democratic elections in the various Soviet republics were held in order to generate new elites who would implement economic reform. For example, elections held in the Russian Soviet Federative Socialist Republic in March 1990 created a new assembly, which chose Boris Yeltsin to be its chairman. Yeltsin was typical of new leaders produced by democracy, in that he believed that Russia had been ill served by the Soviet Union. Societies of every Soviet republic believed that they had been exploited by the system to the benefit of other regions.

The crisis came in summer 1991. Gorbachev's own legitimacy had come from the party, but he was trying to replace the party with a state. To do so, he had to find a formula that would both recognize the status of the republics and create a functional center, in an atmosphere of nationalist discontent, political anxiety, and economic shortfall. His solution was a new union treaty, to be signed that August. A group of Soviet conservatives had Gorbachev arrested in his dacha on the night of August 18, during his vacation. They had little idea of what to do next, aside from broadcasting ballet on television. The victor of the coup proved to be Boris Yeltsin, who defied the plotters in Moscow, stood on a tank, and made himself a popular hero. Gorbachev was able to return to Moscow, but Yeltsin was now in charge.

Once Yeltsin became its most important politician, the days of the Soviet Union were numbered. Western leaders feared instability and campaigned to keep the USSR intact. In August 1991, President George H. W. Bush traveled to Kyiv to urge Ukrainians not to leave the Soviet Union: "Freedom is not the same as independence," he instructed them. In October he told Gorbachev: "I hope you know the position of our government: we support the center." In December 1991, Yeltsin removed Russia from the Soviet Union by signing an agreement with newly elected leaders of Soviet Ukraine and Soviet Belarus. The Russian Soviet Federative Socialist Republic of the Soviet Union became an independent state known as the Russian Federation. All of the other former republics of the Soviet Union followed suit.

The new Russian Federation was established as a constitutional republic, legitimated by democracy, where a president and a parliament would be chosen by free elections. On paper, Russia had a succession principle.

ILYIN HAD anticipated a different transition from Soviet to Russian power: fascist dictatorship, the preservation of all Soviet territory, permanent war against the sinful West. Russians began to read him in the 1990s. His ideas had no effect on the end of the Soviet Union, but they did influence how post-Soviet oligarchs consolidated a new kind of authoritarianism in the 2000s and 2010s.

It is impossible for a human being to do what Ilyin imagined a Russian redeemer should: emerge from a realm of fiction and act from the spirit of totality. Yet a feat of scenography by skilled propagandists (or, in the nice Russian phrase, "political technologists") might create the appearance of such an earthly miracle. The myth of a redeemer would have to be founded on lies so enormous that they could not be doubted, because doubting them would mean doubting everything. It was not so much elections as fictions that allowed a transition of power, a decade after the end of the Soviet Union, from Boris Yeltsin to Vladimir Putin. Then Ilyin and Putin rose together, the philosopher and the politician of fiction.

Democracy never took hold in Russia, in the sense that power never changed hands after freely contested elections. Yeltsin was president of the Russian Federation because of an election that took place when Russia was still a Soviet republic, in June 1991. Those taking part in that election were not choosing a president of an independent Russia, since no such thing yet existed. Yeltsin simply remained president after independence. To be sure, such an institutionally ambiguous claim to power was typical as the 1990s began. As the Soviet empire in eastern Europe and then the Soviet Union itself came apart, various backroom compromises, roundtable negotiations, and partly free elections generated hybrid systems of government. In other postcommunist states, free and fair presidential and parliamentary elections quickly followed. The Russian Federation managed no election that might have legitimated Yeltsin or prepared the way for a successor. In a development Ilyin had not foreseen, but which was easy to reconcile with his doctrine, the very rich chose Russia's redeemer.

The wealthy few around Yeltsin, christened the "oligarchs," wished to manage democracy in his favor and theirs. The end of Soviet economic planning created a violent rush for profitable industries and resources and inspired arbitrage schemes, quickly creating a new class of wealthy men. Wild privatization was not at all the same thing as a market economy, at least as conventionally understood. Markets require the rule of law, which was the most demanding aspect of the post-Soviet transformations. Americans, taking the rule of law for granted, could fantasize that markets would create the necessary institutions. This was an error. It mattered whether newly independent states established the rule of law, and above all whether they managed a legal transition of power through free elections.

In 1993, Yeltsin dissolved the Russian parliament and sent armed men against its deputies. He told his western partners that this was streamlining needed to accelerate market reforms, a version of events accepted in the American press. So long as markets were invoked, politicians of inevitability could see an attack on a parliament as a step towards democracy. Yeltsin then used the conflict with parliament as a justification for strengthening the office of the president. In 1996, Yeltsin's team (by its own account) faked elections that won him another term as president.

By 1999, Yeltsin was visibly ill and frequently intoxicated, and the problem of succession became acute. Elections were needed to replace him; from the perspective of the oligarchs these needed to be managed and the outcome controlled. A successor was needed who would allow Yeltsin's family (in both the normal sense of his relatives and in the Russian sense of friendly oligarchs) to stay alive and maintain their wealth. "Operation Successor," as the challenge was known in the Kremlin, had two stages: finding a new man who was not a known associate of Yeltsin, and then inventing a fake problem that he could then appear to solve.

To find his successor, Yeltsin's entourage organized a public opinion poll about favorite heroes in popular entertainment. The winner was Max Stierlitz, the hero of a series of Soviet novels that were adapted into a number of films, most famously the television serial *Seventeen Moments of Spring* in 1973. The fictional Stierlitz was a Soviet plant in German military intelligence during the Second World War, a communist spy in Nazi uniform. Vladimir Putin, who had held a meaningless post in the East German provinces during his career in the KGB, was seen as the closest match to the fictional Stierlitz.* Having

---

* For his part, Putin would describe the fictional Stierlitz character as a teacher, and as president would decorate the actor who portrayed Stierlitz in the television adaptation of 1973. That actor, Vyacheslav Tikhonov, appeared in 2004 and 2010 in films directed by Nikita Mikhalkov, who apparently introduced Putin to the writings of Ilyin.

enriched himself as the assistant to the mayor of St. Petersburg in the 1990s, Putin was known to the Kremlin and thought to be a team player. He had worked for Yeltsin in Moscow since 1998, chiefly as head of the Federal Security Service (FSB, the former KGB). When appointed Yeltsin's prime minister in August 1999, Putin was unknown to the larger public, so not a plausible candidate for national elected office. His approval rating stood at 2%. And so it was time to generate a crisis that he could appear to solve.

In September 1999, a series of bombs exploded in Russian cities, killing hundreds of Russian citizens. It seemed possible that the perpetrators were FSB officers. In the city of Ryazan, for example, FSB officers were apprehended by their local colleagues as suspects in the bombings. Though the possibility of self-terrorism was noticed at the time, the factual questions were overwhelmed by righteous patriotism as Putin ordered a new war against the part of Russia deemed to be responsible for the bombings: the Chechen republic of southwestern Russia, in the Caucasus region, which had declared independence in 1993 and then fought the Russian army to a standstill. There was no evidence that Chechens had anything to do with the bombings. Thanks to the Second Chechen War, Putin's approval rating reached 45% in November. In December, Yeltsin announced his resignation and endorsed Putin as his successor. Thanks to unequal television coverage, manipulation of the vote tally, and the atmospherics of terrorism and war, Putin was accorded the absolute majority needed to win the presidential election of March 2000.

The ink of political fiction is blood.


SO BEGAN a new kind of politics, known at the time as "managed democracy," which Russians would master and later export. Credit for the political technology of Operation Successor was taken by Vladislav Surkov, a brilliant half-Chechen public relations specialist who served as Yeltsin's deputy chief of staff. The stage management of democracy that he pioneered, where a mysterious candidate used manufactured crises to assemble real power, continued as Surkov accepted a series of posts from Putin.

During Putin's first two presidential terms, between 2000 and 2008, Surkov exploited manageable conflicts to gain popularity or change institutions. In 2002, after Russian security forces killed dozens of Russian civilians while retaking a theater from terrorists, television fell under total state control. After a provincial school was besieged by terrorists in 2004, the post of elected regional governor was abolished. Justifying the end of those elected governorships, Surkov (citing Ilyin) claimed that Russians did not yet know how to vote. In Surkov's opinion, Russia "was not ready and could not have been ready for life in the conditions of modern democracy." Nevertheless, Surkov continued, Russia was superior to other post-Soviet states in its sovereignty. He claimed that none of the non-Russian nations of the old Soviet Union was capable of statehood.

Surkov's claims to Russian superiority did not pass a test that Russian leaders at that time still held to be relevant: resemblance to, approval from, and rapprochement with Europe. In 2004, three former republics of the Soviet Union—Lithuania, Latvia, and Estonia—joined the European Union, along with several other east European states that had been Soviet satellites. In order to join the European Union, these countries had to demonstrate their sovereignty in specific ways that Russia had not: by creating a market that could bear competition, an administration that could implement EU law, and a democracy that held free and fair elections.

States that joined the European Union had operative principles of succession. Russia did not. Surkov transformed this failure into a claim of superiority by speaking of "sovereign democracy." In so doing, he conjured away Russia's problem—that without actual democracy, or at least some succession principle, there was no reason to expect that Russia would endure as a sovereign state. Surkov suggested that "sovereign democracy" was a temporary measure that would allow Russia to find its own way to a certain kind of Western political society. Yet his term was celebrated by extreme nationalists, such as the fascist Alexander Dugin, who understood sovereign democracy as a permanent state of affairs, a politics of eternity. Any attempt to make of Russia an actual democracy could now be prevented, thought Dugin, by reference to sovereignty.

Democracy is a procedure to change rulers. To qualify democracy with an adjective—"people's democracy" during communism, "sovereign democracy" thereafter—means eliminating that procedure. At first, Surkov gamely tried to have it both ways, claiming to have preserved the institution of democracy by bringing the right person to power: "I would say that in our political culture the personality is the institution." Ilyin had performed the same trick: he called his redeemer a "democratic dictator" since he supposedly represented the people. Surkov's pillars of Russian statehood were "centralization, personification, and idealization": the state must be unified, its authority granted to an individual, and that individual glorified. Citing Ilyin, Surkov concluded that the Russian people should have as much freedom as they were ready to have. Of course, what Ilyin meant by "freedom" was the freedom of the individual to submerge himself in a collectivity that subjugates itself to a leader.

Surkov's juggling act was possible in the prosperous first decade of the twenty-first century. Between 2000 and 2008, during Putin's first two terms as president, the Russian economy grew at an average rate of almost 7% per annum. Putin won his war in Chechnya. The government exploited high world market prices of natural gas and oil to distribute some export profits throughout the Russian population. The instability of the Yeltsin order had passed, and many Russians were understandably pleased and grateful. Russia also enjoyed a stable position in foreign affairs. Putin offered NATO Russia's support after the terrorist attacks of September 11, 2001. In 2002, he spoke favorably of "European culture" and avoided portraying NATO as an adversary. In 2004, Putin spoke in favor of European Union membership for Ukraine, saying that such an outcome would be in Russia's economic interest. He spoke of the enlargement of the European Union as extending a zone of peace and prosperity to Russia's borders. In 2008, he attended a NATO summit.

In 2004, Putin was accorded the absolute majority necessary to win the office of president and began a second four-year term. Fraudulent or not, regular elections at least assured Russians that there was a time limit for presidential power. Surely, Russians could imagine, in 2008 some new figure would emerge, as Putin had emerged in 2000. According to the Russian constitution, Putin could not legally run for a third term in 2008, and so instead chose his own successor, the unknown Dmitry Medvedev. Once Medvedev was accorded the office of president, he named Putin prime minister. Under Medvedev, the Russian constitution was changed so that the term of president was extended to six years. Putin would be permitted to run again in 2012 and again in 2018. This was clearly his intention: victory of his party, United Russia, in the parliamentary elections of December 2011 and in all elections thereafter; victory in the presidential elections of March 2012 and then again in March 2018—a total of twenty years in office at least, the establishment of political eternity.

Yet the only mechanism for returning to the office of president in 2012 was the (apparently) democratic election. Putin would have to cheat, as before; but this time, when caught cheating, he would admit the deed. This was Surkov's identification of the personality with the institution, or Ilyin's proposition of ritual elections. Because Putin had weakened the mechanism of succession, he would have to insist that Russia did not need one. Killing the political future forced the political present to be eternal; making an eternity of the present required endless crisis and permanent threats.

ON DECEMBER 4, 2011, Russians were asked to grant United Russia a majority in the lower house of the Russian parliament. This was a special moment, since Medvedev, then president, and Putin, then prime minister, had already announced that they intended to switch jobs. Once their party won the parliamentary elections and once Putin won the presidential elections of the coming March, Medvedev would serve Putin as prime minister.

Many Russians found the prospect of eternal Putin unappealing. After the global financial collapse of 2008, Russian growth had slowed. Neither Putin nor Medvedev offered a program that would alter Russia's dependence upon commodity exports or offer the prospect of social mobility. Thus many Russians saw these elections as the last chance to prevent stagnation, and voted accordingly.

By the reckonings of independent Russian electoral observers, United Russia won about 26% of the vote in the December 4 elections. The party was nevertheless accorded enough votes to control a majority in parliament. Russian and international observers criticized unbalanced media coverage, and physical and digital manipulation of the vote. (Nick Griffin, the leader of the British National Party and a Holocaust denier, was present as a regime-friendly "observer." He declared the Russian elections "much fairer than Britain's.") On December 5, the protests began. On December 10, some fifty thousand people gathered in Moscow; on December 24, the figure grew to eighty thousand. Russians gathered in ninety-nine cities over the course of the month, in the largest protests in the history of the Russian Federation. The main slogan was "For Free Elections!"

The fakery was repeated during the March 4, 2012, presidential elections. Putin was accorded the majority that he needed to be named president after one round of balloting. This time most of the electoral manipulation was digital rather than manual. Tens of millions of cybervotes were added, diluting the votes cast by human beings, and giving Putin a fictional majority. In some districts, Putin was accorded votes in round numbers, suggesting that targets set by central authorities had been understood literally by local officials. In Chechnya, Putin was accorded 99.8% of the ballots: the figure likely reflected the total control exercised by his Chechen ally Ramzan Kadyrov. Putin received similar tallies in mental hospitals and in other places subject to state control. In Novosibirsk, protestors complained that vote counts totaled 146% of the population. Once again, independent Russian and international observers noted the irregularities. And once again, regime-friendly foreigners from the far Right endorsed the results.

On March 5, 2012, in Moscow some twenty-five thousand Russian citizens protested the falsified presidential elections. For Putin himself, these months, between December 2011 and March 2012, were a time of choice. He might have listened to criticisms of the parliamentary vote. He might have accepted the outcome of the presidential ballot and won in the second round of voting rather than in the first. To win on the first ballot was a point of pride, nothing more. He might have understood that many of the protestors were concerned about the rule of law and the principle of succession in their country. Instead, he seemed to take personal offense.

Putin chose to regard the transient illusion of winning on the first ballot as more important than law, and his own hurt feelings as more important than the convictions of his fellow citizens. Putin casually accepted that there had been fraud; Medvedev helpfully added that all Russian elections had been fraudulent. By dismissing the principle of "one person, one vote" while insisting that elections would continue, Putin was disregarding the choices of citizens while expecting them to take part in future rituals of support. He thereby accepted Ilyin's attitude to democracy, rejecting what Ilyin had called "blind faith in the number of votes and its political significance," not only in deed but in word. A claim to power was staked: he who fakes wins.

If Putin came to the office of president in 2000 as a mysterious hero from the realm of fiction, he returned in 2012 as the vengeful destroyer of the rule of law. Putin's decision to steal the election under his own spotlight placed Russian statehood in limbo. His accession to the office of president in 2012 was therefore the beginning of a succession crisis. Since the man in power was also the man who had eliminated the future, the present had to be eternal.

In 1999 and 2000, the Kremlin had used Chechens as the necessary enemy. Chechnya had now been defeated, and the Chechen warlord Kadyrov became an important member of Putin's regime. After the fakery of 2011 and 2012, the domestic political emergency was permanent, and so the enemy had to be as well. Some intractable foreign foe had to be linked to protestors, so that they, rather than Putin himself, could be portrayed as the danger to Russian statehood. Protestors' actions had to be uncoupled from the very real domestic problem that Putin had created, and associated instead with a fake foreign threat to Russian sovereignty. The politics of eternity requires and produces problems that are insoluble because they are fictional. For Russia in 2012, the fictional problem became the designs of the European Union and the United States to destroy Russia.

LEONID BREZHNEV'S permanent enemy, the decadent West, had returned: but this time the decadence would be of a more explicitly sexual variety. Ilyin had described opposition to his views as "sexual perversion," by which he meant homosexuality. A century later, this was also the Kremlin's first reaction to democratic opposition. Those who wished to have votes counted in 2011 and 2012 were not Russian citizens who wanted to see the law followed, their wishes respected, their state endure. They were mindless agents of global sexual decadence whose actions threatened the innocent national organism.

On December 6, 2011, the day after the first protest in Moscow, the president of the Russian Federation, then still Dmitry Medvedev, retweeted a message to the effect that a leading protestor was a "stupid cocksucking sheep." Vladimir Putin, still prime minister but about to become president again, said on Russian television that the white ribbons worn by protestors made him think of condoms. Then he compared protestors to monkeys and did a monkey imitation. Visiting Germany, Putin told a surprised Angela Merkel that the Russian opposition was "sexually deformed." Russian Foreign Minister Sergei Lavrov began to claim that the Russian government had to take a stand against homosexuality to defend the innocence of Russian society.

A confidant of Putin, Vladimir Yakunin, developed the sheep image into a theory of geopolitics. In Yakunin's opinion, published in a long article in November 2012, Russia was eternally confronted with a conspiracy of enemies, which has controlled the course of history since time began. This global group had released homosexual propaganda around the world in order to reduce birth rates in Russia and thereby preserve the power of the West. The spread of gay rights was a deliberate policy intended to turn Russians into a "herd" easily manipulable by the global masters of capitalism.

In September 2013, a Russian diplomat repeated this argument at a conference on human rights in China. Gay rights were nothing more than the chosen weapon of a global neoliberal conspiracy, meant to prepare virtuous traditional societies such as Russia and China for exploitation. President Putin took the next step at his personal global summit at Valdai a few days later, comparing same-sex partnerships to Satanism. He associated gay rights with a Western model that "opens a direct path to degradation and primitivism, resulting in a profound demographic and moral crisis." The Russian parliament had by then passed a law "For the Purpose of Protecting Children from Information Advocating for a Denial of Traditional Family Values."

Human sexuality is an inexhaustible raw material for the manufacture of anxiety. The attempt to place heterosexuality within Russia and homosexuality beyond was factually ludicrous, but the facts were beside the point. The purpose of the anti-gay campaign was to transform demands for democracy into a nebulous threat to Russian innocence: voting = West = sodomy. Russia had to be innocent, and all problems had to be the responsibility of others.

The campaign did not depend on a factual demonstration of the heterosexuality of the Russian elite. In the previous four years, when Putin had been prime minister, Surkov had placed him in a series of fur-and-feathers photo shoots. Putin and Medvedev's attempt to present themselves as manly friends by posing in matching whites after badminton matches was similarly unconvincing. Putin divorced his wife just as his anti-gay campaign began, leaving the champion of family values without a traditional family. The question of gender identity clung to the Russian president. In 2016, Putin asserted that he was not a woman who has bad days. In 2017, he denied that he was Donald Trump's groom. That year it became a criminal offense to portray Putin as a gay clown. An attentive female scholar summarized his position: "Putin's kisses are reserved for children and animals."

Putin was offering masculinity as an argument against democracy. As the German sociologist Max Weber argued, charisma can initiate a political system, but it cannot guarantee its continuity. It is normal, Weber observed, to form a political and commercial clan around a charismatic leader. But if that man wishes to go beyond redistributing the booty and planning the next raid, he must find a way to transfer his authority to someone else, ideally by a means that will allow power to be transferred again. Solving this problem of succession is the precondition of establishing a modern state.

Weber defined two mechanisms that would allow a burst of charisma to become durable institutions: (1) through custom, as for example in a monarchy where the eldest son succeeded the father; or (2) through law, as for example in a democracy where regular voting allows parliaments and rulers to be replaced. Putin did not seem to be planning a monarchical succession. He has kept his daughters at a distance from public politics (although the family did benefit from crony capitalism). The logical possibility that remains is thus law, which in the modern world usually means democracy. Putin himself dismissed this alternative. And so the display of masculinity provided a semblance of power at the expense of Russia's integrity as a state.

During self-inflicted catastrophes of this kind, a certain kind of man always finds a way to blame a woman. In Vladimir Putin's case, that woman was Hillary Clinton.

IF THE Kremlin's first impulse was to associate democratic opposition with global sodomy, its second was to claim that protestors worked for a foreign power, one whose chief diplomat was female: the United States. On December 8, 2011, three days after the protests began, Putin blamed Hillary Clinton for initiating them: "she gave the signal." On December 15, he claimed that the demonstrators were paid. Evidence was not provided and was not the point. If, as Ilyin maintained, voting was just an opening to foreign influence, then Putin's job was to make up a story about foreign influence and use it to alter domestic politics. The point was to choose the enemy that best suited a leader's needs, not one that actually threatened the country. Indeed, it was best not to speak of actual threats, since discussing actual enemies would reveal actual weaknesses and suggest the fallibility of aspiring dictators. When Ilyin wrote that the art of politics was "identifying and neutralizing the enemy," he did not mean that statesmen should ascertain which foreign power actually posed a threat. He meant that politics began with a leader's decision about which foreign enmity will consolidate a dictatorship. Russia's real geopolitical problem was China. But precisely because Chinese power was real and proximate, considering Russia's actual geopolitics might lead to depressing conclusions.

The West was chosen as an enemy precisely because it represented no threat to Russia. Unlike China, the EU had no army and no long border with Russia. The United States did have an army, but had withdrawn the vast majority of its troops from the European continent: from about 300,000 in 1991 to about 60,000 in 2012. NATO still existed and had admitted former communist countries of eastern Europe. But President Barack Obama had cancelled an American plan to build a missile defense system in eastern Europe in 2009, and in 2010 Russia was allowing American planes to fly through Russian airspace to supply American forces in Afghanistan. No Russian leader feared a NATO invasion in 2011 or 2012, or even pretended to. In 2012, American leaders believed that they were pursuing a "reset" of relations with Russia. When Mitt Romney referred to Russia as America's "number one geopolitical foe" in March 2012, he was ridiculed. Almost no one in the American public or media was paying attention to Moscow. Russia did not even figure in American public opinion polls about global threats and challenges.

The European Union and the United States were presented as threats because Russian elections were faked. In winter 2011 and spring 2012, Russian television channels and newspapers generated the narrative that all who protested electoral fraud were paid by Western institutions. The effort began on December 8, 2011, with the reporting of Putin's claim that Clinton had initiated the protests. Under the headline "Putin proposes tougher punishment for Western stooges," *Noviie Izvestiia* reported his professed belief that "the Russian opposition forces began mass protests after the 'go-ahead' given by US Secretary of State Hillary Clinton." The association between opposition and treason was axiomatic, the only question that of the appropriate punishment. In March, Russian television released a film, described as a "documentary," which claimed that Russian citizens who took to the streets were paid by devious foreigners.

Precisely because Putin had made the Russian state vulnerable, he had to claim that it was his opponents who had done so. Since Putin believed that "it would be inadmissible to allow the destruction of the state to satisfy this thirst for change," he reserved for himself the right to define views that he did not like as a threat to Russia.


FROM 2012, there was no sense in imagining a worse Russia in the past and a better Russia in the future, mediated by a reforming government in the present. The enmity of the United States and the European Union had to become the premise of Russian politics. Putin had reduced Russian statehood to his oligarchical clan and its moment. The only way to head off a vision of future collapse was to describe democracy as an immediate and permanent threat. Having transformed the future into an abyss, Putin had to make flailing at its edge look like judo.

In 2012, Putin made it clear that he understood democracy as ritualized support for his person. It meant, as he informed the Russian parliament in his annual address for that year, "compliance with and respect for laws, rules, and regulations." Individual Russians had no right to protest against the anti-democratic actions of their government, on Putin's logic, since democracy required them to align their souls with laws that banned such protests. Putin was repeating Ilyin's understanding of both elections and law. Thus "freedom" meant subordination to the words of an arbitrary leader. Indeed, after Putin's return to the office of president in May 2012, the Russian state was transformed in ways that corresponded to Ilyin's proposals. Every important measure brought to life an element of Ilyin's constitutional texts.

Libel was made a criminal offense. A law that banned insults to religious sensitivities made the police the enforcer of an Orthodox public sphere. It became a crime to publish cartoons of Jesus or to play Pokémon Go in a church. The authority and budget of the FSB were increased, and its officers granted broad authority to shoot without warning. A new FSB unit was named after Felix Dzerzhinsky, the founder of the Cheka (predecessor of the GRU, NKVD, KGB, and FSB). The definition of treason was expanded to include the provision of information to nongovernmental organizations beyond Russia, which made telling the truth over email a high crime. Undefined "extremism" was outlawed. Nongovernmental organizations deemed to work "against Russia's interests" were banned. Those that had received funding from abroad—a very general notion that included any form of international cooperation, such as holding a conference—were required to register themselves as "foreign agents."

On the morning that the "foreign agent" law went into effect, graffiti appeared across Moscow on the headquarters of nongovernmental organizations reading FOREIGN AGENT USA. One target was *Memorial*, a storehouse of materials on the history of Russia in the twentieth century. Russia's own past became a foreign threat. *Memorial* had documented the suffering of Soviet citizens, including Russians, during the Stalinist period. Of course, if all of Russia's problems came from the outside, there was little sense in dwelling on such matters. The politics of eternity destroys history.

IN THE politics of eternity, the past provides a trove of symbols of innocence exploited by rulers to illustrate the harmony of the homeland and the discord of the rest of the world. Putin's third response to the protests of 2011 and 2012 was to explicitly endorse and propagate Ilyin's version of the politics of eternity, to imagine Russia as a virginal organism troubled only by the threat of foreign penetration.

On December 15, 2011, ten days after the protests against electoral fraud began, and two decades after the dissolution of the USSR, Putin imagined a Russia where historical conflicts were literary problems. Sitting in a radio studio with the fascist writer Alexander Prokhanov, Putin mused about a Russia that would honor Soviet monuments to the terror against Soviet citizens, specifically to the Cheka and its founder, Felix Dzerzhinsky. If something had gone wrong in Russian history, said Putin, it was the end of the Soviet Union. A historical event in which Putin's patron Yeltsin had been the central figure, and which had enabled Putin's own career, was now a mysterious passage to national malaise. What Russia needed, proposed Putin, was a different sense of the word *revolution*: a cycle that returned over and over, to the same place.

"Can we say," Putin asked millions of radio listeners, "that our country has fully recovered and healed after the dramatic events that have occurred to us after the Soviet Union collapsed, and that we now have a strong, healthy state? No, of course she is still quite ill; but here we must recall Ivan Ilyin: 'Yes, our country is still sick, but we did not flee from the bed of our sick mother.'" The remark suggested that Putin had been reading rather deeply in the Ilyin corpus, but his interpretation of the passage was odd. For Ilyin, it had been the foundation of the USSR, not its dissolution, that was the wound to Russia. Ilyin had wished to remain with his actual mother, but could not do so because he was expelled from the Soviet Union by the Cheka. Ilyin told his Cheka interrogator, "I consider Soviet power to be an inevitable historical outcome of the great social and spiritual disease which has been growing in Russia for several centuries."

As a former KGB officer, Putin was a Chekist, as Russians still say, who wished to rule Russia through the Russian Orthodox Church. He wanted a reconciliation of what he called the traditions of Red and White, communist and Orthodox, terror and God. A sense of history would have required some confrontation with both aspects of Russian history. The politics of eternity allowed Putin the freedom to accept both Red and White as innocent Russian responses to external threats. If all conflicts were the fault of the outsider, there was no need to consider Russians, their choices, or their crimes. The extreme Right and Left should instead be drawn together as a bicephalous icon. Putin banished contradictions. He oversaw a revival of Ilyin's work in which Ilyin's criticism of the Soviet Union was ignored. It would have been gauche to mention that Ilyin had recommended that Chekists be purged from politics in a post-Soviet Russia.

In 2005, Putin had reburied Ilyin's corpse at a monastery where the Soviet secret state police had incinerated the corpses of thousands of Russian citizens executed during the Great Terror. At the moment of Ilyin's reburial, the head of the Russian Orthodox Church was a man who had been a KGB agent in Soviet times. At the ceremony, a military band struck up the Russian national anthem, which has the same melody as the Soviet national anthem. The man who seems to have exposed Putin to Ilyin's writings, the film director Nikita Mikhalkov, was the son of the composer responsible for both versions. Mikhalkov was an avid student of Ilyin, as his political manifesto reveals: Russia was a "spiritual-material unity," a "thousand-year-old union of multiple nationalities and tribes," exhibiting a "particular, supranational, imperial consciousness." Russia was the center of Eurasia, "an independent, cultural-historic continent, organic, national unity, geopolitical and sacred, center of the world."

When Putin laid flowers on Ilyin's grave in 2009, he was in the company of his favorite Orthodox monk, Tikhon Shevkunov, who was willing to see the Soviet executioners as Russian patriots. Putin himself, speaking a few years later, had no trouble seeing the values of communism as biblical: "A certain ideology dominated in the Soviet Union, and regardless of our feelings about it, it was based on some clear, in fact quasi-religious, values. The Moral Code of the Builder of Communism, if you read it, is just a pathetic copy of the Bible." A number of Ilyin's contemporaries had called Ilyin a "Chekist for God." He was reburied as such, with honors conferred by the Chekists and the men of God, and by the men of God who were Chekists, and by the Chekists who were men of God.

Ilyin was returned, body and soul, to the Russia he had been forced to leave. And that very return, in its endorsement of contradiction and its disregard of fact, was the purest expression of respect for Ilyin's tradition. To be sure, Ilyin opposed the Soviet system. But once it no longer existed it was history; and for Ilyin the facts of the past were nothing but raw material for the construction of a myth of innocence. Modifying Ilyin's views ever so slightly, it was possible to see the Soviet Union not as an external imposition upon Russia, as he had seen it, but as Russia, and therefore immaculate. And so Russians could recall the Soviet system as an innocent Russian reaction to the hostility of the world. Their rulers honored their own Soviet past by reburying an enemy of the Soviet Union.

Vasily Grossman, the great Soviet novelist and chronicler of the crimes of National Socialism and Stalinism, wrote, "Everything flows, everything changes. You cannot enter the same transport twice." He meant "transport to a concentration camp," and was referring to the adage of Heraclitus: "Everything flows, everything changes. You cannot step into the same river twice." In Ilyin's sensibility, adapted by Putin, time was not a river flowing forward, but a cold round pool where ripples flowed ever inward towards a mysterious Russian perfection. Nothing new ever happened, and nothing new ever could happen; the West assaulted Russian innocence over and over again. History in the sense of the study of the past must be rejected, because it would raise questions.

In Mikhalkov's 2014 film *Sunstroke*, he had ethnic Russians sentenced to death by a female Jewish secret police officer, thereby suggesting that any unjust killing was done by people who might be considered alien by nationality or gender. In 2017, when Russia had to somehow address the centenary of the Bolshevik Revolution, Russian television aired a multipart drama about Leon Trotsky, thereby coding the revolution as Jewish. The hero at the end of the drama was none other than Ivan Ilyin. And so Russia celebrated a centennial of revolution by enshrining a counterrevolutionary philosopher who said that Russians should think of the past in terms of cycles of innocence. A lesson had been learned.

AS PUTIN endorsed Ilyin's politics of eternity, he accepted Ilyin's definition of the Russian nation. On January 23, 2012, just after the parliamentary elections, and just before the presidential elections, Putin published an article in which he developed Ilyin's understanding of the national question. By claiming that political opposition was sexual and foreign, Putin had already located all responsibility for Russian problems beyond the Russian redeemer or the Russian organism. By arguing that Russia was an inherently innocent "civilization," Putin closed the logical circle. Russia was by its nature a producer and exporter of harmony, and must be allowed to bring its variety of peace to its neighbors.

In this article, Putin abolished the legal borders of the Russian Federation. Writing as its future president, he described Russia not as a state but as a spiritual condition. Citing Ilyin by name, Putin claimed that Russia had no conflicts among nationalities and indeed could not have had any. The "nationality question" in Russia was, according to Ilyin, an invention of enemies, a conceptual import from the West that had no applicability to Russia. Like Ilyin, Putin wrote of Russian civilization as eliciting fraternity. "The Great Russian mission," wrote Putin, "is to unify and bind civilization. In such a state-civilization there are no national minorities, and the principle of recognition of 'friend or foe' is defined on the basis of a common culture." That politics begins from "friend or foe" is the basic fascist idea, formulated by the Nazi legal theorist Carl Schmitt and endorsed and propagated by Ilyin.

In writing of Russia as a civilization, Putin meant everyone whom he regarded as part of that civilization. Rather than speaking of the Ukrainian state, whose sovereignty, territorial integrity, and borders Russia officially recognized, Putin preferred to imagine the Ukrainians as a folk scattered across the broad expanse of what he defined as Russian territory, "from the Carpathians to Kamchatka," and thus as an element of Russian civilization. If Ukrainians were simply one more Russian group (like "Tatars, Jews, and Belarusians"), then Ukrainian statehood was irrelevant and Putin as a Russian leader had the right to speak for the Ukrainian people. He concluded with a cry of defiance, telling the world that Russians and Ukrainians would never be divided, and threatening war to those who failed to understand: "We have lived together for centuries. Together we triumphed in the most horrible of wars. And we will continue to live together. And to those who want to divide us, I can only say one thing: the day will never come."

When Putin threw down that gauntlet, in January 2012, no one in the West was paying attention. The issue in the headlines was that of Russian voters and their discontents; no one in Europe, America, or Ukraine was considering Russian-Ukrainian relations. And yet Putin, moving very quickly, had formulated a politics of eternity that transformed Russians' protests against his fake elections into a European and American offensive against Russia in which Ukraine would be the field of battle. It was not, according to Putin, that individual Russians had been wronged because their votes did not count. It was that Russia as a civilization had been wronged because the West did not understand that Ukraine was Russian. It was not that Putin had weakened the Russian state by undermining its succession principle. It was that Europeans and Americans were challenging Russian civilization by recognizing Ukraine. In his first address to the Russian parliament as president in 2012, Putin affirmed this concept of the civilization-state.

No one was trying to divide the Russian Federation as a sovereign state with borders. But Ukraine was also a sovereign state with borders. That Ukraine was a different sovereign state than Russia was an elementary matter of international law, just as Canada was not the United States, and Belgium was not France. By presenting the banal legal status quo as a violation of Russia's immaculate civilization, Putin was overthrowing a prevailing concept of law, one that Russia had observed for the previous two decades, in favor of particular claims from culture. Russia was not only innocent but generous, went his reasoning, since only through Russian civilization could Ukrainians understand who they truly were.

Even the most servile of Ukraine's leaders would have difficulty accepting Putin's description of their society. The president of Ukraine at the time, Viktor Yanukovych, was a known quantity in Russia and hardly a threat. Yanukovych had been disgraced in 2004 when a presidential election was stolen on his behalf, and Putin had been embarrassed when the election was held again and someone else won. The American political strategist Paul Manafort, at work on a plan to increase Russia's influence in the United States, was dispatched to Kyiv to help Yanukovych. Under Manafort's tutelage,

Yanukovych acquired some skills; thanks to the corruption of his rivals, he gained a second chance.

Yanukovych won the election of 2010 legitimately and began his term by offering Russia essentially everything that Ukraine could give, including basing rights for the Russian navy on Ukraine's Crimean peninsula until the year 2042. This made it impossible for Ukraine to consider joining the NATO alliance for at least three decades, as Ukrainians, Russians, and Americans understood at the time. Russia announced that it would expand its presence on the Black Sea by adding warships, frigates, submarines, troop-landing ships, and new naval aircraft. A Russian expert pronounced that Russian forces would remain in their Black Sea ports "until doomsday."

Suddenly, in 2012, Putin's new doctrine challenged the very notion that Ukraine and Russia were legal equals who could sign a treaty. In 2013 and 2014, Russia would try to transform Yanukovych from a servile client into a powerless puppet, thereby inducing Ukrainians to rebel against a government that suspended their rights, copied repressive Russian legislation, and applied violence. Putin's idea of Russian civilization and his bullying of Yanukovych would bring revolution to Ukraine.

ASKED BY students of history to name a historical authority, Putin could only think of one name: Ivan Ilyin. Now, Ilyin was many things, but he was no historian. If Ilyin's timeless regularities could replace historical time, if identity could replace policy, then the question of succession could perhaps be delayed.

In his first address to the Russian parliament as president in 2012, Putin described his own place in the Russian timescape as the fulfillment of an eternal cycle: as the return of an ancient lord of Kyiv whom Russians call *Vladimir*. The politics of eternity requires points in the past to which the present can cycle, demonstrating the innocence of the country, the right to rule of its leader, and the pointlessness of thinking about the future. Putin's first such point was the year 988, when his namesake, an early medieval warlord known in his time as Volodymyr or Valdemar, converted to Christianity. In Putin's myth of the past, Volodymyr/Valdemar was a Russian whose conversion linked forever the lands of today's Russia, Belarus, and Ukraine.

Putin's monastic friend Tikhon Shevkunov maintained that "he who loves Russia and wishes it well can only pray for Vladimir, placed at the head of Russia by God's will." In this formulation, *Vladimir* Putin is the Russian redeemer who emerges from beyond history ("by God's will") and mystically incorporates a millennial Russian past simply by bearing a name. Time became a mystical loop, vacant of factuality. When a statue of Volodymyr/Valdemar was unveiled in

Moscow (with the modern Russian spelling "Vladimir"), the Russian media was careful not to mention that the city of Moscow had not existed when Volodymyr/Valdemar ruled. Instead, Russian television repeated that the new monument was the first such homage to the leader of Rus. This was untrue. In fact, a statue of Volodymyr/Valdemar had been standing in Kyiv since 1853.

In history, the person in question was known as Volodymyr (as ruler of Kyiv) and Valdemar (to his Scandinavian relatives). He belonged to a clan of Vikings, known as the Rus, who had worked their way south along the Dnipro River in order to sell slaves at southerly ports. The Rus made Kyiv their main trading post and eventually their capital. The death of each Viking warlord caused bloody struggles. Volodymyr/Valdemar had been prince of Novgorod, where (according to Arab sources) he had converted to Islam in order to trade with nearby Muslim Bulgars. To win Kyiv, Volodymyr/Valdemar made for Scandinavia to seek military assistance against his brothers. He won the campaign and control of Rus. Volodymyr formalized the pagan rites of Kyiv and had local Christians sacrificed to the god of thunder. At some point Volodymyr married the sister of the Byzantine emperor, a political coup that required his conversion to Christianity. Only then did Christianity rather than official paganism became the source of legitimation of the ruler of Kyiv.

Christianity did not prevent parricidal, fratricidal, and filicidal warfare, because it did not provide a succession principle. Volodymyr had imprisoned his son Sviatopolk and was marching on his son Yaroslav when he died in 1015. After Volodymyr's death, Sviatopolk killed three of his brothers, only to be defeated on the battlefield by his brother Yaroslav. Sviatopolk then brought in the Polish king and a Polish army to defeat Yaroslav, who, for his part, recruited an army of Pechenegs (people who had drunk from his grandfather's skull) to defeat Sviatopolk, who was killed in battle. Then yet another brother, Mstislav, marched on Yaroslav and defeated him, creating the conditions for a truce and joint rule between those two brothers. After Mstislav died in 1036, Yaroslav ruled alone. And so the succession from father Volodymyr to son Yaroslav took seventeen years, and was complete only after ten sons of Volodymyr were dead. The life and rule of Volodymyr/Valdemar of Kyiv, if seen as history rather than within a politics of eternity, does offer a lesson: the importance of a principle of succession.

No doubt the Russian state can be maintained, for a time, by elective emergency and selective war. The very anxiety created by the lack of a succession principle can be projected abroad, creating real hostility and thus starting the whole process anew. In 2013, Russia began to seduce or bully its European neighbors into abandoning their own institutions and histories. If Russia could not become the West, let the West become Russia. If the flaws of American democracy could be exploited to elect a Russian client, then Putin could prove that the world outside is no better than Russia. Were the European Union or the United States to disintegrate during Putin's lifetime, he could cultivate an illusion of eternity.

## CHAPTER THREE

# INTEGRATION OR EMPIRE (2013)

Europe, however serious its numerous shortcomings and misdemeanors, has nevertheless acquired an awesomely precious, indeed priceless, dowry of skills and know-how which it can still share with the rest of a planet that needs them now more than ever for its survival.

—ZYGMUNT BAUMAN, 2013

A state with a principle of succession exists in time. A state that arranges its foreign relations exists in space. For Europeans of the twentieth century, the central question was thus: After empire, what? When it was no longer possible for European powers to dominate large territories, how could the remnants and fragments maintain themselves as states? For a few decades, from the 1950s through the 2000s, the answer seemed self-evident: the creation, deepening, and enlargement of the European Union, a relationship among states known as integration. European empires had brought the first globalization, as well as its disastrous finales: the First World War, the Great Depression, the Second World War, the Holocaust. European integration provided a fundament for a second globalization, one that, in Europe at least, promised to be different.

European integration lasted long enough that Europeans could take it for granted, and forget the resonance and power of other political models. Yet history never ends, and alternatives always emerge. In 2013, the Russian Federation proposed an alternative to integration under the name "Eurasia": empire for Russia, nation-states for everyone else. One problem with this proposal was that the nation-state had proven itself to be untenable in Europe. In the history of Europe's great powers, imperialism blended into integration, with the nation-state hardly appearing. The major European powers had never been nation-states: before the Second World War they had been empires, where citizens and subjects were unequal; afterwards, as they lost their empires, they had joined a process of European integration in which sovereignty was shared. The east European nation-states that had been founded as such had collapsed in the 1930s or 1940s. In 2013, there was every reason to suspect that, absent a larger European system, European states would also dissolve. One form of disintegration, that of the European Union, would very likely lead to another, the disintegration of the states of Europe.

Russian leaders seemed to understand this. Unlike their European counterparts, they were openly discussing the 1930s. Russia's Eurasia project had its roots in the 1930s, precisely the decade when European nation-states collapsed into war. Eurasia became plausible in Russia as its leaders made integration impossible for their people. At the same time, the Kremlin rehabilitated fascist thinkers of the era, and promoted contemporary Russian thinkers who recalled fascist ideas. The major Eurasianists of the 2010s—Alexander Dugin, Alexander Prokhanov, and Sergei Glazyev—revived or remade Nazi ideas for Russian purposes.

In his time, Ivan Ilyin was in the mainstream when he believed that the future, like the past, belonged to empires. In the 1930s, the major question seemed to be whether the new empires would be of the extreme Right or the extreme Left.

The First World War brought the collapse of the old European land empires: not only Ilyin's Russia, but the Habsburg monarchy, the German Empire, and the Ottoman Empire. Thereafter, an experiment in the creation of nation-states was undertaken on their territories. France tried to support these new entities, but during the Great Depression ceded influence in central and eastern Europe to

FINLAND

NORWAY
Kristiania

Helsinki

Stockholm    Tallinn
ESTONIA

RUSSIAN
S.F.S.R.

°Edinburgh    SWEDEN    LATVIA
North    DENMARK    Riga    Moscow
Dublin    UNITED    Sea    Copenhagen    Baltic    LITHUANIA
IRISH FREE    KINGDOM    Sea    Kaunas
STATE    Danzig    EAST    Wilno
NETHERLANDS    PRUSSIA    Minsk    U.S.S.R.
Amsterdam    (Ger.)    BELARUSIAN
London    Berlin    S.S.R.
Brussels    GERMANY    Warsaw
BELGIUM    POLAND
Paris    LUX.    Prague    Cracow    Lwów    Kyiv    Kharkiv
CZECHOSLOVAKIA    Dnipro
FRANCE    Munich    UKRAINIAN S.S.R.
Bern    Vienna    Budapest    Chisinau
Bay of    SWITZERLAND    AUSTRIA    Odessa
Biscay    HUNGARY    ROMANIA    CRIMEAN
A.S.S.R.
Belgrade    Bucharest    (RSFSR)
ITALY    YUGOSLAVIA    Danube    Black Sea
Madrid    Rome    BULGARIA
SPAIN    Sofia
Tirana    Istanbul
ALBANIA    Ankara
GREECE    TURKEY
Athens

Malta
(UK)

Cyprus
(UK)

EUROPE
c. 1930

Mediterranean Sea

fascist Italy and Nazi Germany. When a Polish regional governor or a Romanian fascist pronounced that the era of liberal democracy was over, they were voicing a general European conviction, indeed one that was widely shared on the other side of the Atlantic. In the 1930s the United States was an empire, in the sense that a large number of its Native American and African American subjects were not full citizens. Whether or not it would become a democracy was an open question; many of its influential men thought not. George Kennan, an American diplomat who would become his country's outstanding strategic thinker, proposed in 1938 that the United States should "go along the road which leads through constitutional change to the authoritarian state." Using the slogan "America First," the famous aviator Charles Lindbergh called for sympathy with Nazis.

The Second World War also taught Europeans that the choice was between fascism and communism, empires of the far Right or far Left. It began with an unstoppable alliance of the two extremes, a German-Soviet offensive military pact of August 1939 that quickly destroyed the European system by eliminating whole states. Germany had already demolished Austria and Czechoslovakia; the Wehrmacht and the Red Army together invaded and destroyed Poland; and then the Soviet Union occupied and annexed Lithuania, Latvia, and Estonia. With Soviet economic backing, Germany invaded and defeated France in 1940. The second stage of the war began in June 1941, when Hitler betrayed Stalin and Germany invaded the Soviet Union. Now the extremes were on opposite sides. Berlin's war aim was imperial: the control of the fertile soil of Soviet Ukraine which, Hitler thought, would make of Germany a self-sufficient economy and a world power. As allies or as enemies, the far Right and the far Left seemed the only viable options. Even resistance to Nazi rule was usually led by communists.

In general, the defeat of Nazi Germany in 1945 discredited fascism: either because Europeans came to see fascism as a moral disaster, or because fascism claimed to be about winning and lost. After the Red Army drove the Wehrmacht from the Soviet Union and eastern Europe, Soviet power was established again in Estonia, Latvia, and Lithuania, and communist regimes took over in Romania, Poland, and Hungary—all countries where right-wing authoritarianism had seemed the work of destiny just a few years before. By 1950, communism extended across almost the entirety of the zone of nation-states that had been formed after the First World War. In the aftermath of the Second World War, as in the aftermath of the First, the European nation-state proved unsustainable.

American economic power had been decisive to the course of the war. Although the United States was late to enter the military conflict in Europe, it supplied its British and Soviet allies. In postwar Europe, the United States subsidized economic cooperation in order to support the political center and undermine the extremes and thus, in the long run, create a stable market for its exports. This recognition that markets required a social basis was of a piece with American domestic policy: in the three postwar decades, the gap between rich and poor in the United States was narrowed. In the 1960s, the vote was extended to African Americans, reducing the imperial character of American politics. Although the Soviet Union and its east European satellites refused American aid after the war, west European states undertook a renewed experiment with the rule of law and democratic elections, with American financial support. Although the policies differed considerably from state to state, in general Europe in these decades built a system of health care and social insurance that later generations would take for granted. In western and central Europe, the state would no longer be dependent upon empire, but could be rescued by integration.

European integration began in 1951. Ilyin died only three years later. Like the Russian thinkers and leaders who revived him a half century later, he never took European integration seriously. He preserved his Manichean view of politics until the end: Russian empire meant salvation, and all other regimes marked various points on the slippery slope to Satanism. When Ilyin looked at postwar Europe he saw Spain and Portugal, maritime empires governed by right-wing dictators. He believed that Francisco Franco and António de Oliveira Salazar had preserved the fascist legacy and would reconstitute the European fascist norm. In postwar Britain and France, Ilyin saw empires rather than a constitutional monarchy and a republic, and presumed that the imperial element was the durable one.

If European states were empires, wrote Ilyin, it was natural that Russia was one and should remain one. Empire was the natural state of affairs; fascist empires would be most successful; Russia would be the perfect fascist empire.

IN THE half century between Ilyin's death and his rehabilitation, a Europe of integration replaced the Europe of empire. Germany began the pattern. Defeated in war and divided thereafter, Germans accepted a proposition from neighboring France, and along with Belgium, the Netherlands, Luxembourg, and Italy established a European Coal and Steel Community in 1951. West Germany's leaders, Konrad Adenauer in particular, saw that the path to national sovereignty and unification led through European integration. As other European empires also lost their colonial wars and their colonial markets, this project broadened. Even Great Britain, the imperial superpower, joined the undertaking (along with Denmark and Ireland) in 1973. Portugal and Spain set a new pattern of losing colonies, replacing authoritarianism with parliamentary democracy, and then joining the European project (both in 1986). Europe was a soft landing after empire.

By the 1980s, democracy through integration had become the norm in much of Europe. All of the members of what was then called the European Community were democracies, most of them markedly more prosperous than the communist regimes to their east. In the 1970s and 1980s, the gap in living standards between western and eastern Europe grew, as changes in communications made it harder to hide. As Mikhail Gorbachev tried to repair a Soviet state to rescue the Soviet economy, west European states were building a new political framework around economic cooperation. In 1992, a few months after the Soviet Union ceased to exist, the European Community was transformed into the European Union (EU). This EU was the practice of the coordination of law, the acceptance of a shared high court, and an area of free trade and movement. It later became, for most of its members, a zone with a common border and a common currency.

For most of the communist states of eastern Europe, the European Union also proved to be a secure destination after empire, though in a different way. In the 1930s and 1940s, the east European states established after the First World War fell prey to German empire, or to Soviet empire, or to both. After the revolutions of 1989, newly elected leaders of the east European states that emerged from Soviet domination expressed their aspiration to join the European project. This "return to Europe" was a reaction to the lesson of 1918 and 1945: that without some larger structure, the nation-state is untenable. In 1993 the EU began to sign association agreements with east European states, beginning a legal relationship. Three principles of membership were established in the 1990s: market economies able to handle competition; democracy and human rights; and the administrative capacity to implement European laws and regulations.

In 2004 and 2007, seven post-communist states (Poland, Hungary, Romania, Bulgaria, the Czech Republic, Slovakia, Slovenia) and three former Soviet republics (Lithuania, Latvia, and Estonia) joined the European Union. In 2013, Croatia also joined the EU. The kind of small political unit that had failed after 1918 and after 1945 could now endure, because there was a European order to support sovereignty. As of 2013, the EU included the metropoles of the old maritime empires that had disintegrated after the Second World War, as well as the former peripheries of the land empires that had disintegrated during or after the First.

What the EU had not done by 2013 was extend to territory that had been within the original borders of the Soviet Union as established in 1922. In 2013, twenty years after its western neighbors, Ukraine was negotiating an association agreement with the EU. At some later point, Ukrainian membership in the European Union might overcome this final barrier. Ukraine was the axis between the new Europe of integration and the old Europe of empire. Russians who wished to restore empire in the name of Eurasia would begin with Ukraine.

The politics of integration were fundamentally different from the politics of empire. The EU was like an empire in that it was a large economic space. It was unlike an empire in that its organizing principle was equality rather than inequality.

**EUROPE**
c. 1956

An imperial power does not recognize the political entities that it encounters in what it regards as colonial territories, and so it destroys or subverts them while claiming that they never existed. Europeans in Africa could claim that African political units did not exist, and were not therefore subject to international law. Americans expanding westward could sign treaties with native nations, and then disregard them on the logic that those nations were not sovereign. Germans invading Poland in 1939 argued that the Polish state did not exist; Soviets meeting them in the middle of the country made the exact same argument. Moscow denied the sovereign status of its neighbors when it occupied and annexed Lithuania, Latvia, and Estonia in 1940, even going so far as to claim that prior service to those states was a crime. When Germany invaded the Soviet Union in 1941, it denied that it was invading a state, treating the peoples of the Soviet Union as colonial subjects.

Throughout the history of European imperialism, European powers assumed that international law applied to their dealings with European peers—though not to their colonial domains where they accumulated power and wealth. In the Second World War, Europeans applied colonial principles to one another. Postwar integration was a return to the idea that law governed dealings among Europeans, as Europeans lost their colonies in Europe and then around the world. In the EU, treaties were meant to change economics, after which economics would alter politics. Recognition of sovereignty was the condition of the entire enterprise. European integration proceeded from the assumption that state borders were fixed, and that change must proceed within and between states rather than by one invading another. Each member of the EU was supposed to be a rule-of-law state, with integration among them governed by law.

The result by 2013 was a formidable if vulnerable creation. The EU's economy was larger than that of the United States, larger than that of China, and about eight times larger than that of Russia. With its democratic procedures, welfare states, and environmental protection, the EU offered an alternative model to American, Russian, and Chinese inequality. It included most of the states regarded as the world's least corrupt. Lacking unified armed forces and convincing institutions of foreign policy, the EU depended upon law and economics for diplomacy as well as internal functioning. Its implicit foreign policy was to persuade leaders and societies who wished for access to European markets to embrace the rule of law and democracy. Citizens of non-member states who wanted European markets or values would pressure governments to negotiate with the EU, and vote out leaders who failed to do so. This seemed to work in the 1980s, 1990s, and 2000s.

The EU's vulnerability was the European politics of inevitability: *the fable of the wise nation.* Citizens of west European member states thought that their nations had long existed and had made better

choices as they learned from history, in particular learning from war in Europe that peace was a good thing. As European empires were forced to abandon colonies and joined the process of integration, this fable of the wise nation smoothed the process, allowing Europeans to look away from both defeat in colonial wars and the atrocities they committed as they lost.

In history there was no era of the nation-state: generally (with exceptions such as Finland), empire ended while integration began, with no interval in between. In the indispensable cases of Germany, France, Britain, Italy, the Netherlands, Spain, and Portugal there was no moment between empire and integration when the nation was sovereign and the state flourished in isolation. It is true that citizens of these countries unreflectively believe that their country has a history as a nation-state: generally, after a moment of reflection, they realize that this is not the case. Such reflection does not usually take place, because history education throughout Europe is national. Lacking serious education in their own imperial pasts, and lacking the comparative knowledge that would allow them to see patterns, Europeans settled for a falsehood. The fable of the wise nation, learned in childhood, comforted adults by allowing them to forget the true difficulties of history. By reciting the fable of the wise nation, leaders and societies could praise themselves for choosing Europe, when in fact Europe was an existential need after empire.

By the 2010s, citizens of east European states were making the same mistake, albeit in a different way. Although most of the anti-communist dissidents had seen the need for a "return to Europe" after 1989, actual membership in the European Union after 2004 or 2007 allowed for forgetfulness. The crises after the First and Second World Wars, when the nation-state as such had proven untenable, were recast as unique moments of national victimhood. Young east Europeans were not taught to reflect on the reasons for state failure in the 1930s or 1940s. Seeing themselves exclusively as innocent victims of German and Soviet empire, they celebrated the brief interwar moment when nation-states could be found on the territory of eastern Europe. They forgot that these states were doomed not just by malice but also by structure: without a European order, they had little chance to survive.

The EU never attempted to establish a common historical education for Europeans. As a result, the fable of the wise nation made it seem possible that nation-states, having chosen to enter Europe, could also choose to leave. A loop back to an imagined past could seem possible, even desirable. And so a politics of inevitability created an opening for a politics of eternity.

In the 2010s, nationalists and fascists who opposed the EU promised Europeans a return to an imaginary national history, and their opponents rarely saw the real problem. Because everyone accepted the fable of the wise nation, the EU was defined by both its supporters and opponents as a national choice rather than as a national necessity. The United Kingdom Independence Party (UKIP) of Nigel Farage in Great Britain, the *Front National* of Marine Le Pen in France, and the *Freiheitliche* party of Heinz-Christian Strache in Austria, for example, all resided comfortably in the politics of eternity. The leaders of one EU member state, Hungary, built a right-wing authoritarian regime inside the EU beginning in 2010. Another EU member state, Greece, faced financial collapse after the world financial crisis in 2008. Its voters moved to the far Right or far Left. Hungarian and Greek leaders began to see Chinese and Russian investment as an alternative route to the future.

The explicit Russian rejection of a European future was something new. Russia was the first European post-imperial power not to see the EU as a safe landing for itself, as well as the first to attack integration in order to deny the possibility of sovereignty, prosperity, and democracy to others. When the Russian assault began, Europe's vulnerabilities were exposed, its populists thrived, and its future darkened. The great question of European history was again open, because certain possibilities in Russia had been closed.

RUSSIA UNDER Putin was unable to create a stable state with a succession principle and the rule of law. Because failure had to be presented as success, Russia had to present itself as a model for Europe, rather than the other way around. This required that success be defined not in terms of prosperity and freedom but in terms of sexuality and culture, and that the European Union (and the United States) be defined as threats not because of anything they did but because of the values they supposedly represented. Putin executed this maneuver with stunning rapidity as he returned to office as president in 2012.

Until 2012, Russian leaders spoke favorably of European integration. Yeltsin accepted Europe as a model, at least rhetorically. Putin described the approach of the EU to Russia's border as an opportunity for cooperation. The eastward enlargement of NATO in 1999 was not presented by Putin as a threat. Instead, he tried to recruit the United States or NATO to cooperate with Russia to address what he saw as common security problems. After the United States was attacked by Islamist terrorists in 2001, Putin offered to cooperate with NATO in territories that bordered Russia. Putin did not present the EU enlargement of 2004 as a threat. On the contrary, he spoke favorably that year of future EU membership for Ukraine. In 2008, Putin attended the NATO summit in Bucharest. In 2009, Medvedev allowed American aircraft to fly over Russia to supply troops in Afghanistan. In 2010, Russia's ambassador to NATO, the radical nationalist Dmitry Rogozin, expressed his concern that NATO would leave Afghanistan. Rogozin complained of NATO's lack of fighting spirit, its "mood of capitulation." He wanted NATO troops at Russia's border.

The basic line of Russian foreign policy through 2011 was not that the European Union and the United States were threats. It was that they should cooperate with Russia as an equal. The decade of the 2000s was the lost opportunity for the creation of a Russian state that might have been seen as such. Russia managed no democratic changes of executive power. What had been an oligarchy of contending clans in the 1990s was transformed into a kleptocracy, in which the state itself became the single oligarchical clan. Rather than monopolizing law, the Russian state under Putin monopolized corruption. To be sure, the state provided a measure of stability to its citizens in the 2000s, thanks to exports of natural gas and oil. It did not deliver the promise of social advancement to the bulk of the Russian population. Russians who founded businesses could be arrested at any time for any imagined violation of the law, and very often they were.

In matters of peace and war, Moscow also took actions that made it harder for Europeans to see Russia as an equal. In April 2007, Estonia was crippled for weeks in a major cyberattack. Although the event was confusing at the time, it was later understood to be the first salvo in a Russian cyberwar against Europe and the United States. In August 2008, Russia invaded its neighbor Georgia and occupied some of its territories. The conventional assault was accompanied by cyberwar: the president of Georgia lost control of his website, Georgian news agencies were hacked, and much of the country's internet traffic was blocked. Russia invaded Georgia to make European integration impossible for its neighbor, but was in fact renouncing it for itself.

By the 2010s, oligarchy in the Russian Federation had made reform not just impossible but unthinkable. Writing for the German press in November 2010, Putin tried to have it both ways, arguing that the EU should integrate with Russia without expecting Russia to change in any way. Since the Russian Federation could not follow Europe's principles, went his reasoning, Europe should forget those principles. Putin was beginning to imagine a reverse integration in which European states would become more like Russia, which would have meant the end of the EU.

A signal difference between a Europe of empire and a Europe of integration was the attitude towards law. On this issue, Putin the politician was following the course of Ilyin the philosopher: an early faith in law yielded to an endorsement of lawlessness as patriotic. Ilyin's great concern as a young man in Russia before the revolution had been the spirit of the law. He believed that Russians needed to imbibe it, but could not see how.

A century later, the boring EU had solved this problem. Its tedious process of accession involved the export of the spirit of the law. European integration was a means of transporting the idea of the rule of law from places where it functioned better to places where it functioned worse. In the 1990s, association agreements signed between the EU and aspiring members initiated legal relationships that included the implicit promise of a deeper legal relationship, namely full membership. The prospect of future membership made clear the benefits of the rule of law, in a way that individual citizens could understand.

The mature Ilyin rejected the rule of law in favor of the arbitrariness—*proizvol*—of fascism. Having given up hope that Russia could be governed by law, he presented lawlessness (*proizvol*) as a patriotic virtue. Putin followed the same trajectory, citing Ilyin as his authority. When he first ran for president in 2000, he spoke of the need for a "dictatorship of the law." Those two concepts contradicted each other, and one of them fell away. Running for president in 2012, Putin rejected the idea of a European Russia, which meant ignoring external incentives that favored the rule of law. Instead, *proizvol* would be presented as redemptive patriotism. The operative concept in the Russian language today is *bespredel*, boundary-less-ness, the absence of limits, the ability of a leader to do anything. The word itself arose from criminal jargon.

On this logic, Putin was not a failed statesman but a national redeemer. What the EU might describe as failures of governance were to be experienced as the flowering of Russian innocence.


PUTIN CHOSE empire over integration. If the EU did not accept Russia's proposition to integrate with Russia, Putin explained in 2011 and 2012, Russia would help Europe to become Eurasian, more like itself. A Eurasian Customs Union with neighboring post-Soviet dictatorships Belarus and Kazakhstan was established on January 1, 2010, while Putin was prime minister. As a presidential candidate in late 2011 and early 2012, Putin proposed a more ambitious "Eurasian Union," an alternative to the EU that would include its member states and thus assist in its demise. He described the Eurasian idea as the beginning of a new ideology and geopolitics for the world.

Writing in the newspaper *Izvestiia* on October 3, 2011, Putin announced the grand project of Eurasia. Russia would bring together states that had not proven to be plausible members of the European

Union (and implicitly, in the future, states that exited a collapsing European Union). This meant present and future dictatorships. In *Nezavisimaia Gazeta* on January 23, 2012, Putin claimed, citing Ilyin, that integration was not about common achievement, as the Europeans thought, but about what Putin called "civilization." On Putin's logic, the rule of law ceased to be a general aspiration and became an aspect of a foreign Western civilization. Integration in Putin's sense was not about working with others but about praising oneself; not about doing but being. There was no need to do anything to make Russia more like Europe. Europe should be more like Russia.

Of course, for the EU, coming to resemble Russia would have meant an undoing. In a third article, in *Moskovskie Novosti* on February 27, 2012, Putin drew that very conclusion. Russia could never become a member of the EU because of "the unique place of Russia on the world political map, its role in history and in the development of civilization." Eurasia would therefore "integrate" its future members with Russia without any of the troubling burdens associated with the EU. No dictator would have to step down; no free elections would have to be held; no laws would have to be upheld. Eurasia was a spoiler system, designed to prevent states from joining the EU and prevent their societies from thinking that this was possible. In the long run, Putin explained, Eurasia would overwhelm the EU in a larger "Union of Europe," a "space" between the Atlantic and the Pacific, "from Lisbon to Vladivostok." Not to join Eurasia, Putin said, would be "to promote separatism in the broadest sense of the word."

As a presidential candidate in 2011 and 2012, Putin promised the release of Russia from general standards and the extension of Russian particularities to others. If Russia could be portrayed as a pristine source of civilizational values that others had lost, then the question of reforming Russian kleptocracy would become irrelevant. As a beacon for others, Russia should be celebrated but not altered. Putin was matching his words with his deeds, since he had made European integration unthinkable for his people. The way that Putin assumed the office of president made his Eurasian turn irreversible. The abandonment of democratic procedures in 2011 and 2012 mocked a basic criterion of EU membership. To clear protestors from the street by violence and then portray them as agents of Europe was to define the EU as an enemy.

Russia had no plausible principle of succession, and the future of the Russian state was uncertain, but none of this could be said. Putin could control the state but not reform it. So foreign policy had to take the place of domestic policy, and diplomacy had to be about culture rather than security. In effect, this meant exporting Russian chaos while speaking of Russian order, spreading disintegration in the name of integration. Once inaugurated as president in May 2012, Putin presented Eurasia as an instrument to dissolve the EU in order to simplify the world order so that empires could compete for territory. The black hole at the center of his system could not be filled, but it could draw in neighbors. At his inauguration, Putin proposed that Russia become "a leader and a center of gravity for the whole of Eurasia." Addressing parliament that December, he spoke of a coming catastrophe that would commence a new era of colonial resource wars. At such a moment, it would be frivolous to propose reform or to imagine progress. During this permanent emergency, Putin proclaimed, Russia would rely on its native genius within "great Russian spaces."

The reference to "great spaces," a concept from the Nazi legal thinker Carl Schmitt, was not even the most striking moment of the address. Using the odd word "passionarity," Putin evoked a special Russian ability to thrive amidst global chaos. Such "passionarity" would determine, according to Putin, "who will take the lead and who will remain outsiders and inevitably lose their independence." The strange term was the invention of one Russian thinker, Lev Gumilev. Unlike Ilyin, who had to be rediscovered, Gumilev was a Soviet citizen. His signature term "passionarity" was recognizable to Russians, even if unnoticed elsewhere. As Russians knew, Gumilev was the modern exemplar of Eurasian thought.

**LONG BEFORE** Putin announced his Eurasian policy, Eurasian thought had represented a specific Russian proposal to dominate and transform Europe. This important intellectual tendency had arisen in the 1920s as a response to the earlier Russian disagreement between "slavophiles" and "westernizers." The westernizers of the nineteenth century believed that history was unitary, and that the path to progress was singular. For them, Russia's problem was backwardness, and so reform or revolution was needed to push Russia to a modern European future. The slavophiles believed that progress was illusory and that Russia was endowed with a particular genius. Orthodox Christianity and popular mysticism, they maintained, expressed a depth of spirit unknown in the West. The slavophiles imagined that Russian history had begun with a Christian conversion in Kyiv a thousand years before. Ilyin began as a westernizer and ended as a slavophile, a trajectory that was very common.

The first Eurasianists were exiled Russian scholars of the 1920s, contemporaries of Ilyin, who rejected both the slavophile and the westernizer attitudes. They agreed with the slavophiles that the West was decadent, but denied the slavophile myth of Christian continuity with ancient Kyiv. The Eurasianists saw no meaningful connection between the ancient Rus of Volodymyr/Valdemar and modern Russia. They focused instead on the Mongols, who had easily defeated the remnants of Rus in the early 1240s. In their vision, the happy conventions of Mongol rule allowed for the foundation of a new city, Moscow, in an environment safe from European corruptions such as the classical heritage of Greece and Rome, the Renaissance, the Reformation, and the Enlightenment. Modern Russia's destiny was to turn Europe into Mongolia.

The Eurasianists of the 1920s soon scattered, and some of them renounced their earlier views. They had one gifted acolyte within the Soviet Union: Lev Gumilev (1912–1992). Gumilev was born to an extraordinary family, and lived one of the most tragically and gar-ishly Soviet lives imaginable. Lev's parents were the poets Nikolai Gumilev and Anna Akhmatova. When Lev was nine years old, his father was executed by the Cheka; his mother then wrote one of the most famous poems in modern Russia, which included the verse: "it loves, it loves droplets of blood, the Russian land." With such parents, Lev had difficulty submerging himself into his university studies in the 1930s; he was observed closely by the secret police and denounced by his colleagues. In 1938, during the Great Terror, he was sentenced to five years in the Gulag, to a camp at Norilsk. This inspired his mother's famous *Requiem*, in which Anna referred to Lev as "my son, my horror." In 1949, Gumilev was once again sentenced to the Gulag, this time to ten years near Karaganda. After Stalin's death in 1953 he was released, but the years in the Gulag left their mark. Gumilev saw the inspirational possibilities in repression, and believed that the basic biological truths of life were revealed in extreme settings.

Writing as an academic in the Soviet Union of the 1960s, 1970s, and 1980s, Gumilev revived the Eurasian tradition. He agreed with his teachers that Mongolia was the source of Russian character and its shelter from Western decadence. Like the émigré scholars of the 1920s, he portrayed Eurasia as a proud heartland that extended from the Pacific Ocean to a meaningless and sick European peninsula at the western extreme.

Whereas the original Eurasians had been serious scholars with disciplinary training in the universities of the Russian Empire, Gu-milev was a typical Soviet autodidact, an enthusiastic amateur in sev-eral fields. To define the boundary between Eurasia and Europe, for example, he relied upon climate. He used the average January tem-perature to draw a line that ran through Germany. On one side was Eurasia and on the other Europe. It just so happened that, when Gu-milev made this argument, East Germany was under Soviet domina-tion and West Germany was not.

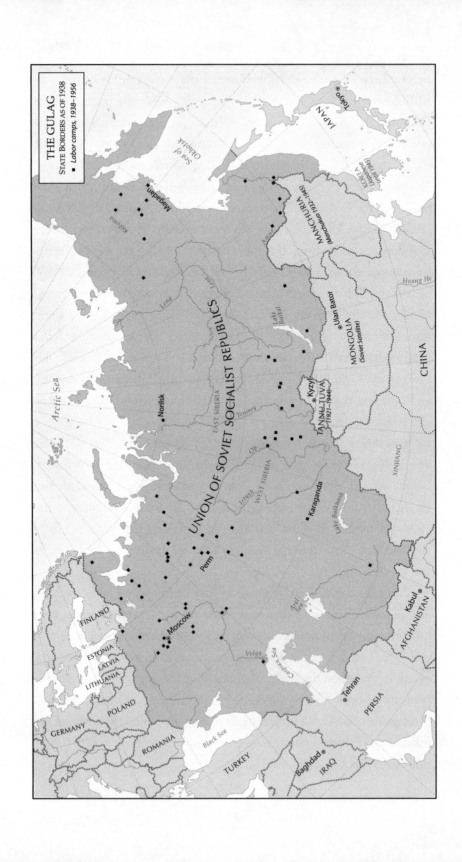

Gumilev's contribution to Eurasianism was his theory of ethnogenesis: an explanation of how nations arise. It began from a specific understanding of astrophysics and human biology. Gumilev maintained that human sociability was generated by cosmic rays. Some human organisms were more capable than others of absorbing space energy and retransmitting it to others. These special leaders, in possession of the "passionarity" Putin mentioned in his 2012 speech, were the founders of ethnic groups. According to Gumilev, the genesis of each nation could therefore be traced to a burst of cosmic energy, which began a cycle that lasted for more than a thousand years. The cosmic rays that enlivened Western nations had been emitted in the distant past, and so the West was dead. The Russian nation arose from cosmic emissions on September 13, 1380, and was therefore young and vibrant.

Gumilev also added a specific form of antisemitism to the Eurasian tradition, one that enabled Russians to blame their own failings on the Jews and the West at the same time. The relevant concept was that of the "chimera," or false nation. Healthy nations such as the Russian, warned Gumilev, must beware "chimerical" groups that draw life not from cosmic rays but from other groups. He meant the Jews. For Gumilev, the history of Rus did not show that Russia was ancient, but it did show that Jews were an eternal threat. Gumilev claimed that in medieval Rus it was the Jews who had traded slaves, establishing themselves as a "military-commercial octopus." These Jews, according to Gumilev, were agents of a permanently hostile Western civilization that sought to weaken and defame Rus. He also claimed that Rus had to pay tribute to Jews in blood. Gumilev therefore advanced three basic elements of modern antisemitism: the Jew as the soulless trader, the Jew as the drinker of Christian blood, and the Jew as the agent of an alien civilization.

Despite his years in the Gulag, Gumilev came to identify himself with the Soviet Union as his Russian homeland. He made friends and taught students, and his influence even after his death in 1992 was considerable. The economist Sergei Glazyev, who advised Yeltsin and Putin, referred to Gumilev and used his concepts. Glazyev spoke of an economic union with state planning "based on the philosophy of Eurasianism." Gumilev was friendly with the philosopher Yuri Borodai and his son Alexander. The younger Borodai dreamed of the "armed passionary," people who would be "catalyzers of powerful movements" that would liberate "the entire territory of Eurasia."

As president, Vladimir Putin would not only cite Gumilev on the Eurasian project, but he would appoint Sergei Glazyev his advisor on Eurasia. Not long after, Alexander Borodai would take an important part in the Russian invasion of Ukraine.

TO SPEAK of "Eurasia" in the Russia of the 2010s was to refer to two distinct currents of thought that overlapped at two points: the corruption of the West and the evil of the Jews. The Eurasianism of the 2010s was a rough mixture of a Russian tradition developed by Gumilev with Nazi ideas mediated by the younger Russian fascist Alexander Dugin (b. 1962). Dugin was not a follower of the original Eurasianists nor a student of Gumilev. He simply used the terms "Eurasia" and "Eurasianism" to make Nazi ideas sound more Russian. Dugin, born half a century after Gumilev, was an antiestablishment kid of the Soviet 1970s and 1980s, playing his guitar and singing about killing millions of people in ovens. His life's work was to bring fascism to Russia.

As the Soviet Union came to an end, Dugin traveled to western Europe to find intellectual allies. Even as Europe integrated, there were marginal thinkers of the far Right who preserved Nazi ideas, celebrated national purity, and decried economic, political, and legal cooperation as part of some global conspiracy. These were Dugin's interlocutors. An early influence was Miguel Serrano, author of *Hitler: The Last Avatar*, who claimed that the Aryan race owed its superiority to its extraterrestrial origins. Dugin, like Gumilev, found Ilyin's Russian redeemer by seeking beyond earth. If the leader must arrive untainted by events, he must come from somewhere beyond history.

Ilyin resolved the issue by presenting a redeemer who emerged from fiction in a poof of erotic mysticism. The mature Gumilev and the young Dugin looked to the stars.

In the early 1990s, Dugin became close to the French conspiracy theorist Jean Parvulesco, who spoke to him of the ancient conflict between people of the sea (Atlanticists) and people of the earth (Eurasianists). In Parvulesco's idea, the Americans and British yield to abstract Jewish ideas because their maritime economies separate them from the earthy truths of human experience. Alain de Benoist of the French neo-fascist movement known as the *Nouvelle Droite* explained to Dugin the centrality of the United States to such schemes, as the representative abstract (Jewish) culture. These were updates of Nazi ideas, as Dugin well understood. At the time, Dugin was writing under the pen name "Sievers," a reference to Wolfram Sievers, a German Nazi executed for war crimes in 1947 who had been known for collecting the bones of murdered Jews.

Dugin's European contacts allowed him to bring Nazi concepts home to Russia. In 1993, Dugin and Eduard Limonov, who called Dugin the "St Cyril and Methodius of fascism," founded the National Bolshevik Party. Its members raised their fists while hailing death. In 1997, Dugin called for a "fascism, borderless and red." Dugin exhibited standard fascist views: democracy was hollow; the middle class was evil; Russians must be ruled by a "Man of Destiny"; America was malevolent; Russia was innocent.

Dugin shared with Ilyin a debt to Carl Schmitt. It was Schmitt who had formulated a vision of world politics without laws and states, grounded instead in the subjective desires of cultural groups for ever more land. Schmitt dismissed "the empty concept of state territory" and regarded the nation as "fundamentally an organism." In his view, the Eurasian landmass was a "great space" to be mastered by whoever could take it. Schmitt claimed that maritime powers such as Great Britain and the United States were bearers of abstract, Jewish notions of law. He formulated a concept of international law by which the world would be divided into a few "great spaces" from which "spatially alien powers" should be excluded. He meant that the United States should have no influence in Europe. Dugin preserved these ideas while simply changing the entity that was supposedly threatened by Jews, America, and law: no longer Nazi Germany but instead contemporary Russia.

Dugin dismissed Ilyin as an inferior philosopher who served nothing more than a "technical function" in the Putin regime. Nevertheless, much of Dugin's writing reads like a parody of Ilyin. "The West," claimed Dugin in a typical expostulation, "is the place where Lucifer fell. It is the center for the global capitalist octopus." The West, Dugin continued, "is the matrix of rotten cultural perversion and wickedness, deceit and cynicism, violence and hypocrisy." It was so decadent that it would collapse at any moment, and yet it was a constant threat. Democracy was not its renewal, but the sign of a coming cataclysm. Dugin regarded the reelection of Barack Obama as president of the United States in 2012 in these terms: "Let him ruin this country, let justice finally prevail, so that this monstrous colossus on clay feet, this new Carthage, which spreads its abominable economic and political power across the entire world, and tries to fight with all and against all, so that it quickly disappears." These characterizations of the West are axioms, not observations. The facts of the present are irrelevant, as are the facts of the past. For Dugin, as for Ilyin, the past only matters as a reservoir of symbols, of what Dugin called "archetypes." The past provided Dugin with what Russians called "the spiritual resource," a source of images to be used to alter the present.

Writing in the early twenty-first century, Dugin was confronted with the success of the European Union, a hyperlegal entity that rescued states after empire. Dugin never pronounced its name. When asked to comment upon the EU, Dugin asserted that it was doomed. Long before Putin began to speak of a Eurasia that must include Ukraine as an element of Russian civilization, Dugin defined the independent Ukrainian state as the barrier to Russia's Eurasian destiny. In 2005, Dugin founded a state-supported youth movement whose members urged the disintegration and russification of Ukraine. In

2009, Dugin foresaw a "battle for Crimea and eastern Ukraine." The existence of Ukraine, in Dugin's view, constituted "an enormous danger for all of Eurasia."

Concepts from the three interflowing currents of Russian fascism—Ilyin's Christian totalitarianism, Gumilev's Eurasianism, and Dugin's "Eurasian" Nazism—appeared in Putin's discourse as he sought an exit from the dilemma he created for his country in 2012. Fascist ideas burst into the Russian public sphere during the Obama administration's attempt to "reset" relations with the Russian Federation. The dramatic change in Russia's orientation bore no relation to any new unfriendly action from outside. Western enmity was not a matter of what a Western actor was *doing*, but what the West was portrayed as *being*.

IN 2012, fascist thinkers were placed in the Russian mainstream by a Russian president who seemed to think that he needed them. Ilyin had been granted as full a resuscitation as a state can give a philosopher. Gumilev was cited by Putin in his most important address. Dugin became a frequent guest on Russia's largest television channel. The Eurasian idea was a preoccupation of a new think tank, the Izborsk Club. Its members included Dugin, Glazyev, and Tikhon Shevkunov—Putin's favorite monk and his companion at Ilyin's gravesite. Shevkunov was the author of the cyclical idea that Putin reincarnated Volodymyr/Valdemar of Rus—and also the author of the bestselling book in Russia of 2012.

The founder and moving spirit of the Izborsk Club was the fascist novelist Alexander Prokhanov, Putin's companion in that radio program of December 2011 where Putin had cited Ilyin. Like Dugin, Prokhanov used the notion of Eurasia to mean the return of Soviet power in fascist form. Also like Dugin, he repeated the ideas of Carl Schmitt; if Prokhanov had a core belief, it was the endless struggle of the empty and abstract sea-people against the hearty and righteous land-people. Like Adolf Hitler, Prokhanov blamed world

Jewry for inventing the ideas that enslaved his homeland. He also blamed them for the Holocaust. Like Dugin, Prokhanov openly embraced political fiction, seeking to create drastic images that would exude meaning before people had the chance to think for themselves. An example of his creative mind was his reaction to the election of Barack Obama as president of the United States. Discussing a meeting of Obama with Russians, Prokhanov moaned that it was "as if they had all been given a black teat, and they all suck at it with lust and mammalian smacking . . . In the end, I was humiliated by this."

Amidst the ceaseless ink-flood of Prokhanov's publications, the most pertinent to Eurasia was an interview he gave in Kyiv, Ukraine, on August 31, 2012, right before the opening of the Izborsk Club. That March, Ukraine and the European Union had initialed an association agreement, and the Ukrainian government had undertaken an action plan to prepare the country for the signing of the accord the following year. Baffled by Prokhanov's attitude towards Europe, his interviewer asked him questions that revealed basic Eurasian themes: the precedence of fiction over fact; the conviction that European success was a sign of evil; the belief in a global Jewish conspiracy; and the certainty of Ukraine's Russian fate.

When asked about the high standard of living in the EU, Prokhanov responded: "Swim across the Dnipro River and find mushrooms growing great under the sun!" A momentary vision of a primal Slavic experience was more important than a durable way of life created by decades of work for the benefit of hundreds of millions of people. Prokhanov's next move was to claim that factuality was hypocrisy: "Europe is vermin that has learned to call heinous and disgusting things beautiful." Whatever Europeans might seem to be doing or saying, "you don't see their faces under the masks." In any event, Europe was dying: "The white race is perishing: gay marriages, pederasts rule the cities, women can't find men." And Europe was killing Russia: "We didn't get infected with AIDS, they deliberately infected us."

The fundamental problem, said Prokhanov in this interview, was the Jews. "Antisemitism," he said, "is not a result of the fact that

Jews have crooked noses or cannot correctly pronounce the letter 'r.' It is a result of the fact that Jews took over the world, and are using their power for evil." In a move that was typical of Russian fascists, Prokhanov deployed the symbolism of the Holocaust to describe world Jewry as a collective perpetrator and everyone else as the victims: "Jews united humanity in order to throw humanity into the furnace of the liberal order, which is now suffering a catastrophe." The only defense against the international Jewish conspiracy was a Russian redeemer. Eurasianism was Russia's messianic mission to redeem mankind. It "has to encompass the entire world."

This grand redemptive project, said Prokhanov, would begin when Russia, Ukraine, and Belarus merge. "When I speak of Russia," said Prokhanov, "I have in view people living in Ukraine and Belarus." Ukraine had before it a "colossal messianic mission," because the destiny of Kyiv was to bow before Moscow and thus commence the Russian conquest of the world. "If the first empire was established here," said Prokhanov, meaning Rus a thousand years before, "the future empire has already been proclaimed by Putin. It is the Eurasian Union, and Ukraine's contribution to this empire could be grandiose." In the end, asked Prokhanov, "why be at the outskirts of London when you can be at the center of Eurasia?" Prokhanov was concerned that Ukraine's president Viktor Yanukovych might not be able to fulfill this assignment. Perhaps, he mused, the government of Ukraine would have to be changed.

The Izborsk Club, the intellectual hub of the new Russian nationalism, was inaugurated a few days later, on September 8, 2012. Its manifesto began with the claim, familiar from Ilyin, that factuality was a Western weapon against Russia:

> The Russian state has once again been exposed to the deadly threat posed from liberal centers: a threat from within Russian society and from beyond its borders. The lethal ideological and informational "machine" that destroyed all the bases and values of the "White" Romanov empire and then destroyed all the foundations of the

"Red" Soviet empire is everywhere at work. The fall of these empires transformed the great Eurasian space into a chaos of warring peoples, faiths and cultures on fields of blood. This liberal "machine" was built with the help of anthropologists and historians, social scientists and specialists in "chaos theory," economists and masters of information wars. It disintegrates the fundamental principles by which the unified Eurasian state is constructed. It suppresses the underlying codes of national consciousness that the nation needs to be victorious and to extend its existence in history. This battering "machine" pounds at the Orthodox Church, the spiritual basis of the nation. It prevents the construction of a national security apparatus, leaving Russia unarmed at a time of rising military conflict. It sows discord amidst the harmony of Russia's main religious confessions. It prevents the reconciliation of Russia's historical epochs. It prolongs the ruinous Russian Time of Troubles, demonizing the Russian leader and all institutions of authority.

No reference was made in the manifesto to any specific European or American policy. The problem was not what Europeans or Americans did, but that the European Union and the United States existed. As Prokhanov had made clear already, the enmity of the West was to be taken as a given, even when Western actors pursued friendly policies to Russia. The manifesto's authors replaced history with eternity: the cyclical pattern of Western perfidy and Russian innocence. According to the manifesto, previous Eurasian empires had

flourished as no empires had before, and then crashed into a "black hole," from which, as it seemed, there was no return. But the state was again reborn, in another form, with another historical center, and again rose and flourished before declining and disappearing. This circularity, the death of the state and its triumph over death, confer upon Russian history a resurrectionary character, in which Russian civilization inevitably rises from the dead. The first empire was that of Kyiv-Novgorod. The second was Muscovy. The third empire was that of the Romanov dynasty. The fourth empire was the Soviet Union. Today's Russian State, despite the loss of great territories, still carries the mark of empire. The geopolitics of the Eurasian continent once again forcefully gathers spaces that had been lost. This is the legitimation of the "Eurasian project" initiated by Putin.

Rather than using Russian history to establish interests or evaluate perspectives within Russian society, Eurasia offered poetic utterances meant to create a lyrical unity from prior bloodshed. If Soviet terror murdered countless Russian Orthodox priests in the 1930s, all is well and good, because their spirits arose in the 1940s to bless the Red Army:

> The unification of two historical eras, a strategic alliance of "Reds" and "Whites" in the face of the liberal peril—this is the enormous worldview mission of true statesmen. Such an alliance is possible in the light of the mystical Russian Victory of 1945, when the "Red" system had the prayerful support of all the Saints killed in the years when the church was persecuted, and the arms of the "Red Victory" became holy Russian arms. The future Russian Victory demands the union of "Reds" and "Whites." It demands the creation of a state in which, as V. V. Putin said, "Red" commissars can live together with "White" officers.

The celebration of both the far Left and the far Right in the past elided Russia's present problem: the absence of a center, a political fulcrum, a succession principle that would allow power to shift from left to right or right to left while preserving the state. Since all political activity was ruled out as foreign, differences of opinion or acts of opposition had to be a result of the malignant designs of Europeans and Americans who resent Russia's immaculate innocence:

The Russian messianic consciousness, grounded in the teaching of an "earthly paradise," in an ideal existence, in the Orthodox dream of divine justice—all of this summons the negation of Russia at the level of worldview, the attacks on her faith, culture, and historical codes. A military invasion of Russia—the consequence of that intolerance and profound hostility. And so the theme of Russian weapons is a holy theme for Russia. Russian weapons protect not only cities, territories, the boundless richness of the earth. They protect the entire religious and cultural order of Russia, all of Russia's secular and holy shrines.

These lines were published in the midst of a new armament program, which doubled Russia's annual weapons procurement budget between 2011 and 2013. The authors of the manifesto dreamed of a militarized totalitarian Russia that permanently mobilized the entire population and promised nothing but sacrifice:

Russia does not need hasty political reform. It needs arms factories and altars. The loss of the historical moment after the destruction of the "Red" empire, the strategic backwardness by comparison to the "liberal" West, demand from Russia a developmental leap. This leap involves a "mobilization project" which would concentrate all of the nation's resources upon the preservation of sovereignty and the defense of the people.

After this initial salvo, further articles by members of the Izborsk Club elaborated its position. The liberal order that produced factuality, one member wrote, was the work of "the world backstage, the core of which are the Zionist leaders." Other members of the Izborsk Club explained that Putin's Eurasian Union was "the project of restoring Russia as a Eurasian empire." They presented the EU as an existential threat to Russia, since it enforced law and generated prosperity. Russian foreign policy should therefore support the extreme Right within EU member states until the EU collapses, as Prokhanov ecstatically anticipated, into a "constellation of European fascist states." Ukraine, as one Izborsk Club expert wrote, "is all ours, and eventually it will all come back to us." According to Dugin, the annexation of Ukrainian territory by Russia was the "necessary condition" of the Eurasian imperial project.

For the Eurasianists of the Izborsk Club, facts were the enemy, Ukraine was the enemy, and facts about Ukraine were the supreme enemy. An intellectual task of the Izborsk Club was to produce the narratives that transported any such facts towards oblivion. Indeed, the mission of the Izborsk Club was to serve as a barrier to factuality. "Izborsk" was chosen as the name of the think tank because the town of Izborsk is the site of a historical Muscovite fortress that had resisted, as the club's website recalled, "the Livonians, Poles, and Swedes." Now the invader was the "liberal machine" of factuality.

One of Russia's long-range bombers, a Tu-95 built to drop atomic bombs on the United States, was renamed "Izborsk" in honor of the club. In case anyone failed to notice this sign of Kremlin backing, Prokhanov was invited to fly in the cockpit of the aircraft. In the years to come, this and other Tu-95s would regularly approach the airspace of the member states of the European Union, forcing them to activate their air defense systems and to escort the approaching bomber away. The Tu-95 "Izborsk" would be used to bomb Syria in 2015, creating refugees who would flee to Europe.

SERGEI GLAZYEV, advisor of Putin, reader of Gumilev, follower of Schmitt, member of Izborsk, linked Eurasian theory to practice. After Glazyev was fired from the Yeltsin administration for corruption in 1993, he got a helping hand from the American conspiracy theorist Lyndon LaRouche, who held similar views. In 1999 LaRouche published an English translation of Glazyev's tract *Genocide: Russia and the New World Order*, which posited that a cabal of (Jewish) neoliberals had deliberately destroyed Russia in the 1990s. Like other Russian fascists, Glazyev used terms associated with the Holocaust (e.g., "genocide") to suggest that Jews were the real perpetrators and Russians the real victims. He was elected to parliament as a communist in 1999, and then helped to found the radical nationalist party *Rodina* in 2003. This was not as much of a contradiction as it seemed. In Russia's "managed democracy," *Rodina* was meant to draw votes away from the communist party towards a group trusted by Putin. Glazyev thought that that a planned economy should serve the interests of the Russian nation, which in his view included Ukraine: "We cannot forget the historical importance of Little Russia [Ukraine] for us. We have never divided Russia and Ukraine, in our minds."

Russian foreign policy arose, Glazyev wrote, "from the philosophy of Eurasianism." Following Schmitt, Glazyev maintained that states were obsolete. The Eurasian project was "based on a fundamentally different spatial concept": Schmitt's idea of "great spaces" dominated by a great power. America must stay away, Glazyev decreed, since it was not part of the Eurasian great space. Since the EU was a bastion of state sovereignty it must fall, and the citizens of its member states must be granted the fascist totality for which they long. "Europeans," wrote Glazyev, "have lost their sense of direction. They live in a mosaic, in a fragmented world with no shared relationships." Happily, Russian power could return them to what Glazyev regarded as "reality."

Glazyev did not discuss the preferences of the people who lived in the European Union. Did Europeans really need to discover firsthand the profundity of a Russian system where life expectancy in 2012 was 111th in the world, where the police could not be trusted, bribes and blackmail were the stuff of everyday life, and prison was a middle-class experience? In its distribution of wealth, Russia was the most unequal country in the world; the EU's far greater wealth was also far more evenly shared among its citizens. Glazyev helped his master maintain Russian kleptocracy by changing the subject from prosperity to values, to what Putin called "civilization."

Beginning in 2013, the principles of Eurasia guided the foreign policy of the Russian Federation. The official Foreign Policy Concept for that year, published on February 18 under the signature of Foreign Minister Sergei Lavrov with the special endorsement of President Vladimir Putin, included, amidst the boilerplate that remained unaltered from year to year, a series of changes corresponding to the ideas of Ilyin, the Eurasianists, and their fascist traditions.

The Foreign Policy Concept repeated Putin's characterization of the future as roiling chaos and resource grabs. As states weakened, great spaces would reemerge. In such a world there can be no "oasis" from "global turbulence," so the EU was doomed. Law would give way to a contest of civilizations. "Global competition demands, for the first time in contemporary history, a civilizational dimension." Russia was responsible not for the well-being of its citizens but for the safety of undefined "compatriots" beyond its borders. Eurasia was a "model of unification," open to the former republics of the Soviet Union and also to members of the current European Union. Its basis of cooperation was "the preservation and extension of a common cultural and civilizational heritage."

The Concept made clear that the process of supplanting the EU with Eurasia was to begin immediately, in 2013, at a time when Ukraine was in negotiations with the EU over the terms of an association agreement. According to the Concept, if Ukraine wished to negotiate with the EU, it should accept Moscow as its intermediary. In Eurasia, Russian dominance was the order of things. In the long term, Eurasia would overcome the EU, leading to "the creation of a unified humanitarian space from the Atlantic to the Pacific Ocean." Lavrov later repeated this aspiration, citing Ilyin as its source.

BECAUSE THE EU is a consensual organization, it was vulnerable to campaigns that raised emotions. Because it was composed of democratic states, it could be weakened by political parties that advocated leaving the EU. Because the EU had never been meaningfully opposed, it never occurred to Europeans to ask whether debates on the internet were manipulated from outside with hostile intent. The Russian policy to destroy the EU took several corresponding forms: the recruitment of European leaders and parties to represent the Russian interest in European disintegration; the digital and televisual penetration of public discourse to sow distrust of the EU; the recruitment of extreme nationalists and fascists for public promotion of Eurasia; and the endorsement of separatism of all kinds.

Putin befriended and supported European politicians who were willing to defend Russian interests. One was Gerhard Schröder, the retired German chancellor, who was in the employ of the Russian gas company Gazprom. A second was Miloš Zeman, elected president of the Czech Republic in 2013 after a campaign partly financed by the Russian oil company Lukoil, and reelected in 2018 after a campaign financed by unknown sources. A third was Silvio Berlusconi, who shared vacations with Putin before and after leaving the office of Italian prime minister in 2011. In August 2013, Berlusconi was convicted of tax fraud and banned from public office until 2019. Putin suggested that Berlusconi's true problem was the persecution of heterosexuals: "If he were gay, no one would ever lay a finger on him." Here Putin was enunciating a basic principle of his Eurasian civilization: when the subject is inequality, change it to sexuality. In 2018, Berlusconi began a political comeback.

In the post-communist east European member states of the European Union, such as the Czech Republic, Slovakia, Hungary, and Poland, Russia financed and organized internet discussion outlets to cast doubt on the value of EU membership. These sites purported to provide news on various themes but in every case suggested that the EU was decadent or unsafe. In the larger west European media markets, the international English-, Spanish-, German-, and French-language television network RT was more important. RT became the media home of European politicians who opposed the EU, such as Nigel Farage of the United Kingdom Independence Party (UKIP) and Marine Le Pen of the *Front National* in France.

Farage and Le Pen proposed a return to a nonexistent past, when Europeans lived in nation-states without immigrants. They were eternity politicians, urging their fellow citizens to reconsider the 1930s as a golden age. Both Great Britain and France had been maritime empires that, as their colonies won independence, joined a European integration project. Never in modern history was either country a nation-state separated from the world. Thanks to the fable of the wise nation, their citizens generally did not understand their own history, and so did not appreciate the stakes of the debate about EU membership. Because Britain and France had no modern history as nation-states, an exit from the European Union would be a step into the unknown rather than the comfortable homecoming promised by nationalism. It would mean joining Russia as the remnant state of a European empire beyond the reach of European integration. Thus Farage and Le Pen were natural partners for a Russia whose approach to history was annihilation.

In 2013, a preoccupation with gay sex brought together Russian and French politicians of eternity. That May, the French parliament extended rights to same-sex couples. Marine Le Pen and her *Front National* then joined Russian activists to resist what they characterized as a global sodomite conspiracy. In June, Le Pen visited Russia and enthusiastically joined in Russia's new campaign for "civilization." She advanced the Russian argument that gay rights were the sharp end of a global neoliberal conspiracy against innocent nations. In her words, "homophilia is one of the elements of globalization," and Russia and France must together resist "a new international empire infected by the virus of commercialization." That particular turn of phrase was a gesture to the belief, common among Russian nationalists, that Russians were too innocent to have contracted AIDS, and that therefore its presence in Russia was a result of biological warfare. Le Pen was happy to agree that Russians were the victim of a "new cold war that the EU is carrying out against Russia." Aymeric Chauprade, her advisor on foreign policy, promised his Russian audience that the *Front National* would destroy the European Union if it came to power.

At that same moment, a few reliable Americans were also invited to defend Russia's new gender politics. RT interviewed Richard Spencer, the leading American white supremacist, on the question of American-Russian relations. As it happened, Spencer was married to Nina Kouprianova, Dugin's translator. Since Spencer admired Putin and believed that Russia was "the sole white power in the world," it was not surprising that he was quick to blame the Obama administration for starting a "cold war" over Russia's anti-sodomy campaign. Three years later, Spencer would lead his followers in a modified Nazi chant: "hail Trump, hail our people, hail victory."

As it happened, Donald Trump was the second high-profile American to support Putin that summer, during the vulnerable moment when official Russia claimed for itself the role of protector of heterosexuality. Trump was in the midst of a long campaign to delegitimize the president of his own country by claiming, falsely, that Barack Obama had not been born in the United States. RT tried to make this notion plausible. Trump was eager, however, to flatter the president of another country. On June 18, 2013, Trump wondered in a tweet whether Putin "will become my new best friend?"

Trump's contribution to global heterosexuality was to bring a beauty pageant to the Moscow suburbs, or rather to look on as Russians did so. In principle he was the organizer; in fact he was paid twenty million dollars to oversee the work of his Russian colleagues. This was a pattern of relations between Russians and Trump that was by then long established: Trump was paid so that his name could assist Russians who knew something about money and power. Just a few weeks earlier, in April 2013, the FBI had arrested twenty-nine men suspected of running two gambling rings inside Trump Tower. According to investigators, the operation was overseen by Alimzhan Tokhtakhounov, a Russian citizen who also ran a money-laundering operation from a condo directly under Trump's own. As the FBI searched for him, Tokhtakhounov attended the Miss Universe pageant and sat a few seats away from Trump. (The United States attorney who had authorized the Trump Tower raid was Preet Bharara. Upon becoming president, Trump fired Bharara.)

The Russian property developer Aras Agalarov was Trump's partner in bringing the beauty pageant to Russia. Agalarov, whose father-in-law had been KGB chief in Soviet Azerbaijan, was an oligarch who specialized in relations with other oligarchs. He built shopping malls, gated communities, and, later, two soccer stadiums for Putin to accommodate the 2018 World Cup. He did the work for the Miss Universe pageant: it was hosted on his property, his wife was a judge, his son sang. Trump said that during the pageant he "was with all the top people." Be that as it may, his relationship with the Agalarov family continued. Trump sent Agalarov's son, the pop star Emin, a video greeting on his birthday. The Agalarov family offered its help when Trump decided to run for president. Among the many instances of contact between the Trump campaign and prominent Russians was a meeting in Trump Tower in June 2016, in which a Russian lawyer, briefed by the chief prosecutor of the Russian Federation, offered the Trump campaign materials about Hillary Clinton. It was the Agalarov family that initiated the contact and brought the group together. When Donald Trump Jr. heard of the possibility of cooperating with a foreign power against the Clinton campaign, he replied, "I love it."

The love began that summer of 2013. Agalarov was awarded the Order of Honor from Putin right before the Miss Universe pageant was held. On the day when Trump wondered if Putin would become his "new best friend," Le Pen was touring the Russian parliament. In the years to come, Le Pen and Trump would each support the other's aspirations to the presidency. Their 2013 visits to Moscow, superficially about homosexuality and heterosexuality, deepened political and financial debts to Russia. In late 2013 and early 2014, both Marine Le Pen and her father, Jean-Marie Le Pen, the founder of her party, announced that the *Front National* was funded by Russia. A mediator in the financial transactions between Russia and the *Front*

*National* was Aymeric Chauprade, who was himself allowed to borrow 400,000 euros as a reward for arranging a loan from a Russian bank to Jean-Marie Le Pen.

Although the *Front National* was pleased to join the Kremlin in its anti-sodomy campaign, its major issue at home in France was immigration and Islam. Accordingly, actors in Russia tried to drive French voters towards the *Front National* by spreading fear of Islamist terrorism. In April 2015, Russian hackers took over the transmission of a French television station, pretended to be the Islamist terrorist group ISIS, and then broadcast a message designed to frighten French voters. That November, when 130 people were killed and 368 injured in a real terrorist attack in Paris, Prokhanov predicted that terrorism would drive Europe towards fascism and Russia.

In the 2017 French presidential campaign, Marine Le Pen praised her patron Putin. She finished second in the first round of elections that April, defeating every candidate from France's traditional parties. Her opponent in the second round was Emmanuel Macron, whom Russian propaganda insinuated was the gay candidate of the "gay lobby." In the second round, Le Pen received 34% of the ballots. Though she lost to Macron, she did better than any other far Right candidate in the history of postwar France.

TO SUPPORT the *Front National* was to attack the European Union. France was, after Germany, the EU's most important member, and Le Pen the EU's most powerful critic. In 2013, Russia's financing of the *Front National* seemed much more likely to alter the future of the EU than its support of Nigel Farage and "Brexit," his project to remove Britain from the European Union. Farage, like Le Pen, Spencer, and Trump, supported Putin during his turn to Eurasia. On July 8, 2013, Farage claimed on RT that the "European project is actually beginning to die."

The first order of business for Russian foreign policy in the United Kingdom was actually Scottish separatism. The Scottish National

Party was urging Scots to vote for independence in a referendum. In the weeks before it was held on September 18, 2014, Russian media falsely suggested that Scotland would lose its health service and its football team if it remained in Great Britain. After a majority of Scottish voters elected to remain in the United Kingdom, videos appeared on the internet that seemed to cast doubt about the validity of the vote. One of them showed actual vote rigging in Russia, presented as Scotland. These videos were then promoted over Twitter by accounts based in Russia. Then a Russian official proclaimed that the result "was a total falsification." Although no actual irregularities were reported, roughly a third of Scottish voters gained the impression that something fraudulent had taken place. It would have been a victory for Russia had Scotland left the United Kingdom; but it was also a victory for Russia if the inhabitants of the United Kingdom came to distrust their institutions. After the Conservative Party won the May 2015 general election in the United Kingdom, RT published an opinion piece on its website claiming that the British electoral system was rigged.

Although Britain's Conservative Party could form a government by itself after those elections, it was divided on the issue of Britain's membership in the European Union. In order to end the intra-party dispute, Prime Minister David Cameron agreed to a non-binding national referendum on the question. This was extremely good news for Moscow, although it was not entirely a surprise. Russia had been preparing for such a possibility for some time. In 2012, Russian intelligence had founded, in Britain, a front organization called the Conservative Friends of Russia. One of its founding members, the British lobbyist Matthew Elliott, served as the chief executive of Vote Leave, the official organization making the case for a British exit from the EU. Nigel Farage, leader of the political party founded on the program of leaving the EU, kept appearing on RT, and expressed his admiration for Putin. One of his senior staffers took part in a Russian smear campaign against the president of Lithuania, who had criticized Putin.

All of the major Russian television channels, including RT, supported a vote to leave the EU in the weeks before the June 23, 2016, poll. A persuasion campaign on the internet, although unnoticed at the time, was probably more important. Russian internet trolls, live people who participated in exchanges with British voters, and Russian Twitter bots, computer programs that sent out millions of targeted messages, engaged massively on behalf of the Leave campaign. Four hundred and nineteen Twitter accounts that posted on Brexit were localized to Russia's Internet Research Agency—later, every single one of them would also post on behalf of Donald Trump's presidential campaign. About a third of the discussion of Brexit on Twitter was generated by bots—and more than 90% of the bots tweeting political material were not located in the United Kingdom. Britons who considered their choices had no idea at the time that they were reading material disseminated by bots, nor that the bots were part of a Russian foreign policy to weaken their country. The margin of the vote was 52% for leaving and 48% for staying.

This time, no Russian voice questioned the result, presumably since the voting had gone the way Moscow had wished. Brexit was a triumph for Russian foreign policy, and a sign that a cyber campaign directed from Moscow could change reality.

For some time, Russian politicians had been urging Britain to separate from the European Union. In 2015 Konstantin Kosachev, the chairman of the international affairs committee of the Duma, had instructed the British about the "myth" that the European Union was "infallible and invulnerable." After the referendum, Vladimir Putin provided a soothing argument in favor of the disintegration of the EU: that the British had been exploited by others. In fact, many of the districts of Great Britain most heavily subsidized by the EU voted to leave it. Putin gently supported the misunderstandings and prejudices that led to things falling apart: "No one wants to feed and subsidize weaker economies, support other states, whole peoples—it is an obvious fact." Moscow had weaponized the fable of the wise nation. In fact, Britain had never been a state that had decided to support others, but a collapsing empire whose statehood was rescued by European integration. Pervyi Kanal, the most important Russian television station, soothingly confirmed the myth that Britain could go it alone because it had always done so: "For this nation it is important that none of its alliances or commitments are binding." Under the mistaken impression that they had a history as a nation-state, the British (the English, mainly) voted themselves into an abyss where Russia awaited.

Russia's support of Austrian enemies of the EU was ostentatious. Like Great Britain and France, Austria was the metropole of an old European empire that had joined the integration process. Austria had been the heart of the Habsburg monarchy, and then during the 1920s and 1930s a failed nation-state, then for seven years a part of Nazi Germany. Some of the leaders of its *Freiheitliche* party were connected by family or ideology (or both) to the Nazi period. This was the case with Johann Gudenus, who studied in Moscow and spoke Russian.

During the 2016 Austrian presidential campaign, the *Freiheitliche* were negotiating a cooperation agreement with Putin's party in Russia, apparently in the expectation that their candidate Norbert Hofer would win. He almost did. In April he won the first round of the election. He narrowly lost the second round, which was then repeated after a claim of electoral violations. In December 2016, Hofer lost the second round again. He did take 46% of the total vote, the most a *Freiheitliche* candidate had received in an Austrian national election.

As in France, Russia's candidate did not win, but performed far better than would have been expected when Russia's campaign to destroy the EU began. In December 2016, *Freiheitliche* leaders flew to Moscow to sign the cooperation agreement they had negotiated with Putin's political party. In October 2017, the *Freiheitliche* won 26% in Austria's parliamentary elections, and then joined a coalition government that December. A far Right party in open partnership with Moscow was helping to govern an EU member.

INTEGRATION OR empire? Would Russia's new Eurasian imperialism destroy the EU? Or would European integration reach territory that had been part of the Soviet Union in 1922? That was the European question of 2013. As Moscow persistently sought that year to destroy the EU, Kyiv was finalizing an association agreement with it. The trade pact was popular in Ukraine: oligarchs wanted access to EU markets; owners of small businesses wanted the rule of law to compete with those oligarchs; students and younger people wanted a European future. Although President Viktor Yanukovych tried hard not to see it, he was facing a choice. If Ukraine signed an association agreement with the EU, it would not be able to join Putin's Eurasia.

The Eurasianists themselves took a clear position. Dugin had long urged the destruction of Ukraine. Prokhanov had suggested in July 2013 that Yanukovych might have to be removed. In September 2013, Glazyev said that Russia could invade Ukrainian territory if Ukraine did not join Eurasia. In November 2013, Yanukovych failed everyone: he did not sign the completed association agreement, nor did he bring Ukraine into Eurasia. In February 2014, Russia invaded Ukraine. A Russian politics of eternity was engaging a European politics of inevitability. Europeans had little idea what to do: the EU had never been resisted, let alone combated. Few realized that an attack on integration was also an attack on their own fragile states. Moscow was continuing the campaign against the EU on what it believed would be the yielding territory of Ukraine.

Because they failed to understand the stakes of the conflict in Ukraine, Europeans proved to be more vulnerable to Russian attack than Ukrainians. Because Ukrainians were aware that their own state was fragile, many had no trouble seeing the EU as a precondition for a future with law and prosperity. They saw Russia's intervention as cause for a patriotic revolution, since they understood EU membership as a stage in the construction of a Ukrainian state.

Other Europeans had forgotten this connection, and so experienced the political problem posed by Russia's war in Ukraine as cultural difference. Europeans proved vulnerable to soporific Russian propaganda suggesting that Ukraine's problems showed its distance from the European mainstream.

The Russian politics of eternity easily found the blindness at the center of the European politics of inevitability. Russians had only to say, as they would in 2014 and 2015, that Ukrainians were not a wise nation, since they had not learned the lessons of the Second World War. Europeans who nodded sagely and did nothing reinforced a basic misunderstanding of their own history, and placed the sovereignty of their own states in jeopardy.

The only escape from the alternatives of inevitability and eternity was history: understanding it or making it. Ukrainians, seeing their situation for what it was, had to do something new.

## CHAPTER FOUR

# NOVELTY OR ETERNITY (2014)

Beginning, before it becomes a historical event, is the supreme capacity of man; politically, it is identical with man's freedom.
  —HANNAH ARENDT, 1951

The Russian politics of eternity reached back a thousand years to find a mythical moment of innocence. Vladimir Putin claimed that his millennial vision of the baptism of Volodymyr/Valdemar of Kyiv made Russia and Ukraine a single people. While visiting Kyiv in July 2013, Putin read souls and spoke of God's geopolitics: "Our spiritual unity began with the Baptism of Holy Rus 1025 years ago. Since then, much has happened in the lives of our peoples, but our spiritual unity is so strong that it is not subject to any action by any authority: neither government authorities nor, I would even go so far as to say, church authorities. Because regardless of any existing authority over the people, there can be none that is stronger than the authority of the Lord—nothing can be stronger than that. And this is the most solid foundation for our unity in the souls of our people."

In September 2013 at Valdai, his official presidential summit on foreign policy, Putin expressed his vision in secular terms. He cited Ilyin's "organic model" of Russian statehood, in which Ukraine was an inseparable organ of the virginal Russian body. "We have common traditions, a common mentality, a common history and a common culture," said Putin. "We have very similar languages. In that respect, I want to repeat again, we are one people." The association agreement between the EU and Ukraine was to be signed two months later. Russia would attempt to halt this process on the grounds that nothing new can happen within its spiritual sphere of influence—"the Russian world," as Putin began to say. His attempt to apply a Russian politics of eternity beyond Russia's borders had unintended consequences. Ukrainians responded by creating new kinds of politics.

Nations are new things that refer to old things. It matters how they do so. It is possible, as Russian leaders have done, to issue ritual incantations designed to reinforce the status quo at home and justify empire abroad. To say that "Rus" is "Russia," or that Volodymyr/Valdemar of Rus in the 980s is Vladimir Putin of the Russian Federation in the 2010s, is to remove the centuries of interpretable material that permits historical thought and political judgment.

It is also possible to see in the thousand years since the baptism of Volodymyr/Valdemar of Kyiv a history rather than a story of eternity. To think historically is not to trade one national myth for another, to say that Ukraine rather than Russia is the inheritor of Rus, that Volodymyr/Valdemar was a Ukrainian and not a Russian. To make such a claim is merely to replace a Russian politics of eternity with a Ukrainian one. To think historically is to see how something like Ukraine might be possible, just as something like Russia might be possible. To think historically is to see the limits of structures, the spaces of indeterminacy, the possibilities for freedom.

The configurations that make Ukraine possible today are visible in the medieval and early modern periods. The Rus of Volodymyr/Valdemar was fractured long before the defeat of its warlords by the Mongols in the early 1240s. After the Mongol invasions, most of the territory of Rus was absorbed by the Grand Duchy of Lithuania in the thirteenth and fourteenth centuries. The Christian warlords of Rus then became leading figures of pagan Lithuania.

The Grand Duchy of Lithuania adopted the political language of Rus for its laws and courts. From 1386, the Lithuanian grand dukes generally ruled Poland as well.

The idea of a "Ukraine" to designate part of the lands of ancient Rus emerged after 1569, when the political relationship between Lithuania and Poland changed. In that year, the Kingdom of Poland and the Grand Duchy of Lithuania formed a commonwealth, a constitutional union of the two realms. During the bargaining, most of the territory of present-day Ukraine was shifted from the Lithuanian to the Polish part of the new common entity. This set off conflicts that created the political idea of Ukraine.

After 1569 on the territory of today's Ukraine, the eastern Christian traditions of Rus were challenged by western Christianity, which was in the midst of fertile transformations. Polish Catholic and Protestant thinkers, aided by the printing press, challenged the hold of eastern Christianity on the lands of Rus. Some of the Orthodox warlords of Rus converted to Protestantism or Catholicism and adopted the Polish language for communication among themselves. Following Polish models (and the example of Polish nobles who moved east), these local magnates began to transform the fertile Ukrainian steppe into great plantations. This meant binding the local population to the land as serfs in order to exploit their labor. Ukrainian peasants who tried to flee serfdom often found another form of bondage, since they could be sold into slavery by neighboring Muslims, in the extreme south of what is today Ukraine. These Muslims, known as Tatars, were under the suzerainty of the Ottoman Empire.

Serfs sought refuge with the Cossacks, free men who lived by raiding, hunting, and fishing at the southeastern edge of the steppe, in the no-man's-land between Polish and Ottoman power. They built their fortress, or *Sich*, on an island in the middle of the Dnipro River, not far from the present-day city that bears the river's name. In wartime, thousands of Cossacks fought as contract soldiers in the Polish army. When Cossacks fought as infantry and the Polish nobility as cavalry, the Polish army rarely lost. In the early seventeenth century, the Polish-Lithuanian Commonwealth was the largest state in Europe, and even briefly took Moscow. It was a republic of nobles, in which every nobleman was represented in parliament. In practice, of course, some noblemen were more powerful than others, and the wealthy magnates of Ukraine were among the most important citizens of the commonwealth. Cossacks wanted to be ennobled, or at least to have fixed legal rights within the commonwealth. This was not granted them.

In 1648, these tensions brought rebellion. The Polish-Lithuanian Commonwealth was about to undertake a campaign against the Ottoman Empire. The Cossacks who were preparing to take the field

against the Ottomans instead found a leader, Bohdan Khmelnyts'kyi, who persuaded them to rebel against local polonized landlords. Knowing that he needed allies, Khmelnyts'kyi recruited the Tatars, to whom he offered local Ukrainian Christians as slaves. When the Tatars deserted him, he needed a new ally, and Moscow was the only one he could find. There was nothing fated about this alliance. The Cossacks and the Muscovites both saw themselves as inheritors of Rus, but they had no common language and needed translators to communicate. Though a rebel, Khmelnyts'kyi was a child of the Renaissance, Reformation, and Counter-Reformation, whose languages were Ukrainian, Polish, and Latin (but not Russian). The Cossacks were accustomed to legal contracts binding on both parties. They saw as a temporary arrangement what the Muscovite side regarded as permanent subjugation to the tsar. In 1654, Muscovy invaded the Polish-Lithuanian Commonwealth. In 1667, the lands that are now Ukraine were split along the Dnipro River, with the Cossack strongholds falling to Muscovy. The status of Kyiv was at first uncertain, but it too was ceded to Muscovy.

Muscovy now turned westward after its long Asian career. The city of Kyiv had existed for about eight hundred years without a political connection to Moscow. Kyiv had passed through the Middle Ages, the Renaissance and the Baroque, the Reformation and the Counter-Reformation, as a European metropolis. Once joined to Muscovy, its academy became the major institution of higher learning in the realm, which after 1721 was known as the Russian Empire. Kyiv's educated men filled the professional classes of Moscow and then St. Petersburg. The Cossacks were assimilated into the Russian imperial armed forces. Empress Catherine took a Cossack lover and deployed the Cossacks to conquer the Crimean Peninsula. At the end of the eighteenth century, the Russian Empire partitioned the Polish-Lithuanian Commonwealth out of existence, with the help of Prussia and the Habsburg monarchy. In this way, almost all of the ancient lands of Rus became part of the new Russian Empire.

In the nineteenth century, Russian imperial integration called forth a Ukrainian patriotic reaction. The Russian imperial university in Kharkiv was the first center of a Romantic tendency to idealize the local peasant and his culture. In mid-century Kyiv, a few members of ancient noble families began to identify with the Ukrainian-speaking peasantry rather than with Russian or Polish power. At first, Russian rulers saw in these tendencies a laudable interest in "south Russian" or "little Russian" culture. After Russia's defeat in the Crimean War of 1853–1856 and a Polish uprising of 1863–1864, Russian imperial authorities defined Ukrainian culture as a political danger, and banned publications in the Ukrainian language. The

Statutes of the Grand Duchy of Lithuania, with their echoes of the ancient law of Rus, lost their force. The traditional place of Kyiv as the center of eastern Orthodoxy was assumed by Moscow. The Uniate Church, formed in 1596 with an eastern liturgy but a western hierarchy, was abolished.

The one land of Rus that remained outside the Russian Empire was Galicia. When the Polish-Lithuanian Commonwealth had been partitioned out of existence at the end of the eighteenth century, Habsburg rulers ended up with these territories. As a Habsburg crownland, Galicia preserved certain features of Rus civilization, such as the Uniate Church. The Habsburg monarchy renamed it "Greek Catholic" and educated its priests in Vienna. Children and grandchildren of these men became Ukrainian national activists, editors of newspapers, and candidates to parliament. When the Russian Empire restricted Ukrainian culture, Ukrainian writers and activists moved to Galicia. After 1867, the Habsburg monarchy had a liberal constitution and a free press, so these political immigrants had the freedom to continue Ukrainian work. Austria held democratic elections, so party politics became national politics throughout the monarchy. Refugees from the Russian Empire defined Ukrainian politics and history as a matter of a continuous culture and language rather than imperial power. As for the peasants themselves, the vast bulk of the population that spoke the Ukrainian language was mainly concerned with owning land.

After the Bolshevik Revolution of November 1917, a Ukrainian government declared independence. Yet unlike other east European peoples, Ukrainians were unable to form a state. No Ukrainian claim was recognized by the powers that won the First World War. Kyiv changed hands a dozen times among the Red Army, its White Russian opponents, a Ukrainian army, and the Polish army. Beleaguered Ukrainian authorities made an alliance with newly independent Poland, and together the Polish and Ukrainian armies took Kyiv in May 1920. When the Red Army counterattacked, Ukrainian soldiers fought alongside Poles all the way back to Warsaw. But when Poland and Bolshevik Russia signed their peace treaty at Riga in 1921, the lands that Ukrainian activists saw as theirs were divided: almost all of what had been in the Russian Empire fell to the emerging Soviet Union, whereas Galicia and another western district, Volhynia, fell to Poland. This was not exceptional but hypertypical. A Ukrainian nation-state lasted months, whereas its western neighbors lasted years, but the lesson was the same, and best learned from the Ukrainian example: the nation-state was difficult and in most cases untenable.

———

UKRAINIAN HISTORY brings into focus a central question of modern European history: After empire, what? According to the fable of the wise nation, European nation-states learned a lesson from war and began to integrate. For this myth to make sense, nation-states must be imagined into periods when in fact they did not exist. The fundamental event of the middle of the European twentieth century has to be removed: the attempts by Europeans to establish empires within Europe itself. The crucial case is the failed German attempt to colonize Ukraine in 1941. The rich black earth of Ukraine was at the center of the two major European neoimperial projects of the twentieth century, the Soviet and then the Nazi. In this respect as well, Ukrainian history is hypertypical and therefore indispensible. No other land attracted as much colonial attention within Europe. This reveals the rule: European history turns on colonization and decolonization.

Joseph Stalin understood the Soviet project as self-colonization. Since the Soviet Union had no overseas possessions, it had to exploit its hinterlands. Ukraine was therefore to yield its agricultural bounty to Soviet central planners in the First Five-Year Plan of 1928–1933. State control of agriculture killed between three and four million inhabitants of Soviet Ukraine by starvation. Adolf Hitler saw Ukraine as the fertile territory that would transform Germany into a world power. Control of its black earth was his war aim. As a result of the German occupation that began in 1941, more than three million more inhabitants of Soviet Ukraine were killed, including about 1.6 million Jews murdered by the Germans and local policemen and militias. In addition to those losses, some three million more inhabitants of Soviet Ukraine died in combat as Red Army soldiers. Taken together, some ten million people were killed in a decade as a result of two rival colonizations of the same Ukrainian territory.

After the Red Army defeated the Wehrmacht in 1945, the borders of Soviet Ukraine were extended westward to include districts taken from Poland, as well as minor territories from Czechoslovakia and Romania. In 1954, the Crimean Peninsula was removed from the Russian Soviet Federative Republic of the Soviet Union and added to Soviet Ukraine. This was the last of a series of border adjustments between the two Soviet republics. Since Crimea is connected to Ukraine by land (and an island from the perspective of Russia), the point was to connect the peninsula to the Ukrainian water supplies and electricity grids. The Soviet leadership took the opportunity to explain that Ukraine and Russia were unified by fate. Because the year 1954 was the three hundredth anniversary of the agreement that had united the Cossacks and Muscovy against the Polish-Lithuanian Commonwealth, Soviet factories produced cigarette packs and nightgowns with the logo 300 YEARS. This was an early example of the Soviet politics of eternity: legitimating rule not by present achievement or future promise but by the nostalgic loop of a round number.

Soviet Ukraine was the second most populous republic of the USSR, after Soviet Russia. In Soviet Ukraine's western districts, which had been part of Poland before the Second World War, Ukrainian nationalists resisted the imposition of Soviet rule. In a series of deportations in the late 1940s and early 1950s, they and their families were sent by the hundreds of thousands to the Soviet concentration camp system, the Gulag. In just a few days in October 1947, for example, 76,192 Ukrainians were transported to the Gulag in what was known as Operation West. Most of those who were still alive at the time of Stalin's death in 1953 were released by his successor, Nikita Khrushchev. In the 1960s and 1970s, Ukrainian communists joined their Russian comrades in governing the largest country in the world. During the cold war, southeastern Ukraine was a Soviet military heartland. Rockets were built in Dnipropetrovsk, not far from where the Cossacks once had their fortress.

Though Soviet policy had been lethal to Ukrainians, Soviet leaders never denied that Ukraine was a nation. The governing idea was that nations would achieve their full potential under Soviet rule, and then dissolve once communism was achieved. In the early decades of the Soviet Union, the existence of a Ukrainian nation was taken for granted, from the journalism of Joseph Roth to the statistics of the League of Nations. The famine of 1932–1933 was also a war against the Ukrainian nation, in that it wrecked the social cohesion of villages and coincided with a bloody purge of Ukrainian national activists. Yet the vague idea remained that a Ukrainian nation would have a socialist future. It was really only in the 1970s, under Brezhnev, that Soviet policy officially dropped this pretense. In his myth of the "Great Fatherland War," Russians and Ukrainians were merged as soldiers against fascism. When Brezhnev abandoned utopia for "really existing socialism," he implied that the development of non-Russian nations was complete. Brezhnev urged that Russian become the language of communication for all Soviet elites, and a client of his ran Ukrainian affairs. Schools were russified, and universities were to follow. In the 1970s, Ukrainian opponents of the Soviet regime risked prison and the psychiatric hospital to protest on behalf of Ukrainian culture.

To be sure, Ukrainian communists joined wholeheartedly and in great numbers in the Soviet project, helping Russian communists to govern Asian regions of the USSR. After 1985, Gorbachev's attempt to bypass the communist party alienated such people, while his policy of *glasnost,* or open discussion, encouraged Soviet citizens to air national grievances. In 1986, his silence after the nuclear disaster at Chernobyl discredited him among many Ukrainians. Millions of inhabitants of Soviet Ukraine were needlessly exposed to high doses of radiation. It was hard to forgive his specific order that a May Day parade go forward under a deadly cloud. The senseless poisoning of 1986 prompted Ukrainians to begin to speak of the senseless mass starvation of 1933.

In summer 1991, the failed coup against Gorbachev opened the way for Boris Yeltsin to lead Russia from the Soviet Union. Ukrainian communists and oppositionists alike agreed that Ukraine should follow suit. In a referendum, 92% of the inhabitants of Soviet

Ukraine, including a majority in every Ukrainian region, voted for independence.

AS IN the new Russia, the 1990s in the new Ukraine were marked by takeovers of Soviet assets and clever arbitrage schemes. Unlike in Russia, in Ukraine the new class of oligarchs formed themselves into durable clans, none of which dominated the state for more than a few years at a time. And unlike in Russia, in Ukraine power changed hands through democratic elections. Both Russia and Ukraine missed an opportunity for economic reform in the relatively good years before the world financial crisis of 2008. Unlike in Russia, in Ukraine the European Union was seen as a cure for the corruption that hindered social advancement and a more equitable distribution of wealth. EU membership was consistently promoted, at least rhetorically, by Ukrainian leaders. The Ukrainian president from 2010, Viktor Yanukovych, promoted the idea of a European future, even as he pursued policies that made such a future less likely.

Yanukovych's career demonstrates the difference between Ukrainian oligarchical pluralism and Russian kleptocratic centralism. He had run for president for the first time in 2004. The final count had been manipulated in his favor by his patron, the outgoing president Leonid Kuchma. Russian foreign policy was also to support his candidacy and declare his victory. After three weeks of protests on Kyiv's Independence Square (known as the Maidan), a ruling of the Ukrainian supreme court, and new elections, Yanukovych accepted defeat. This was an important moment in Ukrainian history; it confirmed democracy as a succession principle. So long as the rule of law functioned at the heights of politics, there was always hope that it might one day extend to everyday life.

After his defeat, Yanukovych hired the American political consultant Paul Manafort to improve his image. Although Manafort maintained a residence in Trump Tower in New York, he spent a great deal of time in Ukraine. Under Manafort's tutelage, Yanukovych got a better haircut and better suits, and began to talk with his hands. Manafort helped him to pursue a "Southern strategy" for Ukraine reminiscent of the one that his Republican Party had used in the United States: emphasizing cultural differences, making politics about being rather than doing. In the United States, this meant playing to the grievances of whites even though they were a majority whose members held almost all the wealth; in Ukraine it meant exaggerating the difficulties of people who spoke Russian, even though it was a major language of politics and economics of the country, and the first language of those who controlled the country's resources. Like Manafort's next client, Donald Trump, Yanukovych rose to power on a campaign of cultural grievance mixed with the hope that an oligarch might defend the people against an oligarchy.

After winning the presidential election of 2010, Yanukovych concentrated on his own personal wealth. He seemed to be importing Russian practices by creating a permanent kleptocratic elite rather than allowing the rotation of oligarchical clans. His dentist son became one of the richest men in Ukraine. Yanukovych undermined the checks and balances among the branches of the Ukrainian government, for example by making the judge who had misplaced his criminal record the chief justice of the Ukrainian supreme court. Yanukovych also tried to manage democracy in the Russian style. He put one of his two major opponents in prison, and had a law passed that disqualified the other from running for president. This left him running for a second term against a handpicked nationalist opponent. Yanukovych was certain to win, after which he could tell Europeans and Americans that he had saved Ukraine from nationalism.

As a new state, Ukraine had enormous problems, most obviously corruption. An association agreement with the EU, which Yanukovych promised to sign, would be an instrument to support the rule of law within Ukraine. The historical function of the EU was precisely the rescue of the European state after empire. Yanukovych might not have understood this, but many Ukrainian citizens did.

For them, only the prospect of an association agreement made his regime tolerable. So when Yanukovych suddenly declared, on November 21, 2013, that Ukraine would not sign the association agreement, he became intolerable. Yanukovych had made his decision after speaking with Putin. The Russian politics of eternity, ignored by most Ukrainians until then, was suddenly at the doorstep.

It is the investigative journalists who bring oligarchy and inequality into view. As chroniclers of the contemporary, they react first to the politics of eternity. In the oligarchical Ukraine of the twenty-first century, reporters gave their fellow citizens a chance at self-defense. Mustafa Nayyem was one of these investigative journalists, and on November 21, he had had enough. Writing on his Facebook page, Nayyem urged his friends to go out to protest. "Likes don't count," he wrote. People would have to take their bodies to the streets. And so they did: in the beginning, students and young people, thousands of them from Kyiv and around the country, the citizens with the most to lose from a frozen future.

They came to the Maidan, and they stayed. And in so doing they took part in the creation of a new thing: a nation.


WHATEVER THE flaws of the Ukrainian political system, Ukrainians after 1991 had come to take for granted that political disputes would be settled without violence. Exceptions, such as the murder of the popular investigative reporter Georgiy Gongadze in 2000, brought protests. In a country that had seen more violence in the twentieth century than any other, the civic peace of the twenty-first was a proud achievement. Alongside the regularity of elections and the absence of war, the right to peaceful assembly was one way that Ukrainians themselves distinguished their country from Russia. So it came as a shock when riot police attacked the protestors on the Maidan on November 30. News that "our children" had been beaten spread through Kyiv. The spilling of "the first drop of blood" stirred people to action.

Ukrainian citizens came to Kyiv to help the students because they were troubled by violence. One of them was Sergei Nihoyan, a Russian-speaking ethnic Armenian from the southeastern district of Ukraine known as the Donbas. A worker himself, he expressed solidarity with "students, citizens of Ukraine." The reflex of protecting the future, triggered in the minds of students by the fear of losing Europe, was triggered in others by the fear of losing the one generation raised in an independent Ukraine. Among the representatives of older generations who came to the Maidan to protect the students were the "Afghans"—veterans of the Red Army's invasion of Afghanistan. The protests of December 2013 were less about Europe and more about the proper form of politics in Ukraine, about "decency" or "dignity."

On December 10, 2013, the riot police were sent in a second time to clear the Maidan of protestors. Once again the word went out, and Kyivans of all walks of life decided to put their bodies in front of batons. A young businesswoman recalled that her friends "were shaving and putting on clean clothes in case they should die that night." A middle-aged literary historian ventured forth with an elderly couple, a publisher and a physician: "My friends were an invalid who is well over 60, and his wife of about the same age—next to them I seemed rather young, strong and healthy (I am a 53-year-old woman, and of course at my age it is difficult to think of physically overcoming armed men). My friends are both Jews and I am a Polish citizen, but we walked together, as Ukrainian patriots, convinced that our lives would be of no value if the protests were crushed now. We made it to the Maidan, not without some difficulties. My friend Lena, a doctor, the gentlest being in the world, is only a meter and a half tall—I had to keep her at a distance from the riot police, because I knew that she would tell them exactly what she thought of them and the whole situation." On December 10, the riot police could not move the crowd.

On January 16, 2014, Yanukovych retroactively criminalized the protests and legalized his own use of force. The official parliamentary record included a raft of legislation which the protestors called "dictatorship laws." These measures severely limited freedom of expression and freedom of assembly, banning undefined "extremism," and requiring nongovernmental organizations that received money from abroad to register as "foreign agents." The laws were introduced by deputies with ties to Russia and were copies of Russian legislation. There were no public hearings, no parliamentary debate, and indeed no actual vote: a show of hands was improperly used instead of an electronic count, and the number of hands raised was short of a majority. The laws were nevertheless entered into the books. Protestors recognized that they would be treated as criminals if apprehended.

Six days later, two protestors were shot dead. From the perspective, say, of either the United States or Russia, both much more violent societies, it is hard to appreciate the weight of these two deaths for Ukrainians. The mass killings by sniper fire four weeks later would overshadow these first two deaths. The Russian invasion of Ukraine that began five weeks later brought so much more bloodshed that it can seem impossible to recall how the killing began. And yet to the society actually concerned, there were specific moments that seemed intolerable breaches of common decency. In the final week of January, Ukrainian citizens who had not previously supported the Maidan protests began to arrive, in large numbers, from all over the country. Because it seemed that Yanukovych had now bloodied his hands, his further rule was inconceivable to many Ukrainians.

Protestors experienced this moment as the warping of their own political society. A demonstration that had begun in defense of a European future had become a defense of the few tenuous gains in the Ukrainian present. By February the Maidan was a desperate stand against Eurasia. Until then, few Ukrainians had given any thought to the Russian politics of eternity. But protestors did not want what they saw on offer: violence leading to a futureless life amid wisps of what might have been.

As February began, Yanukovych was still the president, and Washington and Moscow had ideas about how he might remain in power. A telephone call between an American assistant secretary of state and the American ambassador in Kyiv, apparently recorded by a Russian secret service and leaked on February 4, revealed that American policy was to support the formation of a new government under Yanukovych. This proposal was out of line with the demands of the Maidan and, indeed, completely out of touch. Yanukovych's rule was already over, at least in the minds of those who chose to risk their lives on the Maidan after the killings of January 22, 2014. A survey showed that only 1% of protestors would accept a political compromise that left Yanukovych in office. On February 18, parliamentary discussions began, with hope that some compromise could be found. Instead, the next day saw a bloody confrontation that made the continuation of Yanukovych's regime even less likely.

The history of the Maidan between November 2013 and February 2014, the work of more than a million people presenting their bodies to the cold stone, is not the same thing as the history of the failed attempts to put it down. Bloodshed had been unthinkable for protestors within Ukraine; only bloodshed made Americans and Europeans notice the country; bloodshed served Moscow as an argument to send the Russian army to bring much more. And so the temptation is strong to recall Ukraine as it was seen from the outside, the arc of narrative following the arc of bullets.

For those who took part in the Maidan, their protest was about defending what was still thought to be possible: a decent future for their own country. The violence mattered to them as a marker of the intolerable. It came in bursts of a few moments or a few hours. But people came to the Maidan not for moments or hours but for days, weeks, and months, their own fortitude suggesting a new sense of time, and new forms of politics. Those who remained on the Maidan could do so only because they found new ways to organize themselves.

THE MAIDAN brought four forms of politics: the civil society, the economy of gift, the voluntary welfare state, and the Maidan friendship.

Kyiv is a bilingual capital, something unusual in Europe and unthinkable in Russia and the United States. Europeans, Russians, and Americans rarely considered that everyday bilingualism might bespeak political maturity, and imagined instead that a Ukraine that spoke two languages must be divided into two groups and two halves. "Ethnic Ukrainians" must be a group that acts in one way, and "ethnic Russians" in another. This is about as true as to say that "ethnic Americans" vote Republican. It is more a summary of a politics that defines people by ethnicity, proposing to them an eternity of grievance rather than a politics of the future. In Ukraine, language is a spectrum rather than a line. Or, if it is a line, it is one that runs inside of people rather than between them.

Ukrainian citizens on the Maidan spoke as they did in everyday life, using Ukrainian and Russian as it suited them. The revolution was begun by a journalist who used Russian to tell people where to put the camera, and Ukrainian when he spoke in front of it. His famous Facebook post ("Likes don't count") was in Russian. On the Maidan, the question of who spoke what language was irrelevant. As the protestor Ivan Surenko remembered, writing in Russian: "The Maidan crowd is tolerant on the language question. I never heard any discussions about the matter." In one survey, 59% of the people on the Maidan defined themselves as Ukrainian speakers, 16% as Russian speakers, and 25% as both. People switched languages as the situation seemed to demand. People spoke Ukrainian from the stage erected at the Maidan, since Ukrainian is the language of politics. But then the speaker might return to the crowd and speak to friends in Russian. This was the everyday behavior of a new political nation.

The politics of this nation were about the rule of law: first the hope that an association agreement with the European Union could reduce corruption, then the determination to prevent the rule of law from disappearing entirely under the waves of state violence. In surveys, protestors most often selected "the defense of the rule of law" as their major goal. The political theory was simple: the state needed civil society to lead it toward Europe, and the state needed Europe to lead it away from corruption. Once the violence began, this political theory expressed itself in more poetic forms. The philosopher Volodymyr Yermolenko wrote, "Europe is also a light at the end of a tunnel. When do you need a light like that? When it is pitch dark all around."

In the meantime, civil society had to work in darkness. Ukrainians did so by forming horizontal networks with no relationship to political parties. As the protestor Ihor Bihun recalled: "There was no fixed membership. There was no hierarchy either." The political and social activity of the Maidan from December 2013 through February 2014 arose from temporary associations based upon will and skill. The essential idea was that freedom was responsibility. There was thus pedagogy (libraries and schools), security (*Samoobrona,* or self-defense), external affairs (the council of Maidan), aid for victims of violence and people seeking missing loved ones (Euromaidan SOS), and anti-propaganda (InfoResist). As the protestor Andrij Bondar remembered, self-organization was a challenge to the dysfunctional Ukrainian state: "On the Maidan a Ukrainian civil society of incredible self-organization and solidarity is thriving. On the one hand, this society is internally differentiated: by ideology, language, culture, religion and class, but on the other hand it is united by certain elementary sentiments. We do not need your permission! We are not going to ask you for something! We are not afraid of you! We will do everything ourselves."

The economy of the Maidan was one of gift. In its first few days, as Natalya Stelmakh recalled, the people of Kyiv gave with extraordinary generosity: "Within two days other volunteers and I were able to collect in *hryvnia* the equivalent of about $40,000 in cash from simple residents of Kyiv." She remembered trying and failing to prevent an elderly pensioner from donating half of a monthly check. Aside from donations in cash, people provided food, clothes, wood, medications, barbed wire, and helmets. A visitor would be surprised to find deep order amidst apparent chaos, and realize that what seemed at first like extraordinary hospitality was in fact a spontaneous welfare state. The Polish political activist Sławomir Sierakowski was duly impressed: "You walked through the Maidan and you are presented with food, clothing, a place to sleep, and medical care."

In early 2014, the vast majority of the protestors, some 88% of the hundreds of thousands of people who appeared, were from beyond Kyiv. Only 3% came as representatives of political parties, and only 13% as members of nongovernmental organizations. According to surveys taken at the time, almost all of the protestors—about 86%—made up their own minds to come, and came as individuals or families or groups of friends. They were taking part in what the art curator Vasyl Cherepanyn called "corporeal politics": getting their faces away from screens and their bodies among other bodies.

Patient protest amidst increasing risks generated the idea of the "Maidan friend," the person you trusted because of common trials. The historian Yaroslav Hrytsak described one way that new acquaintances were made: "On the Maidan, you are a pixel, and pixels always work in groups. Groups were mostly formed spontaneously: you or your friend bumped into somebody you or your friend know; and the person whom you met did not walk alone—he or she would be also accompanied by his or her friends. And thus you start to walk together. One night I walked with an unlikely group of 'soldiers of fortune': my friend the philosopher and a businessman whom I know. He was accompanied by a tiny man with sad eyes. He looked like a sad clown, and I found out that he was indeed a professional clown who organized a charitable group that worked with children who had cancer."

Having come as individuals, Ukrainian citizens on the Maidan joined new institutions. In practicing corporeal politics they were placing their bodies at risk. As the philosopher Yermolenko put it: "We are dealing with revolutions in which people make a gift of themselves." People often expressed this as a kind of personal transformation, a choice unlike other choices. Hrytsak and others recalled the French philosopher Albert Camus and his idea of a revolt as the moment when death is chosen over submission. Posters on the Maidan quoted a 1755 letter by the American Founding Father Benjamin Franklin: "Those who would give up Essential Liberty, to purchase a little Temporary Safety, deserve neither Liberty nor Safety."

A group of Ukrainian lawyers waited on the Maidan, day after day, holding a sign reading LAWYERS OF THE MAIDAN. People who had been beaten or otherwise abused by the state could report the wrongdoing and begin a legal case. Lawyers and others on the Maidan were not thinking of the enduring problem of Russian political philosophy: how to generate a spirit of law in an autocratic system. And yet, by their actions on behalf of a vision of law, they were addressing the very problem that had haunted Ilyin.

A hundred years before, in the waning years of the Russian Empire, Ilyin had wished for a Russia ruled by law, but could not see how its spirit would ever reach the people. After the Bolshevik Revolution, he accepted that lawlessness from the far Left must be met by lawlessness from the far Right. At the very moment that Putin was applying Ilyin's notion of law to Russia, Ukrainians were demonstrating that the authoritarian shortcut could be resisted. Ukrainians demonstrated their attachment to law by cooperating with others and by risking themselves.

If Ukrainians could solve Ilyin's riddle of law by invoking Europe and solidarity, surely Russians could too? That was a thought that Russian leaders could not permit their citizens to entertain. And so, two years after the protests in Moscow, Russian leaders applied the same tactics to Kyiv: the homosexualization of protest to evoke a sense of eternal civilization, and then the application of violence to make change seem impossible.

IN LATE 2011, when Russians protested faked elections, their leaders associated the protestors with homosexuality. In late 2013, confronted with the Maidan in Ukraine, the men of the Kremlin made the same move. After two years of anti-gay propaganda in the Russian Federation, the ideologues and entertainers were sure of themselves. Their starting point was that the European Union was homosexual, and so the Ukrainian movement towards Europe must be as well. The Izborsk Club claimed that the EU "groans under the weight of the LGBT lobby's domination."

In November and December 2013, the Russian media covering the Maidan introduced the irrelevant theme of gay sex at every turn. When covering the very first day of protests by Ukrainian students in favor of the association agreement, the Russian media sought to fascinate its readers by conflating Ukrainian politics with handsome men and gay sex. A social media page of Vitali Klitschko, a heavyweight boxer who led a Ukrainian political party, was hacked and gay material introduced. Then this was presented as a news story for millions of Russians on a major television station, NTV. Before Russians could apprehend that pro-European protests were underway in a neighboring country, they were invited to contemplate taboo sex.

Right after students began their protests on the Maidan, the Russian television channel NTV warned of "homodictatorship" in Ukraine. Viktor Shestakov, writing for *Odna Rodina*, claimed that "a specter is haunting the Maidan, the specter of homosexuality. The fact that the first and the most zealous integrators in Ukraine are local sexual perverts has long been known."

Dmitry Kiselev, the leading figure in Russian television media, warmed to the theme. In December 2013 he was appointed the director of a new media conglomerate known as Rossiia Segodnia, or Russia Today. Its aim was to dissolve the Russian state media's pursuit of news as such into a new pursuit: of useful fiction. He greeted his new staff with the words "objectivity is a myth" and set the new editorial line as "love for Russia."

On December 1, 2013, the world press reported the beating of students by Ukrainian riot police the previous night. As Ukrainian students huddled in a church tending their wounds, Kiselev found a way to formulate their protests as sexual geopolitics. That evening on

*Vesti Nedeli,* recalling to his viewers the Great Northern War of the early eighteenth century, he described the European Union as a new alliance turned against Russia. This time, however, Kiselev claimed, the Swedish, Polish, and Lithuanian enemies were warriors of sexual perversion. Poland and Lithuania were not in fact enemies of Russia in the Great Northern War. Getting one's own history wrong is essential to eternity politics.

In another episode, Kiselev expressed his delight to have discovered a magazine with a nude photo shoot of Klitschko from a decade earlier. On the set, Kiselev stroked the black riot gear worn by the Ukrainian police as the camera zoomed in. Meanwhile, the newspaper *Segodnia* breathlessly praised itself for publishing a photograph that framed Klitschko together with a gay Ukrainian writer. In the Ukrainian context, these were two activists at a press conference. In the Russian press, the sexual orientation of the one and the male beauty of the other was the story.

European integration was interpreted by Russian politicians to mean the legalization of same-sex partnerships (which was not an element of Ukraine's association agreement with the EU) and thus the spread of homosexuality. When the German foreign minister visited Kyiv on December 4, the newspaper *Komsomol'skaia Pravda* headlined the meeting as "Gay firewood on the Maidan fire."

WHILE THE Putin regime had crushed protests at home in 2011 and 2012, it sought to redefine politics as innocence rather than action. Rather than asking how past experience might instruct reformers of the present about possibilities for the future, Russians were meant to adapt their minds to a news cycle which instructed them on their own innocence. One eternal verity of Russian civilization turned out to be sexual anxiety. If Russia were indeed a virginal organism threatened by the world's uncomprehending malice, as Ilyin had suggested, then Russian violence was a righteous defense against penetration. For Putin as for Ilyin, Ukraine was part of that national body. For Eurasia to come into being, Ukrainian domestic politics would have to become more like Russian domestic politics.

When Yanukovych announced that he would not sign the EU association agreement in November 2013, this was celebrated by the Russian government as a victory. But Yanukovych had not actually agreed to join Eurasia, a move that would have been even more unpopular among Ukrainians. In December 2013 and January 2014, the Kremlin tried to help Yanukovych crush protest and thereby make it possible for him to complete his turn from the EU towards Eurasia. Yanukovych claimed that both Europe and Russia wanted Ukraine, and each needed to pay him off. While the EU refused, Putin was ready to offer Yanukovych money.

On December 17, 2013, Putin offered Yanukovych a package of $15 billion in bond purchases and reduced prices for natural gas. The aid seemed to be conditional: it was offered along with Russian requests that the streets of Kyiv be cleared of protestors. By then the Ukrainian riot police had already failed twice in this mission, on November 30 and December 10. They had also been abducting individual protestors thought to be leaders and beating them. None of this was working, so Russians came to help. A group of twenty-seven Russian specialists in the suppression of protests, officers of the FSB and instructors from the ministry of internal affairs, arrived in Kyiv. On January 9, 2014, the Russian ambassador to Ukraine informed Yanukovych that Ukrainian riot policemen would be given Russian citizenship after the coming operation to crush the Maidan. This was a very important assurance, since it meant that these policemen did not need to fear the consequences of their actions. If the opposition won in the end, they would still be safe.

Moscow apparently calculated in January 2014 that a more competent application of violence would break the protests and transform Yanukovych into a puppet. It did not enter into Russian calculations that Ukrainian citizens were on the Maidan for patriotic reasons of their own. When the Yanukovych regime introduced the Russian-style dictatorship laws of January 16, 2014, this suggested massive violence to come. Russian-style laws did not have the same consequences in Ukraine as in Russia. Ukrainian protestors saw them as offensive foreign implants. When those two protestors were killed on January 22, the Maidan grew as never before. Remote-control counterrevolution had failed. Moscow was unable to move Ukraine into Eurasia by helping Yanukovych to repress the opposition. It was time for a shift in strategy. By early February 2014, it appeared Moscow no longer aimed to maneuver Yanukovych and Ukraine into Eurasia. Instead, Yanukovych would be sacrificed in a campaign to provoke chaos throughout the country.

A MAJOR actor in the new policy was Igor Girkin, a colonel in Russian military intelligence (GRU) who was employed by Konstantin Malofeev. Known in Russia as the "Orthodox oligarch," Malofeev was an anti-sodomy activist and an outspoken Russian imperialist. In his view, "Ukraine is part of Russia. I can't consider the Ukrainian people as non-Russian." Ukraine had to be saved by Russia from Europe because otherwise Ukrainian citizens "would have had to spread sodomy as a norm in traditional Ukrainian society." This was not true in any factual sense. Malofeev was expressing the orientation of Russian policy: to present Europe as a civilizational enemy, homosexuality as the war, and Ukraine as the battleground.

Malofeev's employee Girkin was experienced in irregular warfare. He had fought as a Russian volunteer on the Serbian side in the Yugoslav Wars, taking part in engagements in Bosnian towns and UN-declared "safe areas" where ethnic cleansing and mass rape took place. He had also fought in Russia's wars in Transnistria and Chechnya, and had written about these experiences for media edited by the fascist Alexander Prokhanov. Girkin spent the days between January 22 and February 4, 2014, in Kyiv, and then, it seems, recommended to the Kremlin that Ukraine be invaded and dismembered.

A memorandum that circulated in the Russian presidential administration in early February 2014, apparently based on the work of Girkin, anticipated the change in the course of Russian policy. It began from the premise that "the Yanukovych regime is utterly bankrupt. Its diplomatic, financial, and propaganda support by the Russian state no longer makes any sense." Russian interests in Ukraine were defined as the military-industrial complex of Ukraine's southeast and "control over the gas transport system" in the entire country. Russia's main goal should be "the disintegration of the Ukrainian state." The proposed tactic was to discredit both Yanukovych and the opposition by violence, while invading southern Ukraine and destabilizing the Ukrainian state. The memorandum included three propaganda strategies meant to provide cover for such a Russian intervention: (1) to demand that Ukraine federalize itself in the interests of a supposedly oppressed Russian minority, (2) to define opponents of the Russian invasion as fascists, and (3) to characterize the invasion as a civil war stoked by the West.

In a policy paper of February 13, 2014, the Izborsk Club repeated the contents of the confidential Kremlin memorandum. The Maidan might inspire Russians to act and was therefore intolerable; Yanukovych was finished; therefore Russia should invade Ukraine and take what it could. As with the presidential memorandum, the guiding concept of the Izborsk policy paper was that Russia should seize some Ukrainian territory and then wait for the state to collapse. The Izborsk Club also proposed that Russian television channels justify the intervention in Ukraine by the deliberate, premeditated fiction that "a fascist coup is coming"; this would indeed be a major line of Russian propaganda once war began.

On the day that the Izborsk Club was propagating this general idea, Vladislav Surkov, Putin's propaganda genius, arrived in the south Ukrainian province of Crimea. The next day, Surkov flew from Crimea to Kyiv. Foreign Minister Lavrov chose that very day (February 14, 2014) to formalize the idea that Russian civilization was an innocent body defending itself from Western perversion. In the newspaper *Kommersant*, Lavrov repeated Ilyin's idea that "society is a living organism" that had to be protected from Europe's hedonistic "refusal of traditional values." Lavrov presented the Ukrainians who were struggling, and by that point dying, for European ideas of law as the prey of European sexual politics. Even as Russian troops were mobilizing to invade Ukraine and overturn its government, Lavrov presented Russia as the victim. The true aggressors, according to Lavrov, were the international gay lobbyists who "propagated with missionary insistence both inside their own countries and in relations with neighbors." Surkov left Kyiv on February 15. Live ammunition was distributed to the Ukrainian riot police on February 16. On February 18, Ukrainians waited while parliamentary deputies discussed a constitutional compromise. Instead, protestors on the Maidan were surprised by massive and lethal violence.

Now European actors finally began to move. Although the protests had been pro-European from the beginning, they had not been meaningfully supported by the European Union, its member states, or any Western actor. European public opinion took little notice of the Maidan before the violence began. Politicians issued bland and interchangeable calls for both sides to avoid violence. Once the violence began, diplomats expressed official concern. Diplomatic discourse became a cause for mockery on the Maidan, as people who risked their lives found themselves alone and isolated. As violence increased, the mockery turned to pathos. Ukrainian protestors on the Maidan flew flags of an imagined "United States of Russia" to express their view that the great powers shared a common indifference or hostility.

The most significant initiative came from a European diplomat. Polish Foreign Minister Radosław Sikorski persuaded his French and German colleagues to join him in Kyiv for talks with Yanukovych on February 20. A Russian diplomat joined the group. Over the course of a long and difficult day of negotiations, Yanukovych agreed to leave office at the end of 2014, before his term was over. As impressive as this diplomatic resolution might have seemed, it was outdated before it was signed. Russian authorities had already concluded that Yanukovych was doomed, and the Russian invasion force was already on the move. Signing the agreement allowed Russia to blame others for failing to fulfill its terms, even as the Russian invasion that followed four days later drastically changed the conditions under which it had been signed.

The moment had passed when Ukrainian protestors might have accepted Yanukovych as president. Had there been any doubt that he had to resign on the morning of February 20, it had dissipated by the end of the day. On February 20, there was another Russian delegation in Kyiv, led by Vladislav Surkov, and including Sergei Beseda, a general of the FSB. These Russians were not there to negotiate. As others did so, snipers hidden near the Maidan shot and killed about a hundred people, most of them protestors, a few of them Ukrainian riot policemen. It was unclear what (if any) part of the Ukrainian government was involved in these shootings.

After the mass killing, Yanukovych was abandoned by the parliamentary deputies who had supported him and the policemen who had protected him. He fled his garish residence, leaving behind a trove of documents—including records of large cash payments to his advisor Paul Manafort, who two years later surfaced as the campaign manager of Donald Trump.

THE SNIPER massacre and the flight of Yanukovych marked the shift from Russia's first Eurasian plan to its second. Russian leaders had accepted that Yanukovych was useless. His bloody downfall, foreseen in Moscow, created the chaos that served as cover for the second strategy: military intervention designed to make the state as a whole disintegrate. In the few days between the sniper massacre of February 20 and the Russian invasion of Ukraine on February 24, shocking but fictitious reports appeared about Ukrainian atrocities in Crimea, and about refugees from the peninsula who needed urgent assistance. Russian military intelligence created fictitious personae on the internet to spread these stories. A group of internet trolls in St. Petersburg, known as the Internet Research Agency, was at work to confuse Ukrainian and international opinion. This was by now a signature of Russian foreign policy: the cyber campaign that would accompany a real war.

By the time Yanukovych surfaced in Russia, the Russian invasion of Ukraine was under way. It began from Crimea, the southern peninsula of Ukraine, where by treaty Russia had naval bases. Some 2,000 naval infantry were permanently stationed in Sevastopol alone. These troops had been reinforced since the previous December by soldiers arriving from the Russian Federation. Russian army units 27777, 73612, 74268, and 54607 were among the 22,000 troops brought from Russia. Girkin had visited Crimea in January. In February he was accompanied by his friend Alexander Borodai: a Eurasianist, an admirer of Gumilev, a writer for Prokhanov's media, and the head of public relations for Malofeev.

Beginning on February 24, 2014, some ten thousand Russian special forces, in uniform but without insignia, moved northward through the Crimean peninsula. The moment they left their bases they were engaged in an illegal invasion of Ukraine. Kyiv was caught by surprise at a moment when chains of command were uncertain and the main concern was to avoid further violence. Provisional Ukrainian authorities ordered Ukrainian forces on the peninsula not to resist. By the night of February 26, Russian soldiers had seized the regional parliament building in the city of Simferopol and raised the Russian flag. According to Girkin, he was in command of the concurrent operation to seize the Simferopol airport. On February 27, Putin's Eurasia advisor Sergei Glazyev placed a telephone call to Crimea to arrange the new government. A local Russian gangster named Sergei Aksionov was proclaimed prime minister of Crimea; Borodai was his media advisor. On February 28, the Russian parliament endorsed the incorporation of Ukrainian territory into the Russian Federation. On that day, the president of the United States said that he was "deeply concerned by reports of military movements taken by the Russian

Federation inside of Ukraine." This was Barack Obama's first public statement about the crisis.

The public spectacle of the Russian invasion was provided by the Night Wolves, a Russian biker gang that served as a paramilitary and propaganda arm of the Putin regime. On February 28, the day that the Russian parliament voted for annexation, the Night Wolves were dispatched to Crimea. The bikers had been organizing rallies in Crimea for years, accompanied personally by Putin in 2012. (Putin cannot ride a motorcycle, so he was given a trike). Now the Night Wolves provided the face that Russia chose to show of itself. A few months earlier, one of the Night Wolves had described their worldview: "You have to learn to see the holy war underneath the everyday. Democracy is a fallen state. To split 'left' and 'right' is to divide. In the kingdom of God there is only above and below. All is one. Which is why the Russian soul is holy. It can unite everything. Like in an icon. Stalin and God." Here was Ilyin's philosophy, Surkov's geopolitics, and Putin's civilization expressed in a few words.

The Night Wolves found concise ways to translate sexual anxiety into geopolitics and back again. As a male-only club devoted to black leather, the Night Wolves naturally had a strong position on homosexuality, which they defined as an attack by Europe and the United States. A year later, celebrating the Russian invasion, their supreme leader Alexander Zaldostanov remembered their proud parade around Crimea in this way: "For the first time we showed resistance to the global Satanism, the growing savagery of Western Europe, the rush to consumerism that denies all spirituality, the destruction of traditional values, all this homosexual talk, this American democracy." According to Zaldostanov, the slogan of the Russian war against Ukraine should be "death to faggots." The association of democracy with gay Satan was a way to make law and reform foreign and unthinkable.

Having invaded Ukraine, Russian leaders took the position that their neighbor was not a sovereign state. This was the language of empire. On March 4, Putin explained that Ukraine's problem had been democratic elections that led to changes in power. Such functional elections, he suggested, were an alien American implant. He said that the situation in Ukraine was like that of Russia during the Bolshevik Revolution of 1917. Russia could go back in time and correct the mistakes of the past. "Logically," said Alexander Dugin on March 8, "Ukraine as it was during twenty-three years of its history has ceased to exist." Russian international lawyers, who during those previous twenty-three years had paid obsessive attention to the need to respect territorial boundaries and state sovereignty, argued that invasion and annexation were justified by the disappearance of the Ukrainian state—in other words, by the chaos caused by the Russian invasion. In Dugin's mind, the war to demolish the Ukrainian state was a war against the European Union: "we must take over and destroy Europe."

On March 16, some of the Ukrainian citizens of Crimea took part in an electoral farce that the Russian occupiers called a referendum. Prior to the vote, all public propaganda pushed in the same direction. Posters proclaimed that the choice was between Russia and Nazism. Voters had no access to international or Ukrainian media. On the ballots were two options, both of which affirmed the annexation of Crimea by Russia. The first option was to vote for the annexation of Crimea by Russia. The second was to restore the autonomy of the Crimean authorities, who had just been installed by Russia and requested annexation by Russia. According to internal information of the Russian presidential administration, the turnout was about 30% and the vote split between the two options. According to the official results, participation was about 90%, with almost all voters choosing the variant that led most directly to annexation. In Sevastopol, official turnout was 123%. Qualified observers were absent, although Moscow did invite a few European politicians of the extreme Right to endorse the official results. The *Front National* sent Aymeric Chauprade to Crimea, and Marine Le Pen personally endorsed the results. Within the Russian presidential administration, people were reminded to "thank the French."

In a grand ceremony in Moscow, Putin accepted what he called the "wishes" of the Crimean people and extended the boundaries of the Russian Federation. This violated basic consensual principles of international law, the United Nations Charter, every treaty signed between independent Ukraine and independent Russia, as well as a number of assurances that Russia had offered Ukraine about the protection of its frontiers. One of these was the Budapest Memorandum of 1994, in which the Russian Federation (along with the United Kingdom and the United States) had guaranteed Ukrainian borders when Ukraine agreed to give up all nuclear weapons. In what was perhaps the greatest act of nuclear disarmament in history, Ukraine handed over some 1,300 intercontinental ballistic missiles. By invading a country that had engaged in complete nuclear disarmament, Russia offered the world the lesson that nuclear arms should be pursued.

In March and April, Russian media conveyed the propaganda themes that had been discussed by the presidental administration and the Izborsk Club in February. There was a burst of enthusiasm for the "federalization" of Ukraine, on the logic that the "voluntary" separation of Crimea required Kyiv to give its other regions similar freedom of action. The Russian foreign ministry was careful to specify that "federalization" meant a specific Russian proposal to dismember the Ukrainian state, not any general principle that might apply to Russia. On March 17, the Russian foreign ministry declared that in view of "the deep crisis of the Ukrainian state," Russia had the right to define Ukraine as a "multinational people" and propose "a new federal constitution" for the country. The word "federalization" appeared in major Russian television media 1,412 times in April. Even in a mood of national euphoria, however, Russian leaders soon saw the risk of "federalization." The name of the Russian state was the "Russian Federation" and it was divided into units; but these had limited legal meaning and were ruled by appointees of the president. Within three months, the word "federalization" all but disappeared from the Russian public sphere.

Vladimir Putin presented the annexation of Crimea as a mystical personal transformation, an exultant passage into eternity. Crimea had to be part of Russia, explained Putin, because the leader of ancient Rus, Volodymyr/Valdemar, whom Putin called Vladimir, had been baptized there a thousand years before. That act by his namesake was recalled by Putin as the powerful gesture of a timeless superhero who "predetermined the overall basis of the culture, civilization, and human values that unite the peoples of Russia, Ukraine, and Belarus" (concepts that did not exist at the time). If the events of our time are "predetermined" by a millennial myth, then no knowledge of the past is necessary and no human choices matter. Vladimir is Volodymyr and Russia is Rus and politics is the eternal pleasure of the wealthy few—and there is nothing more to be said or done.

The parliamentary deputy Tatiana Saenko cited Ilyin to claim that the annexation of Crimea meant the "resurrection and rebirth" of Russia. She claimed that Western objections to the Russian invasion of Ukraine were a matter of "double standards." This common Russian argument made of law not a general principle but a cultural artifact located among non-Russian peoples. Because Western states do not always follow every law, it ran, law had no validity. Russia, too, might violate laws; but since Russia did not accept the rule of law, this was not hypocritical. Since Russia was not hypocritical, it was innocent. If there are no standards, went the reasoning, then there are no double standards. If Europeans or Americans mention international law during a time of such Russian innocence as the invasion of Ukraine, this makes them a spiritual threat. And so references to international law only demonstrated Western perfidy.

This was Ilyin's politics of eternity: a cycle back to the past replaces the forward movement of time; law means what Russia's leader says it means; Russia is repairing God's failed world with violence.

Putin was the redeemer from beyond history who emerged to alter time. Putin himself took up this theme on April 17, characterizing the Russian invasion of Ukraine as a spiritual defense against a permanent Western attack: "The intention to split Russia and Ukraine, to separate what is essentially a single nation in many ways, has been an issue of international politics for centuries." For Malofeev, the Russian invasion was a war against eternal evil: "for those who do battle there, the war looks like a war against hordes fighting under the banner of the anti-Christ with Satanic slogans." What could be more eternal than the campaign against Sodom?

The fall of Crimea encouraged Russian leaders to repeat the same scenario throughout southern and eastern Ukraine. On March 1, Glazyev telephoned confederates in the regional capitals of Ukraine's southern and southeastern districts to help plan coups d'état. Putin's Eurasia advisor ordered that the scenario of Crimea be repeated in other regions of Ukraine: a crowd would "storm the regional state administration building," then some new assembly would be coerced to declare independence and ask for Russian help. In Kharkiv, a crowd of locals and Russian citizens (brought by bus from Russia) did indeed break into the regional state administration building, after first storming the opera house by mistake. These people beat and humiliated Ukrainian citizens who were seeking to protect the building. The Ukrainian writer Serhiy Zhadan refused to kneel and had his skull broken.

In April, Putin publicly recited the goals of Russian policy as outlined in the February memorandum. The idea was still the "disintegration" of the Ukrainian state in the interests of Russia. Dozens of Ukrainian state institutions and companies suddenly faced cyberattacks, as did the most important institutions of the EU. In the southeastern Ukrainian district of Donetsk, a Russian neo-Nazi named Pavel Gubarev proclaimed himself "people's governor" on May 1, on the logic that "Ukraine never existed." The duo of Malofeev employees sent to Crimea, Igor Girkin and Alexander Borodai, returned to Ukraine in April. Borodai would name himself prime minister of an imagined new people's republic in southeastern Ukraine. His justification was similar: "There is no longer any Ukraine." His friend Girkin proclaimed himself the minister of war, and asked Russia to invade the Donbas and establish military bases.

THE RUSSIAN intervention in the Donbas was called the "Russian Spring." It was certainly springtime for Russian fascism. On March 7, 2014, Alexander Dugin rejoiced in "the expansion of liberational (from Americans) ideology into Europe. It is the goal of full Eurasianism—Europe from Lisbon to Vladivostok." The fascist commonwealth was coming into view, boasted the fascist. A few days later, Dugin proclaimed that history had been undone: "Modernity was always essentially wrong, and we are now at the terminal point of modernity. For those who rendered modernity and their own destiny synonymous, or who let that occur unconsciously, this will mean the *end*." The coming struggle would mean "real liberation from the open society and its beneficiaries." According to Dugin, an American diplomat of Jewish origin was "a dirty pig," and a Ukrainian politician of Jewish origin a "ghoul" and a "bastard." Chaos in Ukraine was the work of "Mossad." In the same spirit, Alexander Prokhanov, speaking with Evelina Zakamskaia on Russian television on March 24, blamed Ukrainian Jews for Russia's invasion of Ukraine—and for the Holocaust.

This was a new variety of fascism, which could be called *schizofascism:* actual fascists calling their opponents "fascists," blaming the Holocaust on the Jews, treating the Second World War as an argument for more violence. It was a natural next step in a Russian politics of eternity, in which Russia was innocent and thus no Russian could ever be a fascist. During the Second World War, Soviet propaganda identified the enemy as the "fascists." According to Soviet ideology, fascism arose from capitalism. During the war against Nazi Germany, Russians could imagine that Soviet victory was part of a larger historical shift in which capitalism would disappear, and all men would become brothers. After the war, Stalin celebrated a national triumph, not so much of the Soviet Union as of Russia. This suggested that the "fascist" enemy was the outsider rather than the capitalist, and thus a more permanent conflict. In the 1970s, Stalin's heir, Brezhnev, located the meaning of Soviet (and Russian) history in the victory of the Red Army in the Second World War. In so doing, Brezhnev definitively changed the sense of the word "fascism." It no longer suggested a stage of capitalism that might be overcome, since history was no longer expected to bring change. "Fascism" meant the eternal threat from the West, of which the Second World War was an example.

Thus Russians educated in the 1970s, including the leaders and war propagandists of the 2010s, were instructed that "fascist" meant "anti-Russian." In the Russian language it is practically a grammatical error to imagine that a Russian could be a fascist. In contemporary Russian discourse, it is easier for an actual Russian fascist to call a non-fascist a "fascist" than it is for a non-fascist to call a Russian fascist a "fascist." Thus a fascist like Dugin could celebrate the victory of fascism in fascist language while condemning as "fascist" his opponents. Ukrainians defending their country were "junta mercenaries from the ranks of the Ukrainian swine-fascists." Similarly, a fascist like Prokhanov could describe fascism as a physical substance that spilled in from the West to threaten Russian virginity. In June, Prokhanov wrote of fascism as "black sperm" that threatened "the golden goddesses of Eurasia." His lapidary expression of racial and sexual anxiety was a perfect fascist text. Glazyev also followed the schizofascist protocol. While endorsing Nazi geopolitics, he set a standard for calling Russia's enemies "fascist." Writing in September 2014 for the Izborsk Club, Glazyev called Ukraine "a fascist state, with all the signs of fascism known to science."

Schizofascism was one of many contradictions on display in spring 2014. According to Russian propaganda, Ukrainian society was full of nationalists but not a nation; the Ukrainian state was repressive but did not exist; Russians were forced to speak Ukrainian though there was no such language. Glazyev overcame contradiction by invoking the West. The Americans, he averred, wanted a third world war because of high national debt. Ukraine should have collapsed when Glazyev made a few phone calls. When it did not, this only showed that its government was an American projection, "the Nazi junta that the Americans had installed in Kyiv." To defeat what he characterized as an American occupation, Glazyev maintained that it was "necessary to terminate all its driving forces: the American ruling elite, European bureaucracy and Ukrainian Nazis. The first one is the main aspect, the two others—secondary." Putin's Eurasia advisor was saying that Eurasia required the destruction of American politics. The war for Ukraine and Europe would be won, Glazyev thought, in Washington.

Like his advisor Glazyev, Putin defined Ukrainians who resisted Russian invasion as fascists. Speaking of the chaos that Russia had brought about by invading its neighbor, Putin claimed on March 18 that "nationalists, neo-Nazis, Russophobes and antisemites executed this coup. They continue to set the tone to this day." This claim had a certain schizofascist ring. Russian foreign policy in 2014 bore more than a passing resemblance to certain of the more notorious moments of the 1930s. The replacement of laws, borders, and states with innocence, righteousness, and great spaces was fascist geopolitics. Foreign Minister Lavrov's Foreign Policy Concept, invoked to justify the invasion of Ukraine, repeated the principle that a state might intervene to protect anyone that it defines as a member of its own culture. This was the argument that Hitler had used in annexing Austria, partitioning Czechoslovakia, and invading Poland in 1938 and 1939, and the argument Stalin had used when invading Poland in 1939 and annexing Estonia, Latvia, and Lithuania in 1940.

On March 14, 2014, when a *Ukrainian* was killed by *Russians* in Donetsk, Lavrov claimed this as a justification for Russian intervention in a neighboring sovereign state: "Russia is aware of its responsibility for the lives of its compatriots and nationals in Ukraine and reserves the right to defend those people." Putin said the same on April 17: "The essential issue is how to ensure the legitimate rights and interests of ethnic Russians and Russian speakers in the southeast of Ukraine." The fact that Ukrainian citizens enjoyed greater rights of expression than Russian citizens went unmentioned. Putin later promised to use "the entire arsenal" of available means to protect Russia's "compatriots."

This language of "compatriots" in what Putin called the "Russian world" made citizens of Ukraine hostage to the whims of a foreign ruler. A person disappears into a notional community, defined from a great distance, in the capital of another country. In the rhetoric of a Russian civilization or "Russian world," Ukrainian citizens lost their individuality and became a collective whose culture, as defined by Russians, justified a Russian invasion of Ukraine. The individual disappears into eternity.

IN A war that was supposed to be against fascism, many of Russia's allies were fascists. American white supremacists Richard Spencer, Matthew Heimbach, and David Duke celebrated Putin and defended his war, and Russia repaid them by using an approximation of the Confederate battle flag as the emblem of its occupied territories in southeastern Ukraine. The European far Right also applauded Russia's war. The Polish fascist Konrad Rękas endorsed Putin's Eurasia concept in general and a Russian invasion of Ukraine in particular. In September 2013, he anticipated that Russia would invade Ukraine, and dreamed of leading a Russian-backed government in Poland. Robert Luśnia was a onetime collaborator with the Polish communist secret police and a financial supporter of Antoni Macierewicz, a major figure in the Polish Right. Together with Rękas, he tried to spread the Russian propaganda line that Ukraine was dominated by Jews.

Confederate battle flag          Novorossiia flag

The leader of the Hungarian fascist party Jobbik, invited by Dugin to Moscow, praised Eurasia. The leader of Bulgaria's fascist party launched an electoral campaign in Moscow. The neo-Nazis of Greece's Golden Dawn praised Russia for defending Ukraine from "the ravens of international usury," by which they meant the Jewish international conspiracy. The Italian *Fronte Nazionale* lauded Putin's "courageous position against the powerful gay lobby." America's leading white supremacist, Richard Spencer, tried (but failed) to organize a meeting of the European far Right in Budapest. Among the invitees were Dugin and the German neo-Nazi Manuel Ochsenreiter, a defender of the Russian invasion of Ukraine on Russian media.

A few dozen French far-Right activists came to fight in Ukraine on the Russian side. They were screened by the Russian army and then sent into the field. About a hundred German citizens also came to fight in the company of the Russian army and Russian paramilitaries, as did citizens of a number of other European countries. Russia's war in Ukraine created training grounds for terrorism. In fall 2016, a Serbian nationalist was arrested for planning an armed coup in Montenegro. He had fought on the Russian side in Ukraine, and said that he had been recruited for the plot by Russian nationalists. In January 2017, Swedish Nazis trained by Russian paramilitaries in Russia bombed an asylum center for refugees in Gothenburg.

In 2014, institutions and individuals close to the Kremlin organized Russia's fascist friends. In April 2014, a branch of the *Rodina* party founded a "World National-Conservative Movement." It cited Ilyin in referring to the EU as part of the "global cabal," in other words the international Jewish conspiracy. Alyaksandr Usovsky, a Belarusian citizen and the author of the book *God Save Stalin! Tsar of the U.S.S.R. Joseph the Great,* helped Malofeev coordinate the actions of European fascists. Usovsky paid Poles who were willing to stage anti-Ukrainian protests at the moment when Ukraine was invaded by Russia.

Malofeev personally invited the leaders of the European far Right to a palace in Vienna on May 31, 2014. At this gathering, France was represented by Aymeric Chauprade and Marion Maréchal–Le Pen, the niece of Marine Le Pen. Dugin stole the show with his passionate case that only a united far Right could save Europe from gay Satan.


**THE SCHIZOFASCIST** lies displaced the events in Ukraine and the experiences of Ukrainians. Under the weight of all of the contradictory concepts and hallucinatory visions of spring 2014, who would see or remember the individual on the Maidan, with his or her facts and passions, his or her desire to be in history and make history?

Russians, Europeans, and Americans were meant to forget the students who were beaten on a cold November night because they wanted a future. And the mothers and fathers and grandparents and veterans and workers who then came to the streets in defense of "our children." And the lawyers and consultants who found themselves throwing Molotov cocktails. The hundreds of thousands of people who broke themselves away from television and internet and who journeyed to Kyiv to put their bodies at risk. The Ukrainian citizens who were not thinking of Russia or geopolitics or ideology but of the next generation. The young historian of the Holocaust, the sole supporter of his family, who went back to the Maidan during the sniper massacre to rescue a wounded man, or the university lecturer who took a sniper's bullet to the skull that day.

One can record that these people were not fascists or Nazis or members of a gay international conspiracy or Jewish international conspiracy or a gay Nazi Jewish international conspiracy, as Russian propaganda suggested to various target audiences. One can mark the fictions and contradictions. This is not enough. These utterances were not logical arguments or factual assessments, but a calculated effort to undo logic and factuality. Once the intellectual moorings were loosed, it was easy for Russians (and Europeans, and Americans) to latch on to well-funded narratives provided by television, but it was impossible to work one's way towards an understanding of people in their own setting: to grasp where they were coming from, what they thought they were doing, what sort of future they imagined for themselves.

Ukrainians who began by defending a European future found themselves, once the propaganda and the violence began, fighting for a sense that there could be a past, a present, and a future. The Maidan began as Ukrainian citizens sought to find a solution for Ukrainian problems. It ended with Ukrainians trying to remind Europeans and Americans that moments of high emotion require sober thought. Distant observers jumped at the shadows of the story, only to tumble into a void darker than ignorance. It was tempting, amidst the whirl of Russian accusations in 2014, to make some kind of compromise, as many Europeans and Americans did, and accept the Russian claim that the Maidan was a "right-wing coup."

The "coup" in the story of the Ukrainian revolution took place earlier, and in Russia: in 2011 and 2012, when Putin returned to the office of president with a parliamentary majority in violation of the laws of his own country. The leader who came to power by such means had to divert attention, blame, and responsibility to external enemies. For Putin, the Russian invasion of Ukraine was the latest episode of Russian self-defense from a Europe whose sin was its existence. The Russian claim of a "coup" in Ukraine was among the most cynical of the Kremlin's formulations, since the very Russians who made it had expected Yanukovych to be removed by force, and organized (failed or successful) coups d'état in nine Ukrainian districts.

The issue in Ukraine was the weakness of the rule of law and the associated inequality of wealth and ubiquity of corruption. It was obvious to protesting Ukrainians that the rule of law was the only way to distribute resources collected by oligarchs more equitably through the society, and to allow others to succeed in the economy. Throughout the entire period of the Maidan, social advance in predictable and just conditions was the central goal. The first protestors, in November 2013, were concerned with improving the rule of law by the Europeanization of Ukraine. Those who followed were concerned with protecting the rule of law, such as it was, from a corrupt oligarchical leader who had fallen under the sway of Moscow. In January and February 2014, protestors used the language of human rights.

There were certainly representatives of right-wing and indeed extreme-Right groups on the Maidan, and they were important in the Maidan's self-defense when the government began to torture and kill. The right-wing party *Svoboda*, however, lost much of its support during the Maidan. Right Sector, a new group, could only put about three hundred people on the Maidan. New right-wing groups came to the surface after Russia invaded Ukraine, fighting the Russian army and separatists in the east. On balance, though, the extraordinary thing was how little the war swung popular opinion towards radical nationalism, far less than in the invading country. The far Right did not begin the movement on the Maidan, were never anything like a majority, and did not decide how power changed hands at the end.

Although of course different people took different views, the protests were generally supported by the largest Jewish communities of Ukraine, in Kyiv and Dnipro. Among those who organized self-defense battalions on the Maidan was a veteran of the Israel Defense Forces, who would remember that his men in Kyiv called him "brother." The first two mortal casualties on the Maidan, in January, were the ethnic Armenian Sergei Nihoyan and the Belarusian citizen Mikhail Zhiznevsky. Those killed in the sniper massacre of February represented the diversity of Ukraine and of the protest. Among them was Yevhen Kotlyev, a Russian-speaking environmentalist from Kharkiv, in the extreme northeast of Ukraine. Three unarmed Ukrainian Jews were killed in the massacre, one of them a Red Army veteran. People of Ukrainian, Russian, Belarusian, Armenian, Polish, and Jewish cultures died in a revolution in the name of Europe that was started by a multilingual young man from a Muslim refugee family.

A coup involves the military or the police or some combination of the two. The Ukrainian military stayed in its barracks, and the riot police fought the protestors to the very end. Even when President Yanukovych fled, no one from the military, police, or power ministries sought to take power, as would have been the case during a coup. Yanukovych's flight to Russia placed Ukrainian citizens and lawmakers in an unusual situation: a head of state, during an invasion of his country, sought permanent refuge in the invading country. This was a situation without legal precedent. The agent of transition was a legally elected parliament.

The acting president and the members of the provisional government, far from being right-wing Ukrainian nationalists, were generally Russian speakers from eastern Ukraine. The speaker of parliament, chosen to act as president, was a Baptist minister from southeastern Ukraine. The ministries of defense, internal affairs, and state security were taken over, during the transition period, by Russian speakers. The acting minister of defense was of Roma origin. The minister of internal affairs was half Armenian and half Russian by birth. Of the two deputy prime ministers, one was Jewish. The regional governor of Dnipropetrovsk, a southeastern region threatened by Russian invasion, was also Jewish. Although three of the eighteen cabinet positions of the provisional government of spring 2014 were held by the nationalist *Svoboda* party, this was not a government of the Right in any meaningful sense.

People who carry out coups do not call for a reduction in power of the executive branch, but that is what happened in Ukraine. People who carry out coups do not call elections in order to cede power, but this is what happened in Ukraine. The presidential elections held on

May 25, 2014, were won by Petro Poroshenko, a centrist Russian speaker from southern Ukraine who was best known as a chocolatier. If there was anything like a coup attempt at that moment, it was Russia's attempt to hack Ukraine's Central Election Commission in order to proclaim that a far-Right politician had won, and the announcement on Russian television that he had done so.

In May 2014, two far-Right politicians presented themselves as candidates for the Ukrainian presidency; each of them received less than 1% of the vote. Both of them received fewer votes than a Jewish candidate running on a Jewish platform. The victor Poroshenko then called for parliamentary elections, which were held in September. Again, this is the opposite of what would have been expected during a coup, and again the popularity of the far Right in Ukraine was very limited. Neither of Ukraine's right-wing parties, *Svoboda* and a new one that grew from the paramilitary group Right Sector, cleared the 5% threshold required for participation in parliament. *Svoboda* lost its three ministerial portfolios, and a new government was formed without the Right. The speaker of the new parliament was Jewish; he later became prime minister.

The association agreement with Europe was signed in June 2014. It went into force in September 2017. History went on.

IT MAKES a difference whether young people go to the streets to defend a future or arrive in tanks to suppress one.

For many Ukrainians, the future could not come fast enough. If the Maidan was possible, then political nations, civil societies, economies of gift, and individual sacrifice were possible—and might appear again. Since Ukrainian civil society had defended itself and the Ukrainian state persisted, Ukrainian political history continued. Because Ukraine did not fall apart with the first blow, the Russian politicians of eternity had to keep coming.

The Russian officers sent to command the war in Crimea, and then in other parts of Ukraine, were people who inhabited a timescape of eternal Russian innocence. According to Borodai, Ukraine and Russia belonged to a "common civilization," which he described as "a giant Russian world that was formed over a millennium." The existence of a Ukrainian state was thus conceived as a form of aggression against Russia, since outsiders "want to remove Ukraine from our Russian world." Borodai read Gumilev and worked for Malofeev; similar ideas, though, were held by Russians and Ukrainians who did not read fascist thinkers or work for sodomy-obsessed investment bankers.

The Russian invasion of Ukraine coincided with a spike in popularity of the literature of the "accidental time traveler," a Russian genre of science fiction. In these stories, individuals, groups, weapons, and armies loop back and forth through time in order to correct the overall picture. As in the politics of eternity, facts and continuities disappear, replaced by jumps from point to point. At the crucial junctures, an innocent Russia is always repelling a sinful West. Thus Stalin contacts Putin to help him declare martial law in Russia and war on the United States. Or Russians travel back to 1941 to help the Soviet Union defeat the German invasion.

It became official Russian policy, as it had been official Soviet policy, to recall the Second World War as having begun in 1941 rather than in 1939. The year 1941 is a moment of Russian innocence only if it is forgotten that the Soviet Union had begun the war in 1939 as Germany's ally, and that between 1939 and 1941 had undertaken policies in occupied lands that were not so very different from Germany's own. As recently as 2010, Putin had been willing to speak to the Polish prime minister about the Katyn massacre, the most notorious Soviet crime of the period. By 2014, this attitude had been completely reversed. Putin incorrectly defended the Molotov-Ribbentrop pact of 1939 as merely a nonaggression agreement, which was a throwback to Soviet tradition. If "the Soviet Union did not want to fight," as Putin said in 2014, then why had the Soviet army invaded Poland in 1939 and taken Polish officers prisoner, and why had the Soviet secret police murdered thousands of them at Katyn in 1940? In 2014, Russian law made it a criminal act to suggest that the Soviet Union had invaded Poland, occupied the Baltic States, or committed war crimes between 1939 and 1941. The Russian supreme court later confirmed that a Russian citizen could be convicted of a crime for a re-posting of elementary facts about Russian history on social media.

The axiom of perfect Russian innocence permitted endless Russian imagination. Igor Girkin, who collaborated with Borodai in Crimea and in the subsequent Russian intervention in southeastern Ukraine, was also an inveterate traveler through timescapes. Though an officer of Russian military intelligence and an employee of Malofeev, he found time to write science fiction for children. Before the invasion of Ukraine, Girkin was also a reenactor—someone who likes to dress up in uniforms and act out the battles of the past. In Ukraine, Girkin commented on a real war on a blog devoted to antiques. As an aficio-nado of the First World War and the Russian Civil War, he hoped to decorate the Russian soldiers of 2014 with medals from that epoch. As someone who reenacted the Second World War as a Red officer, Girkin cited orders given by Stalin in 1941 when he executed actual people during the actual Russian invasion of 2014.

For many young Russian men, the intervention in Ukraine took place in an imagined 1941, amidst the remembered glory of their great-grandfathers' defense of the USSR from Nazi Germany. Tele-vision enforced this perspective by its constant invocation of terms associated with the Great Fatherland War. Pervyi Kanal used the phrase "punitive operations" in reference to Ukrainian soldiers more than five hundred times. A reference to German actions during the Second World War, this phrase set the calendar back to 1941 and cast the Ukrainians as the Nazis. Russian soldiers in Crimea, when asked about their actions, changed the subject to the Second World War. After subsequent interventions in southeastern Ukraine, Russians made their prisoners of war march in public, imitating the humili-ation parades of German soldiers Stalin had organized. Ukrainian citizens who chose to fight on the Russian side stole a World War

Two–era tank from a monument. (Its motor was in working order because it had been repaired for a parade the previous year.) One such partisan said that she could not imagine a Ukrainian victory, which would mean "1942." So long as battle was raging, it was always and forever 1941. During a major incursion in summer 2014, young Russians painted the words FOR STALIN! on their tanks.

In Russia, Stalin's (not Putin's, *Stalin's*) approval rating rose to 52%, the highest recorded figure. The approval rating of Leonid Brezhnev also reached a historical high. It was long-dead Brezhnev who had created the cult of even-longer-dead Stalin as the leader who had rescued Russia in the Great Fatherland War. Stalin and Brezhnev not only grew in popularity among the living, but also in resonance in their world. As time passed, ever more Russians expressed an opinion about their dead leaders. Stalin and Brezhnev were not receding into the past, but cycling back into the eternal present. Indeed, the simple fact that Russians in the second decade of the twenty-first century responded to regular political surveys about leaders from the twentieth was strongly suggestive. The politics of eternity has more than a whiff of the undead.

The war in Ukraine was not a contest of historical memories. Rather, the Russian invasion broke what had been a common Soviet myth about a common Russian and Ukrainian past. The name of the official war museum in Kyiv was changed from "Great Fatherland War" to "Second World War" when captured Russian tanks from the war of 2014 were placed on its lawn.

The Russian war against Ukraine was something more profound: a campaign of eternity against novelty. Must any attempt at novelty be met with the cliché of force and the force of cliché? Or was it possible, along with the Ukrainians of the Maidan, to make something new?

## CHAPTER FIVE

# TRUTH OR LIES (2015)

He who is deceived is turned into a thing.
—MIKHAIL BAKHTIN, 1943

Black milk of daybreak we drink in the evening
we drink in the evening we drink in the morning
we drink and we drink
we dig a grave in the air, there's room for us all
—PAUL CELAN, 1944

Russia arrived first at the politics of eternity. Kleptocracy made the political virtues of succession, integration, and novelty impossible, and so political fiction had to make them unthinkable.

Ivan Ilyin's ideas gave form to the politics of eternity. A Russian nation bathed in the untruth of its own innocence could learn total self-love. Vladimir Surkov showed how eternity could animate modern media. While working for Putin, he wrote and published a novel, *Almost Zero* (2009), that was a kind of political confession. In the story, the only truth was our need for lies, the only freedom our acceptance of this verdict. In a story within the larger plot, the hero was troubled by a flatmate who only slept. An expert issued a report: "We will all be gone," the expert confided, "as soon as he opens his eyes. Society's duty, and yours in particular, is to continue his dream." The perpetuation of the dream state was Surkov's job description. If the only truth was the absence of truth, the liars were honorable servants of Russia.

To end factuality is to begin eternity. If citizens doubt everything, they cannot see alternative models beyond Russia's borders, cannot carry out sensible discussions about reform, and cannot trust one another enough to organize for political change. A plausible future requires a factual present. Following Ilyin, Surkov spoke of the "contemplation of the whole" which enabled a vision of "geopolitical reality": that foreigners tried to draw Russians away from their native innocence with their regular attacks. Russians were to be loved for their ignorance; loving them meant perfecting that ignorance. The future held only more ignorance about the more distant future. As he wrote in *Almost Zero:* "Knowledge only gives knowledge, but uncertainty gives hope."

Like Ilyin before him, Surkov treated Christianity as a gateway to his own superior creation. Surkov's God was a reclusive colleague with limitations, a fellow demiurge to be bucked up with a few manly slaps. As Ilyin had done, Surkov invoked familiar biblical verses in order to invert their meanings. In his novel, he has a nun refer to First Corinthians 13:13: "Uncertainty gives hope. Faith. Love." If citizens can be kept uncertain by the regular manufacture of crisis, their emotions can be managed and directed. This is the opposite of the plain meaning of the biblical passage Surkov was citing: hope, faith, and love are the trinity of virtues that articulate themselves as we learn to see the world as it is. Just before this passage is the famous one about maturity as seeing from the vantage of another: "For now we see through a glass, darkly; but then face to face: now I know in part; but then shall I know even as also I am known." The first thing we learn when we see from the perspective of another is that we are not innocent. Surkov meant to keep the glass dark.

In the Russia of the 2010s, the dark glass was a television screen. Ninety percent of Russians relied upon television for their news. Surkov was the head of public relations for Pervyi Kanal, the country's most important channel, before he became a media manager for Boris Yeltsin and Vladimir Putin. He oversaw the transformation of

Russian television from a true plurality representing various interests into a false plurality where images differed but the message was the same. In the mid-2010s, the state budget of Pervyi Kanal was about $850 million a year. Its employees and those of other Russian state networks were taught that power was real but that the facts of the world were not. Russia's deputy minister of communications, Alexei Volin, described their career path: "They are going to work for The Man, and The Man will tell them what to write, what not to write, and how this or that thing should be written. And The Man has the right to do it, because he pays them." Factuality was not a constraint: Gleb Pavlovsky, a leading political technologist, explained, "You can just say anything. Create realities." International news came to substitute for regional and local news, which all but disappeared from television. Foreign coverage meant the daily registration of the eternal current of Western corruption, hypocrisy, and enmity. Nothing in Europe or America was worthy of emulation. True change was impossible—that was the message.

RT, Russia's television propaganda sender for foreign audiences, had the same purpose: the suppression of knowledge that might inspire action, and the coaxing of emotion into inaction. It subverted the format of the news broadcast by its straight-faced embrace of baroque contradiction: inviting a Holocaust denier to speak and identifying him as a human rights activist; hosting a neo-Nazi and referring to him as a specialist on the Middle East. In the words of Vladimir Putin, RT was "funded by the government, so it cannot help but reflect the Russian government's official position." That position was the absence of a factual world, and the level of funding was about $400 million a year. Americans and Europeans found in the channel an amplifier of their own doubts—sometimes perfectly justified—in the truthfulness of their own leaders and the vitality of their own media. RT's slogan, "Question More," inspired an appetite for more uncertainty. It made no sense to question the factuality of what RT broadcast, since what it broadcast was the denial of factuality.

As its director said: "There is no such thing as objective reporting." RT wished to convey that all media lied, but that only RT was honest by not pretending to be truthful.

Factuality was replaced by a knowing cynicism that asked nothing of the viewer but the occasional nod before sleep.

"INFORMATION WAR is now the main type of war." Dmitry Kiselev was in a position to know. He was the coordinator of the Russian state agency for international news, and the host of a popular Sunday evening program, *Vesti Nedeli,* that led the information offensive against Ukraine.

The first men the Kremlin sent to Ukraine, the spearpoint of the Russian invasion, were the political technologists. A war where Surkov commands is fought in unreality. He was in Crimea and Kyiv in February 2014, and served as Putin's advisor on Ukraine thereafter. The Russian political technologist Alexander Borodai was the press officer for Crimea during its annexation. In summer 2014, the "prime ministers" of two newly invented "people's republics" in Ukraine's southeast were Russian media managers.

A modest affair in military terms, the Russian invasion of southern and then southeastern Ukraine involved the most sophisticated propaganda campaign in the history of warfare. The propaganda worked at two levels: first, as a direct assault on factuality, denying the obvious, even the war itself; second, as an unconditional proclamation of innocence, denying that Russia could be responsible for any wrong. No war was taking place, and it was thoroughly justified.

When Russia began its invasion of Ukraine on February 24, 2014, President Putin lied with purpose. On February 28 he claimed, "We have no intention of rattling the sabre and sending troops to Crimea." He had already sent troops to Crimea. At the moment he uttered these words, Russian troops had been marching through Ukrainian sovereign territory for four days. For that matter, the Night Wolves were in Crimea, following Russian soldiers around in a loud display of revving engines, a media stunt to make the Russian presence unmistakable. Even so, Putin chose to mock reporters who noted the basic facts. On March 4, he asserted that Russian soldiers were local Ukrainian citizens who had purchased their uniforms at local stores. "Why don't you have a look at the post-Soviet states," Putin proposed. "There are many uniforms there that are similar. You can go to a store and buy any kind of uniform."

Putin was not trying to convince anyone in that post-Soviet world that Russia had not invaded Ukraine. Indeed, he took for granted that Ukrainian leaders would not believe his lie. The provisional Ukrainian government understood that Ukraine was under Russian attack, which is why it pled for an international response rather than reacting with military force. Had leaders in Kyiv believed Putin, they certainly would have ordered resistance. Putin's aim was not to fool Ukrainians but to create a bond of willing ignorance with Russians, who were meant to understand that Putin was lying but to believe him anyway. As the reporter Charles Clover put it in his study of Lev Gumilev: "Putin has correctly surmised that lies unite rather than divide Russia's political class. The greater and the more obvious the lie, the more his subjects demonstrate their loyalty by accepting it, and the more they participate in the great sacral mystery of Kremlin power."

Putin's direct assault on factuality might be called *implausible deniability*.* By denying what everyone knew, Putin was creating unifying fictions at home and dilemmas in European and American

---

* The older idea of *plausible* deniability, constructed by Americans in the 1980s, was to make claims in an imprecise way that allowed an escape from accusations of racism. This strategy was memorably formulated by the strategist Lee Atwater: "You start out at 1954, by saying, 'Nigger, nigger, nigger.' By 1968, you can't say 'Nigger'—that hurts you. Backfires. So you say stuff like forced busing, states' rights, and all that stuff. You're getting so abstract now that you're talking about cutting taxes, and all these things you're talking about are totally economic things, and a by-product of them is blacks get hurt worse than whites." If someone who spoke like this was accused of racism, he could plausibly say that he was not speaking about blacks.

newsrooms. Western journalists are taught to report the facts, and by March 4 the factual evidence that Russia had invaded Ukraine was overwhelming. Russian and Ukrainian journalists had filmed Russian soldiers marching through Crimea. Ukrainians were already calling Russian special forces "little green men," a joking suggestion that the soldiers in their unmarked uniforms must have come from outer space. The soldiers could not speak Ukrainian; local Ukrainians were also quick to notice Russian slang particular to Russian cities and not used in Ukraine. As the reporter Ekaterina Sergatskova pointed out, "the 'little green men' do not conceal that they are from Russia."

Western journalists are also taught to report various interpretations of the facts. The adage that there are two sides to a story makes sense when those who represent each side accept the factuality of the world and interpret the same set of facts. Putin's strategy of implausible deniability exploited this convention while destroying its basis. He positioned himself as a side of the story while mocking factuality. "I am lying to you openly and we both know it" is not a side of the story. It is a trap.

Western editors, although they had the reports of the Russian invasion on their desks in the late days of February and the early days of March 2014, chose to feature Putin's exuberant denials. And so the narrative of the Russian invasion of Ukraine shifted in a subtle but profound way: it was not about what was happening to Ukrainians, but about what the Russian president chose to say about Ukraine. A real war became reality television, with Putin as the hero. Much of the press accepted its supporting role in the drama. Even as Western editors became more critical over time, their criticism was framed as their own doubts about Kremlin claims. When Putin later admitted that Russia had indeed invaded Ukraine, this only proved that the Western press had been a player in his show.

After implausible deniability, Russia's second propaganda strategy was the proclamation of innocence. The invasion was to be understood not as a stronger country attacking a weaker neighbor at a moment of extreme vulnerability, but as the righteous rebellion of an oppressed people against an overpowering global conspiracy. As Putin said on March 4: "I sometimes get the feeling that across the huge puddle, in America, people sit in a lab and conduct experiments, as if with rats, without actually understanding the consequences of what they are doing." The war was not taking place; but were it taking place, America was to be blamed; and since America was a superpower, all was permitted in response to its omnipotent malice. If Russia had invaded, which it was somehow both doing and not doing, Russians would be justified in whatever they were doing and not doing.

The choice of tactics in the invasion served this strategy of innocence. The absence of insignia on Russian uniforms and the absence of markings on Russian weapons, armor, equipment, and vehicles did not convince anyone in Ukraine. The point was to create the ambience of a television drama of heroic locals taking unusual measures against titanic American power. Russians would be expected to believe the preposterous: that the soldiers whom they saw on their television screens were not their own army but a ragtag band of can-do Ukrainian rebels defending the honor of their people against a Nazi regime supported by infinite American power. The absence of insignia was not meant as evidence, but as a cue about how Russian viewers were supposed to follow the plot. It was not meant to convince in a factual sense, but to guide in a narrative sense.

Real soldiers pretending for dramatic reasons to be local partisans can use partisan tactics, thus endangering real civilians. As a tactic of war, this might be called *reverse asymmetry*. Normally, "asymmetrical warfare" means the use of unconventional tactics by a partisan force or terrorist group against a stronger regular army. In the Russian invasion, the strong used the weapons of the weak—partisan and terrorist tactics—in order to pretend to be the weak. During what was already an illegal invasion, the Russian army broke the basic laws of war, by design and from the outset. Putin endorsed this manner of warfare even as he denied that a Russian invasion was under way. On

March 4, he predicted that Russian soldiers would hide among civilians. "And let's see those [Ukrainian] troops try to shoot their own people, with us behind them—not in front, but behind. Let them just try to shoot at women and children!"

THE BATTLE for Crimea was easily won by March 2014. The subsequent Russian intervention in southeastern Ukraine continued. In this second campaign, *implausible deniability* would again test the fidelity of Russians and the courage of journalists; and *reverse asymmetry* would again cover an illegal war in the aureole of victimhood. The two tactics confirmed the politics of eternity, where facts vanish amidst the insistence that nothing ever happens except foreign malevolence and legitimate resistance. Assisted by Surkov, Putin invited Russians into a cycle of eternity in which Russia was defending itself as it had always done.

Eternity takes certain points from the past and portrays them as moments of righteousness, discarding the time in between. In this war, Russian leaders had already mentioned two such points: the conversion of Volodymyr/Valdemar in 988, which supposedly made of Ukraine and Russia a single nation forever; and the German invasion of the Soviet Union in 1941, which somehow made a Ukrainian protest movement a fascist threat. To justify the extended intervention in Ukraine's southeast, Putin in April 2014 added a third reference to the past: 1774. That was when the Russian Empire defeated the Ottoman Empire and annexed territories on the north shore of the Black Sea, some of which are now part of Ukraine. These territories were known in the eighteenth century as "Novorossiia," or New Russia. Putin's use of this term set aside the existing Russian and Ukrainian states, while shifting the conversation to ancient rights. In the logic of "Novorossiia," Ukraine was the aggressor because it included territories that were once called Russian and therefore were eternally Russian. The radical reframing of the issue allowed Russians and observers to forget the banal facts of the present—such as, for example, the fact that Moscow had never once, in the twenty-two years of the common existence of the Russian Federation and Ukraine, issued a formal complaint about the treatment of Russians in Ukraine.

Most citizens of the Russian Federation had not heard of "Novorossiia" in this sense before March and April 2014, when Surkov and Dugin first propagated it and then Putin made it policy. The imperial territory of the eighteenth century was different than the regions defined by Putin and then the Russian media: the nine Ukrainian districts of Crimea, Donetsk, Luhansk, Kharkiv, Dnipropetrovsk, Zaporizhia, Mikolaiv, Odessa, and Kherson. When understood historically, the term also had implications other than those Putin had in mind. Empress Catherine spoke of "New Russia" much as British colonizers spoke of a "New England," a "New South Wales," and so on. In that age of empire, regions inhabited by people other than the colonizers were "new" from the colonial perspective. "New" meant that the region had not always belonged to the empire. Such places did not necessarily remain with the colonial power. New England and New South Wales are not parts of Britain, just as New Russia is not part of Russia.

As Surkov and Glazyev tried to organize armed rebellions in southeastern Ukraine in March 2014, maps of "Novorossiia" flooded Russian television screens. They displayed a span of territory that, if taken by Russia, would separate Ukraine from its ports on the Black Sea and unite occupied Crimea (which has no land connection to Russia) with the territory of the Russian Federation.

The Russian army gathered in March in the two Russian districts that bordered Ukraine, Belgorod and Rostov. The basic idea, consistent with Moscow's plans that February, was to organize forceful takeovers of regional administration buildings in eight further Ukrainian districts, have followers declare secession from within those buildings, and make Ukraine disintegrate from within.

And so, in spring 2014, Russian political technologists arrived in Ukraine on a second mission: after Crimea, the much more ambitious

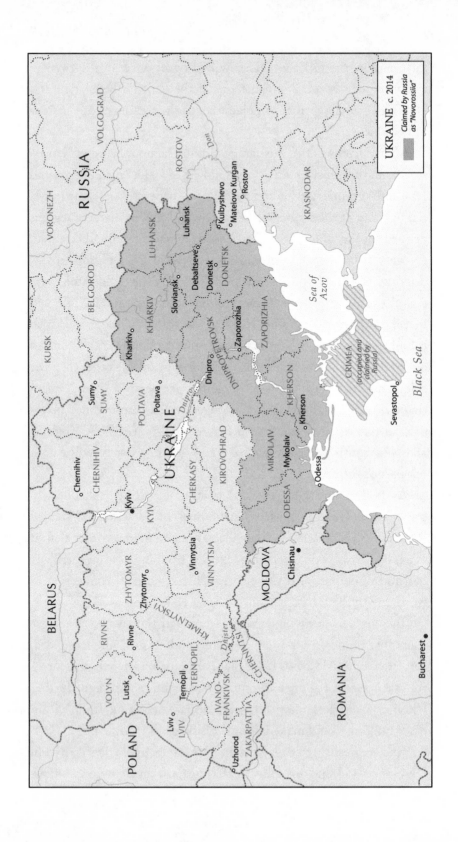

and vaguely defined domination of the Ukrainian southeast. Alexander Borodai was made responsible for the political entities that Russia would subsidize. As Borodai explained, in invading Ukraine "we are fighting for the global Russian idea." His friend Girkin was to handle the military operation in the southeast; he surfaced in April 2014 in the city of Sloviansk. Moscow denied that Borodai and Girkin were its men, or that they were in Ukraine, or both. For Girkin's GRU men in the field in Ukraine, this denial was annoying and, in the end, too much to take. As they set up field headquarters in Sloviansk on April 17, Russian soldiers were irritated that locals believed the Russian propaganda that they were volunteers: "We are special forces from the GRU."

The Ukrainian state was meanwhile under great pressure. Crimea had been occupied by Russia; Russian soldiers were in the southeast; some citizens had high expectations after a revolution that others had opposed; presidential elections had to be organized. Even so, the Russian attempt to seize "Novorossiia" collapsed by summer. The Russian coups in Ukrainian regional capitals in March and April mostly failed. As a rule, when Russians and local confederates tried to stage occupations of regional administration buildings, nothing much happened. To be sure, Ukrainian citizens in these southeastern regions were more likely to list Russian rather than Ukrainian as their first language, more likely to have voted for Yanukovych in 2010, and less likely to have been present on the Maidan. Yet this did not mean that they supported Russian rule or changes of regime by outside forces.

After the annexation of Crimea, the campaign for "Novorossiia" had success in only two of the eight districts concerned, and only in parts of these: Luhansk and Donetsk. Together known as the Donbas, these regions had coal, which Russia did not need. But both bordered the Russian Federation, and their local oligarchs hesitated at crucial moments. Russia failed to get a foothold in regions of much greater interest, such as Kharkiv, Odessa, and Dnipropetrovsk. Kharkiv and Odessa were areas that Russians regarded as centers of

Russian culture, and Dnipropetrovsk was a hub of the two countries' shared military-industrial complex. Dnipropetrovsk became a center of resistance to the Russian invasion under its new governor, Ihor Kolomois'kyi, who put a bounty on the head of Russian soldiers. Although the Russian flag was briefly raised over Kharkiv by a young Russian who liked to climb buildings and take selfies, the regional administration building was returned to Ukrainian control the same day. In Odessa, the initial attempt to storm the regional administration building also failed.

In March and April, local Odessans prepared for a Russian invasion. Prominent local citizens sent an appeal to Putin, explaining that they did not need Russian protection. Others took part in paramilitary training so that they could resist Russian special forces if they arrived. Russian television insisted, day after day, that Ukrainian nationalists were going to storm the province and wreak havoc, although no such thing was happening or would happen. Some Odessans (along with some Russian citizens) marched on May 1 to chant their support for "Novorossiia." The next day, pro-Russian and pro-Ukrainian groups fought on the streets, both sides armed, the pro-Ukrainian side more numerous. People on each side threw Molotov cocktails. When some of the pro-Russian fighters withdrew to a building known as the House of Professors, the battle of Molotov cocktails continued there. The building caught fire, killing a number of the pro-Russian protestors. So ended this particular Russian attempt to inspire internal rebellion within Ukraine.

Prokhanov compared Russia's failed coup in Odessa to the Holocaust; an antisemite invoked the mass murder of the Jews to justify an offensive war. The politics of eternity consumes the substance of the past, leaving only a boundless innocence that justifies everything.

BY MAY 2014, disaster was looming for Russia, even in the parts of the Luhansk and Donetsk regions under Russian control. The small Ukrainian army was more than sufficient to humiliate Girkin's GRU mission in Sloviansk, and defeat the Russian volunteers and Ukrainian separatists whom he had managed to gather. Girkin pled for local help: "I admit that I never expected to find that in the entire region one cannot find even a thousand men willing to risk their lives for their own city." It seemed as if all of the Donetsk and Luhansk regions would soon return to Ukrainian control. A meaningful response to the Ukrainian advance would require more Russian assistance. So the Vostok Battalion, composed largely of Chechens, crossed into Ukraine from Russia. On May 26, its men, together with volunteers from Russia, stormed the Donetsk airport. They were beaten back by Ukrainian defenders and took considerable losses.

At least thirty-one Russian volunteers died in the failed assault. They had left their friends and families behind in Russia because of the media fictions of "fascism" and "genocide" in "Novorossiia." Their deaths went unmentioned in major Russian media. Maria Turchenkova, a Russian journalist who accompanied the corpses on the journey from Ukraine back to Russia for burial, made the point succinctly: "Not a single one of the domestic television channels, which for months have been creating a public notion of a genocide against Russians in eastern Ukraine, have reported that 31 Russians were killed in Donetsk on 26 May."

One of these thirty-one was Evgeny Korolenko. He needed money and had told his wife that he had "perspectives" in the Donbas. Then his wife saw the photograph of his corpse on the internet. Her first and natural reaction was to deny to herself that it was him. "It doesn't look like him," she thought. But then she looked again. The chain that he wore. The shape of his nose. His corpse along with the others was brought to the city of Rostov. An undertaker refused to take the body, fearing it would be seen as provocation: "Please understand: this is a citizen of Russia who fell in combat. And our country is not at war." From a figure of authority she received this characterization of her situation: "You are a mature person. Russia is not carrying out any organized military activities. Your husband went under fire voluntarily in that street."

By the end of June 2014, authorities in Moscow had all but ceased to speak of "Novorossiia," and had shifted to the strategy of making the parts of the Donbas it occupied a permanent source of instability for the Ukrainian state. Some of the Chechens killed in Vostok were replaced by Ossetians, who seemed to think that they had been sent to fight the United States. The name "Vostok" was preserved as the battalion accepted local Ukrainian citizens who found reasons to fight against the Ukrainian state. Some of them were former Ukrainian security officers who were ideologically motivated, such as Alexander Khodakovskii, who said: "We are not really fighting for ourselves here, but for Russia." But it seems that most Ukrainian citizens who fought on the Russian side were drawn into the conflict by the experience of violence, the shelling of cities that resulted from Russia's choice to fight a partisan war.

On July 5, facing defeat by the Ukrainian army, Girkin made the move that Putin had recommended: he turned the local population into human shields. He withdrew his men to Donetsk, and other GRU commanders did the same. This guaranteed, as Girkin noted, that civilians would become the main victims of the war. The Ukrainian side fought Russians and their local allies by shelling cities, while the Russians did the same. In the terminology of partisan war, this was the shift from "positive" to "negative" mobilization: if no one wants to fight for the partisan cause as such (positive motivation), then a partisan commander creates conditions in which the enemy kills civilians (negative motivation). This was Girkin's chosen tactic, as he himself said. One of his Russian interviewers correctly described Girkin as a man who would willingly sacrifice the lives of women and children to advance a military goal. Destroying cities to win recruits was indeed Girkin's signal achievement.

Naturally, Ukrainian citizens in the Donbas did not consider the totality of the situation as the shells exploded. Many blamed the Ukrainian army for using heavy weapons against Ukrainian cities. In interviews, parents spoke of their children learning to distinguish the types of artillery from the sounds of their shells. One mother joined the Russian fight against the Ukrainian army after the yard where her child normally played was hit by a shell. Over and over, Ukrainian citizens who joined the separatists in summer 2014 said that it was the death of women, children, and the aged from artillery that inspired them to take up arms. A survey suggested that this experience (rather than an ideology such as "separatism" or "Russian nationalism") was the main motivation of Ukrainian citizens who chose to fight against the Ukrainian army.

Seeing violent death made people vulnerable to stories that imparted to these deaths some larger sense. These stories were provided by Russian television. It was impossible to know who had launched the shell that landed in your neighborhood; Russian television, all that was available in the parts of Ukraine controlled by Russia, blamed the Ukrainian side. As one Ukrainian citizen who fought on the Russian side remembered, the instruction that the Ukrainian army was a genocidal collective made it easier to think of individual Ukrainian soldiers as "beings in human form" who could and should be shot. Once separatists had brought about the same kind of death that they had seen, the stories of innocence became unimpeachable truth. It is hard to resist lies for which one has already killed.

Having brought the Donbas to this point by summer 2014, Girkin was withdrawn to Russia. The new head of security, Vladimir Antyufeyev, was Russia's leading specialist in the form of geopolitical theater known as "frozen conflict." In a frozen conflict, Russia occupies small parts of a nearby country (Moldova since 1991, Georgia since 2008, Ukraine since 2014), and then presents its own occupation as an internal problem that prevents its neighbors from having closer relations with the European Union or NATO.

In a frozen conflict, the sentiments of local people matter only as a political resource. Locals can be encouraged to kill and die, but their own aspirations cannot be fulfilled, since the point of freezing a conflict is to prevent any resolution. Antyufeyev had spent the previous stage of his career in "Transnistria," a section of Moldova occupied by Russian soldiers, where he had been in charge of security

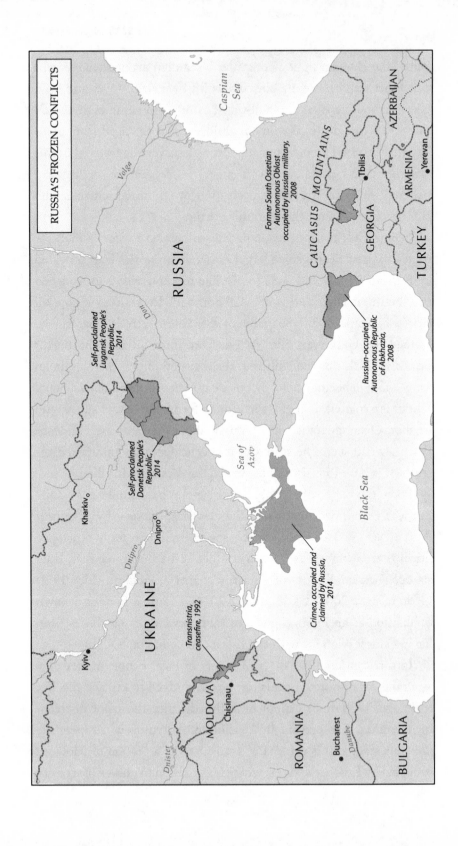

RUSSIA'S FROZEN CONFLICTS

for the unrecognized ministate. His arrival in Donetsk heralded a similar future for the "Donetsk People's Republic." It was to exist, Antyufeyev announced, in permanent limbo. He called it an "independent state," although he also said that no one (including Russia) would recognize it as such. Unification with Russia was also "not a question for today."

For Antyufeyev, the desires of the people of the Donbas were subordinate to the prerogatives of a far grander struggle against the European Union and the United States, which he portrayed as the Satanic West. He promised an offensive that would turn the tide in this global war. The Soviet Union had not collapsed, he said, because of its own problems, but because the West had deployed mysterious "destructive technologies"—this phrase, as in the Izborsk Club manifesto, meant "facts." The Russian invasion of Ukraine, Antyufeyev said, must be understood as the self-defense of innocent Russians from an alliance between "the Freemasons of Europe and the United States" and "the fascists of Ukraine." Antyufeyev had mastered schizofascism. Russia was at war against "fascists," but these fascists were somehow in league with international "Freemasons." The idea of a global conspiracy of Masons is fascist. Antyufeyev was using this fascist portrayal of the world to present himself as an anti-fascist.

Since Ukraine was the focus of the efforts of the global anti-Russian conspiracy, victory there, Antyufeyev thought, might change the world. The Russian intervention in Ukraine, Antyufeyev explained, was a defense of Russia's natural gas and fresh water from a rapacious United States. It was all one struggle, but it could be won. In Antyufeyev's view, "Ukraine is a disintegrating state. Exactly like the United States." The destruction of the United States was both desirable and inevitable. "If the world were saved from demonic constructions such as the United States, it would be easier for everyone to live. And one of these days it will happen."

---

THE RUSSIAN counterattack against the Ukrainian army was launched in July 2014 from the territory of the Russian Federation. It began with massive artillery barrages launched from the Russian side of the border. Evgeny Zhukov, one of the Ukrainian soldiers clearing a stretch of the border in the Luhansk region, recorded the consequences of the first Russian artillery barrage of July 11. Writing on his Facebook page that evening, he wished to correct reports that he and his men had been in a battle. That was not the case. They had been targeted, as he correctly stated, in "a carefully prepared, precisely rehearsed, and successful artillery strike on our military base at the Luhansk border from the Russian side." He described as many of the seventy-nine people who were killed as he could. At the end of his post, he offered them all "a low bow."

Zhukov was describing the first strike in a massive Russian artillery campaign directed against the Ukrainian army. It lasted for four weeks. Until August 8, Russian artillery fired regularly from at least sixty-six positions on the Russian side of the border. Units such as Zhukov's were helpless. Ukraine was at a permanent disadvantage in the information war—some European and American observers were still uncertain that a war was going on, or that Russia was the aggressor. In this fog of stupefaction, a Ukrainian attack on Russian territory would have been a political disaster. And so the information war determined the conditions of the war on the ground. Russia could shell Ukraine from its own territory without consequences, but Ukraine could not consider responding in kind. Some Ukrainian soldiers under artillery fire even fled across the border to Russia, because they knew that Russian territory would be safe. Meanwhile, Russian journalists at the Russian-Ukrainian border had no difficulty in seeing that "Russia is shelling Ukraine from Russian territory." Russian citizens in the border zone took videos of Russian soldiers in action. The Russian soldier Vadim Gregoriev, stationed in Mateiovo Kurgan, in Russia, posted proudly that "all night we pounded Ukraine."

Armies usually evacuate civilians from an artillery range so that they will not be killed by the enemy's return fire. Russian authorities gave no such orders, presumably because they were confident no counterstrike was coming. Children on the Russian side of the border, unlike children on the Ukrainian side of the border, learned to sleep through shelling: it was not directed at them. Some local Russians felt ill at ease about this one-way war, in which their farmsteads were used to rain down death on people not so different from themselves. But a sense of safety combined with television propaganda helped to resolve guilt: "It's awful, but we've understood already that the shooting is not at us, but from us." And if the shooting is "from us," it must be right and good: "Our people are cleansing the border of fascists." After all, said a local Russian, if "Nazis are committing genocide" on the Ukrainian side, then such unusual measures must be justified.

The Russian journalists who reported on the shelling were placing themselves at risk. One of them, Elena Racheva, found herself speaking to FSB officers in Kuibyshevo as the daily cannonade began. "Is that a Grad?" she asked, after they had all paused to listen to the roar characteristic of that artillery piece. All the FSB men smiled. "It was thunder," said one. "I didn't hear a thing," said a second. "It was my wife calling," was the joke of a third. "It's a military salute," was the final witticism. "You understand," said Racheva, "that I can write about this." And the threatening reply: "And then my colleagues will come and explain more persuasively that this was a salute."

The Ukrainian army could not shell Russia, but it could shell Russian soldiers and their allies inside Ukraine. The Russian artillery campaign began only six days after Girkin withdrew his men to the city of Donetsk, and continued thereafter for three more weeks. As Ukrainian soldiers were cut to pieces by Russian Grads firing from Russia, their comrades did not hesitate to aim their own Grads at Ukrainian cities where Russian soldiers, Russian volunteers, and their local allies were hiding. "The shelling so far in Donetsk," admitted Girkin, "I am responsible." The Russian journalist Natalya Telegina distinguished the fable of television, where heroic soldiers defend civilians, from the artillery war she saw: "But that reality exists only on television screens, not around you. Around you is simply war, where both sides are shooting, and no one spares the civilian population."

That was a fact.

ONE DAY after Russia began shelling Ukraine, Russian television provided a compelling escalation in the competition for innocence. On July 12, 2014 Pervyi Kanal told a stirring—and entirely fictional—story of a three-year-old Russian boy who was crucified by Ukrainian soldiers in Sloviansk. No evidence was provided, and independent Russian journalists noted the story's problems: none of the people in the story existed, nor did the "Lenin Square" where the atrocity supposedly transpired. When confronted with this, Russia's deputy minister for communications, Alexei Volin, said that ratings were all that mattered. People watched the cruci-fiction, so all was well.

It seems that Alexander Dugin personally invented the cruci-fiction, a version of which had already appeared on his personal social media. The image of a murdered innocent made Russia the Christ of nations and its war of aggression a response to diabolical cruelty. The purpose of the Russian intervention was nominally to protect speakers of Russian, or as Putin said, "the Russian world." Since everyone on all sides of the conflict spoke Russian, the Russian intervention was killing Russian speakers rather than protecting them. The inconvenience of the factual was overcome by what Dugin liked to call "an archetype," the killing of Jesus. A bloody and confusing war started by flawed Russian leaders that killed thousands of Russian speakers became the martyrdom of an innocent Russian body.

Russian television was the instrument of implausible deniability. It denied the presence of Russian special forces, secret services, commanders, volunteers, and weapons. Prominent Russian citizens such as Girkin, Borodai, and Antyufeyev appeared on Russian television screens, described as activists of "Novorossiia" or administrators of the "Donetsk People's Republic." The same Russian television channels that claimed Russian soldiers were Ukrainian volunteers released video of men at war in Ukraine with what were unmistakably advanced Russian weapons systems. The most modern Russian tanks, not available for foreign sale and never before seen outside Russia, appeared on Ukrainian territory. Russians were not meant to decide the factual question of whether or not their army was in Ukraine, which was obviously the case. They were meant to follow the cues of a television drama: if the voiceover instructed that Russians and their weapons were local, then that was the story to be followed.

A CRUCIAL Russian weapons system delivered from Russia and deployed by Russian soldiers was anti-aircraft batteries. These changed the course of the war in May and June 2014. The Ukrainian army, small as it was, was routing the Russians and their local allies so long as it maintained control of the air. In May, Russia began to supply anti-aircraft weapons and the teams that operated them, and the Ukrainian air force was quickly depleted; four helicopters were shot down. In June, two fixed-wing aircraft were shot down; in July, four fixed-wing aircraft. The Ukrainian command had to cease flying over the Donbas, which gave the Russians their chance.

One of the numerous Russian military convoys left its base in Kursk on June 23, 2014. It was a detachment of the Russian 53rd Air Defense Brigade, bound for Donetsk with a Buk anti-aircraft missile system marked 332. On the morning of July 17, this Buk system was hauled from Donetsk to Snizhne, then brought under its own power to a farmstead south of that town. Meanwhile, Malaysia Airlines Flight 17, bound for Kuala Lumpur from Amsterdam, was crossing over southeastern Ukraine. It was flying on an authorized route, at a normal altitude, in regular contact with air traffic controllers—until a ground-to-air missile suddenly destroyed it.

At 1:20 p.m., Malaysia Airlines Flight 17 was struck by hundreds of high-energy metal projectiles released from the explosion of a 9N314M warhead carried by a missile fired from that Russian Buk launcher at Snizhne. The projectiles ripped through the cockpit and instantly killed the pilots, from whose corpses some of the metal was later extracted. The aircraft flew apart ten kilometers above the earth's surface, its passengers and their possessions scattered over a radius of fifty kilometers. Girkin boasted that his people had shot down another plane over "our sky," and other commanders made similar remarks. Alexander Khodakovskii told the press that a Russian Buk was active in the theater at the time. The Buk was hastily withdrawn from Ukraine back to Russia, and photographed along the way with an empty missile silo. What had happened was quite clear.

The law of gravity seemed to challenge, at least for a few hours on the afternoon of July 17, 2014, the laws of eternity. Surely the passengers who died were the victims, not the Russian soldiers who fired the missile? Even the Russian ambassador to the United Nations was thrown for a moment, using the excuse of "confusion" to explain how a Russian weapon had brought down a civilian airliner. Yet Surkov's apparatus acted quickly to restore the Russian sense of innocence. In a typical mark of tactical brilliance, Russian television never denied the actual course of events: that a Malaysian airliner had been brought down by a Russian weapon fired by Russian soldiers taking part in an invasion of Ukraine. Denying the obvious only suggests it; defeating the obvious means engaging it from the flanks. Even under stress, Russian media managers had the presence of mind to try to change the subject by inventing fictional versions of what had happened.

On the very day the plane was shot down, all of the major Russian channels blamed a "Ukrainian missile," or perhaps a "Ukrainian aircraft," for the downing of MH17, and claimed that the "real target" had been "the president of Russia." The Ukrainian government, according to the Russian media, had planned to assassinate Putin, but by accident had shot down the wrong aircraft. None of this was vaguely plausible. The two planes were not in the same place. The failed assassination story was so ludicrous that RT, after trying it on foreign audiences, did not pursue it. But within Russia itself, the moral calculus was indeed reversed: by the end of a day on which Russian soldiers had killed 298 foreign civilians during a Russian invasion of Ukraine, it had been established that Russia was the victim.

The following day, July 18, 2014, Russian television scattered new versions of the event. Myriad inventions were added to the multiple fictions, not to make any of them coherent, but to introduce further doubts about simpler and more plausible accounts. Thus three Russian television channels claimed that Ukrainian air traffic controllers had asked the pilots of MH17 to reduce their altitude. This was a lie. One of the networks then claimed that Ihor Kolomois'kyi, the Ukrainian Jewish oligarch who was governor of the Dnipropetrovsk region, was personally responsible for issuing the (fictional) order to the air traffic controllers. In an echo of Nazi racial profiling, another network later provided an "expert" on "physiognomy" who claimed that Kolomois'kyi's face demonstrated his guilt.

Meanwhile, five Russian television networks, including some that had peddled the air traffic control story, claimed that Ukrainian fighter aircraft had been on the scene. They could not get straight just which kind of aircraft this might have been, providing pictures of various jets (taken at various places and times), and proposing altitudes that were impossible for the aircraft in question. The claim about the presence of fighter planes was untrue. A week after the disaster, Russian television generated a third version of the story of the downing of MH17: Ukrainian forces had shot it down during training exercises. This too had no basis in fact. Girkin then added a fourth version, claiming that Russia had indeed shot down MH17—but that no crime had been committed, since the CIA had filled the plane with corpses and sent it over Ukraine to provoke Russia.

These fictions were raised to the rank of Russian foreign policy. When asked about MH17, Russian Foreign Minister Sergei Lavrov repeated the inventions of Russian media about air traffic controllers and nearby Ukrainian fighters. Neither of his claims was backed by evidence and both were untrue.

Russian media accounts were impossible not only as journalism but also as literature. If one tried to accept, one by one, the claims of Russian television, the fictional world thus constructed would be impossible, since its various elements could not coexist. It could not have been the case that the plane was shot down both from the ground and from the air. If it had been shot down from the air, it could not have been shot down by both a MiG and an Su-25. If it had been shot down from the ground, this could not have been the result of both a training accident and an assassination attempt. Indeed, the Putin assassination story contradicted everything else that the Russian media claimed. It made no sense to say that Ukrainian air traffic controllers had communicated with the Malaysian pilots of MH17 as part of a plot to shoot down the Russian presidential aircraft.

But even if all of these lies could not make a coherent story, they could at least break a story—one that happened to be true. Although there were certainly individual Russians who grasped what had happened and apologized, the Russian population as a whole was denied the possibility to reflect on its responsibility for a war and its crimes. According to the surveys of the one reliable sociological institute in Russia, in September 2014 86% of Russians blamed Ukraine for shooting down MH17, and 85% continued to do so in July 2015, by which point the actual course of events had been investigated and was clear. Russian media urged Russians to be outraged that they were blamed.

Ignorance begat innocence, and the politics of eternity went on.

RUSSIANS WHO watched television in summer 2014 learned nothing of the Russian artillery that continued to pound Ukrainian positions, nor of the Russian invasion force assembling at the Ukrainian border. As in Crimea in February, the face of Russia at war during the summer campaign would be a biker gang. On August 9, 2014, the day after the Ukrainian army had fled the border under Russian shelling, the Night Wolves staged a motorcycle exhibition in Sevastopol, a Ukrainian city that Russia had annexed along with Crimea. RT described it for Europeans and Americans as an "Epic Night Wolves Biker Rally." In fact, the motorcycle tricks were mediocre and secondary. Most important was the long televised introduction, which brought fascist themes to millions of Russians.

The Sevastopol "bike show" began in darkness in a vast hall. A spotlight revealed Alexander Zaldostanov, the leader of the Night Wolves, as he was raised towards the rafters in a cargo elevator. Wearing a bandanna and a leather vest over tight black clothing, he began to intone: "My motherland delivered ten Stalinist blows to fascism's hirsute body. Even as the earth still settled on the graves of thirty million heroes, even as the cinders of the burned villages still glowed, Stalin gave the order to plant orchards. And among the flowering orchards, we rebuilt the devastated cities, and we thought that the flowering would never end." Zaldostanov was reciting Alexander Prokhanov's manifesto of a few months earlier, "Our New Victory Day."

In that text, Prokhanov was rehabilitating Stalinism by associating it with victory in the Second World War, and justifying the Russian invasion of Ukraine by claiming that it was like the defense of the Soviet Union against Nazi Germany. Rather than a Soviet republic that was invaded by Germany, rather than the main target of Hitler's colonial plans, rather than the major battlefield of the Second World War, rather than a land that lost three million soldiers and another three million civilians to the German occupation, Ukraine suddenly became a wartime enemy of Russia. In his text, Prokhanov made the war between Russian innocence and Western decadence explicitly sexual, dreaming of flowering without deflowering. At just this point in Zaldostanov's recitation, the stage lights came on to reveal Russia's pregnant virgins: a group of women with pillows under their clothes to create a baby bulge, others pushing empty prams.

Prokhanov blamed Russia's problems on foreigners who intervened in what he called the "nightmarish 1990s." His text implored

Russians to ignore the facts around them and to fall instead into a trance before the "icon" of the "red flower." He meant that the Soviet victory in the Second World War made Russians innocent of all wrongdoing for all time. Russians, as they dismember Ukraine, should bow down before the blossom in sensuous worship. "And on this icon once again the scarlet blossom began to open, a marvelous scarlet bud. We inhaled its scent, drank in its marvelous juices." The invasion of Crimea was a climax. "As a gift for our patience and stoicism, our labor and faith, God has sent us Crimea. The Russian people, once divided by enemies, are again united in victorious embraces."

Then Prokhanov (intoned by the biker Zaldostanov to a live audience of tens of thousands, and to a televised audience of millions) specified his fear of penetration. The enemy of the Russian idyll was the giant black penis of Satan. (Barack Obama was at this time the president of the United States.) Taking for granted the myth that Kyiv was the site of Russia's virgin birth, Prokhanov imagined its cathedral as a Russian holy-of-holies. He then fantasized about a diabolical orgasm: "the black sperm of fascism splashed upon Kyiv, the mother of all Russian cities. In the golden apse of St. Sofia, among the temples and shrines, was conceived a deformed embryo with a hairy face and black horns, like the devil in a church fresco."

In Prokhanov's fantasy, fascism was thus not an ideology or an aesthetic. If fascism were such things, the spectacle of a man in black leather intoning a message of national blamelessness and necessary war would be its perfect instantiation. For the schizofascists, fascism was a substance from the dissolute outside world that threatened the virginal Russian organism: "Like a decadent dough it overflowed its Kyiv bowl and spread through all Ukraine." Ultimately to blame for this unspeakable aggression were Barack Obama and Angela Merkel, "who smell of burnt flesh." This last gesture of Prokhanov's was the normal closing flourish of schizofascist prose. A fascist text written by an antisemite to justify a war of aggression exploits the symbols of the Holocaust—here, the ovens of Auschwitz-Birkenau—to direct blame towards others. The travesty was intentional: Prokhanov's invocation of "black sperm" was a profanation of the most justly famous poem of the Holocaust, Paul Celan's "Death Fugue."

Ukrainian society and Ukrainian history were dismissed or suppressed in every line of Prokhanov's manifesto—read by Zaldostanov as Russian artillery shells were exploding in Ukraine, and as Russian soldiers handed in their phones and checked their weapons while they prepared to cross the Ukrainian border. Kyiv was not a Ukrainian city, though it was the capital of Ukraine; Ukraine was an enemy, although Ukrainians suffered more than Russians during the Second World War; the Maidan was not a civic protest but a demonic bastard born of the rape of virgin Russia by black Satan. The drastic images had to overwhelm the prosaic reality of people who wanted a future with the rule of law.

The political preliminaries to the "bike show" went on and on: "A new battle against fascism is inevitable," pronounced Zaldostanov. "The eleventh Stalinist blow is inevitable." Then from the loudspeakers resounded the recorded voices of Obama, Merkel—and Hitler. On the stage, beneath a tarp, a shape began to move, summoned by the voices: the dough overflowing its bowl. From beneath the tarp emerged black figures, who danced in the form of a swastika. Then giant mechanical hands appeared above the stage, one finger bearing a ring with an eagle: the American puppet master. The black figures became Ukrainian protestors who attacked helpless riot police. Zaldostanov condemned "Europe's eternal lackeys, its spiritual slaves." Then the leader of the black demonstrators was lynched.

All of this gave the Russian band 13 Sozvezdie time to prepare its nationalist ska favorite "Why Do Ukrainians Kill Other Ukrainians?" The lyrics asked why Rus had been sold to Europe: an odd question, since Rus was a medieval European realm. As 13 Sozvezdie showed, popular culture could invoke the politics of eternity: Russia was Rus, history never was, invasion is self-defense. In the band's determined if unartful presentation, Ukrainians of today could not have chosen Europe, because Ukraine was Rus and Rus was Russia. Ukrainians must have been manipulated: "Who lied to you today, Ukraine?" Cued by the song, two armored vehicles with Ukrainian markings appeared at the center of the stage and appeared to burn people to death. Heroic Russian volunteers fired thousands of machine-gun rounds at the vehicles while rappelling down cords hung from the rafters. Victorious, the Russian volunteers claimed the vehicles and waved the flags of the "Donetsk People's Republic."

Zaldostanov then spoke again. He linked the existence of Ukraine to the German invasion of the Soviet Union by asking for forgiveness from Red Army soldiers "sleeping in mass graves who, responding to a summons, covered Rus with their hearts." It mattered not at all that a very large number of those Red Army soldiers had been Ukrainians. Russia needed a monopoly on martyrdom. In order to preserve it, Russia would make war on a nation with a far greater record of suffering (the Ukrainians), while abusing the memory of a people with a still greater record of victimhood (the Jews). As the rap group Opasnye now explained in their song "Donbas," Ukrainians needed "fraternal assistance" from big brother Russia. "Fraternal assistance" had been Brezhnev's term for military interventions to sustain communist regimes in other countries.

When this song was over, Zaldostanov called for the conquest of more Ukrainian territory by Russia. The motorcycle exhibition at long last began. Like the preceding ska and rap, the stunts were an unremarkable example of a North American art form. The "bike show" was exceptional only in its rehabilitation of a long-discredited European art form: the Nazi *Gesamtkunstwerk*, the total work of art meant to replace world with worldview, and history with eternity.

THE CRUCI-FICTION (July 10), the MH17 cacophony (July 17), and the "bike show" (August 9) were only three examples of the televised propaganda to which Russians were exposed in the summer of 2014.

This creative ignorance invited Russians into a sense of innocence. It is hard to know what effect all of this had on Russian citizens in general. It certainly persuaded men to travel to Ukraine to fight.

After Russian artillery had cleared sections of the border of Ukrainian troops (by August 8), the way was open for still larger deployments of Russian volunteers (and weapons). As Russian recruiters said (even as Russian spokesmen denied it abroad), the Russian government used unmarked white trucks (which it called "humanitarian") as troop transports. Russian volunteers started their journey because of what they had seen on Russian television about the war in Ukraine. One recruiter, a special forces veteran, explained: "Our press and television present the dramatic facts."

Some of these Russian volunteers assumed that Ukraine did not exist. One Russian from distant Asia—from the point where Russia meets China, Mongolia, and Kazakhstan—declared that Russians and Ukrainians were a single people. Real for these men, by contrast, was "Novorossiia," a construct vanishing from Russian television screens even as the volunteers arrived in Ukraine. Some volunteers imagined that they were preventing the United States from starting a world war, others that they were hindering global Sodom. When asked why they fought, Russian volunteers spoke of "fascism" and "genocide." The cruci-fiction proved unforgettable. Young men spoke of a "call of the heart" to rescue children.

Russian volunteers arriving at the frontier were massively outnumbered by regular Russian troops. In July and August 2014, Russian officers were giving orders to Russian soldiers at twenty-three camps established near the Ukrainian border. By early August, elements of about thirty units of the Russian armed forces had encamped at the frontier and made their preparations for an invasion of Ukraine. Russian villagers grew accustomed to the presence of young recruits from all over Russia, just as they had gotten used to the sound of artillery fire.

Every now and then the soldiers might attract attention. Young men who are about to go under hostile fire can behave unusually in the days before. On the night of August 11, for example, the villagers of Kuibyshevo, just on the Russian side of the border, watched some unfamiliar dancing. The dancers were soldiers of the 136th Motorized Infantry Brigade, based in Buinask, Dagestan—a Muslim-majority district of the Russian Federation in the Caucasus, bordering Chechnya, a place where less than 5% of the population is Russian. Like many of the soldiers of the Russian Federation sent to kill and die in Ukraine, these soldiers were members of non-Russian ethnic minorities, men whose deaths would not register in media markets. Not long after August 11, the 136th Motorized crossed the Russian-Ukrainian border and engaged the Ukrainian army. By August 22, the corpses of the dancers were arriving in Dagestan.

The 18th Separate Motorized Rifle Brigade, based in Chechnya, was one of the first Russian units to cross during the summer invasion. It was composed largely of refugees from Russia's wars in Chechnya, and had just seen action in Crimea. On July 23, six days after Russia shot down MH17, its men got their orders to report to their base in Chechnya. Three days later they were on their way to a camp at the Russian-Ukrainian border. On August 10, one of the unit's soldiers, Anton Tumanov, told his mother that "they are sending us to Ukraine." The next day he was given ammunition and grenades. He posted on VKontakte, the Russian equivalent of Facebook: "They took my phone, and I went to Ukraine." Tumanov was one of about 1,200 comrades from the 18th Separate Motorized who entered Ukraine on August 12.

On August 13, the men of the 18th Separate Motorized were in Snizhne, where four weeks earlier Russian soldiers had shot down MH17. Ukrainian artillery fire set their ammunition dump aflame, killing some 120 men and wounding about 450 more. Anton Tumanov's family received a report: the place of death was listed as "location of unit"; the time of death as "time of performing military service"; the cause of death as "blood loss after having lost his legs." His mother learned more about how her son died because one of his comrades took the risk of telling her. "What I don't understand,"

Tumanov's mother said, "is what he died for. Why couldn't we let people in Ukraine sort things out for themselves?" It pained her that her son was killed in a war that was not officially taking place. "If they sent our soldiers there, let them admit it." When she posted the facts of her son's death on social media, she was attacked as a traitor.

Konstantin Kuzmin, another soldier of the 18th Separate Motorized, probably died at the same time. He had called his parents in a rush on August 8: "Mama, Papa, I love you. Hi to everyone! Kiss my daughter for me." His mother was told nine days later by an emissary of the Russian army that her son had died in exercises on the Ukrainian border. When she asked, "Do you believe the words you are telling me?" he had the decency to reply that he did not.

One of Kuzmin's comrades, the tank driver Rufat Oroniiazov, survived that artillery strike of August 13. His girlfriend was able to follow the progress of his unit through social media, and knew about the artillery strike and fatalities. The next day, he called her to say that "many of ours have died before my eyes." After August 14, he never called again. "We were waiting for marriage," his girlfriend remembered. "Whenever I said something, he smiled."

On or about August 17, 2014, elements of the 76th Air Assault Division, based in Pskov, crossed into Ukraine. Of the two thousand or so of its men deployed against the Ukrainian army, about one hundred were killed in action. The funerals in Pskov began on August 24. People who tried to photograph the graves were chased away. On August 19, the 137th Parachute Regiment of the 106th Airborne Guards, based in Ryazan, joined the invasion. Sergei Andrianov was killed in action not long thereafter. "Forgive me, my son," wrote his mother, "that I could not shelter you from this evil war." A friend posted on VKontakte: "May he who sent you to fight in a foreign land be damned."

The 31st Airborne Assault Brigade, based in Ulyanovsk, had been summoned for training on August 3. Its men knew that they would be sent to Ukraine: everything was following the pattern of their recent deployment to Crimea. One of them, Nikolai Kozlov, had spent his time in Crimea in a Ukrainian police uniform, apparently as part of Russia's deception campaign. By August 24, the 31st Airborne had entered Ukrainian territory. On that day, Kozlov lost his leg in a Ukrainian attack. At least two of his comrades, Nikolai Bushin and Il'nur Kil'chenbaev, were killed in action. The Ukrainian army took ten soldiers of this unit prisoner, including Ruslan Akhmedov and Arseny Il'mitov.

At about the same time, on or about August 14, Russia's 6th Separate Tank Brigade, based in the Nizhegorod region, joined the battle in Ukraine. Its soldiers posed for photographs in front of Ukrainian road signs. Vladislav Barakov was killed in action in his tank, and at least two of his comrades were taken prisoner by the Ukrainian army.

At some point in August 2014, the 200th Motorized Infantry Brigade, based in Pechenga, entered the battle for the city of Luhansk, the second city (after Donetsk) of the Donbas. The young men of the 200th Motorized painted FOR STALIN!, USSR, and the hammer and sickle on their tanks, and DEATH TO FASCISM! on their howitzers. A self-propelled artillery piece was christened STALIN'S FIST, a reference to the eleventh Stalinist blow that Prokhanov had promised. On one Grad artillery piece the soldiers wrote FOR CHILDREN AND MOTHERS, and on another CHILDREN OF DONETSK. The very real civilian casualties of the Ukrainian army's shelling of cities had been killed by that very weapon: the Grad. The Russian Grads labeled FOR CHILDREN AND MOTHERS probably killed children and mothers in their turn.

Evgeny Trundaev of the 200th Motorized was killed in action in Ukraine and posthumously decorated as a Hero of Russia. His comrades took part in the victorious campaign for the Luhansk airport, and then joined other Russian units in the decisive Battle of Ilovaisk, where much of the Ukrainian army was encircled and destroyed by Russian armor. Despite promises of safe passage, Ukrainian soldiers attempting to exit the pocket were killed.

This Russian victory led to a truce at Minsk on September 5. It specified only that "foreign forces" withdraw. Since Moscow denied that Russian troops were in Ukraine, it interpreted this provision as requiring no action. Russian soldiers remained in Ukraine after the Minsk agreement, and new ones were deployed. Some units that had seen combat during the August invasion were rotated out to the camps at the Russian-Ukrainian border or to their bases, only to return to the war in Ukraine a few months later.

In early 2015, Russian armed forces carried out a third major offensive on the territory of Ukraine. The initial objective was the Donetsk airport. After eight months of combat and siege, the airport no longer existed as such. But its long defense by Ukrainian soldiers (and members of paramilitary militias) was symbolic on both sides of the border. Ukrainians called the defenders "cyborgs," since they seemed to live on despite everything. So in Moscow a decision was taken that these men had to die. After the airport was finally taken by overwhelming Russian force in mid-February, Ukrainian prisoners of war were executed.

The second objective of Russia's January 2015 offensive was Debaltseve, a railway junction that linked the Donetsk and Luhansk regions. It was important to the functioning of the Russia-backed pseudostates known as the "Donetsk People's Republic" and the "Lugansk People's Republic." Among the Russian units fighting at Debaltseve was the 200th Separate Motorized Brigade, which had taken part in the August 2014 invasion. It was joined by two units based in Buriatia, a region inhabited by ethnic Buriats (most of whom are Buddhists), on the Russian-Mongolian border, about six thousand kilometers from Ukraine. These were the 37th Motorized Infantry Brigade, based in Kiakhta, and the 5th Separate Tank Brigade, based in Ulan-Ude.

Bato Dambaev, a soldier of the 37th Motorized, posted photographs on social media of the unit's journey from Buriatia to Ukraine and back. Local people in the Donetsk region joked about the "indigenous Donbas Buriats." Everyone in the Donbas, whatever they thought about the war, was aware that the Russian army was involved; people who made such a joke could be for the Russians, or for the Ukrainian state, or indifferent. Photographs of Buriats cuddling puppies or playing soccer in Ukraine were widely circulated. For their part, the Buriats laughed at the Russian propaganda that denied their presence in Ukraine. Other propaganda they accepted as true. They saw their mission as it had been presented to them in the Russian media: to defeat "killers of children."

Though a second ceasefire was signed at Minsk on February 12, 2015, the Russian assault on Debaltseve continued. Once again, the agreement spoke of "foreign forces," and Russia denied that its soldiers were in Ukraine. The fighting continued until the city was destroyed and the Ukrainian army was routed. As a Russian tank commander recalled: "They were breaking out of the pocket, they wanted to clear the road, they flee, and we have to crush them." These words were spoken by Dorzhy Batomunkuev, one of the tank drivers of the 5th Separate Tank Brigade, who suffered severe burns when his tank was hit during the battle. Other Russians and Ukrainian citizens fighting on the Russian side were killed and wounded in the battle for Debaltseve. But the vast majority of the casualties were encircled Ukrainian soldiers. And so the latest major Russian intervention in the Donbas ended, not surprisingly, in a military victory.

Units of the Russian army remained in Ukraine, training locals and engaging in combat. The 16th Separate Special Forces Brigade of the GRU, for example, was stationed in Ukraine in 2015. At least three of its soldiers—Anton Saveliev, Timur Mamaiusupov, and Ivan Kardopolov—were killed in action in Ukraine on May 5. As a woman from Kardopolov's hometown presented the situation: "I don't know, they say on television that we are not at war, but guys keep coming home dead."

This neighbor could contrast what she saw with her own eyes with what she saw on television. For most Russians most of the time, the essentials of the war were behind Surkov's dark glass. Russians were told by their media that the "Donetsk People's Republic" and "Lugansk People's Republic" were independent entities, while separatists admitted that they were dependent upon the Russian taxpayer. This meant, as one separatist leader put it, that a "call from Moscow was viewed as a call from the office of Lord God himself." By "Moscow" he meant Surkov. Media in the two "republics" followed instructions from Moscow to portray America as the source of fascist evil, to consult Dugin and Glazyev, and to give press credentials to European fascists. The suffering of Ukrainian citizens continued, with some ten thousand killed and about two million displaced.

RUSSIA'S WAR against Ukraine was called a "hybrid war." The problem with phrasings in which the noun "war" is qualified by an adjective such as "hybrid" is that they sound like "war minus" when what they really mean is "war plus." The Russian invasion of Ukraine was a regular war, as well as a partisan campaign to induce Ukrainian citizens to fight against the Ukrainian army. In addition to that, the Russian campaign against Ukraine was also the broadest cyber offensive in history.

In May 2014, the website of Ukraine's Central Election Commission was rigged to display an image showing that a nationalist (who had in fact received less than 1% of the vote) had won the presidential election. Ukrainian authorities caught the hack at the last moment. Unaware that the hack had been spotted, Russian television transmitted the very same graphic as it announced, falsely, that the nationalist had been elected president of Ukraine. In autumn 2015, hackers attacked Ukrainian media companies and the Ukrainian railway system. That December, hackers brought down three transmission stations of the Ukrainian power grid, knocking out fifty substations and denying power to a quarter million people. In autumn 2016, hackers attacked the Ukrainian railway, seaport authority, treasury, and the ministries of finance, infrastructure, and defense. They also carried out a second and far more sophisticated attack on the Ukrainian power grid, bringing down a transmission station in Kyiv.

This cyberwar made no headlines in the West at the time, but it represented the future of warfare. Beginning in late 2014, Russia penetrated the email network of the White House, the State Department, the Joint Chiefs of Staff, and multiple American nongovernmental organizations. Malware that caused blackouts in Ukraine was also planted in the American power grid. Only in 2016, when Russian hacks entered American presidential politics, would Americans begin to pay attention.

The most remarkable element of Russia's 2014 invasion of Ukraine was the information war designed to undermine factuality while insisting on innocence. It, too, continued in the United States, with greater sophistication and more impressive results than in Ukraine. Ukraine lost the information war to Russia in the sense that others did not understand Ukraine's predicament. In general, Ukrainian citizens did. The same cannot be said of Americans.

THROUGHOUT THE war in Ukraine, the Russian leadership engaged in implausible deniability, telling obvious lies and then daring the Western media to seek the facts. On April 17, 2014, Putin categorically denied the Russian presence in southeastern Ukraine in these terms: "Nonsense. There are no Russian units in eastern Ukraine—no special services, no tactical advisors. All this is being done by local residents, and proof of that is that those people have literally removed their masks." The curious thing about this claim is that April 17 was the very day when Russia's special forces in Sloviansk indeed removed their masks and said the exact opposite: "We are special forces from the GRU." On August 23, at the very height of the summer campaign, as Russian units began to close the circle on Ukrainian soldiers at Ilovaisk, Lavrov said: "We view all such stories [of the presence of Russian troops] as part of an information war." On August 29, he claimed that photographs of Russian soldiers were "images from computer games."

Lavrov did not really mean that the facts were other than they seemed. He meant that factuality was the enemy. This was the case made by the Izborsk Club in its manifesto and by the Russian commander Antyufeyev before the summer invasion: facts were "information technologies" from the West, and to destroy factuality was to destroy the West. Opinion polls suggest that the denial of factuality did suppress a sense of responsibility among Russians. At the end of 2014, only 8% of Russians felt any responsibility for events in Ukraine. The vast majority, 79%, agreed with the proposition that "the West will be unhappy no matter what Russia does, so you should not pay attention to their claims."

After all of the goading of Russians to fight in Ukraine, silent terror greeted the returning corpses. The families of the dead and wounded were told that they would not receive benefits from the state if they spoke to the press. The St. Petersburg branch of the Soldiers' Mothers Committee, which was keeping a list of Russian war dead, was declared to be a "foreign agent" by the Russian government. The head of the Soldiers' Mothers Committee in Piatigorsk, seventy-three years old and diabetic, was arrested. Most of the journalists who reported on Russian casualties were beaten. By the end of 2014, Russian reporters did not, or rather could not, cover the story. The lists of the dead trailed off. The war went on, but the lights went out.

**THE UNDERLYING** logic of the Russian war against Ukraine, Europe, and America was *strategic relativism*. Given native kleptocracy and dependence on commodity exports, Russian state power could not increase, nor Russian technology close the gap with Europe or America. Relative power could however be gained by weakening others: by invading Ukraine to keep it away from Europe, for example. The concurrent information war was meant to weaken the EU and the United States. What Europeans and Americans had that Russians lacked were integrated trade zones and predictable politics with respected principles of succession. If these could be damaged, Russian losses would be acceptable since enemy losses would be still greater. In strategic relativism, the point is to transform international politics into a negative-sum game, where a skillful player will lose less than everyone else.

In some respects, Russia did lose in its war in Ukraine. No memorable case for Russian culture was made by the peoples of the Caucasus and Siberia journeying for hundreds or thousands of kilometers to kill Ukrainians who spoke Russian better than they did. The Russian annexation of Crimea and sponsorship of the "Lugansk People's Republic" and "Donetsk People's Republic" did complicate Ukraine's foreign relations. Even so, the frozen conflict was a far cry from the "disintegration" of Ukraine discussed in Russian policy papers and the massive expansion suggested by "Novorossiia." Ukraine fielded an army while holding free and fair elections; Russia fielded an army as a substitute for such.

Ukrainian society was consolidated by the Russian invasion. As the chief rabbi of Ukraine put it: "We're faced by an outside threat called Russia. It's brought everyone together." That overstatement suggested an important truth. For the first time in Ukrainian history, public opinion became anti-Russian. In the 2001 Ukrainian census, 17.3% of the inhabitants of the country identified themselves as ethnically Russian; by 2017, that figure had fallen to 5.5%. Some of that drop was a result of the inaccessibility of Crimea and parts of the Donbas region to the survey. But the bulk of it was the result of the Russian invasion. An invasion to defend speakers of Russian killed such people by the thousand and induced them to identify as Ukrainian by the million.

By invading Ukraine, annexing Crimea, and shooting down MH17, Russia forced the European Union and the United States to respond. The EU and U.S. sanctions were a rather mild response to Russia's announced intention to remake "the world order," as Lavrov put it; but they did isolate Russia from its major partners and deepen Russia's economic crisis. Putin pretended that China was an alternative; Beijing exposed Russia's weakness by paying less for Russian hydrocarbons. Russia's power rests upon its ability to balance between the West and the East; the invasion of Ukraine made Russia dependent on China without forcing the Chinese to do anything in return.

Russia's Eurasian ideologists claimed that the United States planned to steal Russia's resources. Antyufeyev, for example, presented Russia's war in Ukraine as a defensive campaign to prevent the United States from stealing Russia's natural gas and fresh water. This reflected a healthy imagination rather than familiarity with American energy production. Indeed, this attention to resources seemed like a displacement. It was Russia's neighbor China, not the United States, that lacked natural gas and fresh water. By claiming that international law did not protect state borders, Moscow opened the way for Beijing, when and if it so desired, to make a similar argument about the Chinese-Russian border. Almost everyone lost in the Russo-Ukrainian war: Russia, Ukraine, the EU, the United States. The only winner was China.

ON AUGUST 29, 2014, the day when Lavrov compared Russia's war against Ukraine to a computer game, Russian and European fascists and extreme-Right politicians gathered on territory seized from Ukraine to simultaneously deny and celebrate the ongoing Russian invasion.

Sergei Glazyev opened an international conference in Yalta under the heading of "anti-fascism." He was (according to the program) joined by fellow Russian fascists Alexander Dugin and Alexander Prokhanov. The guests were the leaders of Europe's extreme Right: Roberto Fiore from Italy, Frank Creyelman from Belgium, Luc Michel from Belgium, Pavel Chernev from Bulgaria, Márton Gyöngyös from Hungary, and Nick Griffin from Great Britain. Russian and European fascists considered founding an "Anti-Fascist Council." They denied the Russian invasion of Ukraine, though they were meeting in a city Russia had annexed; they denied that Russia was still fighting in eastern Ukraine at the time, though featured guests included Russian military commanders who had left the battlefield to be present.

Within the European Union, it was rare to find a major political party that would take such positions. Yet such an option was emerging in Germany and would benefit from Russian support: a new German right-wing party called the AfD (*Alternative für Deutschland,* Alternative for Germany). Standing somewhere between the radicals at Yalta and more traditional parties, it would become Moscow's darling. Its leader, Alexander Gauland, a former member of the center-right Christian Democratic Union, accepted Russia's line on Crimea and positioned his party as a pro-Russian alternative—even as Moscow attacked the German establishment. In autumn 2014, Russia undertook cyberattacks against the German parliament and German security institutions. In May 2015, the Bundestag was attacked again. In April 2016, the Christian Democratic Union—Germany's largest political party, led by Angela Merkel—was also attacked. But the most important campaign undertaken to support the German extreme Right against the German center would be in public. It would exploit an anxiety that Russians and Germans shared, Islam, against the common enemy of Moscow and the AfD, Chancellor Angela Merkel.

Facing rising numbers of refugees from war in Syria (as well as migrants fleeing Africa), Merkel took an unexpected position: Germany would accept large numbers of refugees, more than its neighbors, more than her voters would have wished. On September 8, 2015, the German government announced that it planned to take half a million refugees per year. By no coincidence, Russia began bombing Syria three weeks later. Speaking at the United Nations on September 28, 2015, Putin proposed a "harmonization" of Eurasia with the European Union. Russia would bomb Syria to generate refugees, then encourage Europeans to panic. This would help the AfD, and thus make Europe more like Russia.

Russian bombs began to fall in Syria the day after Putin spoke. Russian aircraft dropped non-precision ("dumb") bombs from high altitudes. Even if the targets had been military, non-precision bombing would have guaranteed more destruction and more refugees making their way to Europe. But Russia was not generally targeting ISIS bases. Human rights organizations reported the Russian bombing of mosques, clinics, hospitals, refugee camps, water treatment plants, and cities in general. In her decision to accept Syrian refugees, Merkel was motivated by the history of the 1930s, when Nazi Germany made its own Jewish citizens into refugees. The Russian response was in effect to say: If Merkel wants refugees, we will provide them, and use the issue to destroy her government and German democracy. Russia supplied not just the refugees themselves, but also the image of them as terrorists and rapists.

On Monday, January 11, 2016, a thirteen-year-old German girl of Russian origin, Lisa F., hesitated to return to her home in Berlin. She had once again had problems in school, and the way her family treated her had aroused the attention of authorities. She went to the house of a nineteen-year-old boy, visited with him and his mother, and stayed the night. Lisa F.'s parents reported her missing to the police. She returned home the next day, without her backpack and cell phone. She told her mother a dramatic story of abduction and rape. The police, following up the report of the missing girl, went to the residence of the friend and found her things. By speaking to her friend and his mother, finding the backpack, and reading text messages, they established where Lisa F. had been. When questioned, Lisa F. told the police what had happened: she had not wanted to go home, and had gone elsewhere. A medical examination confirmed that the story she had told her mother was untrue.

A Berlin family drama then played as global news on Russian television. On January 16, 2016, a Saturday, Pervyi Kanal presented a version of what Lisa F. had told her parents: she had been abducted by Muslim refugees and gang-raped for an entire night. This was the first of no fewer than forty segments on Pervyi Kanal about an event that, according to a police investigation, had never taken place. In the televised coverage, photographs were pasted from other places and times to add an element of verisimilitude to the story. The Russian propaganda network Sputnik chimed in with the general speculation that refugee rapists were loose in Germany. On January 17, the extreme-Right National Democratic Party organized a demonstration demanding justice for Lisa F. Although only about a dozen people appeared, one of them was an RT cameraman. His footage appeared on YouTube the same day.

The Russian information war had been ongoing for some time; most Germans had not been paying attention. The Lisa F. affair was thus a direct hit on a soft target. The Berlin police issued a tactful press release, explaining its findings, omitting names to protect the family, and requesting responsible use of social media. This was not the sort of thing that would slow a Russian propaganda campaign. The Russian media now proclaimed that "the rape of a Berlin Russian girl was hushed up," and that "the police tried to hide it." The story spread from Pervyi Kanal across Russian television and print media, told the same way everywhere: the German state welcomed Muslim rapists, failed to protect innocent girls, and lied. On January 24, a protest organized by an anti-immigration group was covered by Russian media under the headline "Lisa, we are with you! Germans rally under Merkel's window against migrant rapists."

The information war against Merkel was taken up openly by the Russian state. The Russian embassy in London tweeted that Germany rolled out the red carpet for refugees and then swept their crimes under the carpet. On January 26, Foreign Minister Lavrov, referring unforgettably to a German citizen as "our Lisa," intervened on behalf of the Russian Federation. Lavrov claimed that he was forced to act because Russians in Germany were agitated; they were indeed, because of what they had seen on Russian state television. As in Ukraine, the Russian state was claiming to act on behalf of people who were citizens and residents of another country. As in Ukraine, a fictional wrong was used to generate a sense of Russian victimhood and an occasion for the display of Russian power. Like the image of a crucified boy, that of a raped girl was meant to overwhelm.

Not long before the "our Lisa" affair, Amnesty International had published the first of several reports on Russian bombing of civilian targets in Syria. Physicians for Human Rights was also documenting Russian attacks on clinics and hospitals. On December 8, 2015, for example, Russian airstrikes destroyed the al-Burnas Hospital, the largest children's clinic in rural western Idlib, injuring doctors and nurses and killing others. The actual people who were killed and maimed in Russian attacks, the girls and boys and women and men who died under bombing, were shrouded by the specter of Muslims as a rapist collective. Refugees from Syria, like refugees from Ukraine, were subsumed in a fiction of Russian innocence. The imagined violation of a single girl was meant to reverse the valence of the entire story.

Merkel remained the leader of the largest party in Germany, and the only one capable of forming a government. Her position was weakened by the immigrant issue, in some part because of Russian intervention in German discussions. During the 2017 electoral campaign, Russian-backed social media in Germany portrayed immigration as dangerous, the political establishment as cowardly and mendacious, and the AfD as the savior of Germany. In the elections of September 2017, the AfD won 13% of the total vote, finishing third overall. This was the first time since the Nazis in 1933 that a far Right party had won representation in a German parliament. Its leader, Alexander Gauland, promised to "hunt" Merkel and "to take our country back."

OTHER EUROPEAN politicians were still less fortunate than Merkel. The Polish government of the Civic Platform party under Prime Minister Donald Tusk had supported a European future for Ukraine. Polish flags had flown on the Maidan, as young Poles traveled to Kyiv to support friends. Members of an older generation, participants in the Polish anticommunist opposition, found on the Maidan something that they never thought they would see again: solidarity across social classes and political parties. Polish Foreign Minister Radosław Sikorski had journeyed to Kyiv to seek a negotiated settlement between protestors and government.

That Polish government was then brought down. Tapes emerged of private conversations between Civic Platform politicians at restaurants. The problem was not that the tapes revealed scandals, although they did, but that they allowed Poles to hear how politicians speak in private. It is a rare politician who can survive his constituents knowing how he orders food or tells jokes. Sikorski was recorded issuing some rather sound political judgments, but in a language different from that which he used in public. The man who hired waiters to record the conversations owed $26 million to a company with close ties to Vladimir Putin. Two restaurants where conversations were taped were owned by consortia with connections to Semion Mogilevich, regarded as the don of dons of the Russian mob.

Crossing the line that divides public responsibility and private life was far more consequential than it appeared. The undesired exposure of private conversations was incipient totalitarianism, in a country that had been a focal point of Nazi and Soviet aspirations during the twentieth century. This point was rarely made. Polish memories of German and Soviet aggression tended to congeal around heroism and villainy. What got lost was the memory of how totalitarianism endured into the 1970s and 1980s: not by atrocities where the distinction between the perpetrator and victim is clear, but by an erosion of the line between private and public life that demolishes the rule of law and invites the population to participate in the demolition. Poles returned to a world of bugged conversations, unexpected denunciations, and constant suspicion.

Public life cannot be sustained without private life. It is impossible to govern, even for the best of democrats, without the possibility for discreet conversations. The only politicians who are invulnerable to exposure are those who control the secrets of others, or those whose avowed behavior is so shameless that they are invulnerable to blackmail. In the end, electronic scandals that reveal the "hypocrisy" of politicians who break rules help the politicians who disregard rules. Digital revelations end the careers of those who have secrets and begin the careers of those who promote spectacle. By accepting that the private lives of public figures are the same thing as politics, citizens cooperate in the destruction of a public sphere. This quiet emergence of totalitarianism, visible in Poland during the tapes scandal of 2014, was also on display in the United States in 2016.

It was perhaps no great surprise that Civic Platform lost the parliamentary elections in October 2015 to its right-wing rival, the Law and Justice party. Civic Platform had been in power for almost a decade; and Poles had other reasons, aside from the tapes scandal, for weary skepticism. Yet there was something unexpected about the government that was formed that November: the prominent place of the intemperate nationalist Antoni Macierewicz. During the campaign, Law and Justice had promised that Macierewicz, who over the decades had earned a reputation for jeopardizing Poland's national security, would not be named minister of defense. Then he was.

A politician forever preoccupied with secrets and their revelation, Macierewicz was a natural beneficiary of the tapes scandal. In 1993, he had brought down his own government with his unusual treatment of archival records concerning Polish communism. Entrusted with the delicate task of reviewing communist secret police files to find informers, he instead published a random list of names. The "Macierewicz list" of 1993 left out most of the actual agents, including Macierewicz's own political partner, Michał Luśnia. It did include figures who had nothing to do with the secret police, but who would long suffer trying to clear their names.

In 2006, when the Law and Justice party was in power, Macierewicz was entrusted with a second sensitive task: the reform of Polish military intelligence. He published a report that revealed its methods and named its agents, disabling it for the foreseeable future. He ensured that this report was quickly translated into Russian, employing a Russian translator who in a previous job had cooperated with Soviet secret services. In 2007, as head of the new military counterintelligence organizations that he had founded, Macierewicz transferred secret military documents to Jacek Kotas, a man known in Warsaw as the "Russian connection" because of his work for Russian firms linked to the Russian mobster Semion Mogilevich. As defense minister in 2015, Macierewicz arranged another spectacular breach of national security, organizing an illegal nighttime raid on a NATO center in Warsaw whose assignment was to track Russian propaganda.

Macierewicz, a master of the politics of eternity, managed to submerge Poland's actual history of suffering in a political fiction. In office as minister of defense from 2015, Macierewicz translated a recent human and political tragedy into a tale of innocence that allowed for a new definition of enemies. This was the Smolensk catastrophe of April 2010, the deadly crash of an airplane containing Polish political and civic leaders on their way to Russia to commemorate the Katyn massacre. At the time, the Polish government was led by Prime Minister Donald Tusk of the Civic Platform, whereas the president was Lech Kaczyński of Law and Justice. Tusk brought a governmental delegation to Smolensk for an official commemoration. The leaders of Law and Justice hastily arranged to send a rival delegation to a different set of commemorations.

Only the living can commemorate the dead. The first mistake of the rival delegation was placing so much of the Polish elite on board two airplanes flying to the same place at the same time with essentially zero advance planning. The second mistake was to attempt to land those planes in prohibitive conditions at a military airfield for which the pilots were untrained. Although one found the airstrip through the fog, the second crashed in a forest, killing all passengers on board. In that second aircraft, elementary safety procedures had not been followed: the cockpit door had not been closed, denying the pilots their normal authority. Transcripts from the black box revealed that they had not wished to land, but had been pressured to do so by visitors from the back of the plane, including the commander of the air force. The black box transcripts suggested that President Lech Kaczyński had reserved the decision about landing for himself: his delegate spoke directly to the pilots of a "decision from the president." This was not only inappropriate but disastrous, since it brought about not just his own death, but the death of all of his fellow passengers and the crew.

The catastrophe was caused by avoidable human error. That fact was difficult to face. In the atmosphere evoked by Katyn, emotions ran high. They ran higher still in the Kaczyński family, where twin brothers united by politics were suddenly divided in an unexpected and horrible way. Within the Law and Justice party, the accident brought a strange aftermath: one twin brother (Jarosław, who now became leader of the Law and Justice party) remained alive after the other twin brother (Lech, the president) had died in a confusing tragedy. It made matters worse that the two brothers had spoken a few minutes before the crash: whatever else might have been said, it seemed clear that Jarosław had not discouraged Lech from landing.

Macierewicz understood that the search for meaning after death can be channeled into useful political fiction. He created a mystery cult around the crash, floating implausible and contradictory explanations, with the general implication that Putin and Tusk had cooperated in a political mass murder. His technique was strikingly similar to the way that Russian authorities had treated MH17. In the case of MH17, Russians had shot down a civilian airliner, and sought to deny it. In the case of Smolensk, Russia had not shot down an airliner, but Macierewicz seemed eager to prove that it had. But this difference is less important than the similarity. In both cases, the trail of evidence was abundant and convincing, and led to investigations with clear conclusions. In both cases, politicians of eternity spun tales designed to suppress factuality and confirm victimhood.

Macierewicz required that the list of victims of the Smolensk accident be read in public places, and took part in spirited monthly commemorations. A word in Polish reserved for the heroic dead of wars and uprisings, *polegli*, was applied by Macierewicz and others to the crash victims. After 2015, Smolensk became more important than the Katyn massacre that Polish leaders had wished to commemorate, more important than the entire Second World War, more important than the twentieth century. The commemoration of Smolensk divided Polish society as only a fiction can. It alienated Poles from their allies, since no Western leader could believe in Macierewicz's version of events, or even pretend to believe in it. A quarter century of efforts by historians to convey the horrors of Polish history was wasted in a matter of months: thanks to Macierewicz, the true history of Polish suffering was shrouded under nationalist lies. Tusk was elected president of the European Council, one of the top leadership positions in the European Union. It was difficult for European politicians to process Macierewicz's suggestion that Tusk had conspired with Putin to plan a mass murder.

Macierewicz's accusations of Russia were so outlandish that he seemed like the last person who could be a Russian agent. Perhaps that was the point. Macierewicz promoted his cult of Smolensk while promoting men with connections to Moscow. As his secretary of state he appointed Bartosz Kownacki, a man who had traveled to Moscow to legitimate Putin's fraudulent election in 2012. As head of national cryptography Macierewicz appointed Tomasz Mikołajewski, a man about whom little was known—beyond his inability to pass security background checks. For other appointments, he relied upon Jacek Kotas, "the Russian connection." Kotas had a think tank that prepared cadres for Macierewicz. One of its position papers recommended that the Polish army be deprofessionalized and supplemented by a Territorial Defense that would deter protests against the government. That paper was co-written by Krzysztof Gaj, who had spread Russian propaganda about Ukrainian fascism. Macierewicz made the Territorial Defense subordinate to him personally, thus avoiding the command structure of the Polish armed forces. Soon it was funded at the same level as the entire Polish navy. He fired the vast majority of Poland's high-ranking staff and field generals, replacing them with inexperienced people, some of whom were known for their pro-Russian and anti-NATO views.

Warsaw meanwhile abandoned the one policy that had distinguished it among its NATO and EU peers: the support of Ukrainian independence. Under the Law and Justice government, Warsaw chose to emphasize episodes of Polish-Ukrainian conflict in ways that suggested the total innocence of Poles. This was the Polish policy Malofeev had subsidized in 2014, without much success. Now it seemed that no subsidies were needed. Western allies were confounded. The French were told by Kownacki that Poles had taught them how to use forks. British intelligence concluded that Poland was not a reliable partner.

Macierewicz had maintained some American connections, but these too led back to Russia. In 2010, when Macierewicz sought counsel on how to react to the Smolensk tragedy, he traveled to the United States. His contact in the American House of Representatives was Dana Rohrabacher, an American legislator who distinguished himself with his support of Vladimir Putin and Russian foreign policy. In 2012, the FBI warned Rohrabacher that he was regarded by Russian spies as a source. Kevin McCarthy, the Republican majority leader of the House of Representatives, later named Rohrabacher (along with Donald Trump) as the Republican politician most likely to be in the pay of Russia. In 2015, after Macierewicz became minister of defense, Rohrabacher traveled to Warsaw to meet him. In 2016, Rohrabacher went to Moscow to collect documents that Moscow believed would help the Trump campaign. Interestingly, Macierewicz took the trouble to defend Donald Trump from the charge that his campaign was connected to Russia.

Macierewicz did not deny the facts that connected him to Moscow. Instead he treated factuality as the enemy. When a journalist published a book detailing his Russian links in 2017, Macierewicz did not dispute its claims, nor sue the journalist in a civil court where he would have had to produce evidence. Instead, he claimed that investigative journalism constituted a physical attack on a government minister, and initiated proceedings to try the journalist for terrorism before a military tribunal. He was replaced as minister of defense in January 2018. By that time, the European Union (specifically, its executive body, the European Commission) was proposing to sanction Poland for violating basic principles of the rule of law.

**THERE IS** nothing inherently Russian about political fiction. Ilyin and Surkov arrived at their conclusion because of their experiences in, and aspirations for, Russia. Other societies can yield to the same form of politics, after a shock and a scandal, as in Poland, or as a result of inequality and Russian intervention, as in Great Britain and the United States. In his study of Russian media and society, published in 2014, Peter Pomerantsev concluded with the reflection that "here is going to be there," the West is going to be like Russia. It was Russian policy to accelerate this process.

If leaders were unable to reform Russia, reform had to seem impossible. If Russians believed that all leaders and all media lied, then they would learn to dismiss Western models for themselves. If the citizens of Europe and the United States joined in the general distrust of one another and their institutions, then Europe and America could be expected to disintegrate. Journalists cannot function amidst total skepticism; civil societies wane when citizens cannot count on one another; the rule of law depends upon the beliefs that people will follow law without its being enforced and that enforcement when it comes will be impartial. The very idea of impartiality assumes that there are truths that can be understood regardless of perspective.

Russian propaganda was transmitted by protégés on the European far Right who shared Russia's interest in the demolition of European institutions. The idea, for example, that the Russian war on Sodom (and the associated Russian invasion of Ukraine) was a "new cold war," or a "Cold War 2.0," was formulated by the Izborsk Club. It was a helpful notion in Russia, since it stylized gay bashing (and then the invasion of a helpless neighbor while gay bashing) as a grand confrontation with a global superpower over the shape of civilization. This trope of "a new cold war" was spread by Marine Le Pen, the leader of the *Front National,* who used it on RT beginning in 2011 and during her July 2013 visit to Moscow. The leading American white supremacist, Richard Spencer, used the same term at the same time when interviewed by RT.

The European and American far Right also spread the official Russian claim that Ukrainian protests on the Maidan were the work of the West. The Polish fascist Mateusz Piskorski claimed that Ukrainian protests were the work of "the US embassy." Heinz-Christian Strache, the leader of Austria's *Freiheitliche* party, blamed western security services. Márton Gyöngyös of the Hungarian Jobbik party, whom the Russian press itself had classified as an antisemite and a neo-Nazi in the years before antisemites and neo-Nazis became RT commentators, said that the Maidan protests were arranged by American diplomats. Manuel Ochsenreiter, a German neo-Nazi, spoke of the Ukrainian revolution as "imposed by the West." None of these people produced evidence.

Russian conspiratorial ideas, spread by the European far Right, found traction in some corners of the American Right. The pronouncements of former Republican congressman Ron Paul, who ran for president in 2008 and 2012, were particularly interesting. Paul, who described himself as a libertarian, had mounted powerful critiques of American wars abroad. Now he defended a Russian war abroad. Paul cited Sergei Glazyev with approval—although Glazyev's fascist politics and neocommunist economics contradicted Paul's libertarianism, and Glazyev's warmongering contradicted Paul's isolationism. Paul endorsed the Eurasia project, which was again unexpected, given that its philosophical sources were fascist and its economics involved state planning. Paul, echoing a host of European fascists, claimed that "the U.S. government pulled off a coup" in Ukraine. Like them, he provided no evidence. Instead he cited propaganda from RT.

It was less surprising that Lyndon LaRouche, the leader of an American crypto-Nazi organization, followed Glazyev's line. La-Rouche and Glazyev had been in collaboration for two decades around the idea of an international (Jewish) oligarchy, a genocide of Russians by (Jewish) liberals, and the desirability of Eurasia. In LaRouche's view, Ukraine was an artificial construction created by Jews to block Eurasia. Like Glazyev and other Russian fascists, La-Rouche deployed familiar symbols of the Holocaust to define Jews as the perpetrators and others as the victims. On June 27, 2014, La-Rouche published an article by Glazyev, claiming that the Ukrainian government was a Nazi junta installed by the United States.

Stephen Cohen borrowed Russian media terms of abuse at the same time, on June 30, 2014. Like LaRouche, Cohen endorsed the Russian propaganda claim that the Russian invasion of Ukraine was justified by Ukrainian genocide. The notion that Ukraine was perpetrating genocide was translated into English by RT, and then spread by certain people on the American far Right and the American far Left. This propaganda effort exploited images associated with the Holocaust. These could be used by LaRouche to present Russians to American antisemites as the victims of Jews, or by Cohen to suggest to the American Left and American Jews that Russian victimhood in 2014 was like Jewish victimhood in 1941. Either way, the result was not only to falsify events in Ukraine but also to trivialize the Holocaust.

Writing in *The Nation*, Cohen claimed that the Ukrainian prime minister had spoken of adversaries as "subhuman," which he proposed as evidence of the Nazi convictions and behavior of the Ukrainian government. The Ukrainian prime minister had in fact written a statement of condolence to the Ukrainian families of soldiers killed in action, in which he used the word "inhuman" (*neliudy*) to describe the attackers. Russian media then mistranslated the Ukrainian word into Russian as "subhuman" (*nedocheloveki*), and RT used the word "subhuman" in English-language broadcasts. Cohen served as the final link in the chain, bringing the slander into American media. In one RT account, the mistranslation had been broadcast along with a series of other untruths and accompanied by graphic images of mass murder in Rwanda. The RT segment violated broadcasting standards in the United Kingdom, and was pulled from the internet. Readers looking for the false "subhuman" claim could still turn to *The Nation*.

When Russia shot down MH17 in July 2014, Cohen said: "We've had these shootdowns. We had them in the cold war." The killing of civilians was dismissed by a vague reference to the past. A Russian weapon with a Russian crew during a Russian invasion of Ukraine shot down a civilian airliner and killed 298 people. A state transferred soldiers and weapons; an officer gave an order to fire; pilots were killed in a cockpit as shrapnel ripped through their bodies; a plane was ripped apart ten kilometers above the earth; children, women, and men died in sudden terror, their body parts scattered over the countryside. On July 18, 2014, the day that Cohen said this, Russian television was broadcasting its multiple versions of the event. Rather than explaining to Americans what reporters knew—that multiple Ukrainian aircraft had been shot down by Russian weapons in the same place in prior weeks, and that the Russian GRU officer Igor Girkin had claimed credit for shooting down the aircraft that turned out to be MH17—Cohen changed the subject to the "cold war."

This idea that Russia's anti-gay policies and its invasion of Ukraine were a "new cold war" was a meme spread within Russia by the fascists of the Izborsk Club and then by right-wing politicians on RT: Marine Le Pen, beginning in 2011, and Richard Spencer, beginning in 2013. The term became a mainstay in the pages of *The Nation* in 2014, thanks to articles by Cohen and the journal's publisher, Katrina vanden Heuvel.

On July 24, 2014, vanden Heuvel claimed on television that Moscow was "calling for a cease fire" in a "civil war." In speaking in this way, she was separating Russia from a conflict in which it was the aggressor. At that moment, the prime ministers of the "Donetsk

People's Republic" and the "Lugansk People's Republic" were not Ukrainians but Russian citizens brought in by Russian forces, political technologists with no connection to Ukraine. In their public relations capacity, they were promoting the very "civil war" concept that vanden Heuvel was helping to spread. At the time of her television appearance, the Russian citizen in charge of security was Vladimir Antyufeyev, who characterized the conflict as a war against the international Masonic conspiracy and foretold the destruction of the United States.

Vanden Heuvel was speaking one week after MH17 had been shot down by a Russian weapons system, during a summer in which Russian transfers of weapons across the border were widely reported. She was speaking of a "civil war" during a massive Russian artillery barrage from Russian territory. A Russian journalist at the launch site had reported that "Russia is shelling Ukraine from its own territory" and wrote of "the military aggression of Russia against Ukraine." As vanden Heuvel was speaking, thousands of Russian soldiers from units based all over the Russian Federation were massing at the Russian-Ukrainian border. These elementary realities of the Russian war on Ukraine, known at the time thanks to the work of Russian and Ukrainian reporters, were submerged by *The Nation* in propaganda tropes.

Important writers of the British Left repeated the same Russian talking points. In *The Guardian,* John Pilger wrote in May 2014 that Putin "was the only leader to condemn the rise of fascism." This was an unwise conclusion to draw from current events. Just a few days earlier, neo-Nazis had marched on the streets of Moscow without meeting condemnation from their president. A few weeks earlier, on Russian state television, a Russian anchor had claimed that Jews brought the Holocaust on themselves; and her interlocutor, Alexander Prokhanov, had agreed. Putin's government paid the anchorwoman, and Putin himself made media appearances with Prokhanov (who also took a joyride in a Russian bomber, a rather clear expression of official support). These people were not condemned. Russia at the time was assembling the European far Right—as electoral "observers," as soldiers in the field, and as propagators of its messages. Moscow had organized meetings of European fascists and was subsidizing France's far Right party, the *Front National*.

How were opinion leaders of the Left seduced by Vladimir Putin, the global leader of the extreme Right? Russia generated tropes targeted at what cyberwar professionals call "susceptibilities": what people seem likely to believe given their utterances and behavior. It was possible to claim that Ukraine was a Jewish construction (for one audience) and also that Ukraine was a fascist construction (for another audience). People on the Left were drawn in by stimuli on social media that spoke to their own commitments. Pilger wrote his article under the influence of a text he found on the internet, purportedly written by a physician, detailing supposed Ukrainian atrocities in Odessa—but the doctor did not exist and the event did not take place. *The Guardian*'s correction noted only that Pilger's source, a fake social media page, had "subsequently been removed": far gentler, that, than to say that the most-read article about Ukraine in that newspaper in 2014 was a translation of Russian political fiction into English.

*Guardian* associate editor Seumas Milne opined in January 2014 that "far-right nationalists and fascists have been at the heart of the protests" in Ukraine. This corresponded not to *The Guardian*'s reporting from Ukraine but to the Russian propaganda line. Milne dismissed from the record the labors of about a million Ukrainian citizens to turn the rule of law against oligarchy: an odd turn for a newspaper with a left-wing tradition. Even after Putin had admitted that Russian forces were in Ukraine, Milne was claiming that "the little green men" were mostly Ukrainian. At Putin's presidential summit on foreign policy at Valdai in 2013, the Russian president had claimed that Russia and Ukraine were "one people." Milne chaired a session of the 2014 summit, at Putin's invitation.

None of these people—Milne, Pilger, Cohen, vanden Heuvel, LaRouche, Paul—provided a single interpretation that was not available on RT. In some cases, as with Paul and LaRouche, the debt to Russian propaganda was acknowledged. Even those whose work was published adjacent to actual reporting, in *The Nation* or in *The Guardian*, ignored the investigations of actual Russian and Ukrainian reporters. None of these influential American and British writers visited Ukraine, which would have been the normal journalistic practice. Those who spoke so freely of conspiracies, coups, juntas, camps, fascists, and genocides shied from contact with the real world. From a distance, they used their talents to drown a country in unreality; in so doing, they submerged their own countries and themselves.

Enormous amounts of time were wasted in Britain, the United States, and Europe in 2014 and 2015 on discussions about whether Ukraine existed and whether Russia had invaded it. That triumph of informational warfare was instructive for Russian leaders. In the invasion of Ukraine, the main Russian victories were in the minds of Europeans and Americans, not on the battlefields. Far-Right politicians spread Russia's messages, and left-wing journalists helped to bring them to the center. One of the left-wing journalists then entered the corridors of power. In October 2015, Seumas Milne, having chaired Putin's Valdai summit, became chief of communications for Jeremy Corbyn, the leader of Britain's Labour Party. With Milne as his chief press officer, Corbyn proved a poor advocate for EU membership. British voters chose to leave, and Moscow celebrated.

In July 2016, not long after the Brexit referendum, Donald Trump said, "Putin is not going into Ukraine, you can mark it down." The Russian invasion of Ukraine had begun more than two years before, in February 2014, right after snipers murdered Ukrainians on the Maidan. It was thanks to that very set of events that Trump had a campaign manager. Yanukovych fled to Russia, but his advisor Paul Manafort kept working for a pro-Russian party in Ukraine through the end of 2015. Manafort's new employer, the Opposition Bloc, was precisely the part of the Ukrainian political system that wanted to do business with Russia while Russia was invading Ukraine. This was the perfect transition to Manafort's next job. In 2016, he moved to

New York and took over the management of Trump's campaign. In 2014, Trump had known that Russia had invaded Ukraine. Under Manafort's tutelage, Trump proclaimed Russian innocence.

Lyndon LaRouche and Ron Paul were taking the same line at the time: Russia had done nothing wrong, and Europeans and Americans were to blame for the Russian invasion, which perhaps had happened and perhaps had not. Writing in *The Nation* in the summer and autumn of 2016, Cohen defended Trump and Manafort, and dreamed that Trump and Putin would one day come together and remake the world order. The mendacity and the fascism of the Russian assault upon the European Union and the United States, of which the Trump campaign was a part, was a natural story for the Left. However, few on the Left took Trump and his own political fiction seriously in 2016. Perhaps this was because writers they trusted were not analysts of, but rather participants in, the Russian campaign to undermine factuality. In any event, Ukraine was the warning that went unheeded.

When a presidential candidate from a fictional world appeared in the United States, Ukrainians and Russians noted the familiar patterns, but few on the American Right or the American Left listened. When Moscow brought to bear in the United States the same techniques used in Ukraine, few on the American Right or the American Left noticed. And so the United States was defeated, Trump was elected, the Republican Party was blinded, and the Democratic Party was shocked. Russians supplied the political fiction, but Americans were asking for it.

## CHAPTER SIX

# EQUALITY OR OLIGARCHY (2016)

Nothing was more to be desired than that every practicable obstacle should be opposed to cabal, intrigue, and corruption. These most deadly adversaries of republican government might naturally have been expected to make their approaches from more than one querter, but chiefly from the desire in foreign powers to gain an improper ascendant in our councils. How could they better gratify this, than by raising a creature of their own to the chief magistracy of the Union?

—ALEXANDER HAMILTON, 1788

Ill fares the land, to hastening ills a prey
Where wealth accumulates, and men decay.

—OLIVER GOLDSMITH, 1770

Vladimir Putin's eternity regime challenged political virtues: undoing a succession principle in Russia, assaulting integration in Europe, invading Ukraine to stop the creation of new political forms. His grandest campaign was a cyberwar to destroy the United States of America. For reasons having to do with American inequality, Russian oligarchy won an extraordinary victory in 2016. Because it did, inequality became a still greater American problem.

The rise of Donald Trump was the attack by "these most deadly adversaries of republican government" that Alexander Hamilton had feared. Russian leaders openly and exuberantly backed Trump's candidacy. Throughout 2016, Russian elites said with a smile that

"Trump is our president." Dmitry Kiselev, the leading man of the Russian media, rejoiced that "a new star is rising—Trump." The Eurasianists felt the same way: Alexander Dugin posted a video entitled "In Trump We Trust" and urged Americans to "vote for Trump!" Alexei Pushkov, the chair of the foreign relations committee of the lower house of the Russian parliament, expressed the general hope that "Trump can lead the Western locomotive right off the rails." Some Russians tried to alert Americans: Andrei Kozyrev, a former foreign minister, explained that Putin "realizes that Trump will trample American democracy and damage if not destroy America as a pillar of stability and major force able to contain him."

The Russian media machine was at work on Trump's behalf. As a Russian journalist later explained: "we were given very clear instructions: to show Donald Trump in a positive way, and his opponent, Hillary Clinton, in a negative way." The Russian propaganda outlet Sputnik used the #crookedhillary hashtag on Twitter—a gesture of respect and support for Trump, since the phrase was his—and also associated Clinton with nuclear war. Trump appeared on RT to complain that the U.S. media was untruthful, which for RT was the perfect performance: its entire reason for being was to expose the single truth that everyone lied, and here was an American saying the same thing.

When Trump won the presidential election that November, he was applauded in the Russian parliament. Trump quickly telephoned Putin to be congratulated. Kiselev, the leading man of the Russian media, celebrated Trump as the return of manhood to politics on his Sunday evening program, *Vesti Nedeli*. He fantasized before his viewers about Trump satisfying blondes, including Hillary Clinton. He was pleased that "the words 'democracy' and 'human rights' are not in the vocabulary of Trump." Describing a meeting of Trump and Obama, Kiselev claimed that Obama was "waving his arms, as if he were in the jungle." In his commentary on Trump's inauguration, Kiselev said that Michelle Obama looked like the housekeeper.

THE POLITICS of eternity are full of phantasmagoria, of bots and trolls, ghosts and zombies, dead souls and other unreal beings who escort a fictional character to power. "Donald Trump, successful businessman" was not a person. It was a fantasy born in the strange climate where the downdraft of the American politics of eternity, its unfettered capitalism, met the rising hydrocarbon fumes of the Russian politics of eternity, its kleptocratic authoritarianism. Russians raised "a creature of their own" to the presidency of the United States. Trump was the payload of a cyberweapon, meant to create chaos and weakness, as in fact he has done.

Trump's advance to the Oval Office had three stages, each of which depended upon American vulnerability and required American cooperation. First, Russians had to transform a failed real estate developer into a recipient of their capital. Second, this failed real estate developer had to portray, on American television, a successful businessman. Finally, Russia intervened with purpose and success to support the fictional character "Donald Trump, successful businessman" in the 2016 presidential election.

Throughout the exercise, Russians knew what was fact and what was fiction. Russians knew Trump for what he was: not the "VERY successful businessman" of his tweets but an American loser who became a Russian tool. Although Americans might dream otherwise, no one who mattered in Moscow believed that Trump was a powerful tycoon. Russian money had saved him from the fate that would normally await anyone with his record of failure.

FROM AN American point of view, Trump Tower is a garish building on Fifth Avenue in New York City. From a Russian point of view, Trump Tower is an inviting site for international crime.

Russian gangsters began to launder money by buying and selling apartment units in Trump Tower in the 1990s. The most notorious Russian hit man, long sought by the FBI, resided in Trump Tower. Russians were arrested for running a gambling ring from the apartment beneath Trump's own. In Trump World Tower, constructed between 1999 and 2001 on the east side of Manhattan near the United Nations, a third of the luxury units were bought by people or entities from the former Soviet Union. A man investigated by the Treasury Department for money laundering lived in Trump World Tower directly beneath Kellyanne Conway, who would become the press spokeswoman for the Trump campaign. Seven hundred units of Trump properties in South Florida were purchased by shell companies. Two men associated with those shell companies were convicted of running a gambling and laundering scheme from Trump Tower. Perhaps Trump was entirely unaware of what was happening on his properties.

By the late 1990s, Trump was generally considered to be uncreditworthy and bankrupt. He owed about four billion dollars to more than seventy banks, of which some $800 million was personally guaranteed. He never showed any inclination or capacity to pay back this debt. After his 2004 bankruptcy, no American bank would lend him money. The only bank that did so was Deutsche Bank, whose colorful history of scandal belied its staid name. Interestingly, Deutsche Bank also laundered about $10 billion for Russian clients between 2011 and 2015. Interestingly, Trump declined to pay back his debts to Deutsche Bank.

A Russian oligarch bought a house from Trump for $55 million more than Trump had paid for it. The buyer, Dmitry Rybolovlev, never showed any interest in the property and never lived there—but later, when Trump ran for president, Rybolovlev appeared in places where Trump was campaigning. Trump's apparent business, real estate development, had become a Russian charade. Having realized that apartment complexes could be used to launder money, Russians used Trump's name to build more buildings. As Donald Trump Jr. said in 2008, "Russians make up a pretty disproportionate cross-section of a lot of our assets. We see a lot of money pouring in from Russia."

The Russian offers were hard to refuse: millions of dollars upfront for Trump, a share of the profits for Trump, Trump's name on a building—but no investment required from Trump. These terms suited both sides. In 2006, citizens of the former Soviet Union financed the construction of Trump SoHo, and gave Trump 18% of the profits—although he put up no money himself. In the case of Felix Sater, the apartments were currency laundromats. A Russian American, Sater worked as senior advisor of the Trump Organization from an office in Trump Tower two floors below Trump's own. Trump depended upon the Russian money Sater brought through an entity known as the Bayrock Group. Sater arranged for people from the post-Soviet world to buy apartments using shell companies. From 2007, Sater and Bayrock were helping Trump around the world, cooperating on at least four projects. Some of these failed, but Trump made money regardless.

Russia is not a wealthy country, but its wealth is highly concentrated. It is thus common practice for Russians to place someone in their debt by providing easy money and naming the price later. As a candidate for the office of president, Trump broke with decades of tradition by not releasing his tax returns, presumably because they would reveal his profound dependence on Russian capital. Even after he announced his candidacy for the office of president, in June 2015, Trump was pursuing risk-free deals with Russians. In October 2015, near the time of a Republican presidential debate, he signed a letter of intent to have Russians build a tower in Moscow and put his name on it. He took to Twitter to announce that "Putin loves Donald Trump."

The final deal never went through, perhaps because it would have made the Russian sources of Trump's apparent success just a bit too obvious at the moment when his presidential campaign was gaining momentum. The fictional character "Donald Trump, successful businessman" had more important things to do. In the words of Felix Sater, writing in November 2015, "Our boy can become president of the United States and we can engineer it." In 2016, just when Trump needed money to run a campaign, his properties became extremely popular for shell companies. In the half year between his nomination as the Republican candidate and his victory in the general election, some 70% of the units sold in his buildings were purchased not by human beings but by limited liability companies.

RUSSIA'S "BOY" existed in the American mind thanks to a popular American television program, *The Apprentice,* where Trump portrayed a mogul capable of hiring and firing at will. The role came naturally to him, perhaps because pretending to be such a person was already his day job. On the show, the world was a ruthless oligarchy, where an individual's future depended upon the capricious whims of a single man. The climax in each episode came when Trump brought the pain: "You're fired!" When Trump ran for president, he did so on the premise that the world really was so: that a fictional character with fictional wealth who ignores law, despises institutions, and lacks sympathy can govern people by causing pain. Trump outshone Republican rivals at debates thanks to years of practice at playing a fictional character on television.

Trump was broadcasting unreality, and had been for some time. In 2010, RT was helping American conspiracy theorists spread the false idea that President Barack Obama had not been born in the United States. This fiction, designed to appeal to the weaknesses of racist Americans who wished to imagine away their elected president, invited them to live in an alternative reality. In 2011, Trump became the spokesman of this fantasy campaign. He only had a platform to do so because Americans associated him with the successful businessman he played on television, a role which in turn was only possible because Russians had bailed him out. Fiction rested on fiction rested on fiction.

From a Russian perspective, Trump was a failure who was rescued and an asset to be used to wreak havoc in American reality. The relationship was playacted in Moscow at the Miss Universe pageant of 2013, where Trump preened before Putin, hoping that the Russian president would be his "best friend." Trump's Russian partners knew he needed money; they paid him $20 million while they organized the pageant. They allowed him to play his role as the American with money and power. In a music video filmed for the occasion, Trump was permitted to say "You're fired!" to a successful young pop star, the son of the man who actually ran the pageant. Letting Trump win meant owning him completely.

Trump the winner was a fiction that would make his country lose.

THE SOVIET secret police—known over time as the Cheka, the GPU, the NKVD, the KGB, and then in Russia as the FSB—excelled in a special sort of operation known as "active measures." Intelligence is about seeing and understanding. Counterintelligence is about making that difficult for others. Active measures, such as the operation on behalf of the fictional character "Donald Trump, successful businessman," are about inducing the enemy to direct his own strengths against his own weaknesses. America was crushed by Russia in the cyberwar of 2016 because the relationship between technology and life had changed in a way that gave an advantage to the Russian practitioners of active measures.

The cold war, by the 1970s and 1980s, was a technological competition for the visible consumption of attractive goods in the real world. North American and west European countries were then at an unmistakable advantage, and in 1991 the Soviet Union collapsed. As an unregulated internet entered most American (but not Russian) households in the 2000s and the 2010s, the relationship between technology and life changed—and the balance of power shifted along with it. By 2016, the average American spent more than ten hours a day in front of screens, most of that with devices connected to the internet. In "The Hollow Men," T. S. Eliot wrote that "Between the idea / And the reality / Between the motion / And the act / Falls the shadow." The shadow in the America of the 2010s was the internet, dividing people from what they thought they were doing. By 2016, technology no longer made American society look better to the outside world. Instead, technology offered a better look inside American society, and into individual American minds.

In George Orwell's *1984*, the hero is told, "You will be hollow. We shall squeeze you empty, and then we shall fill you with ourselves." In the 2010s, the competition was not about physical objects that could be consumed, as during the cold war, but about psychological states that could be generated in the mind. The Russian economy did not have to produce anything of material value, and did not. Russian politicians had to use technologies created by others to alter mental states, and did. Once the competition was about the invisible manipulation of personalities, it was not surprising that Russia won.

Russia under Putin declared war not for cause but because the terms were favorable. Ilyin and other Russian nationalists after him had defined the West as a spiritual threat, whose very existence generated facts that could be harmful or confusing to Russians. By that logic, preemptive cyberwar against Europe and America was justified as soon as it was technically feasible. By 2016, Russian cyberwar had been underway for nearly a decade, though it was largely ignored in American discussions. A Russian parliamentarian said that the American secret services "slept through" as Russia chose the American president, and there was justice in his words.

Kiselev called information war the most important kind of war. At the receiving end, the chairwoman of the Democratic Party wrote of "a war, clearly, but waged on a different kind of battlefield." The term was to be taken literally. Carl von Clausewitz, the most famous student of warfare, defined it as "an act of force to compel our enemy to do our will." What if, as Russian military doctrine of the 2010s posited, technology made it possible to engage the enemy's will directly, without the medium of violence? It should be possible, as a Russian military planning document of 2013 proposed, to mobilize the "protest potential of the population" against its own interests, or, as the Izborsk Club specified in 2014, to generate in the United

States a "destructive paranoid reflection."* Those are concise and precise descriptions of Trump's candidacy. The fictional character won, thanks to votes meant as a protest against the system, and thanks to voters who believed paranoid fantasies that simply were not true.

During the 2014 presidential elections in Ukraine, Russia hacked the server of Ukraine's Central Election Commission. Ukrainian officials caught the hack at the last moment. In other realms, Ukrainians were not so lucky. The most terrifying possibility of cyberwar is what the professionals call "cyber-to-physical": an action taken at a keyboard to change computer code has consequences in the three-dimensional world. Russian hackers attempted this several times in Ukraine, for example by shutting down parts of the electrical grid. In the United States in 2016, these two forms of attack were brought together: an attack on a presidential election, this time as cyber-to-physical. The aim of Russian cyberwar was to bring Trump to the Oval Office through what seemed to be normal procedures. Trump did not need to understand this, any more than an electrical grid has to know when it is disconnected. All that matters is that the lights go out.

The Russian war against Ukraine was always an element of the larger policy to destroy the European Union and the United States. Russian leaders made no secret of this; Russian soldiers and volunteers believed that they were engaged in a world war against the United States—and in a sense they were right. In spring 2014, when Russian special forces infiltrated southeastern Ukraine, some soldiers

---

* Russian leaders saw the revolution in Ukraine in these terms: If Ukrainians did not want Russian domination, then someone else must be fighting an information war against Russia, and that someone else could only be the United States. Hence the miscommunication between a Kremlin obsessed with Ukraine and a White House that hardly noticed it: the longer the silences of the Americans, the more the Russians assumed that the enemy was working in secret. And so Russia fought the war against the Ukrainian army as an information and cyberwar against the European Union and the United States.

were clearly thinking about defeating America. One of them told a reporter his dream was that "the T-50 [a Russian stealth fighter] will be flying above Washington!" Similar visions filled the imagination of Ukrainian citizens who fought on the Russian side: one of them fantasized about hanging a red flag on top of the American White House and Capitol. In July 2014, when Russia began its second major military intervention in Ukraine, the commander Vladimir Antyufeyev grouped Ukraine and the United States together as "disintegrating" states, and anticipated that the American "demonic construction" would be destroyed. In August 2014, Alexander Borodai (and many others) passed on a joke in social media about Russia intervening in the United States, which included a racist characterization of its president. In September 2014, Sergei Glazyev wrote that the "American elite" had to be "terminated" for the war in Ukraine to be won. In December 2014, the Izborsk Club published a series of articles on a new cold war directed against the United States, to be fought as an information war. It anticipated "filling information with misinformation." The goal was "the destruction of some of the important pillars of Western society."

The Russian FSB and Russian military intelligence (the GRU), both active in Ukraine, would also both take part in the cyberwar against the United States. The dedicated Russian cyberwar center known as the Internet Research Agency manipulated European and American opinion about Russia's war in Ukraine. In June 2015, when Trump announced his candidacy, the Internet Research Agency was expanded to include an American Department. About ninety new employees went to work on-site in St. Petersburg. The Internet Research Agency also engaged about a hundred American political activists who did not know for whom they were working. The Internet Research Agency worked alongside Russian secret services to move Trump into the Oval Office.

It was clear in 2016 that Russians were excited about these new possibilities. That February, Putin's cyber advisor Andrey Krutskikh boasted: "We are on the verge of having something in the information arena that will allow us to talk to the Americans as equals." In May, an officer of the GRU bragged that his organization was going to take revenge on Hillary Clinton on behalf of Vladimir Putin. In October, a month before the elections, Pervyi Kanal published a long and interesting meditation on the forthcoming collapse of the United States. In June 2017, after Russia's victory, Putin spoke for himself, saying that he had never denied that Russian volunteers had made cyberwar against the United States. This was the precise formulation he had used to describe the Russian invasion of Ukraine: that he had never denied that there were volunteers. Putin was admitting, with a wink, that Russia had defeated the United States in a cyberwar.

American exceptionalism proved to be an enormous American vulnerability. The Russian ground offensive in Ukraine proved to be more difficult than the concurrent cyberwar against Europeans and Americans. Even as Ukraine defended itself, European and American writers conveyed Russian propaganda. Unlike Ukrainians, Americans were unaccustomed to the idea that the internet might be used against them. By 2016, some Americans began to realize that they had been duped about Ukraine by Russian propaganda. But few noticed that the next attack was under way, or anticipated that their country could lose control over reality.

IN A cyberwar, an "attack surface" is the set of points in a computer program that allow hackers access. If the target of a cyberwar is not a computer program but a society, then the attack surface is something broader: software that allows the attacker contact with the mind of the enemy. For Russia in 2015 and 2016, the American attack surface was the entirety of Facebook, Instagram, Twitter, and Google.

In all likelihood, most American voters were exposed to Russian propaganda. It is telling that Facebook shut down 5.8 *million* fake accounts right before the election of November 2016. These had been used to promote political messages. In 2016, about a *million* sites on Facebook were using a tool that allowed them to artificially generate tens of millions of "likes," thereby pushing certain items, often fictions, into the newsfeeds of unwitting Americans. One of the most obvious Russian interventions was the 470 Facebook sites placed by Russia's Internet Research Agency but purported to be those of American political organizations or movements. Six of these had 340 million shares each of content on Facebook, which would suggest that all of them taken together had billions of shares. The Russian campaign also included at least 129 event pages, which reached at least 336,300 people. Right before the election, Russia placed three thousand advertisements on Facebook, and promoted them as memes across at least 180 accounts on Instagram. Russia could do so without including any disclaimers about who had paid for the ads, leaving Americans with the impression that foreign propaganda was an American discussion. As researchers began to calculate the extent of American exposure to Russian propaganda, Facebook deleted more data. This suggests that the Russian campaign was embarrassingly effective. Later, the company told investors that as many as sixty *million* accounts were fake.

Americans were not exposed to Russian propaganda randomly, but in accordance with their own susceptibilities, as revealed by their practices on the internet. People trust what sounds right, and trust permits manipulation. In one variation, people are led towards ever more intense outrage about what they already fear or hate. The theme of Muslim terrorism, which Russia had already exploited in France and Germany, was also developed in the United States. In crucial states such as Michigan and Wisconsin, Russia's ads were targeted at people who could be aroused to vote by anti-Muslim messages. Throughout the United States, likely Trump voters were exposed to pro-Clinton messages on what purported to be American Muslim sites. As in the Lisa F. affair in Germany, Russian pro-Trump propaganda associated refugees with rapists. Trump had done the same when announcing his candidacy.

Russian attackers exploited Twitter's capacity for massive retransmission. Even in normal times on routine subjects, perhaps 10% of Twitter accounts (a conservative estimate) are bots rather than human beings: that is, computer programs of greater or lesser sophistication, designed to spread certain messages to a target audience. Though bots are less numerous than humans on Twitter, they are more efficient than humans in sending messages. In the weeks before the election, bots accounted for about 20% of the American conversation about politics. An important scholarly study published the day before the polls opened warned that bots could "endanger the integrity of the presidential election." It cited three main problems: "first, influence can be redistributed across suspicious accounts that may be operated with malicious purposes; second, the political conversation can be further polarized; third, spreading of misinformation and unverified information can be enhanced." After the election, Twitter identified 2,752 accounts as instruments of Russian political influence. Once Twitter started looking it was able to identify about a million suspicious accounts *per day*.

Bots were initially used for commercial purposes. Twitter has an impressive capacity to influence human behavior by offering deals that seem cheaper or easier than alternatives. Russia took advantage of this. Russian Twitter accounts suppressed the vote by encouraging Americans to "text-to-vote," which is impossible. The practice was so massive that Twitter, which is very reluctant to intervene in discussions over its platform, finally had to admit its existence in a statement. It seems possible that Russia also digitally suppressed the vote in another way: by making voting impossible in crucial places and times. North Carolina, for example, is a state with a very small Democratic majority, where most Democratic voters are in cities. On Election Day, voting machines in cities ceased to function, thereby reducing the number of votes recorded. The company that produced the machines in question had been hacked by Russian military intelligence. Russia also scanned the electoral websites of at least twenty-one American states, perhaps looking for vulnerabilities, perhaps seeking voter data for influence campaigns. According to the Department of Homeland Security, "Russian intelligence obtained and maintained access to elements of multiple U.S. state or local electoral boards."

Having used its Twitter bots to encourage a Leave vote in the Brexit referendum, Russia now turned them loose in the United States. In several hundred cases (at least), the very same bots that worked against the European Union attacked Hillary Clinton. Most of the foreign bot traffic was negative publicity about her. When she fell ill on September 11, 2016, Russian bots massively amplified the scale of the event, creating a trend on Twitter under the hashtag #Hillary Down. Russian trolls and bots also moved to support Trump directly at crucial points. Russian trolls and bots praised Donald Trump and the Republican National Convention over Twitter. When Trump had to debate Clinton, which was a difficult moment for him, Russian trolls and bots filled the ether with claims that he had won or that the debate was somehow rigged against him. In crucial swing states that Trump won, bot activity intensified in the days before the election. On Election Day itself, bots were firing with the hashtag #War AgainstDemocrats. After Trump's victory, at least 1,600 of the same bots that had been working on his behalf went to work against Macron and for Le Pen in France, and against Merkel and for the AfD in Germany. Even at this most basic technical level, the war against the United States was also the war against the European Union.

In the United States in 2016, Russia also penetrated email accounts, and then used proxies on Facebook and Twitter to distribute selections that were deemed useful. The hack began when people were sent an email message that asked them to enter their passwords on a linked website. Hackers then used security credentials to access that person's email account and steal its contents. Someone with knowledge of the American political system then chose what portions of this material the American public should see, and when.

During a presidential election year, each major American political party has its turn at a national convention, with an equal chance to choreograph the choice and presentation of its candidate. Russia denied the Democratic Party this chance in 2016. In March and April, Russia hacked the accounts of people in the Democratic National Committee and the Clinton campaign (and tried to hack Hillary Clinton personally). On July 22, some 22,000 emails were revealed, right before the Democratic National Convention was to be held. The emails that were made public were carefully selected to ensure strife between supporters of Clinton and her rival for the nomination, Bernie Sanders. Their release created division at the moment when the campaign was meant to coalesce.

According to American authorities then and since, this hack was an element of a Russian cyberwar. The Trump campaign, however, supported Russia's effort. Trump publicly requested that Moscow find and release more emails from Hillary Clinton. Trump's son Donald Trump Jr. was in personal communication with WikiLeaks, the proxy that facilitated some of the email dumps. WikiLeaks asked Trump Jr. to have his father publicize one leak—"Hey Donald, great to see your dad talking about our publications. Strongly suggest your dad tweet this link if he mentions us"—which Trump Sr. in fact did, fifteen minutes after the request was made. With his millions of Twitter followers, Trump was among the most important distribution channels of the Russian hacking operation. Trump also aided the Russian endeavor by shielding it from scrutiny, denying repeatedly that Russia was intervening in the campaign.

Leaked emails came to the rescue when Trump faced difficulties. On October 7, Trump seemed to be in trouble when a tape revealed his view that powerful men should sexually assault women. Thirty minutes after that tape was published, Russia released the emails of the chairman of Clinton's campaign, John Podesta, thereby hindering a serious discussion of Trump's history of sexual predation. Russian trolls and bots then went to work, trivializing Trump's advocacy of sexual assault and guiding Twitter users to the leak. Then Russian trolls and bots helped to work the Podesta emails into two fictional stories, one about a pizza pedophile ring and another about Satanic practices. These served to distract Trump's supporters from his own confession of sexual predation and helped them to think and talk about something else.

As in Poland in 2015, so in the United States in 2016: no one considered the totalitarian implications of the selective public release of private communications. Totalitarianism effaces the boundary between the private and public, so that it is normal for us all to be transparent to power all of the time. The information that Russia released concerned real people who were serving important functions in the American democratic process; its release to the public affected their psychological state and political capacity during an election. It mattered that the people who were trying to run the Democratic National Convention were receiving death threats over cell phone numbers that Russia had made public. Since Democratic congressional committees lost control of private data, Democratic candidates for Congress were molested as they ran for office. After their private data was released, American citizens who had given money to the Democratic Party were also exposed to harassment and threats. All of this mattered at the highest level of politics, since it affected one major political party and not the other. More fundamentally, it was a foretaste of what modern totalitarianism is like: no one can act in politics without fear, since anything done now can be revealed later, with personal consequences.

Of course, citizens play their part in creating a totalitarian atmosphere. Those who chose to call and threaten were in the avant-garde of American totalitarianism. Yet the temptation went broader and deeper. Citizens are curious: surely what is hidden is most interesting, and surely the thrill of revelation is liberation. Once all that is taken for granted, the discussion shifts from the public and the known to the secret and the unknown. Rather than trying to make sense of what is around us, we hunger for the next revelation. Public servants, imperfect and flawed to be sure, become personalities whom we think we have the right to know completely. Yet when the difference between the public and the private collapses, democracy is placed under unsustainable pressure. In such a situation, only the shameless politician can survive, one who cannot be exposed. A work of fiction such as "Donald Trump, successful businessman" cannot be shamed because it feels no sense of responsibility for the real world. A work of fiction responds to revelation by demanding more. As a candidate, Trump did just this, calling on Moscow to keep searching and exposing.

If they take as knowledge only what is revealed by foreign hackers, citizens become beholden to hostile powers. In 2016, Americans were dependent upon Russia, without realizing that this was the case. Most Americans followed Vladimir Putin's guidance about reading hacked email: "Is it really important who did this?" he asked. "What is inside the information—that is what is important." But what about all of the open sources from which people are distracted by the thrill of revelation? And what about all the other secrets that are not revealed, because the power in question chooses not to reveal them? The drama of revelation of one thing makes us forget that other things are hidden. Neither the Russians nor their surrogates released any information about the Republicans or the Trump campaign or, for that matter, about themselves. None of the ostensible seekers of truth who released emails over the internet had anything to say about the relationship of the Trump campaign to Russia.

This was a telling omission, since no American presidential campaign was ever so closely bound to a foreign power. The connections were perfectly clear from the open sources. One success of Russia's cyberwar was that the seductiveness of the secret and the trivial drew Americans away from the obvious and the important: that the sovereignty of the United States was under visible attack.

THE OPEN sources revealed extraordinary interactions between Trump's advisors and the Russian Federation. It was no secret that Paul Manafort, who joined the Trump campaign in March 2016 and ran it from June through August, had long and deep connections to eastern Europe. As Trump's campaign manager, Manafort took no salary from a man who claimed to be a billionaire, which was rather unusual. Perhaps he was simply public-spirited. Or perhaps he expected that the real payment would come from other quarters.

Between 2006 and 2009, Manafort had been employed by the Russian oligarch Oleg Deripaska to soften up the United States for Russian political influence. Manafort promised the Kremlin "a model that can greatly benefit the Putin government," and Deripaska reportedly paid him $26 million. After a joint investment project, Manafort found himself in debt some $18.9 million to Deripaska. In 2016, while Manafort was working as Trump's campaign manager, this debt appears to have been of concern to Manafort. He wrote to offer Deripaska "private briefings" on the Trump campaign. He tried to convert his influence into Deripaska's forgiveness, hoping "to get whole." Interestingly, Trump's lawyer Marc Kasowitz also represented Deripaska.

Aside from his history of working for Russia to weaken the United States, Manafort had experience getting Russia's preferred candidates elected president. In 2005, Deripaska recommended Manafort to the Ukrainian oligarch Rinat Akhmetov, who was a backer of Viktor Yanukovych. As an operative in Ukraine between 2005 and 2015, Manafort used the same "Southern strategy" that Republicans had developed in the United States in the 1980s: tell one part of the population that its identity is at risk, and then try to make every election a referendum on culture. In the United States, the target audience was Southern whites; in Ukraine the target audience was speakers of Russian: but the appeal was the same. Manafort managed to get Viktor Yanukovych elected in Ukraine in 2010, though the aftermath was revolution and Russian invasion.

Having brought American tactics to eastern Europe, Manafort now brought east European tactics to the United States. As Trump's campaign manager, he oversaw the import of Russian-style political fiction. It was during Manafort's tenure that Trump told a television audience that Russia would not invade Ukraine—two years after Russia had done so. It was also on Manafort's watch that Trump publicly requested that Russia find and release Hillary Clinton's emails. Manafort had to resign as Trump's campaign manager after it emerged that he had been paid $12.7 million in off-the-books cash by Yanukovych. Right down to the last, Manafort showed the touch of a true Russian political technologist, not so much denying the facts as changing the subject to a spectacular fiction. On the day the story of his cash payments broke, August 14, 2016, Manafort helped Russia to spread an entirely fictional story about an attack by Muslim terrorists on a NATO base in Turkey.

Manafort was replaced as campaign manager by the right-wing ideologue and filmmaker Steve Bannon, whose qualification was that he had brought white supremacists to the mainstream of American discourse. As the director of the Breitbart News Network, Bannon made them household names. America's leading racists, to a man, admired Trump and Putin. Matthew Heimbach, a defender of Russia's invasion of Ukraine, spoke of Putin as the "leader of the anti-globalist forces around the world," and of Russia as "the most powerful ally" of white supremacy and as an "axis for nationalists." Heimbach was such an enthusiast of Trump that he physically re-moved a protestor from a Trump rally in Louisville in March 2016—his legal defense at trial was that he was acting on instructions from Trump. Bannon claimed to be an economic nationalist and thus a champion of the people. Yet he owed his career and his media out-let to one American oligarchical clan, the Mercers; and ran a cam-paign to bring another oligarchical clan, the Trumps, to the Oval Office—in cooperation with a man who had helped open the United States to unlimited campaign contributions in a lawsuit sponsored by yet a third American oligarchical clan, the Kochs.

Bannon's extreme-Right ideology lubricated American oligarchy, much as similar ideas had in the Russian Federation. Bannon was a far less sophisticated and erudite version of Vladislav Surkov. He was intellectually underequipped and easily overmatched. By playing

Russia's game at a low level, he assured that Russia would win. Like Russian ideologues who dismissed factuality as enemy technology, Bannon spoke of journalists as the "opposition party." It was not that he denied the truth of claims made against the Trump campaign. He did not, for example, deny that Donald Trump was a sexual predator. Instead he portrayed the reporters who conveyed the relevant facts as enemies of the nation.

Bannon's films were simplistic and uninteresting in comparison to the literature of Surkov or the philosophy of Ilyin, but the idea was the same: a politics of eternity in which the innocent nation is under regular assault. Like his Russian betters, Bannon rehabilitated forgotten fascists, in his case Julius Evola. Like Surkov, he aimed for confusion and darkness, even if his references were a bit more quotidian: "Darkness is good. Dick Cheney. Darth Vader. Satan. That's power." Bannon believed that "Putin is standing up for traditional institutions." In fact, Russia's ostensible defense of tradition was an attack on the sovereign states of Europe and the sovereignty of the United States of America. The presidential campaign Bannon led was a Russian attack on American sovereignty. Bannon grasped this later: when he learned of a meeting between the top members of the Trump campaign and Russians in Trump Tower in June 2016, he called it "treasonous" and "unpatriotic." In the end, though, Bannon agreed with Putin that the federal government of the United States (and the European Union, which he called "a glorified protectorate") should be destroyed.

Throughout the campaign, regardless of whether Manafort or Bannon was formally in charge, Trump counted on his son-in-law, the real estate developer Jared Kushner. Unlike Manafort, who had a history, and Bannon, who had an ideology, Kushner was linked to Russia only by money and ambition. It is easiest to track those connections by noting his silences. Kushner failed to mention, after his father-in-law's election victory, that his company Cadre held a weighty investment from a Russian whose companies had channeled a billion dollars to Facebook and $191 million to Twitter on behalf of the Russian state. It was also noteworthy that Deutsche Bank, which had laundered billions for Russian oligarchs, and which was the only bank still willing to loan to Kushner's father-in-law, extended to Kushner a loan of $285 million just a few weeks before the presidential election.

After his father-in-law was elected president and after he was given a wide range of responsibilities in the White House, Kushner had to apply for security clearance. In his application, he mentioned no contact with Russian officials. In fact, he had taken part in a June 2016 meeting at Trump Tower, along with Manafort and Donald Trump Jr., in which Moscow offered documents to the Trump campaign as part of (as their intermediary put it) "Russia and the Russian government's support for Trump." The Russian spokeswoman at the meeting, Natalia Veselnitskaya, worked as a lawyer for Aras Agalarov, the man who had brought Trump to Moscow in 2013. Also present at the Trump Tower meeting was Ike Kaveladze, a vice president of Agalarov's company, whose own business involved establishing thousands of anonymous companies in the United States. When knowledge of the Trump campaign's meeting with Russians became public, Trump Sr. dictated to Trump Jr. a misleading press release, claiming that the subject of discussion was adoptions.

In addition to his participation in the Trump Tower meeting with Russians, Kushner had spoken multiple times during the campaign to the Russian ambassador, Sergei Kislyak. On one occasion he smuggled Kislyak into Trump Tower in a freight elevator—for talks about how to set up a secret channel of communication between Trump and Putin.

During the campaign, Trump spoke little about foreign policy, limiting himself to the repeated promise to "get along with Putin" and words of praise for the Russian president. Trump delivered his first foreign policy speech on April 27, almost a year after declaring his candidacy. Manafort chose as Trump's speechwriter the former diplomat Richard Burt, who at the time was under contract to a Russian gas company. In other words, a man who owed money to an important Russian hired a man who was working for Russia to write a speech for Russia's preferred candidate. Burt's firm had been paid $365,000 that same spring for the furtherance of Russian commercial interests. Burt had also been a member of the senior advisory board of Alfa-Bank, whose computer servers made several thousand attempts to establish contact with computers in Trump Tower.

As soon as Trump named foreign policy advisors, they fell immediately into conversations with Russians or Russian intermediaries about how Russia could harm Clinton and help Trump. A few days after learning that he would be serving Trump as a foreign policy advisor in March 2016, George Papadopoulos began conversations with people who presented themselves as agents of the Russian government. On April 26, right after Russian military intelligence hacked the email accounts of Democratic politicians and activists, Papadopoulos was offered emails and "dirt" about Hillary Clinton by his Russian contact. He had just been at work editing Trump's first foreign policy speech, which he discussed with his Russian contacts. They were very impressed, and praised him. Shortly after that exchange, Papadopoulos met Trump and other advisors.

One evening in May, while drinking at a London bar, Papadopoulos told an Australian diplomat that Russia had "dirt" on Clinton. The Australians told the FBI, which began an investigation of the Trump campaign's connections with Russia. For his part, Papadopoulos continued his exchanges with his contacts, who urged him forward. "We are all very excited," his female contact wrote him, "about the possibility of a good relationship with Mr. Trump." Arrested by the FBI, he confessed to lying to American authorities about these interactions.

A second Trump advisor on foreign policy, Carter Page, had once briefly worked for an American firm whose director remembered him as pro-Putin and "wackadoodle." Page then set up shop in a building connected to Trump Tower, and met with Russian spies. In 2013, he supplied Russian spies with documents about the energy industry. Page became a lobbyist for Russian gas companies; while working for the Trump campaign he promised his Russian clients that a Trump presidency would serve their interests. At the moment when he was named an advisor to Trump, he owned shares in Gazprom.

Page traveled as a representative of the Trump campaign to Russia in July 2016, right before the Republican National Convention where Trump was to become the Republican nominee for the office of president of the United States. By his own account, Page was speaking to "senior members" of the Putin administration, one of whom "expressed strong support for Mr. Trump." Page returned to the United States and altered the Republican platform in a way that fulfilled Moscow's desires. At the Republican National Convention, Page and another Trump advisor, J. D. Gordon, substantially weakened the section of the platform about the need for a response to the Russian invasion of Ukraine. Page spoke to the Russian ambassador at the Republican National Convention, and then again shortly thereafter.

A third foreign policy advisor was the retired general Michael Flynn. Although Flynn had been the head of the Defense Intelligence Agency and was under consideration for national security advisor, he illegally took money from foreign governments without reporting that he had done so, while tweeting hither and thither various conspiracy theories. Flynn spread the idea that Hillary Clinton was a sponsor of pedophilia. He was also taken in by the story, enthusiastically spread by Russia, that Democratic leaders took part in Satanic rituals. He used his own Twitter account to spread that story, and thus, like a number of other American conspiracy theorists, became a participant in Russian active measures directed against the United States.

In the fog of mental confusion that surrounded Flynn, it was easy to overlook his peculiar connections to Russia. Flynn was permitted to see the headquarters of Russian military intelligence, which he visited in 2013. When invited to a seminar on intelligence at Cambridge in 2014, he befriended a Russian woman, signing his emails to her "General Misha"—a Russian diminutive meaning "Mike." In summer 2015, he worked to promote a plan to build nuclear power plants across the Middle East with Russian cooperation, and then failed to disclose that he had done so. Flynn was a guest on RT, where he gave the impression of being outwitted by the hosts. In 2015, he appeared in Moscow as a paid guest ($33,750) to celebrate the tenth anniversary of the founding of RT. He sat with Vladimir Putin at the gala dinner. When the American media began to report that Russia had hacked the emails of Democratic activists, Flynn responded by retweeting a message that suggested a Jewish conspiracy was behind that claim of Russian responsibility. On Flynn's Twitter feed his followers read: "Not anymore, Jews. Not anymore." Flynn followed and retweeted no fewer than five fake Russian accounts, pushed at least sixteen Russian memes through the internet, and was sharing Russian content with his followers right down to the day before the election.

On December 29, 2016, weeks after Trump had won the election but weeks before his inauguration, Flynn spoke to the Russian ambassador and then lied to others, including the FBI, about what he was doing. His assignment at the time was to make sure that new sanctions imposed on Russia—as a response to Russia's interference in the presidential election—were not taken seriously by Moscow. As Flynn's aide K. T. McFarland wrote: "If there is a tit-for-tat escalation Trump will have difficulty improving relations with Russia, which has just thrown U.S.A. election to him." There seems to have been little doubt among Trump's advisors that he owed his victory to Putin. After Flynn's phone call with Kislyak, Russia announced that it would not react to the new sanctions.

Barack Obama personally warned Trump not to name Flynn to a position of authority. Trump named him national security advisor, perhaps the most sensitive position in the entire federal government. Acting Attorney General Sally Yates warned senior officials on January 26 that Flynn's lying made him vulnerable to Russian blackmail. Four days later, Trump fired her. Konstantin Kosachev, the chairman of the international affairs committee of the Russian Duma, characterized the revelation of factual information about Flynn as an attack on Russia. Flynn resigned in February 2017, and later pled guilty of lying to federal investigators.

In addition to Flynn, Trump filled his cabinet with people who had startlingly intimate connections to a foreign power. Jeff Sessions, an Alabama senator who was quick to endorse Trump, had multiple contacts with the Russian ambassador in 2016. Sessions lied about this to Congress during his confirmation hearings for the office of attorney general, thereby perjuring himself in order to become the highest law enforcement official in the land.

Trump's secretary of commerce had financial dealings with Russian oligarchs, and indeed with Putin's family. In 2014, Wilbur Ross became the vice chairman of, and a leading investor in, the Bank of Cyprus, an offshore haven for Russian oligarchs. He took the position at a time when Russians who sought to avoid sanctions were transferring assets to such places. He worked alongside Vladimir Strzhalkovsky, who had been a colleague of Putin in the KGB. One major investor in the bank was Viktor Vekselberg, a major Russian oligarch trusted by Putin. It was Vekselberg who had financed the reburial of Ivan Ilyin's remains back in 2005.

Once named secretary of commerce, Ross resigned from his position at the Bank of Cyprus, but retained an undisclosed personal connection to Russian kleptocracy. He was part owner of a shipping company, Navigator Holdings, that transported Russian natural gas for a Russian company known as Sibur. One of Sibur's owners was Gennady Timchenko, Putin's judo partner and close friend. Another was Kirill Shamalov, Putin's son-in-law. Ross was in contact with the very center of Russia's oligarchy, the family. As an American cabinet minister, he was in a position to make money by pleasing Russia. Since American sanctions included a ban on transfers of technology that would help in the extraction of natural gas, Ross was in a position to profit personally from the lifting of sanctions.

The United States had never before had a secretary of state personally decorated with the Order of Friendship by Vladimir Putin. Rex Tillerson was such a person. In office, Tillerson oversaw a vast purge of American diplomats, a group whom Putin regarded as the enemy. In throwing the Department of State into chaos, Tillerson substantially reduced the American capacity to project either power or values. Regardless of the particulars of daily events, this was an unambiguous victory for Russia.

The weakening of American diplomacy was of a piece with Trump's general foreign policy orientation, which was to seek personal flattery while neglecting negotiations. This made him an easy mark. As early as August 2016, three months before the election, he had convinced a former acting director of the CIA that "Mr. Putin has recruited Mr. Trump as an unwitting agent of the Russian Federation." After a year in office, only the "unwitting" part seemed questionable. By then, Trump had convinced a number of leading American intelligence specialists that he was a Russian asset. As one of them put it: "My assessment is that Trump is actually working directly for the Russians." A group of three intelligence specialists summarized: "If the Trump campaign received offers of assistance from Russia, and they did nothing to discourage that help (or even encouraged it), they are indebted to a foreign adversary whose national interests are opposed to those of the United States. You can be sure that at some point, Putin will come to collect, if he has not done so already—and when it comes to protecting our democracy the administration will be a puppet of a foreign adversary, not our country's first line of defense." The Trump administration made a mockery of congressional sanctions against Russia, declining to implement legislation and inviting the sanctioned director of a Russian intelligence agency to the United States.

Trump himself repeatedly characterized all accounts of any connections between his campaign and Russia as a "hoax." The word was well chosen, so long as it was applied to the person who was using it. As president, the hoax had to protect itself from reality. And thus Trump fired U.S. Attorney Preet Bharara, who had ordered the raid on Trump Tower in 2013. He fired Acting Attorney General Sally Yates, who had cautioned him against hiring Michael Flynn. And then he fired James Comey, director of the Federal Bureau of Investigation, for investigating Russia's attack on American sovereignty.

The FBI had been investigating Carter Page as a target of Russian espionage before Page became an advisor to Trump; the FBI began investigating George Papadopoulos because he told a foreign diplomat that Russia was carrying out an influence operation against Hillary Clinton. It could not be said, however, that the FBI had treated Russian interference as a very high priority. Although American intelligence had been warned in late 2015 by allies that members of the Trump campaign were in touch with Russian intelligence, American agencies were slow to react. Even after Russia hacked the Democratic National Committee in spring 2016, the FBI did not communicate that information as if it were urgent or timely. Eight days before the November presidential election, Comey had raised the subject of Clinton's use of a private email server in a context that was bound to hurt her candidacy—the discovery of copies of some of these emails during an investigation of the husband of one of her aides, under investigation for improper sexual contact with a teenaged girl. Comey concluded two days before the election that the emails were of no significance, but by then the damage was done. The episode seemed to help Trump.

Even so, the FBI did continue its investigations of connections between the Trump campaign and Russian intelligence. In January 2017, Trump asked Comey, privately, for "loyalty." In February, Trump specifically asked Comey not to investigate Flynn: "I hope you can see your way clear to letting this go, to letting Flynn go." Not receiving such assurances, Trump fired Comey on May 9, 2017. This was Trump's confession that his own candidacy was a hoax. Trump told the press that he fired Comey in order to halt the investigation of Russia. The day after firing Comey, Trump said the same thing to a pair of visitors to the Oval Office: "I faced great pressure because of Russia. Now that's taken off." The visitors were the Russian ambassador to the United States and the Russian foreign minister. They brought digital gear to the White House, which they used to take and distribute photographs of the meeting. Former U.S. intelligence officers found this unusual. More unusual still was that Trump used the occasion to share with Russia intelligence of the highest level of confidentiality, involving an Israeli double agent inside ISIS.

In the aftermath of the Comey firing, Moscow rushed to Trump's support. Pervyi Kanal claimed that "James Comey was a puppet of Barack Obama." Putin assured the world that the president of the United States "acted within the framework of his competencies, constitution, and laws." Not everyone agreed. After Comey's firing, Robert Mueller was appointed special counsel to continue the investigations. Trump ordered that Mueller be fired in June 2017. His own lawyer, known as the White House counsel, refused to carry out the order, threatening to resign instead. Trump then lied about his attempts to halt the investigations and sought new ways to disrupt and undermine American law and order.

RUSSIA ENABLED and sustained the fiction of "Donald Trump, successful businessman," and delivered that fiction to Americans as the payload of a cyberweapon. The Russian effort succeeded because the United States is much more like the Russian Federation than Americans would like to think. Because Russian leaders had already made the shift from the politics of inevitability to the politics of eternity, they had instincts and techniques that, as it turned out, corresponded to emerging tendencies in American society. Moscow was not trying to project some ideal of their own, only to use a giant lie to bring out the worst in the United States.

In important respects, American media had become like Russian media, and this made Americans vulnerable to Russian tactics. The experience of Russia shows what happens to politics when news loses its moorings. Russia lacks local and regional journalism. Little in Russian media concerns the experiences of Russian citizens. Russian television directs the distrust that this generates against others beyond Russia. In the weakness of its local press, America came to resemble Russia. The United States once boasted an impressive network of regional newspapers. After the financial crisis of 2008, the American local press, already weakening, was allowed to collapse. Every day in 2009, about seventy people lost their jobs at American newspapers and magazines. For Americans who lived between the coasts, this meant the end of reporting about life and the rise of something else: "the media." Where there are local reporters, journalism concerns events that people see and care about. When local reporters disappear, the news becomes abstract. It becomes a kind of entertainment rather than a report about the familiar.

It was an American and not a Russian innovation to present the news as national entertainment, which made the news vulnerable to an entertainer. Trump got his chance in the second half of 2015 because American television networks were pleased with the spectacle he provided. The chief executive officer of a television network said that the Trump campaign "may not be good for America, but it's damn good for CBS." In providing plentiful free airtime for Trump, American networks granted the fictional character "Donald Trump, successful businessman" a far broader viewership. Neither Trump nor his Russian backers spent very much money during the campaign. Television did the advertising for them free of charge. Even the Twitter accounts of MSNBC, CNN, CBS, and NBC mentioned Trump twice as often as they mentioned Clinton.

Unlike Russians, Americans tend to get their news from the internet. According to one survey, 44% of Americans get their news from a single internet platform: Facebook. The interactivity of the internet creates an impression of mental effort while impeding reflection. The internet is an attention economy, which means that profit-seeking platforms are designed to divide the attention of their users into the smallest possible units that can be exploited by advertising messages. If news is to appear on such platforms, it must be tailored to fit a brief attention span and arouse the hunger for reinforcement. News that draws viewers tends to wear a neural path between prejudice and outrage. When each day is devoted to emotional venting about supposed enemies, the present becomes endless, eternal. In these conditions, a fictional candidate enjoyed a considerable advantage.

Though internet platforms became major American news providers, they were not regulated as such in the United States. Two Facebook products, News Feed and Trending Topics, purveyed countless fictions. The people who were in charge of Facebook and Twitter took the complacent position offered by the American politics of inevitability: the free market would lead to truth, so nothing should be done. This attitude created a problem for the numerous American users of the internet, who, having lost access to local press (or preferring news that seems free of charge), read the internet as though it were a newspaper. In this way, the American internet became an attack surface for the Russian secret services, who were able to do what they liked inside the American psychosphere for eighteen months without anyone reacting. Much of what Russia did was to take advantage of what it found. Hyperpartisan stories on Fox News or outbursts on Breitbart gained viewership thanks to retransmission by Russian bots. Russian support helped fringe right-wing sites such as Next News Network gain notoriety and influence. Its videos were viewed about 56 million times in October 2016.

The "pizzagate" and "spirit cooking" fictions show how Russian intervention and American conspiratology worked together. Both fictions began with the Russian hack of the emails of John Podesta, the chairman of Clinton's campaign. Some Americans wished to believe that what is private must be mysterious, and they were coaxed along by Russia. Podesta was in touch with the owner of a pizza restaurant—itself no great revelation. Trolls and bots, some of them Russian, began to spread the fiction that the pizzeria's menu was a code for ordering children for sex, and that Clinton ran a pedophilia ring from its basement. InfoWars, a leading American conspiracy site, also spread the story. This fiction ended with a real American shooting a real gun in a real restaurant. The popular right-wing internet activist Jack Posobiec, who had himself spread the Pizzagate lie on Twitter, claimed that the American who fired the shots was an actor paid to discredit the truth. Podesta was also in touch with someone who invited him to a dinner party that he did not attend. The hostess of the dinner party was an artist who had once titled a painting *Spirit Cooking;* Russian trolls and bots spread the story that the dinner party was a Satanic ritual involving the consumption of human bodily fluids. This idea was then passed on by American conspiracy theorists, such as Sean Hannity of Fox News and the Drudge Report.

Russian platforms served content to American conspiracy sites with enormous viewership. For example, in an email hacked and stolen by Russia, Hillary Clinton wrote a few words about "decision fatigue." This term describes the increasing difficulty of making decisions as the day goes on. Decision fatigue is an observation of psychologists about the workplace, not an illness. Once it was stolen by Russia, the email was released by WikiLeaks, and then promoted by the Russian propaganda sender Sputnik as evidence that Clinton was suffering from a debilitating disease. In this form, the story was picked up by InfoWars.

Russians exploited American gullibility. Anyone who paid attention to the Facebook page for a (nonexistent) group called Heart of Texas should have noticed that its authors were not native speakers of English. Its cause, Texas secession, perfectly expressed the Russian policy of advocating separatism in all countries except Russia itself (the South from the U.S., California from the U.S., Scotland from the United Kingdom, Catalonia from Spain, Crimea from Ukraine, the Donbas from Ukraine, every member state from the EU, etc.). The partisanship of Heart of Texas was extremely vulgar: like other Russian sites, it referred to the Democratic presidential candidate as "Killary." Despite all this, the Heart of Texas Facebook page had more followers in 2016 than those of the Texas Republican Party or the Texas Democratic Party—or indeed both of them combined. Everyone who liked, followed, and supported Heart of Texas was taking part in a Russian intervention in American politics designed to destroy the United States of America. Americans liked the site because it affirmed their own prejudices and pushed them just a bit further. It offered both the thrill of transgression and a sense of legitimacy.

Americans trusted Russians and robots who told them what they wanted to hear. When Russia set up a fake Twitter site that purported to be that of the Tennessee Republican Party, Americans were drawn by its edgy presentation and abundant fictions. It spread the lie that Obama was born in Africa, for example, as well as the spirit-cooking fantasy. The Russian version of the Tennessee Republican Party had ten times more Twitter followers than the actual Tennessee Republican Party. One of them was Michael Flynn, who retweeted its content in the days before the election. In other words, Trump's candidate for national security advisor was serving as a conduit for a Russian influence operation in the United States. Kellyanne Conway, Trump's press spokesperson, also retweeted fake Russian content from the same source. She thus assisted the Russian intervention in an American election—even as her campaign denied that there was such a thing. (She also tweeted "love you back" to white supremacists.) Jack Posobiec was a follower and retweeter of the same fake Russian site. He filmed a video of himself claiming that there was no Russian intervention in American politics. When the Russian site was finally taken down, after eleven months, he expressed confusion. He did not *see* the Russian intervention, since he *was* the Russian intervention.

In 1976, Stephen King published a short story, "I Know What You Need," about the courting of a young woman. Her suitor was a young man who could read her mind but did not tell her so. He simply appeared with what she wanted at the moment, beginning with strawberry ice cream for a study break. Step by step he changed her life, making her dependent upon him by giving her what she thought she wanted at a certain moment, before she herself had a chance to reflect. Her best friend realized that something disconcerting was happening, investigated, and learned the truth: "That is not love," she warned. "That's rape." The internet is a bit like this. It knows much about us, but interacts with us without revealing that this is so. It makes us unfree by arousing our worst tribal impulses and placing them at the service of unseen others.

Neither Russia nor the internet is going away. It would help the cause of democracy if citizens knew more about Russian policy, and if the concepts of "news," "journalism," and "reporting" could be preserved on the internet. In the end, though, freedom depends upon citizens who are able to make a distinction between what is true and what they want to hear. Authoritarianism arrives not because people say that they want it, but because they lose the ability to distinguish between facts and desires.

DEMOCRACIES DIE when people cease to believe that voting matters. The question is not whether elections are held, but whether they are free and fair. If so, democracy produces a sense of time, an expectation of the future that calms the present. The meaning of each democratic election is promise of the next one. If we anticipate that another meaningful election will take place, we know that the next time around we can correct our mistakes, which in the meantime we blame upon the people whom we elect. In this way, democracy transforms human fallibility into political predictability, and helps us to experience time as movement forward into a future over which we have some influence. If we come to believe that elections are simply a repetitive ritual of support, democracy loses its meaning.

The essence of Russia's foreign policy is strategic relativism: Russia cannot become stronger, so it must make others weaker. The simplest way to make others weaker is to make them more like Russia. Rather than addressing its problems, Russia exports them; and one of its basic problems is the absence of a succession principle. Russia opposes European and American democracy to ensure that Russians do not see that democracy might work as a succession principle in their own country. Russians are meant to distrust other systems as much as they distrust their own. If Russia's succession crisis can in fact be exported—if the United States could become authoritarian—then Russia's own problems, although unresolved, would at least seem normal. Pressure on Putin would be relieved. Were America the shining beacon of democracy that its citizens sometimes imagine, its institutions would have been far less vulnerable to Russia's cyberwar. From Moscow's perspective, America's constitutional structure created tempting vulnerabilities. Because of the evident flaws in American democracy and the American rule of law, it was all the easier to intervene in an American election.

The rule of law requires that the government control violence, and that the population expects that government can do so. The presence of guns in American society, which can feel like strength to some Americans, appeared in Moscow as a national weakness. In 2016, Russia appealed directly to Americans to buy and use guns, amplifying the rhetoric of the Trump campaign. Trump called for his supporters to exercise their Second Amendment rights against Hillary Clinton were she elected, which was an indirect but transparent suggestion that they should shoot her to death. The Russian cyber campaign was enthusiastic about the right of Americans to bear arms, celebrating the Second Amendment and calling upon Americans to fear terrorism and to buy firearms to protect themselves.

Meanwhile, Russian authorities were cooperating with the American gun lobby in the real world. A Russian group called Right to Bear Arms cultivated ties with the National Rifle Association (NRA). Its purpose was to influence events within the United States: as its members knew perfectly well, Russians will never have the right to bear arms under the present regime. Two prominent members of Russia's Right to Bear Arms, Maria Butina and Alexander Torshin, were also members of the American NRA. Butina was a student in an American university who cofounded a company with an American working closely with the NRA leadership. Torshin was a Russian central banker wanted in Spain on charges of criminal money laundering. In December 2015, representatives of the NRA visited Moscow, where they met Dmitry Rogozin, a radical nationalist and a deputy prime minister who was under U.S. sanctions.

In February 2016, Butina reported to Torshin from the United States that "Trump (NRA member) really is for cooperation with Russia." Torshin met with Donald Trump Jr. in Kentucky that May. That same month, the NRA endorsed Trump, and eventually gave some $30 million to his campaign. Its official attitude to Russia meanwhile underwent an interesting transformation. Through 2015, the NRA had complained that American policy regarding Russia was too weak. Once the NRA's involvement with Russia began, it said the opposite. Russia's support of the NRA resembled its support of right-wing paramilitaries in Hungary, Slovakia, and the Czech Republic. Once Trump was in office, the NRA took a very aggressive tone, proclaiming in a video that "we're coming for" the *New York Times*. Given that the NRA endorsed and funded Trump, that it was a gun organization, and that Trump called the press an "enemy," it was hard to interpret this as anything other than a threat. Democracy depends upon the free exchange of ideas, where "free" means "without the threat of violence." An important sign of the collapse of the rule of law is the rise of a paramilitary and its merger with government power.

In 2016, the most obvious weakness in American democracy was the disconnect between voting and results. In most democracies, it would be unthinkable that a candidate who received millions more votes than her rival would lose. This sort of thing happens on a regular basis in American presidential elections, thanks to the indirect and approximate electoral system known as the electoral college. The American electoral college accords victory by tallying the electoral votes of states rather than by the number of individual votes. States are allocated electoral votes not by population but according to the number of federal elected representatives. Since all states have two senators, less populous states have a disproportionate number of electoral votes; individual votes in small states count for far more than individual votes in large states. Meanwhile, millions of Americans in territories (as opposed to states) have no vote at all. Puerto Rico has more inhabitants than twenty-one of the fifty American states, but its American citizens have no influence on presidential elections.

American states with small populations are also vastly overrepresented in the Senate, the upper house of the American legislature. The population of the largest state is about eighty times the population of the smallest state, but each has two senators. The lower house of the American legislature, the House of Representatives, is elected according to districts that are often drawn to help one party or another. In interwar Yugoslavia, electoral precincts that were drawn to favor the largest ethnicity were known as "water districts." In the United States, the process is known as "gerrymandering." As a result of gerrymandering, Democratic voters in Ohio or North Carolina in effect have, respectively, about one-half or one-third as much ability to elect a representative in Congress as do Republican voters. Citizens did not have an equal vote.

From an American point of view, all of this might appear to be mundane tradition, just the rules of the game. From Moscow's perspective, the system looks like vulnerability to be exploited. When a minority president and a minority party control the executive and legislative branches of government, they can be tempted into a politics where victory depends not upon policy that pleases majorities but upon further limitation of the franchise. A foreign government that can make the system slightly less representative increases that very temptation, tilting the system towards authoritarianism. Russia's intervention in the 2016 U.S. election was not just an attempt to get a certain person elected. It was also the application of pressure to the structure. The victory of a Russian-backed candidate could be less important, in the long run, than the evolution of the system as a whole away from democracy.

When Russia acted against American democracy, the American system was already becoming less democratic. In the early 2010s, as a new system was consolidated in Russia, the U.S. Supreme Court took two important decisions that shifted the United States towards authoritarianism. In 2010, it ruled that money talked: that corporations were individuals, and their campaign spending was free speech protected by the First Amendment to the United States Constitution. This granted real companies, front companies, and various fake civic entities the right to influence campaigns and, in effect, to try to buy elections. It also prepared the way for Trump to claim, as he did, that in an American oligarchy Americans could only be safe if they elected their own oligarch: himself. In fact, Trump was a creature of Russian cyberwar who never demonstrated that he had any money. But his argument from oligarchy was plausible in a political atmosphere where American voters came to believe that money counted for more than their own preferences.

In 2013, the Supreme Court found that racism was no longer a problem in the United States, and issued a ruling whose consequences proved the falseness of that premise. The Voting Rights Act of 1965 had required states with a history of suppressing the votes of African Americans to clear changes in their voting laws with the courts. Once the Supreme Court ruled that this was no longer necessary, American states immediately suppressed the vote of African Americans (and others). Throughout the American South, polling stations disappeared, often without warning, right before elections. Twenty-two American states passed laws designed to suppress the voting of African Americans and Hispanics—laws that materially affected the 2016 presidential election.

In the election of 2016, in the state of Ohio, some 144,000 fewer people voted in counties with large cities than four years before. In 2016 in Florida, some 23% of African Americans were denied the vote as convicted felons. Felonies in Florida include releasing a helium balloon and harvesting lobsters with short tails. In 2016 in Wisconsin, some sixty thousand fewer people voted than in the previous presidential election. Most of the attrition was in the city of Milwaukee, home to most of the state's African Americans. Barack Obama had won Florida, Ohio, and Wisconsin in 2012. Trump won all three states by narrow margins in 2016, Wisconsin by only 23,000 votes.

American race relations presented Russian cyberwarriors with an obvious target. Russia ran a site arousing the emotions of friends and families of policemen who were killed in the line of duty; a site exploiting the emotions of friends and families of African Americans killed by police; a site portraying blacks brandishing weapons; a site encouraging blacks to prepare themselves for attacks by whites; a site where fake black activists used a slogan of white supremacists; and a site where fake black rappers referred to the Clintons as serial killers. Russians seized on Native American protests against a pipeline that crossed a burial ground. Although the posts in that campaign were sometimes obviously not native (the promotion of Russian vodka by Indian activists, for example, was inconceivable), the sites gained followers.

Barack Obama's race was important in Russian popular culture. In 2013, a deputy of the Russian parliament shared a doctored photograph on social media that portrayed Barack and Michelle Obama staring longingly at a banana. On Barack Obama's birthday in 2014, Russian students in Moscow projected a laser light show on the U.S. embassy building, portraying him performing fellatio on a banana. In 2015, a grocery store chain sold a cutting board featuring two parent chimpanzees with Obama's face inserted for the face of a baby chimpanzee. In 2016, a car wash chain promised to "wash away all the blackness," making its meaning clear with a picture of a frightened-looking Obama. The year 2016 was by Chinese reckoning the year of the monkey; Russians commonly used the term to mean Obama's last year in office. The popular news outlet LifeNews, for example, titled a feature article "Slamming the Door on the Year of the Monkey," with a photograph of the American president to remove any doubt as to what was meant.

Race was on the Russian mind in 2016. Russian leaders had occasion that year to observe as race opened a tremendous gap between the executive and legislative branches of the American government. In February, one of the nine supreme court justices died. The Republican majority leader of the Senate, Mitch McConnell, made clear that the Senate would not consider any nominee of Barack Obama. This broke one of the most important conventions of the federal government of the United States, and was commented upon in Moscow. The Russian press quite rightly noted the "paradoxical situation" of a president unable to exercise his normal rights. It did not escape the attention of the Kremlin that the Republican leaders of Congress declared, almost a year early, that Barack Obama no longer enjoyed the usual prerogatives of the president of the United States. At that moment, Russia began its email hack of Democratic politicians and activists.

In June 2016, Paul Ryan, the Republican speaker of the House of Representatives, was discussing Russia with his fellow Republican congressmen. Republican majority leader Kevin McCarthy expressed the belief that Donald Trump was paid by Russia. Ryan reacted by asking that such suspicions be kept "in the family": an embarrassment within the party was more important than the violation of the sovereignty of the country. The possibility that a Republican candidate for president (who was not yet the party's nominee) was the creation of a foreign power was less worrisome than an awkward press conference at which Republicans would tell citizens what they suspected themselves. This level of partisanship, where the enemy is the opposing party and the outside world is neglected, creates a vulnerability easily exploited by hostile actors in that outside world. The next month, Russia began to release the hacked emails of Democratic politicians and activists. If Moscow's calculation was that Republican leaders would not immediately defend their Democratic colleagues from foreign cyberattack, that was correct.

As Republicans realized that Russia was attacking the United States, the fury of partisanship became the desperation of denial and then the complicity of inaction. That September, McConnell listened to the heads of American intelligence agencies report on the Russian cyberwar, but expressed his doubts as to their veracity. It is unknown what the heads of intelligence said, but it is unlikely to be very different from their later public statement: "We assess Russian President Vladimir Putin ordered an influence campaign aimed at the US presidential election. Russia's goals were to undermine public faith in the US democratic process, denigrate Secretary Clinton, and harm her electability and potential presidency." McConnell let it be known that Republicans would treat the defense of the United States from Russian cyberwar as an effort to help Hillary Clinton. At that point, Russia had been at work in the United States for more than a year. After McConnell categorized the Russian attack as partisan politics, its scope expanded. A massive Russian bot offensive began right then.

At the crucial moment, it was unclear who had more influence over the Republican Party: its human leaders or Russian robots. When indisputable evidence appeared that Trump considered it appropriate to sexually abuse women, McConnell asked him to apologize. But Russian bots and trolls went immediately to work to defend Trump from the charges, and to direct Americans to a disclosure of emails engineered to change the subject. Moscow was attacking, and Congress declined to defend the country. The Obama administration might have acted on its own, but was afraid to deepen partisan divisions. "I feel like we sort of choked," as one of its officials put it. Russia won, which is to say that Trump won. Later, Trump named McConnell's wife, Elaine Chao, to his cabinet as secretary of transportation.

To be sure, a number of Republicans had portrayed Russia as a national security threat to the United States. Back in 2012, the Republican candidate for president, Mitt Romney, had been virtually alone in both parties in portraying Russia as a serious problem. While competing for the 2016 Republican nomination, Ohio governor John Kasich, who was knowledgeable about east European politics, was quick to associate Trump with Putin. Another Republican rival for the 2016 nomination, the Florida senator Marco Rubio, claimed that the weakness of Obama's foreign policy encouraged Russian aggression.

Senator Rubio's accusation, which was plausible enough, disguised a more profound problem. Though Obama's response to the 2014 Russian invasion of Ukraine was indeed very cautious, in 2016 Obama did at least recognize that Russian intervention in a U.S. election was a problem for the country as a whole. Even as Kasich and Rubio took a stand on Russian foreign policy, the crucial Republican legislators surrendered in advance to Russian cyberattack. It was more important to humiliate a black president than it was to defend the independence of the United States of America.

That is how wars are lost.

**THE ROAD** to unfreedom is the passage from the politics of inevitability to the politics of eternity. Americans were vulnerable to the politics of eternity because their own experiences had already weakened inevitability. Trump's proposal to "make America great again" resonated with people who believed, along with him, that the American dream was dead. Russia had reached the politics of eternity first, and so Russians knew the techniques that would push Americans in the same direction.

It is easy to see the appeal of eternity to wealthy and corrupt men in control of a lawless state. They cannot offer social advance to their population, and so must find some other form of motion in politics. Rather than discuss reforms, eternity politicians designate threats. Rather than presenting a future with possibilities and hopes, they offer an eternal present with defined enemies and artificial crises. For this to work, citizens have to meet eternity politicians halfway. Demoralized by their inability to change their station in life, they must accept that the meaning of politics lies not in institutional reform but in daily emotion. They must stop thinking about a better future for themselves, their friends, and their families, and prefer the constant invocation of a proud past. At the top and throughout society, material inequality creates the experiences and the sentiments that can be transformed into a politics of eternity. When Ilyin was portrayed as the heroic opponent of the Russian Revolution on Russian television in 2017, it was with the message that the promise of social advancement for the Russian people was a "Satanic deception."

In 2016, Russia was described by Credit Suisse as the most unequal country in the world, as measured by distribution of wealth. Since the end of the Soviet Union, only Russians who have managed to reach the top 10% of annual earners have made any meaningful gains. Russian oligarchy emerged in the 1990s, but was consolidated as the kleptocratic control of the state by a single oligarchical clan under Putin in the 2000s. According to Credit Suisse, in 2016 the top decile of the Russian population owned 89% of the total household wealth. In the report, the United States had a comparable figure: 76%, and rising. Typically, billionaires control 1–2% of national wealth; in Russia, roughly one hundred billionaires owned about a third of the country. At the very top of Russia's grotesque upside-down wealth pyramid were Vladimir Putin and his personal friends. Most often they gained wealth from Russia's sale of natural gas and oil, without any effort on their part. One of Putin's friends, a cellist, became a billionaire for no reason that he could provide. The appeal of the politics of eternity to such men is all too understandable. Far better to shackle a nation and rattle the world than to risk the loss of so much.

The case of the billionaire cellist, like so much else about oligarchy, came to light thanks to the work of investigative reporters. In the 2010s, some of the best of them, in revealing projects such as the Panama Papers and the Paradise Papers, showed how unregulated international capitalism was creating sinkholes for national wealth. Tyrants first hide and launder their money, then use it to enforce authoritarianism at home—or export it abroad. Money gravitates towards where it cannot be seen, which in the 2010s was in various offshore tax havens. This was a global problem: estimates of just how much money was parked offshore, beyond the reach of national tax authorities, ranged from $7 trillion to $21 trillion. The United States was an especially permissive environment for Russians who wished to steal and then launder money. Much of the Russian national wealth that was supposed to be building the Russian state in the 2000s and 2010s found its way to shell corporations in offshore havens. Many of these were in America.

In June 2016, Jared Kushner, Donald Trump Jr., and Paul Manafort met with Russians in Trump Tower to consider Russian offers to hurt the Clinton campaign. One of the intermediaries was Ike Kaveladze, who worked for Aras Agalarov, the Russian real estate developer who had organized the Miss Universe pageant for Trump in 2013. Kaveladze set up anonymous companies in Delaware (at least two thousand). This was legal, since the state of Delaware, like the states of Nevada and Wyoming, permitted the foundation of companies by ghosts. In Delaware, 285,000 distinct entities were registered at a single physical address.

Russians used shell companies to purchase American real estate, often anonymously. In the 1990s, Trump Tower was one of only two buildings in New York City to allow anonymous purchases of apartment units, an opportunity that the Russian mob quickly exploited. Wherever anonymous real estate purchases were allowed, Russians bought and sold apartments, often hiding behind shell companies, as a way to transform dirty rubles into clean dollars. These practices impoverished Russian society and consolidated the Russian oligarchy during the Putin years—and allowed Donald Trump to claim to be a "a VERY successful businessman." In this particular way, the American politics of inevitability, the idea that unregulated capitalism could only bring democracy, supported the Russian politics of eternity, the certainty that democracy was a sham.

**THE AMERICAN** politics of inevitability also prepared the way for the American politics of eternity more directly: by generating and legitimizing vast economic inequality at home. If there was no alternative to capitalism, then perhaps yawning gaps in wealth and income should be ignored, explained away, or even welcomed? If more capitalism meant more democracy, why worry? These mantras of inevitability provided the cover for the policies that made America more unequal, and inequality more painful.

In the 1980s, the federal government weakened the position of trade unions. The percentage of Americans in unionized jobs fell from about a quarter to under 10%. Private sector union membership fell still more sharply, from about 34% to 8% for men and from about 16% to 6% for women. The productivity of the American workforce grew throughout the period, at about 2% a year, but the wages of traditional workers increased more slowly, if at all. Over the same period, the pay of executives increased, sometimes drastically. At the same time, the United States was very weak on the basic policies that stabilized middle classes elsewhere: retirement pensions, public education, public transport, health care, paid vacation, and parental leave.

The United States had the resources to give its workers and its citizens these basics. Yet a regressive trend in taxation policy made this more difficult. Whereas workers paid an increasing tax burden through payroll taxes, corporations and wealthy families saw theirs drop by half or more. Even as the percentage of income and wealth at the top of the American distribution increased, the percentage of tax expected from the most fortunate decreased. Since the 1980s, the tax rates paid by the top 0.1% of American earners fell from about 65% to about 35%, and for the top 0.01% from about 75% to below 25%.

During the presidential campaign, Trump asked Americans to remember when America was great: what his supporters had in mind were the 1940s, 1950s, 1960s, and 1970s, decades when the gap between the wealthiest and the rest was shrinking. Between 1940 and 1980, the bottom 90% of American earners gained more wealth than the top 1% did. This condition of growing equality was what Americans remember with warmth as the time of American greatness. Unions were strong until the 1980s. The welfare state was expanding in the 1950s and the 1960s. Wealth was more evenly distributed, thanks in large part to government policy.

In the era of inevitability, all of this changed. Inequality of income and wealth grew drastically from the 1980s through the 2010s. In 1978, the top 0.1% of the population, about 160,000 families, controlled 7% of American wealth. By 2012, the position of this tiny elite was even stronger: it controlled about 22% of American wealth. At the very top, the total wealth of the top 0.01%, about 16,000 families, increased by a factor of more than six over the same period. In 1978, a family in the top 0.01% was about 222 times as rich as the average American family. By 2012, such a family was about 1,120 times richer. Since 1980, 90% of the American population has gained essentially nothing, either in wealth or income. All gains have gone to the top 10%—and within the top 10%, most to the top 1%; and within the top 1%, most to the top 0.1%, and within the top 0.1% most to the top 0.01%.

In the 2010s, the United States approached the Russian standard of inequality. Although no American oligarchical clan has as yet captured the state, the emergence of such groups in the 2010s (Kochs, Mercers, Trumps, Murdochs) was hard to miss. Just as Russians used American capitalism to consolidate their own power, Americans cooperated with the Russian oligarchy with the same purpose—in the 2016 Trump presidential campaign, for example. Most likely, Trump's preference for Putin over Obama was not just a matter of racism or rivalry: it was also an aspiration to be more like Putin, to be in his good graces, to have access to greater wealth. Oligarchy works as a patronage system that dissolves democracy, law, and patriotism. American and Russian oligarchs have far more in common with one another than they do with their own populations. At the top of the wealth ladder, the temptations of the politics of eternity will be much the same in America as in Russia. There is little reason to expect that Americans would behave better than Russians when placed in similar situations.

For many Americans, oligarchy meant the warping of time, the loss of a sense of the future, the experience of every day as repetitive stress. When economic inequality suppresses social advance, it is hard to imagine a better future, or indeed any future. As an American worker put it during the Great Depression of the 1930s, fear "does distort your outlook and your feeling. Lost time and lost faith." An American born in 1940 was almost certain to make more money than his parents. An American born in 1984 had about a fifty-fifty chance of doing the same. Billy Joel's 1982 song "Allentown," which was really about the neighboring steel town of Bethlehem, Pennsylvania, caught the moment. It spoke of men of a second postwar generation without the social advancement attained by their fathers, of workers betrayed by narrow nationalism. The fate of the steel industry, like that of the American labor market generally, had much to do with changes in the world economy. The number of manufacturing jobs decreased by about one-third between 1980 and 2016. The problem was that American leaders took globalization as the solution to its own problems, rather than as an invitation to reform the American state. The globalization of the 1990s, 2000s, and 2010s coincided instead with the politics of inevitability and the generation of economic inequality.

Inequality means not only poverty but the experience of difference. Visible inequality leads Americans to reject the American dream as unlikely or impossible. Meanwhile, more and more Americans are unable to change residences, which also makes better futures hard to imagine. In the 2010s, more Americans between the ages of eighteen and thirty-four lived with their parents than in any other configuration. A young person who became a teacher and took a job in a public school in San Francisco could not afford to buy a home anywhere in the city. In other words, an American who completes an education and takes a job of the highest public value is not sufficiently rewarded to start what was once considered a normal life. A sense of doom pressed down especially on youth. More than a fifth of American families reported owing debt for college in the 2010s. Exposure to inequality persuaded American teens to drop out of high school, which then in turn made it very hard for them to earn. Children down to the age of four suffered in testing if they were raised in poorer families.

As Warren Buffett put it, "There's class warfare, all right, but it's my class, the rich class, that's making war, and we're winning." Americans die in this war every day, in large numbers, in incomparably greater numbers than in wars abroad or as a result of terrorism at home. Because the United States lacks a functional public health system, inequality has brought a health crisis, which in turn has accelerated and reinforced inequality. It was in counties where public health collapsed in the 2010s that Trump gained the votes that won him the election.

The factor that most strongly correlated with a Trump vote was a local public health crisis, especially where that crisis included high rates of suicide. About twenty American military veterans killed themselves every day in the 2010s; among farmers, the rate was still higher. Believing that tomorrow will be worse than today, Americans, especially white Americans, engaged in behaviors that were likely to reduce their life span. The association between declining health and Trump voting was strong in important states that Obama had won in 2012 but which Trump took in 2016, such as Ohio, Florida, Wisconsin, and Pennsylvania. When life is short and the future is troubled, the politics of eternity beckons.

A SPECTACULAR consequence of the American politics of inevitability in the 2010s was the legalization and popularization of opioids. For hundreds of years it has been known that such chemicals are addictive. Yet in the absence of normal institutions of public health, and in an atmosphere of unregulated capitalism, such basic wisdom could be overwhelmed by marketing. In effect, the United States declared an opium war against itself, making normal life impossible for millions of people and normal politics much more difficult for everyone. American citizens in the 1990s, already the test subjects in a grand experiment in inequality, were simultaneously exposed to the uncontrolled release of manufactured opioids. Oxycontin, which works like heroin in pill form, was approved for prescription in 1995. Marketing representatives for the company that produced it, Purdue Pharma, told doctors that a miracle had occurred: the pain-killing benefits of heroin without the addictiveness.

In the late 1990s in southern Ohio and eastern Kentucky, Purdue Pharma marketing representatives earned bonuses of more than $100,000 a quarter. In 1998, the first "pill mills" began to emerge in Portsmouth, Ohio; these were purported medical facilities where physicians were paid to prescribe Oxycontin or other opioids. Residents of Portsmouth and then other towns soon became addicts and began to die of overdoses. Some switched to heroin. Scioto County, Ohio, of which Portsmouth is the county seat, has a population of about 80,000 people. In a single year, its residents were prescribed 9.7 million pills, which comes to 120 pills for every man, woman, and child. Extreme though that might seem, such numbers became typical in much of the United States. In the state of Tennessee, for example, about 400 million pills were prescribed one year to a population of about 6 million, so about 70 pills per person.

In Russia and in Ukraine in 2014, 2015, and 2016, people often talked about "zombies" and "zombification." During the Russian occupation of southern and southeastern Ukraine, each side claimed that the other had been "zombified," drawn into a trance by the hypnotic power of its own propaganda. The Donbas was not so very different from Appalachia. Indeed, in the 2010s America had multiple Donbases, places of confusion and hopelessness where deep declines in expectations gave rise to faith in easy solutions. Zombification was as pronounced in America as it was in eastern Ukraine. People in Portsmouth with unwashed hair and gray faces could be seen tearing the metal objects from one another's houses, carrying them through town, and selling them for pills. For about a decade, opioids served as currency in that city, as they did among soldiers or mercenaries on both sides of the war in Ukraine.

The opioid plague was not widely discussed during its first two decades, and so grew national. About half of the unemployed men in the United States have been prescribed pain medication. In the year 2015, some ninety-five million Americans took prescription painkillers. For middle-aged white men, deaths from opioid abuse, along with other deaths of despair, canceled out gains in treatment of cancer and heart disease. Beginning in 1999, mortality among middle-aged white males in the United States began to increase. The death rate from drug overdose tripled between 1999 to 2016, when overdoses killed 63,600 Americans. While life expectancy in developed nations increased around the world, it fell in the United States in 2015 and then again in 2016. When Trump was campaigning for the Republican nomination, he did best in the primary elections in places where middle-aged white males were at greatest risk of death.

Anyone who suffers from pain knows that a pill can mean getting through a day, or even getting out of bed. But Oxycontin and heroin create their own special sort of pain through pleasure, overwhelming the *mu*-receptors in our spines and brains, creating in us a craving for ever more. Opioids hinder the development of the frontal cortex of the brain, which is where the capacity to make choices forms in adolescence. Persistent opioid use makes it harder for people to learn from experience, or to take responsibility for their actions. The drug colonizes the mental and social space needed for children, spouses, friends, jobs, the world. At the extreme of addiction, the world becomes a mute and isolated experience of pleasure and need. Time collapses into a cycle from this hit to the next one. The shift from the sense that everything is wonderful to the sense that everything is dark and foreboding becomes normal. Life itself becomes a manufactured crisis, one which seems to have no end except life's end.

Americans were prepared by drugs for the politics of eternity, for the sense of doom interrupted only by the quick hit. At least two million Americans were addicted to opioids at the time of the 2016 presidential election, and tens of millions more were taking pills. The correlation between opioid use and Trump voting was spectacular and obvious, notably in the states that Trump had to win. In New Hampshire, traumatized counties such as Coös swung from Obama in 2012 to Trump in 2016. Every Pennsylvania county that Obama won in 2012 but Trump won in 2016 was in opioid crisis. Mingo County, West Virginia, was one of the places in America most touched by opioids. A town in Mingo County with a population of 3,200 was shipped about two million opioid pills per year. Mingo County went Republican in 2012, but in 2016 Trump took 19% more votes than did Mitt Romney four years earlier. With one exception, every Ohio county in opioid crisis posted significant gains for Trump in 2016 over Romney in 2012, which helped him to win a state that he had to take to win the election. In Scioto County, Ohio, ground zero of the American opioid epidemic, Trump took a spectacular 33% more votes than Romney had.

It was in the localities where the American dream had died that Trump's politics of eternity worked. He called for a return to the past, to a time when America was great. Without inequality, without a sense that the future was closed, he could not have found the supporters he needed. The tragedy was that his idea of governance was to transform a dead dream into a zombie nightmare.

**THE POLITICS** of eternity triumphs when fiction comes to life. A leader from the realm of fiction tells lies without remorse or apology, because for him untruth is existence. The fictional creation "Donald Trump, successful businessman" filled the public space with untruth and never apologized for lies, since doing so would be to recognize that such a thing as truth existed. On 91 of his first 99 days in office, Trump made at least one claim that was blatantly wrong; in the course of his first 298 days he made 1,628 false or misleading claims. In a half-hour interview, he made twenty-four false or misleading claims, which (allowing for the time the interviewer was speaking), is about one per minute. It is true that all presidents lie: the difference is that for Trump, telling the truth was the exception.

Many Americans did not see the difference between someone who constantly lied and never apologized and someone who almost never did and corrected his or her mistakes. They were accepting the description of the world offered by Surkov and RT: no one really ever tells the truth, perhaps there is no truth, so let us simply repeat the things we like to hear, and obey those who say them. That way lies authoritarianism. Trump adopted the Russian double standard: he was permitted to lie all the time, but any minor error by a journalist discredited the entire profession of journalism. Trump made the move, copied from Putin, of claiming that it was not he but the reporters who lied. He referred to them as an "enemy of the American people" and claimed that what they produced was "fake news." Trump was proud of both of these formulations, although both were Russian.

In the Russian model, investigative reporting must be marginalized so that news can become a daily spectacle. The point of spectacle is to summon the emotions of both supporters and detractors and to confirm and strengthen polarization; every news cycle creates euphoria or depression, and reinforces a conviction that politics is about friends and enemies at home, rather than about policy that might improve the lives of citizens. Trump governed just as he had run for office: as a producer of outrage rather than as a formulator of policy.

THE POLITICS of eternity tempts with a cycle of nostalgia and delivers a cycle of conflict. Trump arrived in the Oval Office at a moment when levels of inequality in the United States approached those of Russia. Wealth and income in the United States had not been so unevenly distributed between the top 0.1% and the rest of the population since 1929, the year before the Great Depression. When Trump spoke of "making America great again," his followers thought of the decades after the Second World War, a time when inequality was shrinking. Trump himself meant the disastrous 1930s—and not just the Great Depression as it had actually happened, but something even more extreme and frightful: an alternative world where nothing was done, at home or abroad, to address its consequences.

The slogan of Trump's campaign and his presidency was "America First." This was a reference to the 1930s, or rather to an alternative America of increasing racial and social inequality that was not met with public policy. In the 1930s, the phrase "America First" was used to oppose both the welfare state proposed by Franklin D. Roosevelt and the entrance of the United States into the Second World War. The public face of the America First movement, the pilot Charles Lindbergh, argued that the United States ought to make common cause with Nazis as fellow white Europeans. To say "America First" in the 2010s was to establish a point of mythical innocence in an American politics of eternity, to embrace inequality as natural, to deny that anything should have been done back then or could be done now.

In Trump's politics of eternity, the Second World War lost its meaning. In previous decades Americans had come to think that a virtue of the war was the fight against Nazi racism, which in its turn offered lessons for improving the United States. The Trump administration undermined this American memory of "the good war." In a speech to Navaho veterans, Trump permitted himself a racist reference to a political rival. He managed to mark Holocaust Remembrance Day without mentioning Jews. His spokesman Sean Spicer claimed that Hitler did not kill "his own people." The idea that German Jews were not part of the German people is how the Holocaust began. The politics of eternity demands that effort be directed against the enemy, which can be the enemy within. "The people" always means, as Trump himself put it, "the real people," not the entire citizenry, but some chosen group.

Like his Russian patrons, Trump portrayed the presidency of Barack Obama as an aberration. Along with RT, Trump promoted the fiction that Obama was not an American, an idea meant to strengthen the notion that "the people" are whites. Like Putin with his monkey imitation, like Ilyin and his obsession with jazz as white emasculation, like Prokhanov with his nightmares of black milk and black sperm, Trump dwelled in fantasies of black power. When Trump won the presidency, Kiselev exulted that Obama was "now like a eunuch who cannot do anything." Trump was the only presidential candidate in American history to brag publicly about his penis. His white supremacist supporters called Republicans who would not support Trump's racism "cuckservatives." The reference was to the pornographic meme of a white husband, cuckold to a white wife, who watches her perform fellatio on a black man. To sexualize the enemy was to make politics into biological conflict, and to trade the hard work of reform and freedom for endless anxious preening.

In an American eternity, the enemy is black, and politics begins by saying so. Thus the next point of innocence in Trump's politics of eternity, after the 1930s-era racist isolationism of America First, was an alternative 1860s in which the Civil War was never fought. In actual American history, African Americans were enfranchised a few years after the American Civil War of 1861–1865. If blacks are to be excluded from "the people," an American politics of eternity has to keep them in bondage. And thus, just as the Trump administration questioned the wisdom of fighting Hitler, it also questioned the wisdom of fighting slavery. Speaking of the Civil War, Trump asked: "Why could that one not have been worked out?" His chief of staff, John Kelly, claimed that the cause of the Civil War was the absence of compromise, suggesting that if people had been more reasonable the United States might have reasonably remained a country where black people were reasonably enslaved. In the minds of some of Trump's supporters, the approval of the Holocaust and the endorsement of slavery were intertwined: in a major extreme-Right demonstration, in Charlottesville, Virginia, Nazi and Confederate symbols appeared together.

To proclaim "America First" was to deny any need to fight fascism either at home or abroad. When American Nazis and white supremacists marched in Charlottesville in August 2017, Trump said that some of them were "very fine people." He defended the Confederate and Nazi cause of preserving monuments to the Confederacy. Such monuments in the American South were raised in the 1920s and 1930s, at a time when fascism in the United States was a real possibility; they memorialized the racial purification of Southern cities that was contemporary with the rise of fascism in Europe. Contemporary observers had no difficulty seeing the connection. Will Rogers, the great American entertainer and social commentator of his time, saw Adolf Hitler in 1933 as a familiar figure: "Papers all state that Hitler is trying to copy Mussolini. Looks to me it's the KKK he's copying." The great American social thinker and historian W. E. B. Du Bois could see how the temptations of fascism worked together with American myths of the past. He rightly feared that American whites would prefer a story about enmity with blacks to a reforming state that would improve prospects for all Americans. Whites distracted by racism could become, as he wrote in 1935, "the instrument by which democracy in the nation was done to death, race provincialism deified, and the world delivered to plutocracy," what we call oligarchy.

An American politics of eternity takes racial inequality and makes it a source of economic inequality, turning whites against blacks, declaring hatred normal and change impossible. It begins from fictional premises and makes fictional policy. Americans living in the countryside tend to believe that their taxes are distributed to people in the cities, although the opposite is the case. Many white Americans, especially whites who voted for Trump, believe that whites suffer more from discrimination than do blacks. This is a legacy of American history that reaches back to the immediate aftermath of the Civil War, when President Andrew Johnson defined political equality for African Americans as discrimination against whites. Believers in the politics of inevitability might imagine that, in the course of time, people will become more educated and commit fewer errors. Believers in public policy might try to design reforms that would help people to overcome inequalities regardless of their beliefs. A politician of eternity such as Trump uses false beliefs about past and present to justify fictional policies that reaffirm those false beliefs, making of politics an eternal struggle against enemies.

An eternity politician defines foes rather than formulating policies. Trump did so by denying that the Holocaust concerned Jews, by using the expression "son of a bitch" in reference to black athletes, by calling a political opponent "Pocahontas," by overseeing a denunciation program that targeted Mexicans, by publishing a list of crimes committed by immigrants, by transforming an office on terrorism into an office on Islamic terrorism, by helping hurricane victims in Texas and Florida but not in Puerto Rico, by speaking of "shithole countries," by referring to reporters as enemies of the American people, by claiming that protestors were paid, and so on. American citizens could read these signs. A Republican congressional candidate physically attacked a reporter who was asking him a question about health care. An American Nazi attacked two women on a train in Portland and stabbed two men to death when they tried to protect them. In Washington State a white man ran over two Native Americans in his car while shouting racial slurs. Teachers reported in multiple surveys that the Trump presidency was increasing racial tension in their classrooms. The word "Trump" became a racial taunt at school sporting events.

Insofar as the American politics of eternity generates policy, its purpose is to inflict pain: regressive taxes that transfer wealth from the majority of the country to the very rich, and the reduction or elimination of health care. The politics of eternity works as a negative-sum game, where everyone but the top 1% or so of the population does worse, and the resulting suffering is used to keep the game going. People get the feeling of winning because they believe that others are losing. Trump was a loser since he could only win thanks to Russia; Republicans were greater losers since he had trapped their party;

Democrats were still greater losers since they were excluded from power; and the Americans who suffer from deliberately engineered inequality and health crisis were the greatest losers of all. So long as enough Americans understood losing as a sign that others must be losing still more, the logic could continue. If Americans could be induced to see politics as racial conflict rather than as work for a better common future, they would expect nothing better.

Trump was called a "populist." A populist, however, is someone who proposes policies to increase opportunities for the masses, as opposed to the financial elites. Trump was something else: a sado-populist, whose policies were designed to hurt the most vulnerable part of his own electorate. Encouraged by presidential racism, such people could understand their own pain as a sign of still greater pain inflicted upon others. The only major policy of 2017 was to increase pain: a tax regression law that created a budgetary argument against funding domestic programs, and which included among its provisions the deprivation of health care from many of those who needed it most. In Trump's words, "I've ended the individual mandate" for health insurance. This means that the Affordable Care Act, which had extended health insurance among uninsured Americans, was in his words "basically dead over time." According to the Congressional Budget Office, the health care provisions of the 2017 tax bill will result in the loss of health insurance for thirteen million Americans. As an envoy from the United Nations warned, these policies could make the United States "the most unequal country in the world." From an outside perspective, it was easy to conclude that pain was the purpose of such policies.

On one level, a poor person, unemployed worker, or opioid addict who votes away health care is just giving money to the rich that they do not need and perhaps will not even notice. On another level, such a voter is changing the currency of politics from achievement to suffering, from gain to pain, helping a leader of choice establish a regime of sadopopulism. Such a voter can believe that he or she has chosen who administers their pain, and can fantasize that this leader will hurt enemies still more. The politics of eternity converts pain to meaning, and then meaning back into more pain.

In this respect, America under President Trump was becoming like Russia. In strategic relativism, Russia hurt but aimed to make others hurt more—or at least to convince the Russian population that others were hurting more. Russian citizens took the pain of European and American sanctions after the Russian invasion of Ukraine because they believed that Russia was in a glorious campaign against Europe and America and that Europeans and Americans were getting their just deserts for their decadence and aggression. A fictional justification for war creates real pain that then justifies the continuation of a real war. In winning a battle of that war, in helping Trump to become president, Moscow was spreading this very logic inside the United States.

Moscow won a negative-sum game in international politics by helping to turn American domestic politics into a negative-sum game. In the Russian politics of eternity, Russian citizens trade the prospect of a better future for the vision of a valiant defense of Russian innocence. In an American politics of eternity, white Americans trade the prospect of a better future for the vision of a valiant defense of American innocence. Some Americans can be persuaded to live shorter and worse lives, provided that they are under the impression, rightly or wrongly, that blacks (or perhaps immigrants or Muslims) suffer still more.

If people who support the government expect their reward to be pain, then a democracy based upon policy competition between parties is endangered. Under Trump, Americans came to expect the administration of pain and pleasure, the daily outrage or triumph. For supporters and opponents alike, experience of politics became an addictive behavior, like time spent online or on heroin: a cycle of good and bad moments spent all alone. Few expected that the federal government could generate new and constructive policies. In the short term, a government that does not seek to legitimate itself with policy will be tempted to do so with terror, as in Russia. In the long term, a government that cannot assemble a majority through reforms will destroy the principle of rule by majority.

Such a turn away from democracy and the rule of law seemed to be Trump's preferred course. Trump was the first presidential candidate to say that he would reject the vote tally if he did not win the election, the first in more than a hundred years to urge his followers to physically beat his opponent, the first to suggest (twice) that his opponent should be murdered, the first to suggest as a major campaign theme that his opponent should be imprisoned, and the first to communicate internet memes from fascists. As president, he expressed his admiration for dictators around the world. He won the presidency, and his party its majority in both chambers of the American legislature, thanks to the undemocratic elements of the American system. Trump was keenly aware of the fact, tediously repeating that he did not really lose the popular vote, even though he had done so by a wide margin. His Russian supporters tried to make him feel better: Pervyi Kanal falsely reported, for example, that Clinton had only won the popular election because millions of "dead souls" had cast their ballots for her.

The electoral logic of sadopopulism is to limit the vote to those who benefit from inequality and to those who like pain, and take the vote away from those who expect government to endorse equality and reform. Trump began his administration by naming a voter suppression committee with the mandate to exclude voters from federal elections, evidently so that an artificial majority could be constructed at the federal level in the future, as is already the case in some states. Without the work of such commissions at the state level, it would have been harder for Trump to win in 2016. The hope was apparently to hold future elections under still more restrictive conditions, with ever fewer voters. The dark scenario for American democracy was the possible combination of some shocking act, perhaps one of domestic terrorism, with an election that was then held under a state of emergency, further limiting the right to vote. More than once Trump mused about such a "major event."

The temptation Russia offered Trump was the presidency. The temptation Trump offered Republicans was that of a one-party state, government by rigged elections rather than by political competition, a racial oligarchy in which the task of leaders was to bring pain rather than prosperity, to emote for a tribe rather than perform for all. If all the federal government did was maximize inequality and suppress votes, at some point a line would be crossed. Americans, like Russians, would eventually cease to believe in their own elections; then the United States, like the Russian Federation, would be in permanent succession crisis, with no legitimate way to choose leaders. This would be the triumph of the Russian foreign policy of the 2010s: the export of Russia's problems to its chosen adversaries, the normalization of Russia's syndromes by way of contagion.

Politics is international, but repair must be local. The presidential campaign of 2016, the biography of Donald Trump, the anonymous businesses, the anonymous real estate purchases, the domination of internet news, the peculiarities of the Constitution, the astonishing economic inequality, the painful history of race—to Americans, all of this can seem like a matter of a special nation and its exceptional history. The politics of inevitability tempted Americans to think that the world had to become like the United States and therefore more friendly and democratic, but this was not the case. In fact, the United States was itself becoming less democratic in the 2010s, and Russia was working to accelerate the trend. Russian methods of rule appealed to America's would-be oligarchs. As in Russia, the risk was that fascist ideas would consolidate oligarchy.

To break the spell of inevitability, we must see ourselves as we are, not on some exceptional path, but in history alongside others. To avoid the temptation of eternity, we must address our own particular problems, beginning with inequality, with timely public policy. To make of American politics an eternity of racial conflict is to allow economic inequality to worsen. To address widening disparities of opportunity, to restore a possibility of social advance and thus a sense of the future, requires seeing Americans as a citizenry rather than as groups in conflict.

America will have both forms of equality, racial and economic, or it will have neither. If it has neither, eternity politics will prevail, racial oligarchy will emerge, and American democracy will come to a close.

# EPILOGUE (20—)

To experience its destruction is to see a world for the first time. Inheritors of an order we did not build, we are now witnesses to a decline we did not foresee.

To see our moment is to step away from the stories supplied for our stupefaction, myths of inevitability and eternity, progress and doom. Life is elsewhere. Inevitability and eternity are not history but ideas within history, ways of experiencing our time that accelerate its trends while slowing our thoughts. To see, we must set aside the dark glass, and see as we are seen, ideas for what they are, history as what we make.

Virtues arise from the institutions that make them desirable and possible. As institutions are destroyed, virtues reveal themselves. A history of loss is thus a proposal for restoration. The virtues of equality, individuality, succession, integration, novelty, and truth depend each upon all the others, and all of them upon human decisions and actions. An assault upon one is an assault upon all; strengthening one means affirming the rest.

Thrown into a world we do not choose, we need equality so that we learn through failure but without resentment. Only collective public policy can create citizens with the confidence of individuals. As individuals we seek to understand what we can and should do together and apart. We might join in a democracy with others who have voted before, and will vote after, and in so doing create a principle of succession and a sense of time. With this assured, we might see our country as one among others, recognize the necessity of integration, and choose its terms. The virtues reinforce one another, but not automatically; any harmony demands human virtuosity, the incessant regulation of the old by the new. Without novelty, virtues die.

All of the virtues depend upon truth, and truth depends upon them all. Final truth in this world is unattainable, but its pursuit leads the individual away from unfreedom. The temptation to believe what feels right assails us at all times from all directions. Authoritarianism begins when we can no longer tell the difference between the true and the appealing. At the same time, the cynic who decides that there is no truth at all is the citizen who welcomes the tyrant. Total doubt about all authority is naïveté about the particular authority that reads emotions and breeds cynicism. To seek the truth means finding a way between conformity and complacency, towards individuality.

If it is true that we are individuals, and if it is true that we live in a democracy, then each of us should have a single vote, not greater or lesser power in elections as a result of wealth or race or privilege or geography. It should be individual human beings who make the decisions, not the dead souls (as the Russians call cybervotes), not the internet robots, not the zombies of some tedious eternity. If a vote truly represents a citizen, then citizens can give time to their state, and the state can give time to citizens. That is the truth of succession.

That no country stands alone is the truth of integration. Fascism is the falsehood that the enemy chosen by a leader must be the enemy for all. Politics then begins from emotion and falsehood. Peace becomes unthinkable, since enmity abroad is necessary for control at home. A fascist says "the people" and means "some people," those he favors at the moment. If citizens and residents are recognized by law, then other countries might also be recognized by law. Just as the state requires a principle of succession to exist over time, it needs some form of integration with others to exist in space.

If there is no truth, there can be no trust, and nothing new appears in a human vacuum. Novelty arises within groups, be they entrepreneurs or artists, activists or musicians; and groups need trust. In conditions of distrust and isolation, creativity and energy veer towards paranoia and conspiracy, a feverish repetition of the oldest mistakes. We speak of freedom of association, but freedom *is* association: without it we cannot renew ourselves or challenge our rulers.

The embrace of equality and truth is close and tender. When inequality is too great, the truth is too much for the miserable, and too little for the privileged. Communication among citizens depends upon equality. At the same time, equality cannot be achieved without facts. An individual experience of inequality might be explained away by some story of inevitability or eternity, but the collective data of inequality demand policy. If we do not know just how unequal the distribution of the world's wealth is, or how much of it is hidden from the state by the wealthy, we cannot know where to begin.

If we see history as it is, we see our places in it, what we might change, and how we might do better. We halt our thoughtless journey from inevitability to eternity, and exit the road to unfreedom. We begin a politics of responsibility.

To take part in its creation is to see a world for a second time. Students of the virtues that history reveals, we become the makers of a renewal that no one can foresee.

# ACKNOWLEDGMENTS

I think often about the historians who, decades or centuries hence, will make sense of the moment we experience now. What will we leave behind that they will be able to read? "Information" in the digital sense is infinite, knowledge ever scarcer, and wisdom fleeting. I expect that the prose of honest investigative journalists, perhaps even in paper form, will provide a starting point. Certainly my own very contemporary history depends heavily on reporters who took risks to understand. *The Road to Unfreedom* is dedicated to them.

At a certain point, I thought I was close to finishing a book about contemporary Russia, Ukraine, and Europe, only to realize that its subject was much more British and American than I had thought. Research on the Russian and Ukrainian aspects was supported by a Carnegie Fellowship. At the Institute of Human Sciences in Vienna in 2013–2014, I learned from Ukrainian and Russian colleagues, and from the directors of the program "Ukraine in European Dialogue," Kate Younger and Tatiana Zhurzhenko. I owe a great deal to exchanges among my colleagues Krzysztof Czyżewski, Yaroslav

Hrytsak, and the late Leonidas Donskis at a summer school that took place at the Borderland Foundation in Krasnogruda, Poland, in 2016.

In late 2016, I wrote a political pamphlet called *On Tyranny* and spent much of 2017 discussing American politics with Americans (and trying to explain America to Europeans, while reminding Europeans of the basic similarity of certain problems). Many of the concepts developed here arose in these public discussions. Since I was speaking constantly between the publication of that book and this one, I cannot acknowledge each forum: but I can acknowledge that I was inspired to think by others' determination to work. Throughout this busy and complex time, I have been very fortunate to have the support of my agent, Tina Bennett, and my editor, Tim Duggan.

This book was begun in Vienna and revised in Krasnogruda, but it was completed in New Haven, Connecticut. It was in preparation for a discussion with undergraduate students at Yale, at a lecture organized by Declan Kunkel, that I thought of the concepts of "inevitability" and "eternity" that frame the argument of his book. I thank Yale's Department of History, Jackson Institute, and MacMillan Center for a perfect setting for thought and writing. My extraordinary assistant Sara Silverstein created the environment, intellectual and logistical, in which my work of these last three years could be accomplished. I wish her happiness and success as she continues her career as a historian at the University of Connecticut.

I had the assistance of a fabulous group of researchers: Tory Burnside Clapp, Max Landau, Julie Leighton, Ola Morehead, Anastasiya Novotorskaya, David Shimer, and Maria Teteriuk. Friends and colleagues were kind enough to read chapters. They include Dwayne Betts, Susan Ferber, Jörg Hensgen, Dina Khapaeva, Nikolay Koposov, Daniel Markovits, Paweł Pieniążek, Anton Shekhovtsov, Jason Stanley, Vladimir Tismaneanu, and Andreas Umland. Oxana Mikhaevna shared with me transcripts of interviews with Ukrainian separatists and Russian volunteers fighting in eastern Ukraine. Max Trudolyubov and Ivan Krastev got me thinking about the ideas that became chapters 1 and 2. Paul Bushkovitch kindly shared thoughts about the history of succession in Russia, and Izabela Kalinowska helped me to see connections between contemporary and classical Russian culture. In their own encounter, Nataliya Gumenyuk and Christine Hadley Snyder helped me see connections between Ukrainian and American preoccupations.

I would not have become the historian who wrote this book without my doctoral supervisor, Jerzy Jedlicki (1930–2018), who died as I was writing these final lines. He survived the worst of the tyrannies of the twentieth century and became an exemplar of an east European historiography that was both rigidly analytical and morally engaged. He was one of the few in Poland or elsewhere to be completely untouched by what I call here the politics of inevitability. It grieves me that we will not discuss this book in his Warsaw apartment.

My debts to Marci Shore are many and grow by the day; here they are chiefly philosophical.

Responsibility for this book and for its flaws is my own.

# ENDNOTES

Notes are keyed to the first words of paragraphs. The body of the note clarifies the relationship between the sources and the text. This allows interested readers to check sources without burdening the main text with superscript numbers. The system is simpler than it sounds. The issue of transliteration is not. Sources cited are in Russian, Ukrainian, German, French, Polish, and English. Russian and Ukrainian are spelled in the Cyrillic alphabet, and so Russian and Ukrainian words must be transliterated. In the main text, Russian and Ukrainian names are generally transliterated into familiar forms, or into forms preferred by the people concerned. In the endnotes a simplified version of the Library of Congress transliteration system is used.

Each source will be cited in full at first mention, and thereafter in an abbreviated form. Frequently cited media are abbreviated as follows: BI: *Business Insider*; DB: *Daily Beast*; EDM: *Eurasia Daily Monitor*; FAZ: *Frankfurter Allgemeine Zeitung*; FT: *Financial Times*; GW: *Gazeta Wyborcza*; HP: *Huffington Post*; KP: *Komsomol'skaia Pravda*; LM: *Le Monde*; NG: *Novaia Gazeta*; NPR: *National Public Radio*; NW: *Newsweek*; NY: *New Yorker*; NYR: *New York Review of Books*; NYT: *New York Times*; PK: *Pervyi Kanal*; RFE/RL: *Radio Free Europe/Radio Liberty*; RG: *Russkaia Gazeta*; RK: *Russkii Kolokol*; TG: *The Guardian*; TI: *The Interpreter*; UP: *Ukrains'ka Pravda*; VO: *Vozrozhdenie*; WP: *Washington Post*; WSJ: *Wall Street Journal*.

## CHAPTER 1

15 *Eternity arises* These concepts of inevitability and eternity are new, but the notion of timescapes is not. I have been greatly aided by Hans Ulrich Gumbrecht, *Nach 1945,* trans. Frank Born (Berlin: Suhrkampf, 2012); Johann Chapoutot, "L'historicité nazie," *Vingtième Siècle,* No. 117, 2013, 43–55; Reinhart Koselleck, *Futures Past,* trans. Keith Tribe (Cambridge, Mass.: MIT Press, 1985); Mary Gluck, *Georg Lukács and His Generation, 1900–1918* (Cambridge, Mass.: Harvard University Press, 1991).

16 *Russia reached the politics* Czesław Miłosz, *Zniewolony umysł* (Paris: Kultura, 1953), 15.

16 *The fascism of the 1920s* Wealth and inequality in Russia are discussed in chapter 6, where sources will be cited.

17 *Ivan Ilyin, born to a noble* On the intellectual origins of fascism, see Zeev Sternhell, *Les anti-Lumières* (Paris: Gallimard, 2010). As I will suggest, Ilyin was closest to the Romanian fascists, who were also Orthodox Christians. The problem of Christianity and fascism is a broad one. For background on Western cases, see Susannah Heschel, *The Aryan Jesus* (Princeton: Princeton UP, 2010); John Connelly, *From Enemy to Brother* (Cambridge, Mass.: Harvard UP, 2012); Brian Porter-Szűcs, *Faith and Fatherland* (New York: Oxford UP, 2011).

17 *After a new Russian Federation* The book that led to the revival was I. Ilyin, *Nashi zadachi: Stat'i 1948–1954 gg.* (Paris: Izdanie Russkago obshche-voinskago soiuza, 1956). Its return in the 1990s: Oleg Kripkov, "To Serve God and Russia: Life and Thought of Russian Philosopher Ivan Il'in," doctoral dissertation, Department of History, University of Kansas, 1998, 205. Early Putin addresses: Address to Federal Assembly, April 25, 2005; Address to Federal Assembly, May 10, 2006. Burial: "V Moskve sostoialas' tseremoniia perezakhoroneniia prakha generala A. I. Denikina i filosofa I. A. Il'ina," *Russkaia Liniia,* Oct. 3, 2005. On Ilyin's papers: "MSU will digitize archives of Ilyin," newsru.com. On Putin's speechwriting: Maxim Kalinnikov, "Putin i russkie filosofy: kogo tsitiruet prezident," Rustoria.ru, Dec. 5, 2014. Putin on foreign affairs and invasion of Ukraine, with direct or indirect reference to Ilyin: "Vladimir Putin called the annexation of Crimea the most important event of the past year," PK, Dec. 4, 2014; "Blok NATO razoshelsia na blokpakety," *Kommersant,* April 7, 2008; Vladimir Putin, "Rossiia: natsional'nyi vopros," *Nezavisimaia Gazeta,* Jan. 23, 2012; Vladimir Putin, Address to Federal Assembly, Dec. 12, 2012; Vladimir Putin, Meeting with Representatives of Different Orthodox Patriarchies and Churches, July 25, 2013; Vladimir Putin, Remarks to Orthodox-Slavic Values: The Foundation of Ukraine's Civilizational Choice conference, July 27, 2013; Vladimir Putin, "Excerpts from the transcript of the meeting of the Valdai International Discussion Club," Sept. 19, 2013; Vladimir Putin, interview with journalists in Novo-Ogarevo, March 4, 2014. Putin on Ilyin's authority: "Meeting with young scientists and history teachers," Moscow, 2014, Kremlin, 46951.

18 *The Russian political class* Surkov on Ilyin: Vladislav Surkov, "Speech at Center for Party Studies and Personnel Training at the United Russia Party," Feb. 7, 2006, published in *Rosbalt*, March 9, 2006; Iurii Kofner, "Ivan Il'in—Evraziiskii filosof Putina," *Evraziia-Blog*, Oct. 3, 2015; Aleksei Semenov, *Surkov i ego propaganda* (Moscow: Knizhnyi Mir, 2014). Medvedev on Ilyin: D. A. Medvedev, "K Chitateliam," in I. A. Ilyin, *Puti Rossii* (Moscow: Vagrius, 2007), 5–6. Ilyin in Russian politics: Tatiana Saenko, "Parlamentarii o priniatii v sostav Rossiiskoi Federatsii novykh sub'ektov," *Kabardino-Balkarskaya Pravda*, no. 49, March 18, 2014, 1; Z. F. Dragunkina, "Dnevnik trista sorok deviatogo (vneocherednogo) zasedaniia soveta federatsii," *Biulleten' Soveta Federatsii*, vol. 254 (453); V. V. Zhirinovskii, V. A. Degtiarev, N. A. Vasetskii, "Novaia gosudarstvennost," *Izdanie LDPR*, 2016, 14. Vladimir Zhirinovskii, the leader of the misnamed Liberal Democratic Party, certainly read Ilyin before Putin did. Andreas Umland, "Vladimir Zhirinovskii in Russian Politics," doctoral dissertation, Free University of Berlin, 1997. Bureaucrats received a copy: Michael Eltchaninoff, *Dans la tete de Vladimir Poutine* (Arles: Actes Sud, 2015). For examples of mentions by regional governors and officials of similar rank, see kurganobl.ru/10005.html, etnokonf.astrobl.ru/document/621; old.sakha.gov.ru/node/1349#, special.kremlin.ru/events/president/news/17536; gov.spb.ru/law?d&nd=537918692&nh=1.

18 *Ilyin was a politician* These propositions will be demonstrated in chapters 3 and 6.

19 *Our politics of inevitability* On Ilyin's political orientation: Kripkov, "To Serve God and Russia," 13–35 for youthful leftism; Philip T. Grier, "The Complex Legacy of Ivan Il'in," in James P. Scanlan, ed., *Russian Thought after Communism* (Armonk: M. E. Sharpe, 1994), 165–86; Daniel Tsygankov, "Beruf, Verbannung, Schicksal: Iwan Iljin und Deutschland," *Archiv für Rechts- und Sozialphilosophie*, vol. 87, no. 1, 2001, 44–60. Stanley Payne quotation: *Fascism* (Madison: University of Wisconsin Press, 1980), 42. Articles by Ilyin on Mussolini and Italian fascism: "Pis'ma o fashizmie: Mussolini sotsialist," *VO*, March 16, 1926, 2; "Pis'ma o fashizmie: Biografiia Mussolini," *VO*, Jan. 10, 1926, 3; also see "Natsionalsotsializm" (1933), in D. K. Burlaka, ed., *I.A. Il'in—pro et contra* (Saint Petersburg: Izd-vo Russkogo khristianskogo gumanitarnogo in-ta, 2004), 477–84.

19 *Ilyin regarded fascism* Ilyin on fascism: "Natsional-sotsializm." Ilyin on Russian White movement: "O russkom' fashizmie," *RK* no. 3, 1927, 56, 64; see also Grier, "Complex Legacy," 166–67. A useful introduction to the Russian Civil War is Donald J. Raleigh, "The Russian Civil War, 1917–1922," in Ronald Grigor Suny, ed., *Cambridge History of Russia* (Cambridge, UK: Cambridge UP, 2006), vol. 3, 140–67.

19 *Ilyin was similarly impressed* Ilyin on Hitler: "Natsional-sotsializm," 477–84. On the transfer of ideas by White émigrés, see Michael Kellogg, *The Russian Roots of Nazism* (Cambridge, UK: Cambridge UP, 2005), 12, 65, 72–73; also see Alexander Stein, *Adolf Hitler: Schüler der "Weisen von Zion"*

(Karlové Vary: Graphia, 1936) and V. A. Zolotarev, et al., eds., *Russkaia voennaia emigratsiia* (Moscow: Geiia, 1998). Biography: Tsygankov, "Iwan Iljin"; Tsygankov, "Beruf, Verbannung, Schicksal," 44–60; Kripkov, "To Serve God and Russia," 2, 10, 304; I. I. Evlampiev, ed., *Ivan Aleksandrovich Il'in* (Moscow: Rosspen, 2014), 14; Grier, "Complex Legacy."

20 *In 1938, Ilyin left* Biography: Kripkov, "To Serve God and Russia," 72–73, 240, 304; Grier, "Complex Legacy"; Tsygankov, "Iwan Iljin." Swiss reactions: Jürg Schoch, "'Ich möchte mit allem dem geliebten Schweizervolk dienen,'" *Tages-Anzeiger,* Dec. 29, 2014.

20 *Ilyin's political views* "Sud'ba Bol'shevizma" (Sept. 19, 1941), in I. A. Il'in, *Sobranie sochinenii,* ed. Iu. T. Lisitsy (Moscow: Russkaia kniga, 1993–2008), 22 volumes, here vol. 8. Colleagues: Schoch, "'Ich möchte mit allem dem geliebten Schweizervolk dienen.'" Financial support: Kripkov, "To Serve God and Russia," 245.

20 *When the Soviet Union* Felix Philipp Ingold, "Von Moskau nach Zellikon," *Neuer Zürcher Zeitung,* Nov. 14, 2000.

21 *Ilyin was consistent* I am citing throughout the German edition (I. A. Iljin, *Philosophie Hegels als kontemplative Gotteslehre* [Bern: A. Francke Verlag, 1946]), since the philosophical concepts are German. For the purposes of this book I focus on Ilyin in isolation from Russian discussions: for contexts, see Laura Engelstein, "Holy Russia in Modern Times: An Essay on Orthodoxy and Cultural Change," *Past & Present,* 173, 2001, 129–56, and Andrzej Walicki, *A History of Russian Thought from the Enlightenment to Marxism* (Stanford: Stanford UP, 1979).

21 *The one good* Iljin, *Philosophie Hegels,* 9, 351–52, 374. Cioran on totality: E. M. Cioran, *Le Mauvais Démiurge* (Paris: Gallimard, 1969), 14. On Hegel, Hegelians, and the tradition of totality: see Leszek Kołakowski, *Main Currents of Marxism. Vol. 1: The Founders* (Oxford: Oxford UP, 1978), 17–26.

21 *For Ilyin, our human world* Iljin, *Philosophie Hegels,* 310, 337, 371, 372. Cf Roman Ingarden, *Spór o istnienie świata* (Cracow: Nakład Polskiej Akademii Umiejętności), 1947.

21 *By condemning God* Iljin, *Philosophie Hegels,* 307, 335.

22 *The vision was* On evil: I. Ilyin, *O soprotivlenii zlu siloiu* (1925), in *Sobranie sochinenii,* vol. 5, 43. Existence, factuality, middle class: Iljin, *Philosophie Hegels,* 312, 345. It is also possible to begin a defense of individualism at this very point: Józef Tischner, *Spowiedź rewolucjonisty. Czytając Fenomenologię Ducha Hegla* (Cracow: Znak, 1993), 42–43.

22 *Like all immorality* The idea that ethics begins by not making an exception for oneself is associated with Immanuel Kant, by whom the young Ilyin was much influenced.

22 *Ilyin made an exception* Ilyin on contemplation: Iljin, *Philosophie Hegels,* 8; it was also a theme of his lectures in Switzerland, which he published. Codreanu's vision: Constantin Iordachi, *Charisma, Politics, and Violence* (Trondheim: Norwegian University of Science and Technology, 2004),

45. Ilyin on the nation: "Put' dukhovnogo obnovleniia," (1932–1935), *Sobranie sochinenii*, vol. 1, 196.

23 *Innocence took a specific* Organism and fraternal union: V. A. Tomsinov, *Myslitel' s poiushchim serdtsem* (Moscow: Zertsalo, 2012), 166, 168; Tsygankov, "Iwan Iljin." National minorities: Ilyin, *Nashi zadachi*, 250.

23 *Ilyin thought* Foreign threats: Ilyin, "Put' dukhovnogo obnovleniia," in *Sobranie sochinenii*, vol. 1, 210 (and on God and nation at 328); Iljin, *Philosophie Hegels*, 306 (and on Russian spirit at 345); Kripkov, "To Serve God and Russia," 273.

23 *When God created the world* Ilyin's threat construction and "continental blockade": Iljin, ed., *Welt vor dem Abgrund* (Berlin: Eckart-Verlag, 1931), 152, 155; Kripkov, "To Serve God and Russia," 273.

24 *Before the Bolshevik Revolution* Biographical information: Grier, "Complex Legacy," 165. Ilyin quote: "O russkom" fashizmie," 60: "Dielo v' tom', chto fashizm' est spasitelnyi eksstess patrioticheskago proizvola."

24 *Ilyin's use of the Russian* Ilyin on salvation: "O russkom" fashizmie," *RK*, no. 3, 1927, 60–61. Hitler quotation: *Mein Kampf* (Munich: Zentralverlag der NSDAP, 1939), 73.

25 *The men who redeemed* Ilyin on God: Tsygankov, "Iwan Iljin." Divine totality and Christian war: *O soprotivlenii zlu siloiu*, 33, 142. Chivalrous struggle: "O russkom" fashizmie," 54. In a poem in the first number of his journal *Russki Kolokol* Ilyin also wrote: "My prayer is like a sword. And my sword is like a prayer," *RK*, no. 1, 80. Unlike Nietzsche, who sought to transcend Christianity, Ilyin was merely inverting it. Ilyin said that it was necessary to love God by hating the enemy. Nietzsche (in *Ecce Homo*) said that he who seeks knowledge must love his enemy and hate his friends, which is a challenge of a higher order. Ilyin was the Hegelian, but here Nietzsche was surely the superior dialectician.

25 *Because the world was sinful* Power: Ilyin, "Pis'ma o fashizmie: Lichnost' Mussolini," *VO*, Jan. 17, 1926, 3. Beyond history: "Pis'ma o fashizmie: Biografiia Mussolini," *VO*, Jan. 10, 1926, 3. The sensual: Iljin, *Philosophie Hegels*, 320. Manliness: Ryszard Paradowski, *Kościół i władza. Ideologiczne dylematy Iwana Iljina* (Poznań: Wydawnictwo Naukowe UAM, 2003), 91, 114. Redeemer and organ: I. A. Il'in, "Belaia ideia," *Sobranie sochinenii*, vols. 9–10, 312.

26 *The redeemer suppresses* See Jean-Pierre Faye, "Carl Schmitt, Göring, et l'État total," in Yves Charles Zarka, ed., *Carl Schmitt ou le mythe du politique* (Paris: Presses Universitaires de France, 2009), 161–82; Yves-Charles Zarka, *Un detail dans la pensér de Carl Schmitt* (Paris: Presses Universitaires de France, 2005); Raphael Gross, *Carl Schmitt and the Jews*, trans. Joel Golb (Madison: University of Wisconsin Press), 2007. On Schmitt's influence see Dirk van Laak, *Gespräche in der Sicherheit des Schweigens* (Berlin: Akademie Verlag, 1993); Jan-Werner Müller, *A Dangerous Mind* (New Haven: Yale UP, 2003). The Russian recovery of Ilyin should be understood as part of the international rehabilitation of Schmitt, a subject

too broad to consider here. Schmitt's sovereign: Carl Schmitt, *Politische Theologie* (Berlin: Duncker & Humblot, 2004, 1922), 13. Ilyin on nationalism: "O russkom natsionalizmie," 47. Art of politics: *Nashi zadachi,* 56: "Politika est' iskusstvo uznavat' i obezvrezhyvat' vraga."

26 *The redeemer had the obligation* Ilyin on war: Paradowski, *Kościół i władza,* 194. Romanian song: "March by Radu Gyr" from "Hymn of the Legionary Youth" (1936), cited in Roland Clark, *Holy Legionary Youth: Fascist Activism in Interwar Romania* (Ithaca: Cornell UP, 2015), 152. See relatedly Moshe Hazani, "Red Carpet, White Lilies," *Psychoanalytic Review,* vol. 89, no. 1, 2002, 1–47. Ilyin on excess and passion: *Philosophie Hegels,* 306; "Pis'ma o fashizmie," 3. The novels of Witold Gombrowicz, especially *Ferdydurke,* are good introductions to the problem of innocence.

26 *"Everything begins"* Péguey cited in Eugen Weber, "Romania," in Hans Rogger and Eugen Weber, eds., *The European Right: A Historical Profile* (Berkeley: University of California Press, 1965), 516.

27 *Ilyin tried to design* Ilyin on leaders and elections: *Nashi zadachi,* 33, 340–42; Ilyin, *Osnovy gosudarstevnnogo ustroistva* (Moscow: Rarog', 1996), 80; Paradowski, *Kościół i władza,* 114, 191. See also Iordachi, *Charisma, Politics, and Violence,* 7, 48.

27 *Allowing Russians* Elections: I. A. Il'in, "Kakie zhe vybory nuzhny Rossii" (1951), *Sobranie sochinenii,* vol. 2, part 2, 1993, 18–23. Principle of democracy: Paradowski, *Kościół i władza,* 91.

28 *Ilyin imagined society* Quotation: Ilyin, "Kakie zhe vybory nuzhny Rossii," 25. Middle classes: *Philosophie Hegels,* 312–16; *Osnovy gosudarstevnnogo ustroistva,* 45–46. The contempt for the middle classes was typical of the extreme Right and extreme Left in Ilyin's day. For a nice characterization see Miłosz, *Zniewolony umysł,* 20. It is also typical of Russian fascism now: see for example Alexander Dugin, "The War on Russia in its Ideological Dimension," *Open Revolt,* March 11, 2014.

28 *Ilyin used the word "law"* Ilyin's youthful view of law: I. A. Ilyin, "The Concepts of Law and Power," trans. Philip. T. Grier, *Journal of Comparative Law,* vol. 7, no. 1, 63–87. Russian heart: Ilyin, *Nashi zadachi,* 54; Tomsinov, *Myslitel' s poiushchim serdtsem,* 174. Metaphysical identity: *Philosophie Hegels,* 306. Ilyin refers to Romans 2:15, a verse which is important in Orthodox theology. For an alternative reading of the idea of the heart in phenomenological ethics, see Tischner, *Spowiedź rewolucjonisty,* 92–93.

29 *The Russian nation* Cf Cioran, *Le Mauvais Démiurge,* 24; Payne, *Fascism,* 116.

29 *Ilyin placed a human being* Russian victimhood: Paradowski, *Kościół i władza,* 188, 194.

29 *In the 2010s* Oligarchy in Russia is a subject of chapter 6, and sources will be cited there.

30 *To men raised* Masha Gessen makes a different case for the collapse of forward time in *The Future Is History* (New York: Riverhead Books, 2017).

30 *G. W. F. Hegel's ambition* G. W. F. Hegel, *Vorlesungen über die Philosophie der Geschichte,* part 3, section 2, chapter 24.

30 *Karl Marx was critical* Marx as a Left Hegelian: Karl Marx, *The Economic and Philosophic Manuscripts of 1844*, ed. Dirk J. Struik, New York: International Publishers, 1964, for the points here especially 34, 145, 172. On Left Hegelianism: Kołakowski, *Main Currents*, vol. 1, 94–100.

31 *Ilyin was a Right Hegelian* Ilyin's political philosophy: Philip T. Grier, "The Speculative Concrete," in Shaun Gallagher, ed., *Hegel, History, and Interpretation* (State University of New York Press, 1997), 169–93. Ilyin on Marx: *Philosophie Hegels*, 11. Hegel on God: Marx, *The Economic and Philosophic Manuscripts of 1844*, 40. Ilyin on God: *Philosophie Hegels*, 12; Kripkov, "To Serve God and Russia," 164; Ilyin, "O russkom" fashizmie," 60–64.

31 *Vladimir Lenin* Lenin on Ilyin: Kirill Martynov, "Filosof kadila i nagaiki," *NG*, Dec. 9, 2014; Philip T. Grier, "Three Philosophical Projects," in G. M. Hamburg and Randall A. Poole, eds., *A History of Russian Philosophy 1830–1930* (Cambridge, UK: Cambridge UP, 2013), 329.

31 *Ilyin despised Lenin's revolution* Ilyin on Lenin: Kripkov, "To Serve God and Russia." Ilyin on revolution: "O russkom" fashizmie," 60–61; *Nashi zadachi*, 70. Berdyaev on Ilyin: Martynov, "Filosof kadila i nagaiki"; Eltchaninoff, *Dans la tête de Vladimir Poutine*, 50. See also Tischner, *Spowiedź rewolucjonisty*, 211.

32 *As Ilyin aged* Ilyin on jazz: Ilyin, "Iskusstvo," in D. K. Burlaka, ed., *I.A. Il'in—pro et contra* (St. Petersburg: Izd-vo Russkogo khristianskogo gumanitarnogo in-ta, 2004), 485–86. *Pravda* on jazz: Maxim Gorky, "O muzyke tolstykh," *Pravda*, April 18, 1928. Polish fascists had a similar attitude: Jan Józef Lipski, *Idea Katolickiego Państwa Narodu Polskiego* (Warsaw: Krytyka Polityczna, 2015), 47. On jazz as anti-Stalinism, see Leopold Tyrmand, *Dziennik 1954* (London: Polonia Book Fund, 1980). Vyshynskii on law: Martin Krygier, "Marxism and the Rule of Law," *Law & Social Inquiry*, vol. 15, no. 4, 1990, 16. On Stalinist states of exception: Stephen G. Wheatcroft, "Agency and Terror," *Australian Journal of Politics and History*, vol. 53, no. 1, 2007, 20–43; ibid., "Towards Explaining the Changing Levels of Stalinist Repression in the 1930s," in Stephen G. Wheatcroft, ed., *Challenging Traditional Views of Russian History* (Houndmills: Palgrave, 2002), 112–38.

33 *Although Ilyin had initially* Ilyin on the Soviet Union: Ilyin, *Nashi zadachi*; Kripkov, "To Serve God and Russia," 273. Ilyin on Russia and fascism: see sources throughout this chapter, as well as the discussion of I. I. Evlampiev, "Ivan Il'in kak uchastnik sovremennykh diskussii," in Evlampiev, ed., *Ivan Aleksandrovich Il'in* (Moscow: Rosspen, 2014), 8–34. Stalin and Russia: David Brandenberger, *National Bolshevism* (Cambridge, Mass.: Harvard UP, 2002); Serhy Yekelchyk, *Stalin's Empire of Memory* (Toronto: University of Toronto Press, 2004). See also Yoram Gorlizki and Oleg Khlevniuk, *Cold Peace* (Oxford: Oxford UP, 2004); Hiroaki Kuromiya, *Stalin* (Harlow: Pearson Longman, 2005); Vladislav M. Zubok, *A Failed Empire* (Chapel Hill: University of North Carolina Press, 2007).

33 *Stalin's economic policy* See the sources cited above as well as *Nashi zadachi*,

152–55. On this theme from a different perspective, see Shaun Walker, *The Long Hangover* (Oxford: Oxford UP, 2018), "vacuum" at 1 and sic passim.

34 *In the twenty-first century* Some instances of Putin citing Ilyin were cited earlier in this chapter; others will be cited in chapters 2 and 3. For a sense of the Russian discussion about influence, see Yuri Zarakhovich, "Putin Pays Homage to Ilyin," *EDM*, June 3, 2009; Maxim Kalinnikov, "Putin i russkie filosofy: kogo tsitiruet prezident," Rustoria.ru, Dec. 5, 2014; Martynov, "Filosof kadila i nagaiki"; Izrail' Zaidman, "Russkii filosof Ivan Il'in i ego poklonnik Vladimir Putin," *Rebuzhie*, Nov. 25, 2015; Eltchaninoff, *Dans la tête de Vladimir Poutine.*

35 *The politics of eternity cannot make* As another phenomenological Christian argues, "us and them" also divides good and evil perfectly, which is impossible on earth. See Tischner, *Spowiedź rewolucjonisty,* 164.

## CHAPTER 2

37 *The fascists of Ilyin's time* Randa cited in *Iordachi, Charisma, Politics, and Violence,* 7.

38 *In the Soviet Union* Between Marxism and Leninism is Engels: see Friedrich Engels, *Anti-Dühring* (New York: International Publishers, [1878], 1972).

39 *Although the USSR's state-controlled* See Timothy Snyder, *Bloodlands* (New York: Basic Books, 2010).

39 *The Bolshevik Revolution* For a convincing case study see Amir Weiner, *Making Sense of War* (Princeton: Princeton UP, 2001).

40 *The myth of the October Revolution* For personal histories of the suspension of time, see Katja Petrowskaja, *Vielleicht Esther* (Berlin: Suhrkamp, 2014); and Marci Shore, *The Taste of Ashes* (New York: Crown Books, 2013).

40 *The same held* Kieran Williams, *The Prague Spring and Its Aftermath* (New York: Cambridge UP, 1997); Paulina Bren, *The Greengrocer and His TV* (Ithaca: Cornell UP, 2010).

41 *Brezhnev died in 1982* Christopher Miller, *The Struggle to Save the Soviet Economy* (Chapel Hill: University of North Carolina Press, 2016). Nationalist political economy: Timothy Snyder, "Soviet Industrial Concentration," in John Williamson, ed., *The Economic Consequences of Soviet Disintegration* (Washington, D.C.: Institute for International Economics, 1993), 176–243.

41 *Within the Soviet Union* The locus classicus on the national question within the USSR is Terry Martin, *The Affirmative Action Empire: Nations and Nationalism in the Soviet Union, 1923–1939* (Ithaca, NY: Cornell UP, 2001). Invaluable on the relationship between 1989 and 1991 is Mark Kramer, "The Collapse of East European Communism and the Repercussions within the Soviet Union," *Journal of Cold War Studies,* vol. 5, no. 4, 2003; vol. 6, no. 4, 2004; vol. 7, no. 1, 2005.

41  *The crisis came* For a valuable portrait of Yeltsin see Timothy J. Colton, *Yeltsin: A Life* (New York: Basic Books, 2008).

42  *Once Yeltsin became* Bush in Kyiv: "Excerpts From Bush's Ukraine Speech: Working 'for the Good of Both of Us,'" Reuters, Aug. 2, 1991. Bush to Gorbachev: Svetlana Savranskaya and Thomas Blanton, eds., *The End of the Soviet Union 1991*, Washington, D.C.: National Security Archive, 2016, document 151.

42  *It is impossible* Ilyin's idea of redemption was discussed in chapter 1. See especially "O russkom" fashizmie," 60–63.

43  *Democracy never took hold* For a measured introduction to the history of the end of the USSR, see Archie Brown, *The Rise and Fall of Communism* (New York: HarperCollins, 2009).

44  *In 1993, Yeltsin dissolved* Charles Clover, *Black Wind, White Snow: The Rise of Russia's New Nationalism* (New Haven: Yale UP, 2016), 214–23.

44  *By 1999, Yeltsin was visibly* "Proekt Putin glazami ego razrabotchika," *MKRU,* Nov. 23, 2017; Clover, *Black Wind, White Snow,* 246–47.

44  *To find his successor* For the political and media backdrop, see Arkady Ostrovsky, *The Invention of Russia* (London: Atlantic Books, 2015), 245–83. Approval ratings: David Satter, *The Less You Know, the Better You Sleep* (New Haven: Yale UP, 2016), 11.

45  *In September 1999* On the politics of the bombing: Satter, *The Less You Know,* 10–11; Krystyna Kurczab-Redlich, *Wowa, Wolodia, Wladimir* (Warsaw: Wydawnictwo ab, 2016), 334–46, 368.

46  *During Putin's first two* Terrorism and control: Peter Pomerantsev, *Nothing Is True and Everything Is Possible* (New York: Public Affairs, 2014), 56. Regional governors: Satter, *The Less You Know,* 116. Surkov's explanation: "Speech at Center for Party Studies," Feb. 7, 2006, published in *Rosbalt,* March 9, 2006; *Ivanov + Rabinovich,* April 2006.

46  *States that joined* Surkov and sovereign democracy: *Ivanov + Rabinovich,* April 2006, and succeeding note. See also "Pochemu Putin tsitiruet filosofa Il'ina?" *KP,* July 4, 2009. Dugin developed this view in his later book *Putin protiv Putina* (Moscow: Yauza-Press, 2012).

47  *Democracy is a procedure* Vladislav Surkov on democracy and the three pillars of statehood: *Texts 97-10,* trans. Scott Rose (Moscow: Europe, 2010). Ilyin's "democratic dictator": *Nashi zadachi,* 340–42. Citing Ilyin: Surkov, "Suverenitet—eto politicheskii sinonim konkurentosposobnosti," in *Teksty 97-07* (Moscow: 2008). The person is the institution: Surkov, "Russkaia politicheskaia kultura: Vzgliaad iz utopii," Russ.ru, June 7, 2015.

47  *Surkov's juggling act* 2002 quotation: Michel Eltchaninoff, *Dans la tête de Vladimir Poutine* (Arles: Actes Sud, 2015), 37. On Ukraine's EU future: "Putin: EU-Beitritt der Ukraine 'kein Problem,'" *FAZ,* Dec. 10, 2004. See also discussion in chapter 3.

49  *By the reckonings* Results: Vera Vasilieva, "Results of the Project 'Citizen Observer,'" Dec. 8, 2011. See also Michael Schwirtz and David M. Herszenhorn, "Voters Watch Polls in Russia," *NYT,* Dec. 5, 2011.

Protests: "In St. Petersburg, 120 protestors were detained," *NTV*, Dec. 5, 2011; Will Englund and Kathy Lally, "Thousands of protesters in Russia demand fair elections," *WP*, Dec. 10, 2011; "Russia: Protests Go On Peacefully," Human Rights Watch, Feb. 27, 2012; Kurczab-Redlich, *Wowa*, 607. Regime-friendly media praises police: *KP*, Dec. 5, 2011; *Pravda*, Dec. 5, 2011. Griffin: Elena Servettez, "Putin's Far Right Friends in Europe," Institute of Modern Russia, Jan. 16, 2014; Anton Shekhovstov, *Russia and the Western Far Right* (London: Routledge, 2018); also see Kashmira Gander, "Ex-BNP leader Nick Griffin tells right-wing conference Russia will save Europe," *Independent*, March 23, 2015.

49 *The fakery was repeated* The nature of the falsification: "Fal'sifikatsii na vyborakh prezidenta Rossiiskoi Federatsii 4 Marta 2012 goda," *Demokraticheskii Vybor*, March 30, 2012; also see Satter, *The Less You Know*, 91; Kurczab-Redlich, *Wowa*, 610–12. On Polish "observers" Kownacki and Piskorski: Konrad Schuller, "Die Moskau-Reise des Herrn Kownacki," *FAZ*, July 11, 2017. The former would later become a vice minister of defense in the Polish government, whereas the latter would be arrested for espionage.

50 *On March 5, 2012* "Oppozitsiia vyshla na Pushkinskoi," Gazeta.ru, March 5, 2012.

50 *Putin chose to regard* Medvedev: Satter, *The Less You Know*, 65. Putin: "Excerpts from the transcript of the meeting of the Valdai International Discussion Club," Sept. 19, 2013. Ilyin quotation: "Kakie zhe vybory nuzhny Rossii," 22.

51 *Leonid Brezhnev's permanent enemy* Kripkov, "To Serve God and Russia," 65.

51 *On December 6, 2011* Dmitry Medvedev (@MedvedevRussia), Dec. 6, 2011. See Paul Goble, "'Hybrid Truth' as Putin's New Reality," Window on Eurasia, blog, Jan. 30, 2015.

52 *A confidant of Putin* Vladimir Yakunin, "Novyi mirovoi klass' vyzov dlia chelovechestva," *Narodnyi Sobor*, Nov. 28, 2012.

52 *In September 2013* China: "Address on Human Rights, Democracy, and the Rule of Law," Beijing, Sept. 13, 2013. Valdai: Vladimir Putin, address at Valdai, Sept. 19, 2013. Law: "For the Purpose of Protecting Children from Information Advocating for a Denial of Traditional Family Values," June 11, 2013.

52 *The campaign did not depend* Kisses: Tatiana Zhurzenko, "Capitalism, autocracy, and political masculinities in Russia," *Eurozine*, May 18, 2016; see also Kurczab-Redlich, *Wowa*, 717–19. Groom: "Vladimir Putin Says Donald Trump 'Is Not My Bride, and I'm Not His Groom,'" *TG*, Sept. 5, 2017. On masculinity see also Mary Louise Roberts, *Civilization Without Sexes* (Chicago: University of Chicago Press, 1994); Dagmar Herzog, *Sex After Fascism* (Princeton: Princeton UP, 2005); Judith Surkis, *Sexing the Citizen* (Ithaca, NY: Cornell UP, 2006); Timothy Snyder, *The Red Prince* (New York: Basic Books, 2008).

53 *Putin was offering* Weber develops this in his *Wirtschaft und Gesellschaft;* relevant sections are published in English in Max Weber, *On Charisma and Institution Building,* ed. S. N. Eisenstadt (Chicago: University of Chicago Press, 1968). Iordachi considers this problem for Christian fascists in *Charisma, Politics, and Violence,* 12ff.

53 *Weber defined two mechanisms* The theme of masculinity will be developed in chapters 4 and 6.

54 *If the Kremlin's first impulse* Putin's "signal" was widely reported: *Pravda,* Dec. 8, 2011; *Mir24,* Dec. 8, 2011; *Nakanune,* Dec. 8, 2011. Hillary Clinton's recollection: *What Happened* (New York: Simon and Schuster, 2017), 329. December 15 claim: "Stenogramma programmy 'Razgovor s Vladimirom Putinym. Prodolzhenie," *RG,* Dec. 15, 2011. Ilyin: *Nashi zadachi,* 56, which is a reference to Carl Schmitt, who likewise makes the distinction between friend and enemy prepolitical: *The Concept of the Political,* trans. George Schwab (Chicago: University of Chicago Press, 2007), 25–28. For contemporary assessments of China, see Thomas Stephan Eder, *China-Russia Relations in Central Asia* (Wiesbaden: Springer, 2014); Marcin Kaczmarski, "Domestic Sources of Russia's China Policy," *Problems of Post-Communism,* vol. 59, no. 2, 2012, 3–17; Richard Lotspeich, "Economic Integration of China and Russia in the Post-Soviet Era," in James Bellacqua, ed., *The Future of China-Russia Relations* (Lexington: University of Kentucky Press, 2010), 83–145; Dambisa F. Moyo, *Winner Take All: China's Race for Resources and What It Means for the World* (New York: Basic Books, 2012).

54 *The West was chosen as an enemy* U.S. troop levels: United States European Command, "U.S. Forces in Europe (1945–2016): Historical View," 2016. Romney: "Russia is our number one geopolitical foe," *CNN: The Situation Room with Wolf Blitzer,* March 26, 2012; Z. Byron Wolf, "Was Mitt Romney right about Detroit and Russia?" CNN, Aug. 1, 2013.

55 *The European Union* Russian media on protests: "The Agency," *NYT,* June 2, 2015; Thomas Grove, "Russian 'smear' documentary provokes protests," Reuters, March 16, 2012. Stooges: "Putin predlozhil zhestche nakazyvat prispeshnikov zapada," *Novye Izvestiia,* Dec. 8, 2011.

55 *Precisely because Putin* Vladimir Putin, Address to Federal Assembly, Dec. 12, 2012; see also Putin, "Excerpts from the transcript of the meeting of the Valdai International Discussion Club," Sept. 19, 2013.

56 *In 2012, Putin made* Vladimir Putin, Address to Federal Assembly, Dec. 12, 2012.

56 *Libel was made* Libel law: Rebecca DiLeonardo, "Russia president signs law re-criminalizing libel and slander," jurist.org, July 30, 2012. Extremism: Lilia Shevtsova, "Forward to the Past in Russia," *Journal of Democracy,* vol. 26, no. 2, 2015, 30. NGO law: "Russia's Putin signs NGO 'foreign agents' law," Reuters, July 21, 2012. Law on religious orthodoxy: Marc Bennetts, "A New Russian Law Targets Evangelicals and other 'Foreign' Religions," *NW,* Sept. 15, 2016. Treason law: "Russia: New

Treason Law Threatens Rights," Human Rights Watch, Oct. 23, 2012. FSB: Eltchaninoff, *Dans la tête de Vladimir Poutine*, 29.

57 *On the morning* Human Rights Watch, "Russia: Government vs. Rights Groups," Sept. 8, 2017.

57 *On December 15, 2011* Transcript of radio program: *RG*, Dec. 2011, rg.ru/2011/12/15/stenogramma.html; also see "Vladimir Putin," *Russkaia narodnaia liniia*, Dec. 16, 2011.

58 *"Can we say"* Ilyin in 1922: Kripkov, "To Serve God and Russia," 182. Putin: "Vladimir Putin," *Russkaia narodnaia liniia*, Dec. 16, 2011.

58 *As a former KGB officer* On Red and White: "The Red and White Tradition of Putin," *Warsaw Institute*, June 1, 2017. An example of Ilyin's critique of the USSR: *Welt vor dem Abgrund* (on the secret police and terror), 99–118. Ilyin's purge of officers of the secret police: "Kakie zhe vybory nuzhny Rossii," 18.

58 *In 2005, Putin had* Incineration and Mikhalkov: Sophia Kishkovsky, "Echoes of civil war in reburial of Russian," *NYT*, Oct. 3, 2005. Mikhalkov and Ilyin: Izrail' Zaidman, "Russkii filosof Ivan Il'in i ego poklonnik Vladimir Putin," *Rebuzhie*, Nov. 25, 2015; Eltchaninoff, *Dans la tête de Vladimir Poutine*, 15. Mikhalkov's manifesto: N. Mikhalkov, "Manifesto of Enlightened Conservatism," Oct. 27, 2010. See also Martynov, "Filosof kadila i nagaiki."

59 *When Putin laid flowers* Chekist for God: Kripkov, "To Serve God and Russia," 201. On Shevkunov: Yuri Zarakhovich, "Putin Pays Homage to Ilyin," *EDM*, June 3, 2009; Charles Clover, "Putin and the Monk," *Financial Times*, Jan. 25, 2013. Shevkunov's evaluation of executioners: "Arkhimandrit Tikhon: 'Oni byli khristiane, bezzavetno sluzhivshie strane i narodu,'" *Izvestiya*, March 26, 2009. Putin quotation: "Putin priznal stroitelei kommunizma 'zhalkimi' kopipasterami," lenta.ru, Dec. 19, 2013.

60 *In Mikhalkov's 2014 film* Solnechnyi udar, 2014, dir. Nikita Mikhalkov; *Trotskii*, 2017, dir. Aleksandr Kott and Konstantyn Statskii, debate between Trotsky and Ilyin in episode 8, at 26:20–29, 40.

60 *As Putin endorsed* Vladimir Putin, "Rossiia: natsional'nyi vopros," *Nezavisimaia Gazeta*, Jan. 23, 2012.

61 *In this article* Putin: ibid. Ilyin: *Nashi zadachi*, 56. Schmitt: *Concept of the Political*.

61 *In writing of Russia* Putin, "Rossiia: natsional'nyi vopros."

61 *When Putin threw* Vladimir Putin, Address to Federal Assembly, Dec. 12, 2012.

62 *Even the most servile* Plan for Russia: see the discussion and sources in chapter 6; also see Jeff Horwitz and Chad Day, "Before Trump job, Manafort worked to aid Putin," AP, March 22, 2017. For a comparison of the 2004 and 2010 elections, see Timothy Garton Ash and Timothy Snyder, "The Orange Revolution," *NYR*, April 28, 2005; and Timothy Snyder, "Gogol Haunts the New Ukraine," *NYR*, March 25, 2010.

63 *Yanukovych won* On early pro-Russian policies: Steven Pifer, *The Eagle*

*and the Trident* (Washington, D.C.: Brookings, 2017), 282; Luke Harding, "Ukraine extends lease for Russia's Black Sea Fleet," *TG,* April 21, 2010. Quotation: Fred Weir, "With Ukraine's blessing, Russia to beef up its Black Sea Fleet," *Christian Science Monitor,* Oct. 25, 2010. It is noteworthy that the government formed after Yanukovych's fall, and despite a Russian invasion, declared that it was not Ukraine's intention to join NATO. See Meike Dülffer, interview with Foreign Minister Pavlo Klimkin, "Am Ende zahlt die Fähigkeit, uns selbst zu verteidigen," *Die Zeit,* Oct. 2, 2014.

63 *Suddenly, in 2012* This is the subject of chapter 4.

63 *Asked by students of history* "Meeting with young scientists and history teachers," Moscow 2014, Kremlin 46951.

63 *In his first address* Putin, Address to Federal Assembly, 2012.

64 *Putin's monastic friend* Pray for Vladimir: Yuri Zarakhovich, "Putin Pays Homage to Ilyin," *EDM,* June 3, 2009. For Ilyin's attitude, see *Nashi zadachi,* 142. On the statue: Shaun Walker, "From one Vladimir to another: Putin unveils huge statue in Moscow," *TG,* Nov. 4, 2016. On the Putin regime as gothic feudalism, see Dina Khapaeva, "La Russie gothique de Poutine," *Libération,* Oct. 23, 2014. On millennial longings and Christian fascism, see Vladimir Tismaneanu, "Romania's Mystical Revolutionaries," in Edith Kurzweil, ed., *A Partisan Century* (New York: Columbia UP, 1996), 383–92.

65 *In history, the person* On the history of Rus and the Bulgars: Simon Franklin and Jonathan Shepard, *The Emergence of Rus 750–1200* (London: Longman, 1996), xix, 30–31, 61; Jonathan Shepard, "The origins of Rus'," in Maureen Perrie, ed., *The Cambridge History of Russia,* vol. 1 (Cambridge, UK: Cambridge UP, 2006), 47–97. On the etymology of "Rus": Manfred Hildermaier, *Geschichte Russlands* (Munich: C. H. Beck, 2013), 42. On the slave trade: Anders Winroth, *The Conversion of Scandinavia* (New Haven: Yale UP, 2012), 47–57, 92. On Volodymyr: Jonathan Shepard, "The origins of Rus'," 62–72; Omeljan Pritsak, *The Origin of Rus'* (Cambridge, Mass.: Harvard UP, 1991), 23–25. On paganism see: S. C. Rowell, *Lithuania Ascending* (Cambridge, UK: Cambridge UP, 1994). On language see Harvey Goldblatt, "The Emergence of Slavic National Languages," in Aldo Scaglione, ed., *The Emergence of National Languages* (Ravenna: Loggo Editore, 1984). Not surprisingly, Ilyin was obsessed with banishing Vikings from what he saw as Russian history: Kripkov, "To Serve God and Russia," 247.

65 *Christianity did not prevent* On this succession struggle: Franklin and Shepard, *Emergence of Rus,* 185–246. On succession in Rus generally, see Hildermaier, *Geschichte Russlands,*114–115; Karl von Loewe, trans. and ed., *The Lithuanian Statute of 1529* (Leiden: E. J. Brill, 1976), 2–3; Stefan Hundland, *Russian Path Dependence* (London: Routledge, 2005), 19–42; Franklin, "Kievan Rus," 84–85. See also Andrzej B. Zakrzewski, *Wielkie Księstwo Litewski (XVI–XVIII w.)* (Warsaw: Campidoglio, 2013). The skull: Jonathan Shepard, "The origins of Rus'," 143–46.

## CHAPTER 3

68 *In his time, Ivan Ilyin* See Mark Mazower, *Dark Continent* (New York: Knopf, 1999). For a concise fascist description of democracy, see Corneliu Zelea Codreanu, "A Few Remarks on Democracy," 1937; for a sense of the attractions of the far Left see François Furet, *Le passé d'une illusion* (Paris: Robert Laffont, 1995); Marci Shore, *Caviar and Ashes* (New Haven, Yale UP, 2006); Richard Crossman, ed., *The God that Failed* (London: Hamilton, 1950).

68 *The First World War* On the long First World War: Jörn Leonhard, *Die Büchse der Pandora* (Munich: Beck, 2014); Robert Gerwarth, *Die Besiegten* (Munich: Siedler, 2017). On interwar great power politics: Sergei Gorlov, *Sovershenno sekretno, Moskva-Berlin, 1920–1933* (Moscow: RAN, 1999); Jonathan Haslam, *The Soviet Union and the Struggle for Collective Security in Europe, 1933–39* (Houndmills, UK: Macmillan, 1984); Marek Kornat, *Polityka zagraniczna Polski 1938–1939* (Gdańsk: Oskar, 2012); Hans Roos, *Polen und Europa* (Tübingen: J. C. B. Mohr, 1957); Frank Golczewski, *Deutsche und Ukrainer, 1914–1939* (Paderborn: Ferdinand Schöning, 2010); Hugh Ragsdale, *The Soviets, the Munich Crisis, and the Coming of World War II* (Cambridge, UK: Cambridge UP, 2004); Gerhard L. Weinberg, *The Foreign Policy of Hitler's Germany* (Chicago: University of Chicago Press, 1980); Piotr Stefan Wandycz, *The Twilight of French Eastern Alliances, 1926–1936* (Princeton: Princeton UP, 1988). On interwar political economy and the nation-state, see E. A. Radice, "General Characteristics of the Region Between the Wars," in Michael Kaser, ed., *An Economic History of Eastern Europe*, vol. 1 (New York: Oxford UP, 1985), 23–65; Joseph Rothschild, *East Central Europe Between the World Wars* (Seattle: University of Washington Press, 1992), 281–311; Bruce F. Pauley, "The Social and Economic Background of Austria's *Lebensunfähigkeit*," in Anson Rabinbach, ed., *The Austrian Socialist Experiment* (Boulder: Westview Press, 1985), 21–37. The Polish regional governor: "Protokoł z zebrania polskiej grupy parlamentarnej Wołynia," Centralne Archiwum Wojskowe, Rembertów, I.302.4.122. Kennan: Ira Katznelson, *Fear Itself* (New York: Norton, 2013), 32.

70 *The Second World War* On the Molotov-Ribbentrop Pact, see Gerd Koenen, *Der Russland-Komplex* (Munich: Beck, 2005); Sławomir Dębski, *Między Berlinem a Moskwą. Stosunki niemiecko-sowieckie 1939–1941* (Warsaw: PISM, 2003); John Lukacs, *The Last European War* (New Haven: Yale UP, 2001); Roger Moorhouse, *The Devils' Alliance* (London: Bodley Head, 2014). On the German war in Poland, see Jochen Böhler, *"Größte Härte": Verbrechen der Wehrmacht in Polen September/Oktober 1939* (Osnabrück: Deutsches Historisches Institut, 2005). On simultaneous Soviet war crimes, see Anna M. Cienciala, Natalia S. Lebedeva, and Wojciech Materski, eds., *Katyn* (New Haven: Yale UP, 2007); Grzegorz Hryciuk, "Victims 1939–1941," in Elazar Barkan, Elisabeth A. Cole, and Kai Struve, eds., *Shared History–Divided Memory* (Leipzig: Leipzig University-Verlag,

2007), 173–200. On the centrality of Ukraine, see Snyder, *Bloodlands*; Timothy Snyder, *Black Earth* (New York: Crown Books, 2015). See also Adam Tooze, *The Wages of Destruction* (New York: Viking, 2007); Rolf-Dieter Müller, *Der Feind steht im Osten* (Berlin: Ch. Links Verlag, 2011); Ulrike Jureit, *Das Ordnen von Räumen* (Hamburg: Hamburger Edition, 2012); Christian Gerlach, *Krieg, Ernährung, Völkermord* (Hamburg: Hamburger Edition, 1998); Alex J. Kay, *Exploitation, Resettlement, Mass Murder* (New York: Berghahn Books, 2006).

70 *In general, the defeat* Guides to this transition: Thomas W. Simons, Jr., *Eastern Europe in the Postwar World* (New York: St. Martin's, 1993); Hugh Seton-Watson, *The East European Revolution* (New York: Praeger, 1956), 167–211; Jan T. Gross, "The Social Consequences of War," *East European Politics and Societies*, vol. 3, 1989, 198–214; Bradley F. Abrams, "The Second World War and the East European Revolutions," *East European Politics and Societies*, vol. 16, no. 3, 2003, 623–64; T. V. Volokitina, et al., eds., *Sovetskii faktor v Vostochnoi Evrope 1944–1953* (Moscow: Sibirskii khronograf, 1997).

70 *American economic power* Alan Milward, *The European Rescue of the Nation-State* (Berkeley: University of California Press, 1992). See also Harold James, *Europe Reborn: A History, 1914–2000* (Harlow: Pearson, 2003).

71 *European integration began Nashi zadachi*, 94–95, 166–168. See Evlampiev, "Ivan Il'in kak uchastnik sovremennykh diskussii," 15, who stresses that Ilyin advocated a national dictatorship "with clear fascist overtones" to the end of his life.

72 *In the half century* A history that considers both decolonization and integration is Tony Judt, *Postwar: A History of Europe Since 1945* (New York: Penguin Press, 2005). On the scale of German losses in the war, see Rüdiger Overmans, *Deutsche militärische Verluste im Zweiten Weltkrieg* (Munich: Oldenbourg, 1999); also see Thomas Urban, *Der Verlust: Die Vertreibung der Deutschen und Polen im 20. Jahrhundert* (Munich: C. H. Beck, 2004).

72 *By the 1980s* The case for economic rationality is made in Andrew Moravcsik, *The Choice for Europe* (Ithaca, NY: Cornell UP, 1998).

72 *For most of the communist states* A classic analysis of the Polish case is Antony Polonsky, *Politics in Independent Poland 1921–1939* (Oxford: Clarendon Press, 1972).

73 *In 2004 and 2007* Timothy Snyder, "Integration and Disintegration: Europe, Ukraine, and the World," *Slavic Review*, vol. 74, no. 4, Winter 2015.

74 *An imperial power* See Mark Mazower, "An International Civilization?" *International Affairs*, vol. 82, no. 3, 2006, 553–66.

75 *Throughout the history* On Italy see Davide Rodogno, *Fascism's European Empire*, trans. Adrian Belton (Cambridge, UK: Cambridge UP, 2006).

76 *In history there was no era* A useful French review is Patrick Weil, *How to be French*, trans. Catherine Porter (Durham: Duke UP, 2008).

78 *The explicit Russian rejection* In 2013 the idea of destroying the European Union was cast by Russian leaders as a merger with Eurasia. With time

the Russian threat to destroy the EU became more explicit: Isabelle Mandraud, "Le document de Poutine qui entérine la nouvelle guerre froide," *LM*, Dec. 6, 2016.

79 *Until 2012, Russian leaders* Russia, Putin, and the EU: Jackie Gower, "European Union–Russia Relations at the End of the Putin Presidency," *Journal of Contemporary European Studies*, vol. 16, no. 2, Aug. 2008, 161–67; Eltchaninoff, *Dans la tête de Vladimir Poutine*, 37. Putin on Ukraine in 2004: "Putin: EU-Beitritt der Ukraine 'kein Problem,'" *FAZ*, Dec. 10, 2004. Rogozin on NATO: Artemy Kalinovsky, *A Long Goodbye: The Soviet Withdrawal from Afghanistan* (Cambridge, Mass.: Harvard UP, 2011), 226.

79 *The basic line* Kleptocracy: The locus classicus is Karen Dawisha, *Putin's Kleptocracy* (New York: Simon and Schuster, 2014). Karl Schlögel makes the point powerfully in his *Entscheidung in Kiew* (Munich: Carl Hanser Verlag, 2015), 78. See also Anders Åslund and Andrew Kuchins, *The Russia Balance Sheet* (Washington, D.C.: Peterson Institute, 2009).

79 *In matters of peace and war* Estonia: Hannes Grassegger and Mikael Krogerus, "Weaken from Within," *New Republic*, Dec. 2017, 18; Marcel Van Herpen, *Putin's Propaganda Machine* (Lanham: Rowman and Littlefield, 2016), 121. Georgia: John Markoff, "Before the Gunfire, Cyberattacks," *NYT*, Aug. 12, 2008; D. J. Smith, "Russian Cyber Strategy and the War Against Georgia," *Atlantic Council*, Jan. 17, 2014; Irakli Lomidze, "Cyber Attacks Against Georgia," Ministry of Justice of Georgia: Data Exchange Agency, 2011; Sheera Frenkel, "Meet Fancy Bear, the Russian Group Hacking the US election," *BuzzFeed*, Oct. 15, 2016.

80 *By the 2010s* Vladimir Putin, "Von Lissabon bis Wladiwostok," *Süddeutsche Zeitung*, Nov. 25, 2010.

80 *A signal difference* Putin's embrace of ideology after 2010 is a subject of this book. On his relationship to law and politics before 2010, and for a complementary argument, see Masha Gessen, *The Man Without a Face* (New York: Riverhead Books, 2013). Young Ilyin: Ilyin, "Concepts of Law and Power," 68; Grier, "Complex Legacy," 167; Kripkov, "To Serve God and Russia," 13.

81 *The mature Ilyin* Ilyin, "O russkom" fashizmie," 60.

81 *Writing in the newspaper* Vladimir Putin, "Novyi integratsionnyi proekt dla Evrazii—budushchee, kotoroe rozhdaetsia segodnia," *Izvestiia*, Oct. 3, 2011. See also Vladimir Putin, "Rossiia: natsional'nyi vopros," *Nezavisimaia Gazeta*, Jan. 23, 2012.

82 *Of course, for the EU* Putin on Eurasia: "Rossiia i meniaiushchiisia mir," *Moskovskie Novosti*, Feb. 27, 2012. Eurasian economic union: Jan Strzelecki, "The Eurasian Economic Union: a time of crisis," *OSW Commentary*, no. 195, Jan. 27, 2016.

82 *As a presidential candidate* See chapter 2.

83 *Russia had no plausible principle* Putin on Eurasia in May: "Vladimir Putin vstupil v dolzhnost' Prezidenta Rossii," kremlin.ru, May 7, 2012. See also Alexander Dugin, "Tretii put' i tret'ia sila," *Izborsk Club*, Dec. 4, 2013,

article 1300. Putin in December: Address to Federal Assembly, Dec. 12, 2012.

84  *Long before Putin announced* According to Kripkov, Ilyin was a westernizer when the First World War began: "To Serve God and Russia," 120. See Martin Malia, *Alexander Herzen and the Birth of Russian Socialism, 1812–1855* (Cambridge, Mass.: Harvard UP, 1961); Andrzej Walicki, *The Controversy over Capitalism* (Oxford, UK: Clarendon Press, 1969).

84  *The first Eurasianists* Clover, *Black Wind, White Snow,* 47–63.

84  *The Eurasianists of the 1920s* On the Gulag and biological truths, see Clover, *Black Wind, White Snow,* 124; Golfo Alexopoulos, *Illness and Inhumanity in the Gulag* (New Haven: Yale UP, 2017). On the Gulag generally, see Oleg V. Khlevniuk, *The History of the Gulag* (New Haven: Yale UP, 2004); Lynna Viola, *The Unknown Gulag* (New York: Oxford UP, 2007); Anne Applebaum, *Gulag: A History* (New York: Doubleday, 2003). See also Barbara Skarga, *Penser après le Goulag,* ed. Joanna Nowicki (Paris: Editions du Relief, 2011). On the Great Terror, see Karl Schlögel, *Terror und Traum* (Munich: Carl Hanser Verlag, 2008); Nicolas Werth, *La terreur et le désarroi* (Paris: Perrin, 2007); Rolf Binner and Marc Junge, "Wie der Terror 'Gross' wurde," *Cahiers du Monde russe,* vol. 42, nos. 2–3–4, 2001, 557–614.

85  *Writing as an academic* Clover, *Black Wind, White Snow,* 139.

87  *Gumilev's contribution* Clover, *Black Wind, White Snow,* 125, 129, 134.

87  *Gumilev also added* Alexander Sergeevich Titov, "Lev Gumilev, Ethnogenesis and Eurasianism," doctoral dissertation, University College London, 2005, 102; Clover, *Black Wind, White Snow,* 129. On Gumilev's antisemitism, see Mark Bassin, *The Gumilev Mystique* (Ithaca, NY: Cornell UP, 2016), 313: "Gumilev was a zealous antisemite."

87  *Despite his years* See generally Andreas Umland, "Post-Soviet 'Uncivil Society' and the Rise of Aleksandr Dugin," doctoral dissertation, University of Cambridge, 2007. Borodai and Gumilev: Titov, "Lev Gumilev," 102, 236; Bassin, *Gumilev Mystique,* 314.

88  *To speak of "Eurasia"* Ovens: Clover, *Black Wind, White Snow,* 155. Dugin and Gumilev: Titov, "Lev Gumilev," 13; Clover, *Black Wind, White Snow,* 180; Bassin, *Gumilev Mystique,* 308–9.

88  *As the Soviet Union* Influences: Shekhovtsov, *Russia and the Western Far Right,* chapter 2.

89  *In the early 1990s* Sievers and De Benoist: Clover, *Black Wind, White Snow,* 158, 177.

89  *Dugin's European contacts* Cyril and Methodius and hailing death: Clover, *Black Wind, White Snow,* 11, 225. Borderless and red: Aleksandr Dugin, "Fashizm—Bezgranichnyi i krasnyi," 1997. Destiny: Alexander Dugin, "Horizons of Our Revolution from Crimea to Lisbon," *Open Revolt,* March 7, 2014.

89  *Dugin shared with Ilyin* In Marlene Laruelle's valuable introduction to Dugin's European influences, she makes the point that he was unable to distinguish Schmitt from the National Socialist tradition. It is an

instructive failure. See "Introduction," in Marine Laruelle, ed., *Eurasianism and the European Far Right* (Lanham: Lexington Books, 2015), 10–11. Schmitt quotations: Carl Schmitt, *Writings on War*, trans. Timothy Nunan (Cambridge, UK: Polity Press, 2011), 107, 111, 124. Nunan's introduction is an excellent guide to Schmitt as a theorist of international relations. On Schmitt's opposition to the conventional state and the Nazi attitude to international law, see Czesław Madajczyk, "Legal Conceptions in the Third Reich and Its Conquests," *Michael: On the History of Jews in the Diaspora*, vol. 13, 1993, 131–59. Madajczyk drew from Alfons Klafkowski, *Okupacja niemiecka w Polsce w świetle prawa narodów* (Poznań: Wydawnictwo Instytutu Zachodniego, 1946), written during the war as a reply to Schmitt. Mark Mazower is one of the few Western scholars to see the significance of this German-Polish discussion: *Governing the World* (New York: Penguin Press, 2012) and *Hitler's Empire* (London: Allen Lane, 2008).

90 *Dugin dismissed Ilyin* Archetypes: Alexander Dugin, "Arkhetip vampirov v soliarnykh misteriiakh," propagandahistory.ru, 51; Clover, *Black Wind, White Snow,* 189. Wickedness: Aleksandr Dugin, "Printsipy i strategiia griadushchei voiny," *4 Pera,* Dec. 20, 2015. Technical function: Eltchaninoff, *Dans la tête de Vladimir Poutine,* 110. On Obama: "Obama rozvalit Ameriku," www.youtube.com/watch?v=9AAyz3YFHhE. Spiritual resource: "Ideinye istoki Vladimira Putina," Odinnadtsatyi Kanal, May 17, 2016.

90 *Writing in the early* Enormous danger: Clover, *Black Wind, White Snow,* 238. Youth movement and battle for Crimea: Anton Shekhovtsov, "How Alexander Dugin's Neo-Eurasianists Geared Up for the Russian-Ukrainian War in 2005–2013," *TI,* Jan. 26, 2016. See also Aleksandr Dugin, "Letter to the American People on Ukraine," *Open Revolt,* March 8, 2014.

91 *In 2012, fascist thinkers* Members: "Manifest Ottsov—Osnovaetlei," *Izborsk Club,* dated Sept. 8, 2012, published Dec. 1, 2012, article 887. On Shevkunov in 2012: Charles Clover, "Putin and the Monk," *Financial Times,* Jan. 25, 2013.

91 *The founder and moving spirit* On Prokhanov, see Clover, *Black Wind, White Snow,* 183–87; for useful background, see G. V. Kostyrchenko, *Gosudarstvennyi antisemitizm v SSSR* (Moscow: Materik, 2005). Reaction to Obama: *Ekho Moskvy,* July 8, 2009, 604015.

92 *When asked about* "Yanukovich i Timoshenko: eto ne lichnosti, a politicheskie mashiny—Aleksandr Prokhanov," News24UA.com, Aug. 31, 2012.

92 *The fundamental problem* "Ukraina dolzhna stat' tsentrom Evrazii—Aleksandr Prokhanov," News24UA.com, Aug. 31, 2012.

93 *This grand redemptive project* Ibid.

93 *The Izborsk Club* This and the following long quotations are from the manifesto: "Manifest Ottsov—Osnovaetlei," Izborsk Club, dated Sept. 8, 2012, published Dec. 1, 2012, article 887.

94 *No reference was made* Prokhanov: Interview for *Ekho Moskvy,* July 8, 2009, 604015.

96 *After this initial salvo* "Zionist leaders": Oleg Platonov, "Missiia vypol-nima," *Izborsk Club*, Feb. 6, 2014, article 2816. Collapse of EU and in-tegration of Europe with Russia: Yuri Baranchik and Anatol Zapolskis, "Evrosoiuz: Imperiia, kotoraia ne sostoialas," Izborsk Club, Feb. 25, 2015, article 4847. Prokhanov: "Parizhskii Apokalipsis," Izborsk Club, Nov. 15, 2015. Izborsk's expert on Ukraine: Valery Korovin, interview, "Ukraina so vremenem vernetsia k Rossii," *Svobodnaia Pressa*, March 22, 2016. Dugin: "Tretii put' i tret'ia sila," Izborsk Club, Dec. 4, 2013.

97 *For the Eurasianists* "Nachalo," Izborsk Club, Sept. 12, 2012, article 887.

97 *One of Russia's* Andrei Volkov, "Prokhanov prokatilsia na novom rake-tonostse Tu-95," *Vesti*, Aug. 16, 2014.

97 *Sergei Glazyev* On Glazyev's economics: Sergei Glazyev and Sergei Tka-chuk, "Eurasian economic union," in Piotr Dutkiewicz and Richard Sakwa, *Eurasian Integration* (New Brunswick: Routledge, 2014), 61–83. On Glazyev and LaRouche: Sergei Glazyev, *Genocide: Russia and the New World Order* (published by *Executive Intelligence Review*, 1999). On Ukraine: Sergei Glazyev, "Eurofascism," *Executive Intelligence Review*, June 27, 2014.

98 *Russian foreign policy arose* Sergei Glazyev, "Who Stands to Win? Political and Economic Factors in Regional Integration," *Global Affairs*, Dec. 27, 2013. Or "Takie raznye integratsii," globalaffairs.ru, Dec. 16, 2013. "Spa-tial concept": Glazyev and Tkachuk, "Eurasian economic union," 82. Mosaic: Sergei Glazyev, "SSh idut po puti razviazyvaniia mirovoi voiny," March 29, 2016, lenta.ru.

99 *The Foreign Policy Concept* Quotations in this and succeeding paragraphs from Ministry of Foreign Affairs of the Russian Federation, "Kontseptsiia vneshnei politiki Rossiiskoi Federatsii (utverzhdena Prezidentom Rossiis-koi Federatsii V.V. Putinym 12 fevralia 2013 g.)"

99 *The Concept made clear* Sergei Lavrov, "Istoricheskaia perspektiva vneshnei politiki Rossii," March 3, 2016.

100 *Putin befriended* Zeman: Péter Krekó et al., *The Weaponization of Culture* (Budapest: Political Capital Institute, 2016), 6, 61; Van Herpen, *Putin's Propaganda Machine*, 109; "Milos Zeman," *TG*, Sept. 14, 2016. Lukoil paid a $1.4 million fine owed by Martin Nejedlý, Zeman's advisor and vice chairman of his party (Roman Gerodimos, Fauve Vertegaal, and Mirva Villa, "Russia Is Attacking Western Liberal Democracies," NYU Jordan Center, 2017). 2018 campaign: Veronika Špalková and Jakub Janda, "Ac-tivities of Czech President Miloš Zeman," Kremlin Watch Report, 2018. Like Putin, Zeman presided over a country that took almost no refugees from Syria; and like Putin, he used the image of threat, speaking of a "super-Holocaust" that Muslims could perpetrate upon Czechs. Zeman also denied the Russian presence in Ukraine, and joined in Russian attacks on gays and Russian political prisoners. Zeman was rewarded by Russian media attention: František Vrobel and Jakub Janda, *How Russian Propa-ganda Portrays European Leaders* (Prague: Semantic Visions, 2016). Putin quotation: "Putin: esli by Berluskoni byl geem, ego by pal'tsem nikto ne

tronul," interfax.ru, Sept. 19, 2013. On Berlusconi: Jochen Bittner et al., "Putins großer Plan," *Die Zeit*, Nov. 20, 2014; Jason Horowitz, "Berlusconi Is Back," *NYT*, Jan. 29, 2018. On Schröder: Rick Noack, "He used to rule Germany. Now, he oversees Russian energy companies and lashes out at the U.S.," *WP*, Aug. 12, 2017; Erik Kirschbaum, "Putin's apologist?" Reuters, March 27, 2014.

100 *In the post-communist* Generally: Van Herpen, *Putin's Propaganda Machine*. Internet interventions: Krekó, "Weaponization of Culture"; Anton Shekhovtsov, "Russian Politicians Building an International Extreme Right Alliance," *TI*, Sept. 15, 2015. Le Pen on RT: Marine Turchi, "Au Front nationale, le lobbying pro-russe s'accélère," *Mediapart*, Dec. 18, 2014; see also Iurii Safronov, "Russkii mir 'Natsional'nogo Fronta'," *NG*, Dec. 17, 2014. RT began broadcasting in Spanish in 2009, in German in 2014, and in French in 2017.

101 *Farage and Le Pen proposed* Nigel Farage, "Leave Euro, Retake Democracy!" RT, July 8, 2013; see also Bryan MacDonald, "Could UKIP's rise herald a new chapter in Russian-British relations," RT, Nov. 25, 2014. Le Pen: Alina Polyakova, Marlene Laruelle, Stefan Mesiter, and Neil Barnett, *The Kremlin's Trojan Horses* (Washington, D.C.: Atlantic Council, 2016); see also the discussion below on loans and gay marriage.

101 *In 2013, a preoccupation* Le Pen and sexual politics in Russia: Polyakova et al., *Kremlin's Trojan Horses*, 10. Le Pen on homophilia: Aleksandr Terent'ev-Ml., interview with Marine Le Pen, "Frantsiia davno uzhe ne svobodnaia strana," *Odnako*, Aug. 6, 2013. Chauprade: Marine Turchi, "Les réseaux russes de Marine Le Pen," *Mediapart*, Feb. 19, 2014; *Sputnik France*, Oct. 16, 2013; Aymeric Chauprade, speech to Russian Duma, *Realpolitik TV*, June 13, 2013. Le Pen on Eurasia: "Au congrès du FN, la 'cameraderie' russe est bruyamment mise en scène," *Mediapart*, Nov. 29, 2014.

102 *At that same moment* Spencer admires Putin: Sarah Posner, "Meet the Alt-Right Spokesman Thrilled by Putin's Rise," *Rolling Stone*, Oct. 18, 2016. "Sole white power": Natasha Bertrand, "Trump won't condemn white supremacists or Vladimir Putin," *BI*, Aug. 14, 2017. Spencer and Kouprianova: Casey Michel, "Meet the Moscow Mouthpiece Married to a Racist Alt-Right Boss," *DB*, Dec. 20, 2016; Spencer's chant: Daniel Lombroso and Yoni Appelbaum, "'Hail Trump!'" *The Atlantic*, Nov. 21, 2016; Adam Gabbatt, "Hitler salutes and white supremacism," *TG*, Nov. 21, 2016.

102 *As it happened* RT's engagement with birtherism and similar ideas: Sonia Scherr, "Russian TV Channel Pushes 'Patriot' Conspiracy Theories," Southern Poverty Law Center Intelligence Report, Aug. 1, 2010; also see Shekhovtsov, *Russia and the Western Far Right*, chapter 5. Tweet: Donald Trump, June 18, 2013.

102 *Trump's contribution* Trump and pageant: Jim Zarroli, "At the 2013 Miss Universe Contest, Trump Met Some of Russia's Rich and Powerful," NPR, July 17, 2017. On Trump's finances: Reuters, "Trump Bankers Question His Portrayal of Financial Comeback," *Fortune*, July 17, 2016;

Jean Eaglesham and Lisa Schwartz, "Trump's Debts Are Widely Held on Wall Street, Creating New Potential Conflicts," Jan. 5, 2017; Trump and Mogilevich and Tokhtakhounov: Craig Unger, "Trump's Russian Laundromat," *New Republic,* July 13, 2017; Tokhtakhounov: Chris Francescani, "Top NY art dealer, suspected Russian mob boss indicted on gambling charges," Reuters, April 16, 2013; David Corn and Hannah Levintova, "How Did an Alleged Russian Mobster End Up on Trump's Red Carpet?" *Mother Jones,* Sept. 14, 2016. See also Tomasz Piątek, *Macierewicz i jego tajemnice* (Warsaw: Arbitror, 2017).

103 *The Russian property developer* Trump and Agalarov: Luke Harding, *Collusion* (New York: Vintage, 2017), 229–37; "Here's What We Know about Donald Trump and His Ties to Russia," *WP,* July 29, 2016; "How Vladimir Putin Is Using Donald Trump to Advance Russia's Goals," *NW,* Aug. 29, 2016; Cameron Sperance, "Meet Aras Agalarov," *Forbes,* July 12, 2017; Shaun Walker, "The Trumps of Russia?" *TG,* July 15, 2017; Mandalit Del Barco, "Meet Emin Agalarov," NPR, July 14, 2017. Agalarov sends Trump information about Clinton: Jo Becker, Adam Goldman, and Matt Apuzzo, "Russian Dirt on Clinton? 'I Love It,' Donald Trump Jr. Said," *NYT,* July 11, 2017.

103 *The love began that summer* Order of Honor: "How Vladimir Putin Is Using Donald Trump to Advance Russia's Goals," *NW,* Aug. 29, 2016. Le Pen visits Moscow: Vivienne Walt, "French National Front Secures Funding from Russian Bank," *Time,* Nov. 25, 2014. Trump supports Le Pen: Aidan Quigley, "Trump expresses support for French candidate Le Pen," *Politico,* April 21, 2017; Aaron Blake, "Trump is now supporting far-right French candidate Marine Le Pen," *WP,* April 21, 2017; Gideon Rachman, "Le Pen, Trump and the Atlantic counter-revolution," *FT,* Feb. 27, 2017. Le Pen supports Trump: James McAuley, "Marine Le Pen's tricky alliance with Donald Trump," April 2, 2017. National Front funded by Russia: Marine Turchi, "Le FN attend 40 million d'euros de Russie," *Mediapart,* Nov. 26, 2014; Karl Laske and Marine Turchi, "Le troisème prêt russe des Le Pen," *Mediapart,* Dec. 11, 2014; Abel Mestre, "Marine Le Pen justifie le prêt russe du FN," *LM,* Nov. 23, 2014; Anna Mogilevskaia, "Partiia Marin Le Pen vziala kredit v rossiiskom banke," *Kommersant,* Nov. 23, 2014.

104 *Although the* **Front National** Russians hack French TV: Frenkel, "Meet Fancy Bear"; Gordon Corera, "How France's TV5 was almost destroyed by 'Russian hackers,'" BBC, Oct. 10, 2016; Joseph Menn and Leigh Thomas, "France probes Russian lead in TV5Monde hacking: sources," Reuters, June 10, 2015. Prokhanov: "Parizhskii Apokalipsis," Izborsk Club, Nov. 15, 2015.

104 *In the 2017 French* Le Pen on Putin: Turchi, "Le Front national décroche les millions russe"; Shaun Walker, "Putin welcomes Le Pen to Moscow with a nudge and a wink," *TG,* March 24, 2017; Ronald Brownstein, "Putin and the Populists," *The Atlantic,* Jan. 6, 2017. Russian propaganda about Macron: Götz Hamann, "Macron Is Gay, Not!" *Zeit Online,* Feb. 24, 2017;

"Ex-French Economy Minister Macron Could Be 'US Agent,'" *Sputnik News*, Feb. 4, 2017.

104 *To support the* **Front National** Farage supports Russia: Patrick Wintour and Rowena Mason, "Nigel Farage's relationship with Russian media comes under scrutiny," *TG*, March 31, 2014. Farage on EU: "Leave Euro, retake democracy!'" RT, July 8, 2015.

104 *The first order of business* Bots and trolls supporting fraud claims: Severin Carrell, "Russian cyber-activists," *TG*, Dec. 13, 2017. "Total falsification": "Russia meddled in Scottish independence referendum," *Daily Express*, Jan. 15, 2017. UK elections fake: Neil Clark, "UK general election," RT, May 10, 2015. Support for referendum: Bryan MacDonald, "Ireland needed guns, but Scots only need a pen for independence," RT, Sept. 3, 2014; see also Ben Riley-Smith, "Alex Salmond: I admire 'certain aspects' of Vladimir Putin's leadership," *Telegraph*, April 28, 2014; Anastasia Levchenko, "Russia, Scotland Should Seek Closer Ties—Ex–SNP Leader," *Sputnik*, May 7, 2015.

105 *Although Britain's Conservative Party* On Farage and RT, see earlier. On Farage and Putin: "Nigel Farage: I admire Vladimir Putin," *TG*, March 2014. Staffer: Stephanie Kirchgaessner, "The Farage staffer, the Russian embassy, and a smear campaign," *TG*, Dec. 18, 2017. Conservative Friends of Russia: Carole Cadwalladr, "Brexit, the ministers, the professor and the spy," *TG*, Nov. 4, 2017.

106 *All of the major* Russian propaganda on referendum: "General referendum may trigger a domino effect in Europe," Rossiia-24, June 24, 2016; RT on Brexit: "Is Parliament preparing to ignore public vote for Brexit?" RT, June 6, 2016; "EU army plans 'kept secret' from British voters until after Brexit referendum," RT, May 27, 2016. For the statistics on bots and Brexit, see Marco T. Bastos and Dan Mercea, "The Brexit Botnet and User-Generated Hyperpartisan News," *Social Science Computer Review*, 2017, at 7 for the conclusion that 90% of relevant bots were outside the UK. The 419: Severin Carrell, "Russian cyber-activists," *TG*, Dec. 13, 2017. For analysis, see Carole Cadwalladr, "The Great British Brexit Robbery," *TG*, May 7, 2017; Gerodimos et al., "Russia Is Attacking Western Liberal Democracies."

106 *For some time, Russian politicians* Kosachev: report on election result, *Telegraph*, Jan. 9, 2015. Commitments not binding: PK, June 3, 2016. Putin: "Vladimir Putin ne ozhidaet 'global'noi katastrofy," PK, June 24, 2016, "V Velikobritanii nabiraet oboroty agitatsionnaia kompaniia za vykhod strany iz Evrosoiuza," PK, May 27, 2016.

107 *Russia's support* On Gudenus and the background of the Austrian far Right's connections with Moscow, see Shekhovtsov, *Russia and the Western Far Right*. On Austria in the twentieth century: Gerald Stourzh, *Vom Reich zur Republik* (Vienna: Editions Atelier, 1990); Walter Goldinger and Dieter Binder, *Geschichte der Republik Österreich 1918–1938* (Oldenbourg: Verlag für Geschichte und Politik, 1992); Anson Rabinbach, *The*

*Crisis of Austrian Socialism* (Chicago: University of Chicago Press, 1983); Wolfgang Müller, *Die sowjetische Besatzung in Österreich 1945–1955 und ihre politische Mission* (Vienna: Böhlau, 2005); Rolf Steininger, *Der Staatsvertrag* (Innsbruck: Studien-Verlag, 2005).

107 *During the 2016* Bernhard Weidinger, Fabian Schmid, and Péter Krekó, *Russian Connections of the Austrian Far Right* (Budapest: Political Capital, 2017), 5, 9, 28, 30.

107 *As in France* Cooperation agreement: "Austrian far right signs deal with Putin's party, touts Trump ties," Reuters, Dec. 19, 2016.

108 *Integration or empire?* "Ukrainian Oligarchs Stay Above the Fray and Let the Crisis Play Out," *IBTimes*, Feb. 26, 2014; "Behind Scenes, Ukraine's Rich and Powerful Battle over the Future," *NYT*, June 12, 2013.

108 *The Eurasianists themselves* Prokhanov: "Yanukovich i Timoshenko." Glazyev threat: Shaun Walker, "Ukraine's EU trade deal will be catastrophic, says Russia," *TG*, Sept. 22, 2013. See Schlögel, *Entscheidung in Kiew*, 80.

## CHAPTER 4

111 *The Russian politics of eternity* Vladimir Putin, "Meeting with members of Holy Synod of Ukrainian Orthodox Church of Moscow Patriarchate," July 27, 2013, Kremlin, 18960. He was saying this sort of thing with increasing frequency in 2013: John Lough, "Putin's Communications Difficulties Reflect Serious Policy Problem," Chatham House, 2014.

111 *In September 2013* Vladimir Putin, "Excerpts from the transcript of the meeting of the Valdai International Discussion Club," Sept. 19, 2013. The "organic model" was discussed in chapter 1.

112 *Nations are new things* Early Rus statehood was discussed in chapter 2. See generally Franklin and Shepard, *Emergence of Rus;* Winroth, *Conversion of Scandinavia*.

112 *It is also possible* Isaiah Berlin, in "The Concept of Scientific History," quotes Lewis Namier to interesting effect: "What is meant by historical sense is the knowledge not of what happened, but of what did not happen."

112 *The configurations that make* On the Commonwealth, see Daniel Stone, *The Polish-Lithuanian State, 1386–1795* (Seattle: University of Washington Press, 2001). On the tensions, see Timothy Snyder, *The Reconstruction of Nations: Poland, Ukraine, Lithuania, Belarus, 1569–1999* (New Haven: Yale UP, 2003); Oskar Halecki, *Przyłączenie Podlasia, Wołynia, i Kijowszczyzny do Korony w Roku 1569* (Cracow: Gebethner and Wolff, 1915); Nataliia Iakovenko, *Narys istorii Ukrainy z naidavnishykh chasiv do kintsia XVIII stolittia* (Kyiv: Heneza, 1997); Jan Rotkowski, *Histoire economique de la Pologne avant les partages* (Paris: Champion, 1927).

113 *After 1569* See David Frick, *Polish Sacred Philology in the Reformation and Counter-Reformation* (Berkeley: University of California Press, 1989); André Martel, *La Langue Polonaise dans les pays ruthènes* (Lille: Travaux et Mémoires de l'Université de Lille, 1938).

114  *Serfs sought refuge* Vitalii Shcherbak, *Ukrains'ke kozatstvo* (Kyiv: KM Akademia, 2000); Tetiana Iakovleva, *Hetmanshchyna v druhii polovini 50-kh rokiv XVII stolittia* (Kyiv: Osnovy, 1998).

114  *In 1648, these tensions* See Jaroslaw Pelenski, "The Origins of the Official Muscovite Claim to the 'Kievan Inheritance,'" *Harvard Ukrainian Studies*, vol. 1, no. 1, 1977, 48–50.

116  *Muscovy now turned westward* See David Saunders, *The Ukrainian Impact on Russian Culture, 1750–1850* (Edmonton: CIUS, 1985); K. V. Kharlampovich, *Malorossiiskoe vliianie na velikorusskuiu tserkovnuiu zhizn'* (Kazan: Golubeva, 1914).

116  *In the nineteenth century* Daniel Beauvois, *Pouvoir russe et noblesse polonaise en Ukraine, 1793–1830* (Paris: CNRS Editions, 2003); Daniel Beauvois, *Le noble, le serf, et le revizor* (Paris: Editions des archives contemporaines, 1985); Jarosław Hrycak, *Historia Ukrainy: 1772–1999* (Lublin: Instytut Europy Środkowo-Wschodniej, 2000); Andreas Kappelar, *Russland als Vielvölkerreich* (Munich: Beck, 1982).

117  *The one land of Rus* Iryna Vushko, *The Politics of Cultural Retreat* (New Haven: Yale UP, 2017); John Paul Himka, *Socialism in Galicia* (Cambridge, Mass.: Harvard UP, 1983); Ivan L. Rudnyts'kyi, *Essays in Modern Ukrainian History* (Edmonton: Canadian Institute for Ukrainian Studies, 1987); Roman Szporluk, "The Making of Modern Ukraine: The Western Dimension," *Harvard Ukrainian Studies*, vol. 25, nos. 1-2, 2001, 57–91; Harald Binder, *Galizien in Wien* (Vienna: Verlag der Österreichischen Akademie der Wissenschaften, 2005); Mykhailo Vozniak, *Iak probudylosia ukrains'ke narodnie zhyttia v Halychyni za Avstrii* (L'viv: Dilo, 1924).

118  *After the Bolshevik Revolution* On continuities from the imperial to the Soviet period: Richard Pipes, *The Formation of the Soviet Union* (Cambridge, Mass.: Harvard UP, 1997). On Ukraine and the Entente powers: Oleksandr Pavliuk, *Borot'ba Ukrainy za nezalezhnist' i polityka SShA, 1917–1923* (Kyiv: KM Akademia, 1996); Caroline Milow, *Die ukrainische Frage 1917–1923 im Spannungsfeld der europäischen Diplomatie* (Wiesbaden: Harrassowitz Verlag, 2002); Mark Baker, "Lewis Namier and the Problem of Eastern Galicia," *Journal of Ukrainian Studies*, vol. 23, no. 2, 1998, 59–104. On the Russo-Polish geopolitics: Andrzej Nowak, *Polska a trzy Rosje* (Cracow: Arcana, 2001); also see Richard Ullman, *Anglo-Soviet Relations 1917–1920* (Princeton: Princeton UP, three volumes, 1961–1973). On the districts that fell to Poland: Werner Benecke, *Die Ostgebiete der Zweiten Polnischen Republik* (Köln: Böhlau Verlag, 1999); Jan Tomasz Gross, *Revolution from Abroad* (Princeton: Princeton UP, 1988); Katherine R. Jolluck, *Exile and Identity* (Pittsburgh: University of Pittsburgh Press, 2002).

119  *Ukrainian history* On German colonialism: Willeke Hannah Sandler, "'Colonizers are Born, Not Made': Creating a Colonial Identity in Nazi Germany, 1933–1945," doctoral dissertation, Duke University, 2012; Lora Wildenthal, *German Women for Empire, 1884–1945* (Durham: Duke UP, 2001); Jürgen Zimmerer, *Von Windhuk nach Auschwitz* (Münster: LIT

Verlag, 2011); Wendy Lower, *Nazi Empire-Building and the Holocaust in Ukraine* (Chapel Hill: University of North Carolina Press, 2005); cf Alexander Victor Prusin, *The Lands Between: Conflict in the East European Borderlands, 1870–1992* (Oxford: Oxford UP, 2010). On the language of Soviet self-colonization: Alvin Gouldner, "Stalinism: A Study of Internal Colonialism," *Telos*, no. 34, 1978, 5–48; Lynne Viola, "Selbstkolonisierung der Sowjetunion," *Transit*, no. 38, 2009, 34–56.

119 *Joseph Stalin understood* On the number of Jews murdered in Ukraine: Alexander Kruglov, "Jewish Losses in Ukraine," in Ray Brandon and Wendy Lower, eds., *The Shoah in Ukraine* (Bloomington: Indiana UP, 2008), 272–90. On the number of fatalities in the Holocaust in the USSR, see Yitzhak Arad, *The Holocaust in the Soviet Union* (Lincoln: University of Nebraska Press and Jerusalem: Yad Vashem, 2009). For further reckonings see Dieter Pohl, *Verfolgung und Massenmord in der NS-Zeit 1933–1945* (Darmstadt: Wissenschaftliche Buchgesellschaft, 2008); Snyder, *Bloodlands*.

119 *After the Red Army* On the agreement itself, see John Basarab, *Pereiaslav 1654* (Edmonton: CIUS, 1982).

120 *Soviet Ukraine was the second* On deportations, see Snyder, *Reconstruction of Nations;* Grzegorz Motyka, *Od rzezi wołyńskiej do akcji "Wisła". Konflikt polsko-ukraiński 1943–1947* (Warsaw: Wydawnictwo Literackie, 2011); Jeffrey Burds, "Agentura: Soviet Informants Networks and the Ukrainian Underground in Galicia," *East European Politics and Societies,* vol. 11, no. 1, 1997, 89–130.

120 *Though Soviet policy* On the famine of 1933, see Andrea Graziosi, *The Great Soviet Peasant War* (Cambridge, Mass.: Harvard UP, 1996); Barbara Falk, *Sowjetische Städte in der Hungersnot 1932/33* (Cologne: Böhlau Verlag, 2005); Robert Kuśnierz, *Ukraina w latach kolektywizacji i wielkiego głodu* (Toruń: Grado, 2005); Anne Applebaum, *Red Famine: Stalin's War on Ukraine* (New York: Doubleday, 2017). A contemporary guide to the 1970s and 1980s were the essays later collected in Roman Szporluk, *Russia, Ukraine, and the Breakup of the Soviet Union* (Stanford: Hoover Press, 2000).

121 *To be sure, Ukrainian communists* On the last decades of Soviet Ukrainian history, see Serhii Plokhy, *The Gates of Europe* (New York: Basic Books, 2015), 291–336.

122 *As in the new Russia* For a brief contemporary contrast: "Ukraine's Biggest Problem: No Money," *American Interest,* Feb. 24, 2014; "On Putin and Oligarchs," *American Interest,* Sept. 19, 2014; "Private Banks Fuel Fortune of Putin's Inner Circle," *NYT,* Sept. 29, 2014. See generally Dawisha, *Putin's Kleptocracy.*

122 *After his defeat* Franklin Foer, "The Quiet American," *Slate,* April 28, 2016; Franklin Foer, "Putin's Puppet," *Slate,* July 21, 2016; Roman Romaniuk, "How Paul Manafort Brought US Politics to Ukraine (and Ukrainian Politics to the US)," *UP,* Aug. 18, 2016; Nick Robins-Early, "Who is Viktor Yanukovych and What's His Connection to Paul Manafort?" *HP,* Oct. 30, 2017; Steven Lee Myers and Andrew Kramer, "How Paul

Manafort Wielded Power in Ukraine Before Advising Donald Trump," *NYT,* July 31, 2016.

123 *After winning* Yanukovych family wealth: Benjamin Bidder, "The Dubious Business of the Yanukovych Clan," *Spiegel Online,* May 16, 2012; Alexander J. Motyl, "Ukraine: The Yanukovych Family Business," *World Affairs,* March 23, 2012; H. E. Hale and R. W. Orttung, *Beyond the Euromaidan,* (Palo Alto: Stanford UP, 2016), 191. Yanukovych jails opposition: Kathy Lally, "Ukraine jails former prime minister," *WP,* Oct. 11, 2011; Luke Harding, "Ukraine's new government puts final nail in coffin of the Orange Revolution," *TG,* March 11, 2010.

123 *As a new state, Ukraine* Association agreement: Amanda Paul, "Ukraine under Yanukovych: Plus ça change?" European Policy Centre, Feb. 19, 2010; "Ukraine protests after Yanukovych EU deal rejection," BBC, Nov. 30, 2013; "How the EU Lost Ukraine," *Spiegel Online,* Nov. 25, 2013.

124 *Whatever the flaws* "Berkut' besposhchadno rastoptal kyevskyy evromaydan," *Fakty UA,* Nov. 30, 2013. Exemplary quotation: "The last drop of our patience was the first drop of blood spilled on the Maidan." Sergei Gusovsky, Dec. 13, 2013, in Timothy Snyder and Tatiana Zhurzhenko, eds., "Diaries and Memoirs of the Maidan," *Eurozine,* June 27, 2014.

125 *Ukrainian citizens* Nihoyan in his own words: interview, Jan. 19, 2014, TSN. See also Daisy Sindelar, Yulia Ratsybarska, and Franak Viachorka, "How an Armenian and a Belarusian Died for the Ukrainian Revolution," *The Atlantic,* Jan. 24, 2014; "First Victims of Maidan Crackdown Remembered in Ukraine," *RFE/RL,* Jan. 22, 2015. On the Donbas and its workers, see Hiroaki Kuromiya, *Freedom and Terror in the Donbas* (Cambridge: Cambridge UP, 1998); Tanja Penter, *Kohle für Stalin und Hitler* (Essen: Klartext Verlag, 2010).

125 *On December 10, 2013* Quotations in this paragraph: Snyder and Zhurzhenko, "Diaries and memoirs of the Maidan."

125 *On January 16, 2014* "Priniaatye Radoi 16 ianvaria skandal'nye zakony opublikovany," *Liga Novosti,* Jan. 21, 2014; Will Englund, "Ukraine enacts harsh laws against protests," *WP,* Jan. 17, 2014; Timothy Snyder, "Ukraine: The New Dictatorship," *NYR,* Feb. 20, 2014.

126 *Six days later* David M. Herszenhorn, "Unrest Deepens in Ukraine as Protests Turn Deadly," *NYT,* Jan. 22, 2014; "Timeline: How Ukrainian Protests Descended into Bloodbath," *RFL/RE,* Feb. 19, 2014; Piotr Andrusieczko, "Ofiary kijowskiego Majdanu nie były daremne," *GW,* Nov. 21, 2014.

126 *As February began* Fond Demokratychni Initsiatyvy im. Il'ka Kucheriva, "Vid Maidanu-taboru do Maidanu-sichi," survey of participants, Feb. 2014.

128 *Ukrainian citizens* Poll: "Vid Maidanu-taboru do Maidanu-sichi," survey of participants, Feb. 2014. Surenko: Snyder and Zhurzhenko, "Diaries and memoirs of the Maidan."

128 *The politics of this nation* Volodymyr Yermolenko, "O dvukh Evropakh," inache.net, Dec. 18, 2013.

129  *In the meantime* Bihun: Leonid Finberg and Uliana Holovach, eds., *Maidan. Svidchennia* (Kyiv: Dukh i Litera, 2016), 89. Andrij Bondar: Snyder and Zhurzhenko, "Diaries and memoirs of the Maidan."

129  *The economy of the Maidan* Economy of gift: Valeria Korablyova, "The Idea of Europe, or Going Beyond Geography," unpublished paper, 2016. Quotations: Snyder and Zhurzhenko, "Diaries and memoirs of the Maidan."

130  *In early 2014* Data: "Vid Maidanu-taboru do Maidanu-sichi." Cherepanyn: personal experience, 2014. See also Natalie Wilson, "Judith Butler's Corporeal Politics: Matters of Politicized Abjection," *International Journal of Sexuality and Gender Studies,* vol. 6, nos. 1-2, 2001, at 119–21.

130  *Patient protest* Snyder and Zhurzhenko, "Diaries and memoirs of the Maidan."

130  *Having come as individuals* Yermolenko: "O dvukh Evropakh." Hrytsak quoted in Snyder and Zhurzhenko, "Diaries and memoirs of the Maidan." Franklin quote: Korablyova, "The Idea of Europe, or Going Beyond Geography."

131  *A group of Ukrainian lawyers* Finberg and Holovach, *Maidan. Svidchennia,* 100.

131  *In late 2011* Vladimir Korovin, "Putin i Evraziiskaia ideologiia," Izborsk Club, April 15, 2014, article 2801.

132  *In November and December 2013* "'Ia ne gei!': khakery vzlomali sotsseti Klichko posle ego prizyva vyiti na Maidan," *NTV,* Nov. 22, 2013, 714256. For useful background, see Oleg Riabov and Tatiana Riabova, "The Decline of Gayropa?" *Eurozine,* Feb. 2013.

132  *Right after students began* Homodictatorship: "V Kieve aktivisty vodili khorovod i protykali puzyr' evrogomointegratsii," *NTV,* Nov. 24, 2014, 735116. "The 'gay' maelstrom of euro-integration," *Trueinform,* Dec. 22, 2013; Viktor Shestakov, "'Goluboi' omut 'evrorevoliutsii,' ili Maidan sdali," *Odna Rodina,* Dec. 21, 2014.

132  *Dmitry Kiselev* Jim Rutenberg, "How the Kremlin built one of the most powerful information weapons of the 21st century," *NYT,* Sept. 13, 2017.

132  *On December 1, 2013* Kiselev on Polish-Lithuanian-Swedish alliance: Dmitrii Kiselev, "Vesti Nedeli," Rossiia-1, Dec. 1, 2013, 928691.

133  *In another episode* Dmitrii Kiselev, "Vesti Nedeli," Rossiia-1, Dec. 8, 2013. *Segodnia*: Nikolai Telepnev, "Gei-Udar Po 'Udaru,'" Dec. 20, 2013, 133168.

133  *European integration* Malofeev: Nataliia Telegina, "Put' Malofeeva: ot detskogo pitaniia k sponsorstvu Donbassa i proshchennym," republic.ru, May 12, 2015, 50662. *KP* article: "Gei-drovishki v koster Maidana," *KP,* May 12, 2013, 3055033.

134  *When Yanukovych announced* "V Kieve aktivisty vodili khorovod i protykali puzyr' evrogomointegratsii," NTV, Nov. 24, 2014.

134  *On December 17, 2013* Natural gas deal: "Putin Pledges Billions, Cheaper Gas to Yanukovych," *RFE/RL,* Dec. 17, 2013; Carol Matlack, "Ukraine Cuts a Deal It Could Soon Regret," *Bloomberg,* Dec. 17, 2013; David Herszenhorn and Andrew Kramer, "Russia Offers Cash Infusion for

Ukraine," *NYT*, Dec. 17, 2013. Ukrainian riot police use of force: Andrew Kramer, "Police and Protestors in Ukraine Escalate Use of Force," *NYT*, Jan. 20, 2014; for the recollection of violence see also Snyder and Zhurzhenko, "Diaries and memoirs of the Maidan"; Finberg and Holovach, *Maidan. Svidchennia.*

135 *A major actor* Ilya Arkhipov, Henry Meyer, and Irina Reznik, "Putin's 'Soros' Dreams of Empire as Allies Wage Ukraine Revolt," *Bloomberg*, June 15, 2014.

135 *Malofeev's employee Girkin* Telegina, "Put' Malofeeva." Girkin's past and self-definition as "special operations officer": Aleksandr Prokhanov, interview with Girkin, "Kto ty, Strelok?" *Zavtra*, Nov. 20, 2014. Girkin defines himself as a "full colonel": Aleksandr Chalenko, interview with Girkin, *Politnavigator*, Dec. 1, 2014.

136 *A memorandum that circulated* Andrei Lipskii, "'Predstavliaetsia pravil'nym initsiirovat' prisoedinenie vostochnykh oblastei Ukrainy k Rossii'," *NG*, Feb. 2015. The memorandum's judgment of the Yanukovych regime: "Vo-pervykh, rezhim V. Yanukovicha okonchatel'no obankrotilsia. Ego politicheskaia, diplomaticheskaia, finansovaia, informatsionnaia podderzhka Rossiskoi Federatsiei uzhe ne imeet nikakogo smysla." For a German translation, see "Russlands Strategiepapier im Wortlaut," *Die Zeit*, Feb. 26, 2016; for discussion, see Steffen Dobbert, Christo Grosev, and Meike Dülffer, "Putin und der geheime Ukraine-Plan," *Die Zeit*, Feb. 26, 2015.

136 *In a policy paper* "Spasti Ukrainu! Memorandum ekspertov Izborskogo Kluba," Feb. 13, 2014.

136 *On the day that the Izborsk Club* Lavrov and hedonism: Sergei Lavrov, "V ponimanii EC i CShA 'svobodnyi' vybor za ukraintsev uzhe sdelan," *Kommersant*, Feb. 13, 2014. Surkov and arms: Kurczab-Redlich, *Wowa*, 667–68.

137 *Now European actors* Do you believe that Victoria Nuland, a U.S. assistant secretary of state at the time, passed out cookies on the Maidan? If so, the version of events that has entered your mind has passed through Russian propaganda. She passed out sandwiches. This discrepancy, not important in itself, serves as a helpful trace. If the story in your mind includes the fictional element "cookies," it includes other fictional elements.

137 *The most significant initiative* Negotiations, shooting, flight: "A Kiev, la diplomatie européenne négocie directement avec Ianoukovitch," *LM*, Feb. 20, 2014; Matthew Weaver and Tom McCarthy, "Ukraine crisis: deadly clashes shatter truce," *TG*, Feb. 20, 2014. Yanukovych resigns: Shiv Malik, Aisha Gani, and Tom McCarthy, "Ukraine crisis: deal signed in effort to end Kiev standoff," *TG*, Feb. 21, 2014; "Ukraine's Parliament, President Agree to Opposition Demands," *RFE/RL*, Feb. 21, 2014; Sam Frizell, "Ukraine Protestors Seize Kiev as President Flees," *Time*, Feb. 22, 2014; Alan Taylor, "Ukraine's President Voted Out, Flees Kiev," *The Atlantic*, Feb. 22, 2014.

138 *The moment had passed* FSB presence February 20–21: Kurczab-Redlich,

*Wowa,* 667–68; Andrei Soldatov, "The True Role of the FSB in the Ukrainian Crisis," *Moscow Times,* April 15, 2014. See also Simon Shuster, "The Russian Stronghold in Ukraine Preparing to Fight the Revolution," *Time,* Feb. 23, 2014; Daniel Boffey and Alec Luhn, "EU sends advisers to help Ukraine bring law and order to rebel areas," *TG,* July 26, 2014.

138 *After the mass killing* Yanukovych loses parliamentary majority: "Parliament votes 328–0 to impeach Yanukovych on Feb. 22; sets May 25 for new election; Tymoshenko free," *Kyiv Post,* Feb. 23, 2014; Uri Friedman, "Ukraine's Government Disappears Overnight," *The Atlantic,* Feb. 22, 2014.

138 *The sniper massacre* Cyber in Crimea: Owen Matthews, "Russia's Greatest Weapon May Be Its Hackers," *NW,* May 7, 2015; Hannes Grassegger and Mikael Krogerus, "Weaken from Within," *New Republic,* Dec. 2017, 21; Adam Entous, Ellen Nakashima, and Greg Jaffe, "Kremlin trolls burned across the Internet," *WP,* Dec. 25, 2017. Internet Research Agency: Adrian Chen, "The Agency," *NYT,* June 2, 2015. For the atmosphere of the invasion's first few days, see the early dispatches from Simon Ostrovsky's "Russian Roulette" series at VICE News online.

139 *By the time Yanukovych surfaced* Unit numbers: Thomas Gutschker, "Putins Schlachtplan," *FAZ,* July 9, 2014. Some early coverage of Russian invasion of Ukraine: "Russian troops in Crimea and the traitor admiral" ("Russkie voiska v Krymu i admiral predatel'") *BigMir,* March 3, 2014; Telegina, "Put' Malofeeva." See also Pavel Nikulin, "Kak v Krymu otneslis' k vvodu rossiiskikh voisk," *Slon,* March 1, 2014; Il'ia Shepelin, "Prorossiiskie soldaty otkryli ogon' v vozdukh, chtoby ne dat' ukrainskim vernut' aerodrom Bel'bek," *Slon,* March 3, 2014.

139 *Beginning on February 24, 2014* Russian invasion of Crimea: Anton Bebler, "Crimea and the Russian-Ukrainian Conflict," *Romanian Journal of Foreign Affairs,* vol. 15, no. 1, 2015, 35–53; Ashley Deels, "Russian Forces in Ukraine," *Lawfare,* March 2, 2014; Anatoly Pronin, "Republic of Crimea," *Russian Law Journal,* vol. 3, no. 1, 2015, 133–42. Simferopol: Mat Babiak, "Russians Seize Simferopol," *Ukrainian Policy,* Feb. 27, 2014; Simon Shuster, "Gunmen Seize Parliament in Ukraine's Russian Stronghold," *Time,* Feb. 27, 2014. Girkin's recollection: Sergei Shargunov, interview with Ivan Girkin, *Svobodnaia Pressa,* Nov. 11, 2014. Glazyev call: "Kiev releases audio tapes," *Meduza,* Aug. 22, 2016; see also Gerard Toal, *Near Abroad* (London: Oxford UP, 2016). Aksionov: Simon Shuster, "Putin's Man in Crimea Is Ukraine's Worst Nightmare," *Time,* March 10, 2014. Obama on Ukraine: Thomas Sparrow, "From Maidan to Moscow: Washington's Response to the crisis in Ukraine," in Klaus Bachmann and Igor Lyybashenko, eds., *The Maidan Uprising, Separatism and Foreign Intervention* (Frankfurt: Peter Lang, 2014), 322–23. Obama quote: Bill Chappell, "Obama Warns Russia Against Using Force in Ukraine," NPR, Feb. 28, 2014.

140 *The public spectacle* Night Wolves in Crimea: "Night Wolves, Putin's 'Biker Brothers', To Ride to Ukraine to Support Pro-Russia Cause," *HP,* Feb. 28,

2014; Harriet Salem, "Crimea's Putin supporters prepare to welcome possible Russian advance," *TG,* March 1, 2014. Alexei Weitz cited in Peter Pomerantsev, "Forms of Delirium," *London Review of Books,* vol. 35, no. 19, Oct. 10, 2013.

140 *The Night Wolves found* Zaldostonov quotations: Damon Tabor, "Putin's Angels," *Rolling Stone,* Oct. 8, 2015; Shaun Walker, "Patriotic group formed to defend Russia against pro-democracy protestors," *TG,* Jan. 15, 2015. Putin: "Vladimir Putin otvetil na voprosy zhurnalistov o situatsii na Ukraine," March 4, 2014.

140 *Having invaded Ukraine* On the Vienna gathering and for Dugin quotation: Bernhard Odehnal, "Gipfeltreffen mit Putins fünfter Kolonne," *Tages-Anzeiger,* June 3, 2014. Ceased to exist: Alexander Dugin, "Letter to the American People on Ukraine," *Open Revolt,* March 8, 2014.

141 *On March 16* Referendum: David Patrikarakos, *War in 140 Characters* (New York: Basic Books, 2017), 92–94, 153; Richard Balmforth, "No room for 'Nyet' in Ukraine's Crimea vote to join Russia," Reuters, March 11, 2014. Results: Paul Roderick Gregory, "Putin's human rights council accidentally posts real Crimean election results," *Kyiv Post,* May 6, 2014; "Krym vybral Rossiiu," Gazeta.ru, March 15, 2014; "Za zlyttia z Rosiieiu proholosovalo 123% sevastopoltsiv," *Ukrains'ka Pravda,* March 17, 2014; "V Sevastopole za prisoedinenie k Rossii progolosovalo 123% naseleniia," UNIAN, March 17, 2014. Thank the French: Agathe Duparc, Karl Laske, and Marine Turchi, "Crimée et finances du FN: les textos secrets du Kremlin," *Mediapart,* April 2, 2015.

142 *In a grand ceremony* Budapest Memorandum: Czuperski et al., "Hiding in Plain Sight," 4. Legal implications: Deels, "Russian Forces in Ukraine"; Ivanna Bilych, et al., "The Crisis in Ukraine: Its Legal Dimensions," Razom report, April 14, 2014; Anne Peters, "Sense and Nonsense of Territorial Referendums in Ukraine," ejiltalk.org, April 16, 2014; Anne Peters, "The Crimean Vote of March 2014 as an Abuse of the Institution of Territorial Referendum," in Christian Calliess, ed., *Staat und Mensch im Kontext des Volker-und Europarechts* (Baden-Baden, Noms Verlag, 2015), 255–80. Disarmament: Sergei L. Loiko and Carol J. Williams, "Ukraine troops struggle with nation's longtime neglect of military," *Los Angeles Times,* Oct. 18, 2014.

142 *In March and April, Russian media* March 17 declaration: Ministry of Foreign Affairs, "Zaiavlenie MID o Gruppe podderzhki dlia Ukrainy," March 17, 2014. See Paul Roderick Gregory, "Putin Demands Federalization for Ukraine, But Declares It Off-Limits for Siberia," *Forbes,* Sept. 1, 2014; Maksim Trudoliubov and Nikolai Iepple, "Rossiiskoe obshchestvo ne vidit sebia," *Vedomosti,* July 2, 2015; "M.I.D. Ukrainy schitaet nepriemlemymi predlozheniia Rossii po uregulirovaniiu krizisa v strane," *Interfax,* March 17, 2014, 196364.

143 *Vladimir Putin presented* Vladimir Putin, Address of the President of the Russian Federation, March 18, 2014.

143 *The parliamentary deputy Tatiana Saenko* Tatiana Saenko, "Parlamentarii

o priniatii v sostav Rossiiskoi Federatsii novykh sub"yektov," *Kabardino-Balkarskaya Pravda*, no. 49, March 18, 2014.

143 *This was Ilyin's politics of eternity* Putin quote: "Priamaia liniia s Vladimirom Putinym," Kremlin, April 17, 2014. Malofeev quote: Dmitrii Sokolov-Mitrich and Vitalii Leibin, "Ostavit' Bogu mesto v istorii," *Russkii Reporter,* March 4, 2015. These are notions of time that begin wars but do not describe them. When I read interviews with the pro-Russian volunteers Malofeev imagined as manly Christian warriors fighting the devil, I could not help but smile to see that the first one I turned to was the testimony of a man of Jewish origin who had taken a Russian literary reference to Satan as his nomme de guerre, and the second was of a woman who described her religion as Satanism. My smile was fleeting: their stories, like those of all local people brought into that war, were very sad. (Separatist interviews (B) and (V), transcripts provided by Oksana Mikhaevna.)

144 *The fall of Crimea* Glazyev: "Ukraine publishes video proving Kremlin directed separatism in eastern Ukraine and Crimea," *Euromaidan Press,* Aug. 23, 2016; "English translation of audio evidence of Putin's adviser Glazyev and other Russian politicians' involvement in war in Ukraine," *Focus on Ukraine,* Aug. 30, 2016. Discussion: Veronika Melkozerova, "Two years too late, Lutsenko releases audio of Russian plan that Ukrainians already suspected," *Kyiv Post,* Aug. 27, 2016; Halya Coynash, "Odesa Smoking Gun Leads Directly to Moscow," *Human Rights in Ukraine,* Sept. 20, 2016; "The Glazyev Tapes," *European Council on Foreign Relations,* Nov. 1, 2016.

144 *In April, Putin publicly recited* Girkin and Borodai return in April: Czuperski et al., "Hiding in Plain Sight," 4, 20. Girkin's and Borodai's positions: Dmitrii Sokolov-Mitrich and Vitalii Leibin, "Ostavit' Bogu mesto v istorii," *Russkii reporter,* March 4, 2015; "Profile of Russian Tycoon's Big New Christian TV Channel," *FT,* Oct. 16, 2015. Gubarev as people's governor of Donetsk: Nikolai Mitrokhin, "Transnationale Provokation," *Osteuropa,* 5–6/2014, 158; Mitrokhin, "Infiltration, Instruktion, Invasion," *Osteuropa* 8/2014, 3–16; "Russian ultra-nationalists come to fight in Ukraine," *StopFake,* March 8, 2014; "After Neutrality Proves Untenable, a Ukrainian Oligarch Makes His Move," *NYT,* May 20, 2014. Gubarev quote: Paweł Pieniążek, *Pozdrowienia z Noworosji* (Warsaw: Krytyka Polityczna, 2015), 18.

145 *The Russian intervention* Russian Spring: "Ukraine and Russia are both trapped by the war in Donbas," *The Economist,* May 25, 2017. Dugin quotations: Alexander Dugin, "Horizons of our Revolution from Crimea to Lisbon," *Open Revolt,* March 7, 2014. Zakamskaya: "Blogery Ishchut Antisemitizm Na 'Rossii 24': 'Korichnevaia Chuma' Raspolzaetsia," *Medialeaks,* March 24, 2014. Neo-Nazis in Moscow: Alec Luhn, "Moscow Holds First May Day Parade Since Soviet Era," *TG,* May 1, 2014.

145 *This was a new variety* Schizofascism is an example of what the philosopher Jason Stanley calls "undermining propaganda": using a concept to

destroy that concept. Here anti-fascism is being used to destroy anti-fascism. *How Propaganda Works* (Princeton: Princeton UP, 2016).

146 *Thus Russians educated in the 1970s* Prokhanov: Alexander Prokhanov, "Odinnadtsatyi stalinskii udar. O nashem novom Dne Pobedy," *Izvestiia*, May 5, 2014; Dugin: "Towards Laocracy," July 28, 2014; Glazyev: "Predotvratit' voinu—pobedit' v voine," Izborsk Club, Sept. 2014, article 3962. See also Pieniążek, *Pozdrowiena z Noworosji*, 167.

146 *Schizofascism was one* Glazyev, "Predotvratit' voinu—pobedit' v voine."

147 *Like his advisor Glazyev* Vladimir Putin, Address of the President of the Russian Federation, March 18, 2014.

147 *On March 14, 2014* Lavrov: "Comment by Russian Ministry of Foreign Affairs," March 14, 2014; see also Damien McElroy, "Moscow uses death of protestor to argue for 'protection' of ethnic Russians in Ukraine," *Telegraph*, March 14, 2014.

148 *In a war that was* American white supremacists: Casey Michel, "Beyond Trump and Putin," *Diplomat*, Oct. 13, 2016. Spencer's defense of Russian invasion: "Russian State Propaganda Uses American Fascist to Blame Ukrainian Fascists for Violence," *Daily Surge*, June 5, 2014. Poles: Piątek, *Macierewicz i jego tajemnice*, 176, 180–81.

149 *The leader of the Hungarian* The quotations from: Shekhovstov, *Russia and the Western Far Right*, chapter 5. See generally P. Krekó et al., "The Weaponization of Culture," *Political Capital Institute*, Aug. 4, 2016, 8, 14, 30–40, 59; Alina Polyakova, "Putinism and the European Far Right," *Atlantic Council*, Nov. 19, 2015, 4. On far-Right responses to Ukrainian conflict: Timothy Snyder, "The Battle in Ukraine Means Everything," *New Republic*, May 11, 2014. Budapest: Anton Shekhovtsov, "Far-right international conferences in 2014," *Searchlight*, Winter 2014. Ochsenreiter: Van Herpen, *Putin's Propaganda Machine*, 73.

149 *A few dozen French* Generally: Patrick Jackson, "Ukraine war pulls in foreign fighters," BBC, Sept. 1, 2014. France: Mathieu Molard and Paul Gogo, "Ukraine: Les docs qui montrent l'implication de l'extrême droite française dans la guerre," *Streetpress*, Aug. 29, 2016. Serbian nationalist: "Serbia arrests suspect linked to Montenegro election plot: report," Reuters, Jan. 13, 2017. Swedish Nazis: "Three Swedish men get jail for bomb attacks on asylum centers," Reuters, July 7, 2017; "Russia trains extremists who may wreak havoc in Europe—probe," UNIAN, July 24, 2017.

149 *In 2014, institutions* World National-Conservative Movement: Anton Shekhovtsov, "Slovak Far-Right Allies of Putin's Regime," *TI*, Feb. 8, 2016. See also "Europe's far right flocks to Russia: International conservative forum held in St. Petersburg," *Meduza*, March 24, 2015. Usovsky: Yaroslav Shimov and Aleksy Dzikawicki, "E-Mail Hack Gives Glimpse into Russia's Influence Drive in Eastern Europe," *RFE/RL*, March 17, 2017; Andrew Higgins, "Foot Soldiers in a Shadowy Battle Between Russia and the West," *NYT*, May 28, 2017. The sources: "Za antiukrainskimi aktsiami v Pol'she stoit Kreml," InfoNapalm, Feb. 22, 2017, 33652.

150  *Malofeev personally invited* Odehnal, *"Gipfeltreffen."*

150  *Russians, Europeans, and Americans* On Mykhailo Martynenko (1992–) and Bohdan Solchanyk (1985–2014) and the perspectives of students and their teachers on revolution, see Marci Shore, *The Ukrainian Night: An Intimate History of Revolution* (New Haven: Yale UP, 2018).

151  *Ukrainians who began* "RF traktuet proiskhodiashchee na Ukraine kak popytku gosperevorota, zaiavil press-sekretar' Prezidenta," PK, Feb. 19, 2014, 52312.

152  *There were certainly representatives* Anton Shekhovtsov, "Spectre of Ukrainian 'fascism': Information wars, political manipulation, and reality," *Euromaidan Press,* June 24, 2015.

153  *The acting president* Olga Rudenko, "Oleksandr Turchynov's Baptist faith may help defuse Ukrainian crisis," *WP,* Feb. 26, 2014; "Ukraine Turns to Its Oligarchs for Political Help," *NYT,* March 2, 2014; "Avakov appointed interior minister of Ukraine," *ArmenPress,* Feb. 22, 2014.

153  *People who carry out coups* Sergei Glazyev persisted in calling Poroshenko a "Nazi." "Glazyev: Poroshenko—natsist, Ukraina—Frankenshtein," BBC, June 27, 2014.

154  *In May 2014* Steven Pifer, "Ukraine's Parliamentary Election," Brookings Institute, Oct. 27, 2014.

154  *The Russian officers* Common civilization: Pavel Kanygin, "Aleksandr Borodai: 'Zakliuchat' mir na usloviiakh kapituliatsii my nikak ne gotovy'," *NG,* Aug. 12, 2014. On timescapes: Tatiana Zhurzenko, "Russia's never-ending war against 'fascism,'" *Eurozine,* Aug. 5, 2015.

155  *The Russian invasion of Ukraine* Konstantin Skorkin, "Post-Soviet science fiction and the war in Ukraine," *Eurozine,* Feb. 22, 2016.

155  *It became official Russian policy* Federal Law of May 5, 2014, N. 128-Fr, "O vnesenii izmenenii v otdel'nye zakonodatel'nye akty Rossiiskoi Federatsii." Putin defending Molotov-Ribbentrop pact: Vladimir Putin, "Meeting with young academics and history teachers," Nov. 5, 2014, Kremlin, 46951. Conviction: Gleb Bugush and Ilya Nuzov, "Russia's Supreme Court Rewrites History of the Second World War," *EJIL Talk!* Oct. 28, 2016.

156  *The axiom of perfect* Issio Ehrich, "Absturz von MH17: Igor Strelkow—'der Schütze,'" N-TV.de, July 24, 2014. Girkin and executions and Stalin: Anna Shamanska, "Former Commander of Pro-Russian Separatists Says He Executed People Based on Stalin-Era Laws," *RFE/RL,* Jan. 29, 2016.

156  *For many young Russian men* Punitive operations: "Ukraine conflict: Turning up the TV heat," BBC, Aug. 11, 2014. Tank: "Lies: Luhansk Gunmen to Wage War on Repaired T-34 Museum Tank," *StopFake,* May 13, 2014. "1942": Separatist interview (B). "For Stalin": "Russia's 200th Motorized Infantry Brigade in the Donbass," *Bellingcat,* Jan. 16, 2016. Soldiers in Crimea: Ekaterina Sergatskova, Artiom Chapai, Vladimir Maksakov, eds., *Voina na tri bukvy* (Kharkiv: Folio, 2015), 24. Tank and prisoners: Zhurzenko, "Russia's never-ending war."

157  *In Russia, Stalin's* Approval ratings: "Praviteli v Otechestvennoi Istorii," Levada Center, March 1, 2016.

157  *The war in Ukraine* "V Kiyeve Pereimenovali Muzei Velikoi Otechestvennoi Voiny," ru.tsn.ua, July 16, 2015. Ukraine did have a second myth of that war, with some nationalists in the western part of the country glorifying the nationalist partisans who fought against the installation of Soviet power. The war of 2014, however, was fought in southeast Ukraine, and predominantly by local soldiers.

## CHAPTER 5

159  *Ivan Ilyin's ideas gave form* The novel: Natan Dubovitsky [Vladislav Surkov], "My ischeznem, kak tol'ko on otkroet glaza. Dolg obshchestva i vash, prezhde vsego—prodolzhat' snitsia emu," *Okolonolia,* Media Group LIVE, Moscow 2009. See also: Peter Pomerantsev, "The Hidden Author of Putinism," *The Atlantic,* Nov. 7, 2014; "Russia: A Postmodern Dictatorship," Institute of Modern Russia, 2013, 6; and above all Pomerantsev, *Nothing Is True.*

160  *To end factuality* Vladislav Surkov, "Russkaia politicheskaia kul'tura. Vzgliad iz utopii," *Russkii Zhurnal,* June 15, 2007.

160  *In the Russia of the 2010s* Maksim Trudoliubov and Nikolai Iepple, "Rossiiskoe obshchestvo ne vidit sebia," *Vedomosti,* July 2, 2015. Pavlovsky was contrasting contemporary Russian with prior Soviet practice. In the Stalinist period, the conspiracies portrayed in show trials did veer towards fiction, and, in some of the most dramatic cases, towards antisemitic conspiracy theory: see Snyder, *Bloodlands;* see also *Proces z vedením protistátního spikleneckého centra v čele s Rodolfem Slánským* (Prague: Ministerstvo Spravedlnosti, 1953); Włodzimierz Rozenbaum, "The March Events," *Polin,* vol. 21, 2008, 62–93; Dariusz Stola, "The Hate Campaign of March 1968," *Polin,* vol. 21, 2008, 16–36. Volin: Masha Gessen, "Diadia Volin," *RFE/RL,* Feb. 11, 2013. 90%: Levada Center, "Rossiiskii Media Landshaft," June 17, 2014. Budget: Peter Pomerantsev, "Unplugging Putin TV," *Foreign Affairs,* Feb. 18, 2015.

161  *RT, Russia's television* Examples of guests: Peter Pomerantsev and Michael Weiss, "The Menace of Unreality: How the Kremlin Weaponizes Information, Culture, and Money," Institute of Modern Russia, Nov. 22, 2014, 15. Putin quotation: Margarita Simonyan interview, RT, June 12, 2013. "No such thing": "Interv'iu/Margarita Simon'ian," *RNS,* March 15, 2017. See also Peter Pomerantsev, "Inside Putin's Information War," *Politico,* Jan. 4, 2015; Peter Pomerantsev, "Inside the Kremlin's hall of mirrors," *TG,* April 9, 2015. RT budget: Gabrielle Tetrault-Farber, "Looking West, Russia Beefs Up Spending in Global Media Giants," *Moscow Times,* Sept. 23, 2014. The slogan "Question More" was created by an American public relations firm.

162  *Factuality was replaced* Cf Pomerantsev, *Nothing Is True,* 73, 228.

162 *"Information war"* Quotation: Peter Pomerantsev, "Inside Putin's Information War," *Politico,* Jan. 4, 2015.

162 *The first men the Kremlin sent* Girkin and Borodai: Sokolov-Mitrich and Leibin, "Ostavit' Bogu mesto v istorii"; "Profile of Russian Tycoon's Big New Christian TV Channel," *FT,* Oct. 16, 2015; Mitrokhin, "Transnationale Provokation, 158, and "Infiltration," 3–16; "Russian ultranationalists come to fight in Ukraine," *StopFake,* March 8, 2014; "After Neutrality Proves Untenable, a Ukrainian Oligarch Makes His Move," *NYT,* May 20, 2014.

162 *When Russia began* Rattling: Kurczab-Redlich, *Wowa,* 671. Uniforms: "Vladimir Putin answered journalists' questions on the situation in Ukraine, March 4, 2014," Kremlin, 20366. Timing of troops: Thomas Gutschker, "Putins Schlachtplan," *FAZ,* July 9, 2014.

163 *Putin was not trying* Clover, *Black Wind, White Snow,* 19.

163 *Putin's direct assault* On "little green men": Miller et al., "An Invasion by Any Other Name," 10, 12, 27, 30, 45, 47; Bebler, "Crimea and the Russian-Ukrainian Conflict," 35–53. Sergatskova: *Voina na tri bukvy,* 24.

163 *The older idea of* For the full interview and the context, see Rick Perlstein, "Lee Atwater's Infamous 1981 Interview on the Southern Strategy," *The Nation,* November 13, 2012.

164 *Western editors* Simon Shuster, "Putin's Confessions on Crimea Expose Kremlin Media," *Time,* March 20, 2015. The act would then be repeated a second time with the Russian intervention in the Donbas. Shaun Walker, "Putin admits Russian military presence in Ukraine for first time," *TG,* Dec. 17, 2015.

164 *After implausible deniability* "Vladimir Putin answered journalists' questions on the situation in Ukraine, March 4, 2014," Kremlin, 20366.

165 *The choice of tactics* The removal of insignia before invasion was a frequent theme in final communications between Russian soldiers and their parents or wives. See, for example, Elena Racheva, "'On sam vybral etu professiiu. Ia sama vybrala ego. Nado terpet'," *NG,* Aug. 30, 2014.

165 *Real soldiers pretending* "Vladimir Putin answered journalists' questions on the situation in Ukraine, March 4, 2014," Kremlin, 20366.

166 *Eternity takes certain points* Sherr, "A War of Perception." Putin's reference to "Novorossiia": "Direct Line with Vladimir Putin," April 17, 2014, Kremlin, 20796.

167 *Most citizens* Dugin spoke of "Novorossiia" on March 3: Clover, *Black Wind, White Snow,* 13.

167 *As Surkov and Glazyev* Mitrokhin, "Infiltration."

167 *And so, in spring 2014* Quotation of soldier: Pavel Kanygin, "Bes, Fiks, Roman i goluboglazyi," *NG,* April 17, 2014. On the presence of Russian soldiers, see Pieniążek, *Pozdrowienia z Noworosji,* 72, 93. See also the video interview with Girkin of April 26, 2014: "Segodnia otkryl litso komanduiushchii otriadom samooborony Slavianska Igor' Strelkov," www.youtube.com/watch?v=8mGXDcO9ugw, and the recollections of the

population in Olha Musafirova, "Po leninskim mestam," *NG,* Oct. 2014; Iulia Polukhna, "Dolgaia doroga v Lugansk," *NG,* Oct. 21, 2014. Borodai quotation: Kanygin, "Aleksandr Borodai."

169 *The Ukrainian state* Czuperski et al., "Hiding in Plain Sight," 4–6; Miller et al., "An Invasion by Any Other Name."

169 *After the annexation* On Kolomois'kyi: Pieniążek, *Pozdrowienia z Noworosji;* "Ukraine's Catch 22 Over Its Oligarch Class," *Johnson's Russia List,* March 25, 2015. Russian raises flag over Kharkiv: "Protestors raise Russian flag in two east Ukrainian cities," Reuters, March 1, 2014. Odessa administrative building takeover: Oksana Grytsenko, "Pro-Russia groups take over government buildings," *TG,* March 3, 2014; Charles King, "Forgetting Odessa," *Slate,* May 8, 2014; Mitrokhin, "Infiltration."

170 *In March and April* Odessa: Ekaterina Sergatskova's journalism from the May 3, 2014, Russian edition of *Ukrains'ka pravda* and Artiom Chapai's May 5 account from *Insider* are reprinted in *Voina na try bukvy,* 64–68, 77–84. See also Natalia Zinets, "More than 40 killed in fire, clashes in Ukraine's Odessa," Reuters, May 2, 2014; Howard Amos and Harriet Salem, "Ukraine clashes," *TG,* May 2, 2014.

170 *Prokhanov compared* Prokhanov, "Odinnadtsatyi stalinskii udar."

170 *By May 2014* On Vostok, see Ekaterina Sergatskova's coverage in the June 2, 2014, Russian edition of *Ukrains'ka Pravda,* reprinted in *Voina na tri bukvy,* 117. See also James Sherr, "A War of Perception," in Keir Giles et al., eds., *The Russian Challenge* (London: Chatham House, 2015); James Rupert, "Russia Allows—or Organizes—Chechen Fighters to Reinforce the Secessionist War in Ukraine," *New Atlanticist,* May 30, 2014. Girkin quotation: Sherr, "A War of Perception."

171 *At least thirty-one Russian* Maria Turchenkova, "Gruz 200," *Ekho Moskvy,* blog, June 4, 2014. On the motivation of volunteers from the Russian Federation: Russian separatist interviews (K) and (L).

171 *One of these thirty-one* Elena Kostiuchenko, "'Vash muzh dobrovol'no poshel pod ostrel'," *NG,* June 17, 2014. Russian families whose sons were killed in Syria faced similar problems. Maria Tsvetkova, "Death certificate offers clues on Russian casualties in Syria," Reuters, Oct. 27, 2017.

172 *By the end of June 2014 Voina na tri bukvy,* 117; Serhyi Kudelia, "The Donbas Rift," *Russian Politics and Law,* vol. 54, no. 1, 2016, 20. Khodakovskii quotation: "Komandir batal'ona 'Vostok': Kiev schel, chto dlia nego region poterian," RIA.ru, June 4, 2014.

172 *On July 5, facing* Interview with Girkin: Alekander Chalenko, *Politnavigator,* Dec. 1, 2014; see also Alekander Prokhanov, interview with Girkin, "Kto ty, Strelok?" *Zavtra,* Nov. 20, 2014; "Igor' Strelkov: Ia sebia s Zhukovym ne sravnivaiu, no, kak i on, shtabnoi raboty ne liubliu," politnavigator.net, Dec. 1, 2014. On the strategic position, see Michael Weiss, "All is not well in Novorossiya," *Foreign Policy,* July 12, 2014.

172 *Naturally, Ukrainian citizens* Survey: Kudelia, "Donbas Rift," 20. Self-defense was a theme in interviews with separatists, including those who also expressed ideological views: Separatist interviews (B) and (V), the

latter also on children and shells. There were of course exceptions: see "Varyag: Moe mirovozzrenie sformirovali trudy Dugina," evrazia.org, Nov. 19, 2015.

173 *Seeing violent death* Separatist interview (V).

173 *Having brought the Donbas* "Vladimir Antiufeev—novyi glava gosbezopasnosti DNR," politikus.ru, July 10, 2014; Irene Chalupa, "Needing Better Control in Ukraine War, Moscow Sends in an Old KGB Hand," *New Atlanticist,* July 17, 2014.

173 *In a frozen conflict* Quotations are from an interview: Pavel Kanygin, "'Pridnestrovskii general' Vladimir Antiufeev, stavshii liderom DNP: 'Slabaki! Ispugalis' sanktsii! Gde klad, tam i serdtse'," *NG,* Aug. 15, 2014. For English excerpts, see "Rebel Leader Blames Ukrainian War on Masons," *Moscow Times,* Aug. 15, 2014.

175 *For Antyufeyev, the desires* Kanygin, "'Pridnestrovskii general' Vladimir Antiufeev."

175 *Since Ukraine was the focus* Ibid.

176 *The Russian counterattack* Evgenii Zhukov, Facebook Post, July 11, 2014.

176 *Zhukov was describing* Gregoriev quotation: "Rossiia obstrelivaet Ukrainu s svoei territorii," *Novoe Vremia,* July 23, 2014. Artillery strikes from Russia: Sean Case, "Smoking GRADs: Evidence of 90 cross-border artillery strikes from Russia to Ukraine in summer 2014," mapinvestigation. blogspot.com, July 16, 2015; "Origin of Artillery Attacks on Ukrainian Military Positions in Eastern Ukraine Between 14 July 2014 and 8 Aug. 2014," *Bellingcat,* Feb. 17, 2015.

176 *Armies usually evacuate* Elena Racheva, "Pogranichnoe sostoianie," *NG,* Aug. 11, 2014.

177 *The Russian journalists* Ibid.

177 *The Ukrainian army could not* Natalya Telegina, "Kak by voina. Reportazh s ukrainskoi granitsy," *Dozhd',* Aug. 5, 2014. Girkin responsible: Alexander Prokhanov, interview with Girkin, "Kto ty, Strelok?" *Zavtra,* Nov. 20, 2014.

178 *One day after Russia began* Crucifixion story: "Bezhenka iz Slavianska vspominaet, kak pri nei kaznili malen'kogo syna i zhenu opolchentsa," PK, July 12, 2014, 37175. Reception of crucifixion story: "Aleksey Volin o siuzhete "Pervogo kanala" pro raspiatogo mal'chika," www.youtube.com/watch?v=7TVV5atZ0Qk, July 15, 2014.

178 *It seems that Alexander Dugin* Dugin's original post: www.facebook.com/alexandr.dugin/posts/811615568848485.

178 *Russian television* Weapons: Miller et al., "An Invasion by Any Other Name," 5–65. See also: NATO Allied Command Operations, "NATO Releases Imagery: Raises Questions on Russia's Role in Providing Tanks to Ukraine," June 14, 2014.

179 *A crucial Russian weapons system* Michael Weiss and James Miller, "How We Know Russia Shot Down MH17," *DB,* July 17, 2015; Miller et al., "An Invasion by Any Other Name," 17–34.

179 *One of the numerous* The Russian detachment: "Pre-MH17 Photograph

of Buk 332 Discovered," *Bellingcat,* June 5, 2017; Wacław Radzinowicz, "Donbas, Syria, zestrzelony boeing," *GW,* May 31, 2017.

179 *At 1:20 p.m.* For further supporting detail, see Bellingcat Investigation Team, "MH-17," 3–16, 36–44, sic passim, www.bellingcat.com/tag/mh17/; Weiss and Miller, "How We Know." Girkin's boast: web.archive.org/web/20140717152227/http://vk.com/strelkov_info. Khodakovskii and others: Pieniążek, *Pozdrowienia z Noworosji,* 199, 210; also "Aleksandr Khodakovskii: Ia znal, chto 'Buk' shel iz Luganska," echo.msk.ru, July 12, 2014.

180 *The law of gravity* Churkov's confusion: Weiss and Miller, "How We Know." As of 2017, the Dutch Safety Board was seeking information on two men who appeared to be high-ranking Russian military officers. "Russian Colonel General Identified as Key MH17 Figure," *Bellingcat,* Dec. 8, 2017. The fictional variations are discussed below.

180 *On the very day* "Istochnik: ukrainskie siloviki mogli pereputat' malaiziiskii 'Boing' s samoletom Putina," *NTV,* July 17, 2014, 1144376; "Minoborony: Riadom s 'boingom' letel ukrainskii shturmovik," life.ru, July 21, 2014, 137035; "Veroiatnoi tsel'iu sbivshikh malaiziiskii 'Boing' mog byt' samolet Prezidenta Rossii," *PK,* July 18, 2014, 37539; "Reports that Putin flew similar route as MH17," *RT,* July 17, 2014, 173672.

181 *The following day, July 18* "Dispetchery vynudili Boeing snizitsia nezadolgo do krusheniia," *TVC,* July 18, 2014, 45179; "Neverov: Kolomoiskii mog otdavat' prikazy dispetcheram po Boeing," *TVC,* July 23, 2014, 45480; "Fizionomist: Ochevidno, chto Kolomoiskii znaet, kto sbil 'boing'," life.ru, Oct. 22, 2014, 3329.

181 *Meanwhile, five Russian* "Dispetcher: riadom s Boeing byli zamecheny dva ukrainskikh istrebitelia," *Vesti,* July 17, 2014, 1807749. Third story: "V silovykh strukturakh Ukrainy est' versiia, chto Boeing sbili na ucheniiakh," ria.ru, July 7, 2014, 20140725. Fourth story: "Igor' Strelkov: chast' liudei iz Boinga umerli za neskol'ko sutok do katastrofy," Rusvesna.su, July 18, 2014.

181 *These fictions were raised* Sergei Lavrov, interview, *Rossiiskaia Gazeta,* Aug. 26, 2014.

182 *But even if all of these lies* "Rassledovanie Katastrofy 'Boinga,'" Levada Center, July 27, 2015.

182 *Russians who watched television* The video may be seen as "Bike Show—2014. Sevastopol," June 15, 2015, https://www.youtube.com/watch?v=8K3ApJ2MeP8.

183 *In that text, Prokhanov* Russians were, of course, not innocent during the German occupation. They collaborated with Germans in much the same way as other Soviet citizens. For discussion, see Snyder, *Black Earth.*

183 *Prokhanov blamed* Prokhanov's text, here and subsequently, is "Odinnadtsatyi stalinskii udar. O nashem novom Dne Pobedy," *Izvestiia,* May 5, 2014. He wrote elsewhere of Eurasia as home to "golden goddesses": "Zolotye bogini Evrazii," *Izvestiia,* June 2, 2014.

185 *Ukrainian society* On the German occupation of Soviet Ukraine, see Karel C. Berkhoff, *Harvest of Despair* (Cambridge, Mass.: Harvard UP, 2004).

187 *After Russian artillery* Quotation and generally: "Glava fonda sverd-lovskikh veteranov spetsnaza: 'Ia pomogaiu dobrovol'tsam otpravit'sia na Ukrainu,'" interview with Vladimir Efimov, Novosti E1.ru, Dec. 24, 2014. See also Miller et al., "An Invasion by Any Other Name," 64. Worth consulting on the period are Aleksei Levinson, "Mentalnaia iama," *NG*, June 4, 2014; Levada Center, "Rossiiskii Media Landshaft," June 17, 2014; Ekaterna Vinokurova, "Ischezaiuschchaia federalizatsiia," *Znak*, Aug. 25, 2014.

187 *Some of these Russian* Motivation and trucks: Elena Racheva, "Tyl," *NG*, Aug. 2014. Distance: Russian volunteer interview (K). Call of the heart: Russian volunteer interview (L). Global Sodom: Dmytro Fionik, "Pryhody Boha v Ukraini," in *Veni, vidi, scripsi: Istoriia nazhyvo* (Kyiv: Tempura, 2015), 73. On recruitment, see "Glava fonda sverdlovskikh vet-eranov spetsnaza." For more portraits of volunteers, see Walker, *The Long Hangover*, prologue, sic passim.

187 *Russian volunteers* Troop surge: Miller et al., "An Invasion by Any Other Name." Camps: Racheva, "Pogranichnoe sostoianie"; Racheva, "Tyl."

187 *Every now and then* Dancing: Racheva, "Pogranichnoe sostoianie." Dagestani soldiers killed: Ruslan Magomedov, "Gruz 200," *Chernovik*, Aug. 22, 2014.

188 *The 18th Separate Motorized* Tumanov: Elena Racheva, "Drugoi raboty-to net," *NG*, Sept. 2014; also see Parfitt, "Secret dead of Russia's un-declared war"; Konrad Schuller and Friedrich Schmidt, "Ein offenes Staatsgeheimnis," *FAZ*, Nov. 22, 2014. On the 18th Separate Motor-ized, see also "Sovet po pravam cheloveka peredal Dozhdiu kopiiu ob-rashcheniia v SK s imenami propavshykh soldat," Dozhd', Sept. 2, 2014; Sergei Kanev, "Lapochka iz Kushchevki," *NG*, Sept. 9, 2014; Evgenii Titov, "Stavropol'skaia pravozashchitnitsa, rasskazavshaia o pogibshikh v Ukraine voennosluzhashchikh, arestovana i dostavlena v Piatigorsk," *NG*, Oct. 19, 2014; Courtney Weaver, "Café encounter exposes reality of Rus-sian soldiers in Ukraine," *FT*, Oct. 22, 2014.

188 *On August 13, the men* Quotations: Parfitt, "Secret dead of Russia's unde-clared war." Social media: Racheva, "Drugoi raboty-to net."

189 *Konstantin Kuzmin* Quotation from Steven Rosenberg, "Ukraine Crisis: Forgotten Death of a Russian Soldier," BBC, Sept. 18, 2014.

189 *One of Kuzmin's* Rufat: Kanev, "Lapochka iz Kushchevki."

189 *On or about August 17, 2014* Sergei: Ivan Zhilin, "On otdal svoiu zhizn', a ego privezli ot tak . . ." *NG*, Nov. 21, 2014. Pskov funerals: Aleksei Ponomarev, "V Pskove proshli zakrytye pokhorony mestnykh desant-nikov," *Slon*, Aug. 25, 2014; also see "K poslednemu moriu," *Pskovskaia Gubernaia*, Sept. 12–13, 2014; and David M. Herszenhorn and Alexandra Odynova, "Soldiers' Graves Bear Witness to Russia's Role in Ukraine," *NYT*, Sept. 21, 2014. 137th Parachute Regiment and Andrianov: Ivan Zhilin, "On otdal svoiui zhizn', a ego privezli ot tak . . ." *NG*, Nov. 21, 2014.

189 *The 31st Airborne* Elena Racheva, "Bilet v odin konets," *NG*, Sept. 8, 2014.

190  *At about the same time* Herszenhorn and Odynova, "Soldiers' Graves Bear Witness."

190  *At some point in August* "Russia's 200th Motorized Infantry Brigade in the Donbass: The Tell-Tale Tanks," *Bellingcat*, July 4, 2016.

190  *Evgeny Trundaev* On Trundaev and the 200th: "Russia's 200th Motorized Infantry Brigade in the Donbass: The Hero of Russia," *Bellingcat*, June 21, 2016. Ilovaisk: "Russia's 6th Tank Brigade," *Bellingcat*, Sept. 22, 2015; Racheva, "Bilet v odin konets"; Miller et al., "An Invasion by Any Other Name," 7, 26–37; "The Battle of Ilovaisk," *TI*, Sept. 15, 2014.

191  *In early 2015* Piotr Andrusieczko, "Lotnisko w Doniecku—ukraiński Stalingrad," *GW*, Oct. 3, 2014; Sergei L. Loiko, "Ukraine fighters, surrounded at wrecked airport, refuse to give up," *Los Angeles Times*, Oct. 28, 2014. Natalia Zinets and Maria Tsvetkova, "Ukraine's Poroshenko tells army not to give up Donetsk airport," Reuters, Dec. 5, 2014. "Cyborgs": Miller et al., "An Invasion by Any Other Name," 8, 36. Ukrainian rebels executed: Oleg Sukhov, "Russian fighter's confession of killing prisoners might become evidence of war crimes," *Kyiv Post*, April 6, 2015.

191  *The second objective* Il'ia Barabanov, "V pampasakh Donbassa," Kommersant.ru, Feb. 19, 2015. For a thorough confirmation of Dambaev's journey from Siberia to Ukraine and back, see Simon Ostrovsky, "Russia Denies That Its Soldiers Are in Ukraine, But We Tracked One There Using His Selfies," *Vice*, June 16, 2015. On the 200th: "Russia's 200th Motorized Infantry Brigade in the Donbass," *Bellingcat*, Jan. 16, 2016.

191  *Bato Dambaev* Barabanov, "V pampasakh Donbassa." Attitude to propaganda: Elena Kostiuchenko, "My vse znali, na chto idem i chto mozhet byt'," *NG*, Feb. 3, 2015.

192  *Though a second ceasefire* Batomunkuev: Kostiuchenko, "My vse znali."

192  *Units of the Russian army* Ruslan Leviev, "Three Graves: Russian Investigation Team Uncovers Spetsnaz Brigade in Ukraine," *Bellingcat*, May 22, 2015.

192  *This neighbor could contrast* Dependence on Russian taxpayer: Konrad Schuller, "Ohne Kohle in Kohlrevier," *FAZ*, Nov. 24, 2014. Call from Moscow: Anton Zverev, "Ex-rebel leaders detail role played by Putin aide in east Ukraine," Reuters, May 11, 2017. Instructions from Moscow: Jochen Bittner, Arndt Ginzel, and Alexej Hock, "Cheerful Propaganda and Hate on Command," *Die Zeit*, Sept. 30, 2016. Statistics: the Ukrainian government provides lists of soldiers killed (under 3,000 as of this writing) and estimates of civilians killed (8,000). There is no official Russian information on Russian soldiers killed, since Russia denies that it is fighting a war in Ukraine. Most likely, Russian and Ukrainian casualties are comparable. For discussion, see "'Traceless regiment': Russian military losses in Donbas," Ukrainian Crisis Media Center, May 17, 2017, which is an abridged version of Oleksiy Bratushchak's article of the same date in *Ukrains'ka Pravda*. The official Ukrainian count of internally displaced people is about 1.6 million, but this includes only those who have registered for the status and is certainly an undercount. See "5 Unreported

Facts About Displaced People in Ukraine," *Hromadske International,* May 18, 2017.

193 *In May 2014* Andy Greenberg, "How an Entire Nation Became Russia's Test Lab for Cyberwar," *Wired,* June 20, 2017; Ellen Nakashima, "U.S. government officially accuses Russia of hacking campaign," *WP,* Oct. 7, 2016; Frenkel, "Meet Fancy Bear." Presidential hack: Patrikarakos, *War in 140 Characters,* 123.

193 *The cyberwar made* U.S. institutions: "Bears in the Midst: Intrusion in the Democratic National Convention," *Crowdstrike,* June 15, 2016. State Department: Ellen Nakashima, "New Details Emerge about Russian Hack," *WP,* April 3, 2017. Malware in grid: Greenberg, "How an Entire Nation." See chapter 6 for further discussion.

194 *The most remarkable* To follow the Ukrainian confrontation with cyberwar, consult *StopFake* and *EuroMaidan Press.*

194 *Throughout the war in Ukraine* Putin quote: "Priamaia liniia s Vladimirom Putinym," Kremlin, April 17, 2014. Special forces: Kanygin, "Bes, Fiks, Roman i goluboglazyi." Lavrov: Maria Gorelova, "Lavrov: Soobshcheniia o vvode voisk RF na Ukrainu—chast' informatsionnoi voiny," *KP,* Aug. 23, 2016; "Lavrov nazval snimki vtorzheniia voisk RF v Ukrainu kadrami iz komp'iuternoi igry," NV.ua, Aug. 29, 2014.

194 *Lavrov did not really mean* Levada Center, press release, Dec. 11, 2014.

195 *After all of the goading* St. Petersburg: Russian Ministry of Justice, Aug. 29, 2014, minjust.ru/ru/press/news/minyustom-rossii-vneseny-dopolneniya-v-reestr-nekommercheskih-organizaciy-1. Piatigorsk: Evgenii Titov, "Stavropol'skaia pravozashchitnitsa, rasskazavshaia o pogibshikh v Ukraine voennosluzhashchikh, arestovana i dostavlena v Piatigorsk," *NG,* Oct. 2014. See Leviev, "Three Graves"; Rosenberg, "Ukraine crisis"; Miller et al., "Invasion by Any Other Name," 64.

195 *The underlying logic* This is a logical application of the "realist" idea in international relations theory that international relations is about relative and not absolute gains: after all, losing less than everyone else is a relative gain. What is important to realize is that theories of international relations which present themselves as "realism" can actually be normative, in the sense that states act in order to make them true. Russia's pursuit of a negative-sum game makes sense from the narrow perspective of a threatened oligarchy, but it is not "realism" in the conventional sense of the word, since its application changes the world. In that sense the constructivists in international relations theory are correct. "Realism" in international relations theory was itself a literary construction at the beginning, and a German one for that matter. It leads back to Carl Schmitt. Matthew Specter is exploring related themes.

196 *Ukrainian society was consolidated* Quotation: "Ukraine chief rabbi accuses Russians of staging antisemitic 'provocations,'" Jewish Telegraphic Agency, March 3, 2014. Statistic: "Only 5.5% of Ukrainian citizens consider themselves 'Russian,'" UNIAN, July 11, 2017.

196 *By invading Ukraine* Lavrov: Lilia Shevtsova, "The Putin Doctrine,"

*The American Interest,* April 14, 2014; "Lavrov rasskazal, chto meshaet formirovaniiu novogo mirovogo poriadka," Ren.tv, 19. For contemporary evaluations of China, see the notes to chapter 3.

197 *Russia's Eurasian ideologists* On water as a precious resource: Steven Solomon, *Water* (New York: HarperCollins, 2010).

197 *Sergei Glazyev opened* "Kremlin Advisor Speaks at Yalta Conference Amid Separatists, European Far Right (August 25–31)," *TI,* Aug. 30, 2014; Robert Beckhusen, "As Russia Invades Ukraine, the Kremlin's Far Right Allies Meet in Yalta," *Medium,* Aug. 31, 2014.

198 *Within the European Union* Gauland: Melanie Amman and Pavel Lokshin, "German Populists Forge Ties with Russia," *Der Spiegel,* April 27, 2016. Bundestag: Swiss Federal Intelligence Service, Situation Report, 2015, 76; Gerodimos et al., "Russia Is Attacking Western Liberal Democracies."

198 *Facing rising numbers* Merkel's decision: Helena Smith and Mark Tran, "Germany says it could take 500,000 refugees a year," *TG,* Sept. 8, 2015. On refugees and the rise of the AfD, compare Timothy Garton Ash, "It's the Kultur, Stupid," *NYR,* Dec. 7, 2017; Mark Leonard, "The Germany Crisis," *New Statesman,* March 5, 2016. Harmonization: Vladimir Putin, "70-ia sessiia General'noi Assamblei OON," *UN,* Sept. 28, 2015. Like Americans, Germans did not generally see the war in Ukraine as concerning them directly; it was usually discussed, in both countries, through exoticizing filters which made this impossible. Karl Schlögel's book, *Entscheidung in Kiew,* was an attempt to explain to Germans the relationship between the Russian assault on truth in Ukraine and their own experience of the fragility of institutions. Some German reporters with knowledge of eastern Europe also tried to mediate: Alice Bota, "Angst vor Ukraines Patrioten," *Die Zeit,* Oct. 24, 2014.

198 *Russian bombs began to fall* On Russian bombing: "Russia air strikes 'strengthen IS,'" BBC, Oct. 2, 2015; Jonathan Marcus, "Syria crisis," BBC, Oct. 8, 2015; Tom Miles and Stephanie Nebehay, "U.N. rights boss warns Russia over Syria air strikes," Reuters, Oct. 4, 2016; Alec Luhn, "Russian media could almost be covering a different war in Syria," *TG,* Oct. 3, 2016; Wacław Radzinowicz, "Donbas, Syria, zestrzelony boeing," *GW,* May 31, 2017.

199 *A Berlin family drama* "Russia's Propaganda War Against Germany," *Der Spiegel,* Feb. 8, 2016. Sputnik and generally: Rutenberg, "How the Kremlin built."

200 *The Russian information war* Pervyi Kanal: "Avstriia vremenno priostanavlivaet deistvie Shengenskogo soglasheniia iz-za sluchaev nasiliia v Germanii," PK, Jan. 16, 2016, 300073. Police statement: Polizei Berlin, Facebook post, Jan. 18, 2016. Quotations 1 and 2: "SMI FRG: iznasilovanie v Berline russkoi devochki zamiali, chtoby ne seat' paniku," *Vesti,* Jan. 18, 2016; Elena Chinkova, "Liza, my s toboy!" *KP,* Jan. 24, 2016. Further coverage: Elena Minenkova, "Bednaia Liza . . ." rg-rb.de, Jan. 20, 2016, 17640; "Pervyi podozrevaemyi v seksual'nykh domogatel'stvakh vo

vremia novogodnikh prazdnikov arestovan v Kol'ne," PK, Jan. 19, 2016, 3166.

200 *The information war against Merkel* Damien McGuinness, "Russia steps into Berlin 'rape' storm claiming German cover-up," BBC, Jan. 27, 2016. Lavrov on Lisa F.: "Vystuplenie i otvety na voprosy SMI Ministra inostrannykh del Rossii S.V.Lavrova," mid.ru, Jan. 26, 2016, 2032328.

201 *Not long before* Amnesty International: "Syria: Russia's shameful failure to acknowledge civilian killings," Amnesty International, Dec. 23, 2015. Physicians for Human Rights: "Russian Warplanes Strike Medical Facilities in Syria," Physicians for Human Rights, Oct. 7, 2015. See also Westcott, "NGO Says Russian Airstrikes Hit Three Syrian Medical Facilities in Two Days," *NW,* Oct. 7, 2015. Russian hackers meanwhile punished those who reported on the bombings: "Pawn Storm APT Group Returns," *SC Magazine,* Oct. 23, 2015.

201 *Merkel remained the leader* Russian cyberwar against Merkel: Sophie Eisentraut, "Russia Pulling Strings on Both Sides of the Atlantic," *The Cipher,* Sept. 22, 2017. Quotation: "Wir werden Frau Merkel jagen," *Der Spiegel,* Sept. 24, 2017.

201 *Other European politicians* For Tusk's position, see "Statement by President Tusk on Maidan Square," *EC-CEU,* April 27, 2015. Aleksandra Kovaleva letter: "Letter on 'Euromaydan,'" Maidan Translations, Feb. 21, 2014.

202 *That Polish government* Rosalia Romaniec, "Curious wiretapping affair rocks Polish government," *Deutsche Welle,* June 23, 2014; Michael E. Miller, "Secret Recordings," *WP,* June 11, 2015.

202 *Crossing the line* See generally Hannah Arendt, *The Origins of Totalitarianism* (New York: Harcourt, Brace, 1951). The best commentary at the time was Marcin Król, "Diabeł ma nas w swych objęciach," *GW,* June 27, 2014.

203 *It was perhaps no great surprise* Promise that Macierewicz will not be minister of defense: Agata Kondzińska, "Na kłopoty z Macierewiczem - generał Gowin," *GW,* Oct. 9, 2015.

203 *In 2006, when the Law* These are the themes of Piątek, *Macierewicz i jego Tajemnice.* See also Wojciech Czuchnowski, "Nocny atak Macierewicza na Centrum Kontrwywiadu NATO," *GW,* Dec. 18, 2015; Julian Borger, "Polish military police raid Nato centre in Warsaw," *TG,* Dec. 18, 2015.

204 *Macierewicz, a master* On the state of the commemoration of the Katyn massacre before Macierewicz, as well as a characterization of the Smolensk disaster (132–53), see Alexander Etkind et al., *Remembering Katyn* (Cambridge, UK: Polity, 2012).

204 *Only the living* Quotation from the black box, as established by Polish government expertise: "'Zmieścisz się śmiało.' Generał Błasik prowadził tupolewa na lotnisko w Smoleńsku," dziennik.pl, April 7, 2015, 4877256. Some essential fragments in English are in "Poland publishes plane crash transcript," BBC, June 10, 2010. The official Polish report: "Raport Koncowy z. Badania zdarzenia lotniczego nr 192/2010/11 samolotu Tu-154M

nr 101 zaistnialego dnia 10 kwietnia 2010 w rejonie lotniska Smolensk Poloczny," Warsaw, Poland, July 29, 2011. The Polish and Russian official reports differed in their account of the behavior of the Russian controllers, but not on the essential point. A valuable summary by a Polish pilot is Jerzy Grzędzielski, "Prawda o katastrofie smoleńskiej."

205 *Macierewicz understood that the search* Macierewicz published a *White Book*: Zespół Parlamentarny ds. Badania Przyczyn Katastrofy TU-154 M z 10 kwietnia 2010 roku, "Raport Smolenski: Stan badań, Wydanie II" (Warsaw: Poland, May 2013), 76.

205 *Macierewicz required that the list* "Monthly Warsaw march," Radio Poland, Nov. 10, 2017, 329891.

206 *Macierewicz's accusations of Russia* Piątek, *Macierewicz i jego Tajemnice*; Schuller, "Die Moskau-Reise."

207 *Warsaw meanwhile* Schuller, "Die Moskau-Reise." On Malofeev, see chapter 3.

207 *Macierewicz had maintained* Aubrey McFate, "Poland's defense ministry met with Dana Rohrabacher," *Daily Kos,* Aug. 18, 2017; Adam Entous, "House majority leader to colleagues in 2016: 'I think Putin pays' Trump," *WP,* May 17, 2017; Nicholas Fandos, "He's a Member of Congress. The Kremlin Likes Him So Much It Gave Him a Code Name," *NYT,* Nov. 21, 2017.

207 *Macierewicz did not deny* "OSCE urges Poland's restraint with investigative reporter," AP, Aug. 4 , 2017.

208 *There is nothing inherently* Pomerantsev, *Nothing Is True,* 227.

208 *Russian propaganda was transmitted* See discussion in chapter 3.

209 *Russian conspiratorial ideas* Ron Paul, "The Ukraine Fuse Has Been Lit," *Money and Markets* podcast, May 16, 2014.

210 *It was less surprising* On Glazyev, see chapters 3, 4, and 5. Glazyev article chez LaRouche: "On Eurofascism," *Executive Intelligence Review,* June 27, 2014. On Jews as responsible for fascism and Ukraine: "British Imperial Project in Ukraine: Violent Coup, Fascist Axioms, Neo-Nazis," *Executive Intelligence Review,* May 16, 2014. In LaRouche publications, "British" means "Jewish." See also Lyndon LaRouche on Ukraine in *Executive Intelligence Review,* Jan. 3, 2014, May 2014.

210 *Stephen Cohen* Stephen F. Cohen, "The Silence of American Hawks About Kiev's Atrocities," *The Nation,* June 30, 2014.

210 *Writing in* The Nation Cohen's characterization: "Silence of American Hawks." The Ukrainian prime minister's statement of condolence: "Arsenyi Iatseniuk vyrazyl soboleznovannia," June 14, 2014, www.kmu.gov .ua. Legal action against RT: Jasper Jackson, "RT sanctioned by Ofcom over series of misleading and biased articles," *TG,* Sept. 21, 2015. See also Pomerantsev and Weiss, "The Menace of Unreality," 32.

211 *When Russia shot down MH17* Quotation: *Democracy Now!,* July 18, 2014. For discussion of the event itself and the Russian distraction campaign, see chapter 4.

211 *This idea that Russia's anti-gay* See previous citations on Spencer and Le

Pen; see also Shekhovtsov, *Russia and the Western Far Right*, chapter 5, for the larger pattern: Russia to intermediaries to public. From 2014 to 2017, articles in *The Nation* employed the term with regularity. For a sober analysis of the comparison between the two eras, see Nikolay Koposov, "Back to Yalta? Stephen Cohen and the Ukrainian crisis," *Eurozine*, Sept. 5, 2014.

211 *On July 24, 2014* Quotation: *Democracy Now!*, July 24, 2014. Political technologists: Mitrokhin, "Infiltration." Antyufeyev was discussed previously.

212 *Vanden Heuvel was speaking* Russian journalism on shelling: for quotations, "Rossiia obstrelivaet Ukrainu s svoei territorii," *Novoe Vremia*, July 23, 2014. The article was made available the same day in English: "Direct Translation: Russian Army Gunner Brags, 'All Night We Pounded Ukraine,'" *New Atlanticist*, July 23, 2014.

212 *Important writers* John Pilger, "In Ukraine, the US is dragging us towards war with Russia," *TG*, May 13, 2014. These events are described above. An English summary of the TV interview: "Jews brought Holocaust on themselves, Russian TV host says," Jewish News Service, March 24, 2014.

213 *How were opinion leaders* Walker, *The Long Hangover*, chapter 11.

213 *Guardian associate editor Seumas Milne* Quotations: Seumas Milne, "In Ukraine, fascists, oligarchs and western expansion are at the heart of the crisis," *TG*, Jan. 29, 2014; Seumas Milne, "It's not Russia that's Pushed Ukraine to the Brink of War," *TG*, April 30, 2014. See also "Projecting the Kremlin line," *Left Foot Forward*, March 15, 2015.

214 *Enormous amounts of time* Stephen Bush, "Jeremy Corbyn appoints Seumas Milne as head of strategy and communications," *New Statesman*, Oct. 20, 2015; Laura Kuenssberg, "Corbyn office 'sabotaged' EU Remain campaign—sources," BBC, June 26, 2016. On Russia and Brexit, see the discussion in chapter 3.

214 *In July 2016* Trump quotation: Melissa Chan, "Donald Trump Says Vladimir Putin Won't 'Go Into Ukraine,'" *Time*, July 31, 2016. Manafort and Opposition Bloc: Kenneth P. Vogel, "Manafort's Man in Kiev," *Politico*, Aug. 18, 2016; Peter Stone and Greg Gordon, "Manafort flight records show deeper Kremlin ties," *McClatchy*, Nov. 27, 2017.

## CHAPTER 6

217 *The rise of Donald Trump* Timothy Snyder, "Trump's Putin Fantasy," *NYR*, April 19, 2016, includes most of these citations and sources. See also: Dugin: "In Trump We Trust," Katekhon Think Tank video, posted March 4, 2016; Kozyrev: "Donald Trump's Weird World," *NYT*, Oct. 12, 2016. For "our president": Ryan Lizza, "A Russian Journalist Explains How the Kremlin Instructed Him to Cover the 2016 Election," *NY*, Nov. 22, 2017.

218 *The Russian media machine* Quotation: Lizza, "Russian Journalist." Sputnik: Craig Timberg, "Russian propaganda effort helped spread 'fake news' during election, experts say," *WP*, Nov. 24, 2016; "Hillary Clinton's Axis

of Evil," Sputnik, Oct. 11, 2016. Trump on RT on Sept. 8: Adam Taylor and Paul Farhi, "A Trump interview may be crowning glory for RT," *WP*, Sept. 9, 2016.

218 *When Trump won* Applause: "Donald Trump has been Made an Honorary Russian Cossack," *The Independent*, Nov. 12, 2016. Kiselev and eunuch, arms, porch, housekeeper: *Vesti Nedeli*, Rossiia Odin, Nov. 13, 2016; Nov. 20, 2016; Dec. 25, 2016; Jan. 22, 2017. I am toning down Kiselev's vulgarity.

219 *The politics of eternity are full* For background: Craig Unger, "Trump's Russian Laundromat," *New Republic*, July 13, 2017; Franklin Foer, "Putin's Puppet," *Slate*, July 4, 2016.

219 *Throughout the exercise* His finances will be discussed below. Quotation: Donald Trump, Tweet, Jan. 6, 2018.

219 *Russian gangsters began* Unger, "Trump's Russian Laundromat."

220 *A Russian oligarch bought* Harding, *Collusion*, 272. Dmitry Rybolovlev: Franklin Foer, "Donald Trump Isn't a Manchurian Candidate," *Slate*, July 27, 2016; Philip Ewing, "Subpoena for Deutsche Bank May Put Mueller on Collision Course with Trump," NPR, Dec. 5, 2017. Bank debts: "Trump Bankers Question His Portrayal of Financial Comeback," *Fortune*, July 17, 2016; Keri Geiger, Greg Farrell, and Sarah Mulholland, "Trump May Have a $300 Million Conflict of Interest with Deutsche Bank," *Bloomberg*, Dec. 22, 2016. $55 million: Luke Harding, *Collusion* (London: Guardian Books, 2017), 13, 283. Deutsche Bank's laundering: Ed Caesar, "Deutsche Bank's $10-billion scandal," *New Yorker*, Aug. 29, 2016.

220 *The Russian offers* Unger, "Trump's Russian Laundromat"; Matt Apuzzo and Maggie Haberman, "Trump Associate Boasted," *NYT*, Aug. 28, 2017; Natasha Bertrand, "The Trump Organization," *BI*, Nov. 23, 2017.

221 *Russia is not a wealthy country* Trump Tower Moscow: Gloria Borger and Marshall Cohen, "Document details scrapped deal," CNN, Sept. 9, 2017. Tweet: Oct. 17, 2015.

221 *The final deal never went through* "Our boy": Apuzzo and Haberman, "Trump Associate Boasted." 70%: Natasha Bertrand, "The Trump Organization," *BI*, Nov. 23, 2017.

222 *Trump was broadcasting unreality* RT and birtherism: Scherr, "Russian TV Channel."

222 *From a Russian perspective* Jon Swaine and Shaun Walker, "Trump in Moscow," *TG*, Sept. 18, 2017. The video: Allan Smith, "Trump once made a cameo," *BI*, July 10, 2017; Mandalist Del Barco, "Meet Emin Agalarov," NPR, July 14, 2017.

223 *The Soviet secret police* V. V. Doroshenko et al., eds., *Istoriia sovetskikh organov gosudarstvennoi bezopasnosti: Uchebnik* (Moscow: KGB, 1977), especially at 206–7; Christopher Andrew and Oleg Gordievsky, *KGB* (London: Hodder & Stoughton, 1990), 67–78; John Dziak, *Chekisty* (Lexington: Lexington Books, 1988), especially at 49; Władysław Michniewicz, *Wielki Blef Sowiecki* (Chicago: Wici: 1991); [Jerzy Niezbrzycki],

"'Trest,'" *VO*, vol. 7, no. 1, 1950, 119–33; Timothy Snyder, *Sketches from a Secret War* (New Haven: Yale UP, 2005); Iuri Shapoval, Volodymyr Prystaiko, Vadym Zolotar'ov, *Ch.K.-H.P.U.-NKVD v Ukraini* (Kyiv: Abrys, 1997); Piotr Kołakowski, *NKWD i GRU na ziemiach polskich 1939–1945* (Warsaw: Bellona, 2002); Rafał Wnuk, *"Za pierwszego Sowieta"* (Warsaw: IPN, 2007).

223 *The cold war, by the 1970s* For similar reflections, see Pomerantsev, *Nothing Is True*, 199, 213. Screen time: Jacqueline Howard, "Americans devote more than 10 hours a day to screen time, and growing," CNN, July 29, 2016.

224 *Russia under Putin* Slept through: Vladimir Nikonov on the program *Voskresnyi vecher s Solov'evym*, Rossiia-24, Sept. 10, 2017; discussion in Zachary Cohen, "Russian politician: US spies slept while Russia elected Trump," CNN, Sept. 12, 2017. The general attitude that war was defensive: Nikita Mironov, interview with Alexander Dugin, *Open Revolt*, March 20, 2014; Vladimir Ovchinskii and Elena Larina, "Kholodnaia voina 2.0," Izborsk Club, Nov. 11, 2014. Previous targets: Matthews, "Russia's Greatest Weapon May Be Its Hackers"; "Seven Years of Malware Linked to Russian State–Backed Cyber Espionage," *Ars Technica*, Sept. 17, 2015; Frenkel, "Meet Fancy Bear"; Gerodimos et al., "Russia Is Attacking Western Liberal Democracies."

224 *Kiselev called information war* 2013: Jochen Bittner et al., "Putins großer Plan," *Die Zeit*, Nov. 20, 2014. Izborsk: Vitaly Averianov, "Novaia staraia kholodnaia voina," Izborsk Club, 23 Dec. 2014, article 4409. Quotation: Rutenberg, "How the Kremlin built." See also Donna Brazile: *Hacks* (New York: Hachette), 67.

225 *During the 2014 presidential* These operations were discussed in chapters 3, 4, and 5. For additional detail on Estonia, see "Estonia and Russia: A cyber-riot," *The Economist*, May 10, 2007; Kertu Ruus, "Cyber War I," *European Affairs*, vol. 9, nos. 1-2, 2008.

225 *The Russian war against Ukraine* T-50: Kanygin, "Bes, Fiks, Romani i goluboglazyi." Red flag: Separatist interview (V). Borodai: "Eks-prem'er DNR posovetoval Obame 'zabrat'sia na pal'mu,'" TopNews.ru, Aug. 21, 2014. Antiufeev quotation: Kanygin, "'Pridnestrovskii general Vladimir Antiufeev." Glazyev quotation: "Predotvratit' voinu—pobedit' v voine," Izborsk Club, Sept. 2014, article 3962. December 2014 Izborsk quotation: Averianov, "Novaia staraia kholodnaia voina."

226 *The Russian FSB* "Fabrika trollei," RBK, Oct. 17, 2017, is the original report; see also Shaun Walker, "Russian troll factory paid US activists," *TG*, Oct. 17, 2017.

226 *It was clear in 2016* Krutskikh: Scott Shane, "The Fake Americans Russia Created," *NYT*, Sept. 7, 2017. Revenge: Massimo Calabresi, "Hacking Democracy," *Time*, May 29, 2017, 32. Pervyi Kanal: Oct. 9, 2016, 31169. Putin: Andrew Higgins, "Maybe Private Russian Hackers Meddled in Election, Putin Says," *NYT*, June 1, 2017.

227 *American exceptionalism proved* Hillary Clinton, who was perhaps the

single American with the most reason to be concerned, did not expect an attack of this kind (*What Happened*, 333). See also Donna Brazile, *Hacks*, 135.

227 *In a cyberwar, an "attack surface"* Elizabeth Dwoskin, Adam Entous, and Craig Timberg, "Google uncovers Russian-bought ads," *NYT*, Oct. 9, 2017; Mike Isaac and Daisuke Wakabayashi, "Russian Influence Reached 126 Million Through Facebook Alone," *NYT*, Oct. 30, 2017, and sources cited below. For Facebook's review, see Jen Weedon, William Nuland, and Alex Stamos, "Information Operations and Facebook," April 27, 2017.

227 *In all likelihood* 5.8 million: Craig Timberg and Elizabeth Dowskin, "Facebook takes down data," *WP*, Oct. 12, 2017; Graham Kates, "Facebook Deleted 5.8 million accounts just before the 2016 election," CBS, Oct. 31, 2017. 470 from Internet Research Agency: Jon Swaine and Luke Harding, "Russia funded Facebook and Twitter investments through Kushner investor," *TG*, Nov. 5, 2017. No disclaimer: April Glaser, "Political ads on Facebook Now Need to Say Who Paid for Them," *Slate*, Dec. 18 2017. Estimates of shares: Craig Timberg, "Russian propaganda," *WP*, Oct. 5, 2017. Events pages: David McCabe, "Russian Facebook Campaign Included 100+ Event Pages," *Axios*, Jan. 26, 2018. 3,000 ads: Mike Snider, "See the fake Facebook ads Russians ran," *USA Today*, Nov. 1, 2017; Scott Shane, "These Are the Ads Russia Bought on Facebook in 2016," *NYT*, Nov. 1, 2017. See also the collection by UsHadrons at medium.com/@ ushadrons. 60 million: Nicholas Confessore et al., "Buying Online Influencers," *NYT*, Jan. 28, 2018.

228 *Americans were not exposed* For the ads, see previous note. Susceptibilities: Calabresi, "Hacking Democracy." See also Adam Entous, Craig Timberg, and Elizabeth Dwoskin, "Russian operatives used Facebook ads," *WP*, Sept. 25, 2017; Nicholas Confessore and Daisuke Wkabayashi, "How Russia Harvested American Rage," *NYT*, Oct. 9, 2017. Rifle example: Rebecca Shabad, "Russian Facebook ad showed black woman," CBS, Oct. 3, 2017. Muslim example: "Russian Propaganda Pushed Pro-Hillary Rally," *DB*, Sept. 27, 2017; "Russians Impersonated Real American Muslims," *DB*, Sept. 27, 2017. This site, interestingly enough, quoted Vladislav Surkov's favorite rapper, Tupac Shakur. Michigan and Wisconsin: Manu Rajy, Dylan Byers, and Dana Bash, "Russian-linked Facebook ads targeted Michigan and Wisconsin," CNN, Oct. 4, 2017. Refugees and rapists: Ben Popken, "Russian trolls pushed graphic, racist tweets to American voters," NBC, Nov. 30, 2017. Trump: in announcing his candidacy, June 15, 2015.

229 *Russian attackers exploited* 10%: Onur Varol et al., "Online Human-Bot Interactions: Detection, Estimation, and Characterization," Proceedings of the Eleventh International AAAI Conference on Web and Social Media, March 27, 2017, estimate 9–15% of accounts. On 20% and quotation: Alessandro Bessit and Emilio Ferrara, "Social bots distort the 2016 U.S. Presidential election online discussion," *First Monday*, vol. 21, no. 11, Nov. 7, 2016. Estimate that bots as active as humans: Marco T. Bastos

and Dan Mercea, "The Brexit Botnet and User-Generated Hyperpartisan News," *Social Science Computer Review*, 2017, 4. 2, 752: Ben Popken, "Russian trolls went on attack during key election moments," NBC, Dec. 20, 2017. Twitter's later reckoning: Confessore, "Buying Online Influencers."

229 *Bots were initially used* Twitter and text-to-vote: Twitter, "Update: Russian Interference in 2016 US Election, Bots, & Misinformation," Sept. 28, 2017. North Carolina: Nicole Perlroth et al., "Russian Election Hacking Efforts," *NYT,* Sept. 1, 2017. Electoral boards: "Assessing Russian Activities and Intentions in Recent U.S. Elections," Intelligence Community Assessment, Jan. 6, 2017, iii.

230 *Having used its Twitter bots* Convention and debate: Ben Popken, "Russian trolls went on attack during key election moments," NBC, Dec. 20, 2017. Swing states: "Study: Fake News on Twitter Flooded Swing States," *DB,* Sept. 29, 2017. Bots from Brexit: Carrell, "Russian cyber-activists." Trend and same 1,600: Selina Wang, "Twitter Is Crawling with Bots," *Bloomberg,* Oct. 13, 2017.

230 *In the United States in 2016* See citations below. Email hacks: M. D. Shear and M. Rosenberg, "Released Emails Suggest the D.N.C. Derided the Sanders Campaign," *NYT,* July 22, 2016; Jenna McLaughlin, Robbie Gramer, and Jana Winter, "Private Email of Top U.S. Russia Intelligence Official Hacked," *Time,* July 17, 2017.

230 *During a presidential election year* Russia hacked: Thomas Rid, U.S. Senate testimony, March 30, 2017; Frenkel, "Meet Fancy Bear." Convention atmosphere: Clinton, *What Happened,* 341; Brazile, *Hacks,* 8, 9, 15.

231 *According to American* The U.S. assessments: NCCIC and FBI Joint Analysis Report, "Grizzly Steppe: Russian Malicious Cyber Activity," Dec. 29, 2016; "Assessing Russian Activities and Intentions in Recent U.S. Elections," Intelligence Community Assessment, Jan. 6, 2017. See also U.S. Department of the Treasury, "Issuance of Amended Executive Order 13694; Cyber-Related Sanctions Designations," Dec. 29, 2016. Trump Jr. and Trump Sr. participation: Jack Shafer, "Week 26," *Politico,* Nov. 18, 2017. Quotations: Marshall Cohen, "What we know about Trump Jr.'s exchanges with WikiLeaks," CNN, Nov. 14, 2017. Trump's denials: Kurt Eichenwald, "Why Vladimir Putin's Russia Is Backing Donald Trump," *NW,* Nov. 4, 2016.

231 *Leaked emails* Guiding to Podesta: "Russia Twitter trolls rushed to deflect Trump bad news," AP, Nov. 9, 2017. Thirty minutes: Adam Entous and Ellen Nakashima, "Obama's secret struggle to punish Russia," *WP,* June 23, 2017.

232 *As in Poland in 2015* See Brazile, *Hacks,* 25, 43, 85.

233 *If they take as knowledge* Putin quotation: Frenkel, "Meet Fancy Bear." According to U.S. intelligence, Russia extracted material about Republicans but did not use it. "Assessing Russian Activities and Intentions in Recent U.S. Elections," Intelligence Community Assessment, Jan. 6, 2017, 3.

233 *The open sources revealed* No salary: Philip Bump, "Paul Manafort: An FAQ about Trump's indicted former campaign chairman," *WP,* Oct. 30,

2017. See also: Kate Brannen, "A Timeline of Paul Manafort's Relationship with Donald Trump," *Slate*, Oct. 30, 2017.

234 *Between 2006 and 2009* Payment: Aggelos Petropolous and Richard Engel, "Manafort Had $60 Million Relationship With a Russian Oligarch," NBC, Oct. 15, 2017. Deripaska has denied that the payments were made. Briefings: Julia Ioffe and Frank Foer, "Did Manafort Use Trump to Curry Favor with a Putin Ally?" *The Atlantic*, Oct. 2, 2017. See also: Andrew Roth, "Manafort's Russia connection: What you need to know about Oleg Deripaska," *WP*, Sept. 24, 2017. Lawyer: Rebecca Ruiz and Sharon LaFrontiere, "Role of Trump's Personal Lawyer Blurs Public and Private Lines," *NYT*, June 11, 2017.

234 *Aside from his history* These events were discussed in chapter 4. See Foer, "Quiet American"; Simon Shuster, "How Paul Manafort Helped Elect Russia's Man in Ukraine," *Time*, Oct. 31, 2017; and especially Franklin Foer, "The Plot Against America," *The Atlantic*, March 2018.

234 *Having brought American tactics* Will not invade: Eric Bradner and David Wright, "Trump says Putin is 'not going to go into Ukraine,' despite Crimea," CNN, Aug. 1, 2016. $12.7 million: Andrew E. Kramer, Mike McIntire, and Barry Meier, "Secret Ledger in Ukraine Lists Cash for Donald Trump's Campaign Chief," *NYT*, Aug. 14, 2016. The Turkey story: Andrew Weisburd and Clint Watts, "How Russia Dominates Your Twitter Feed," *DB*, Aug. 6, 2016; Linda Qiu, "Trump campaign chair misquotes Russian media in bogus claim about NATO base terrorist attack," *Politifact*, Aug. 16, 2016.

235 *Manafort was replaced* Mainstream: Sarah Posner, "How Donald Trump's New Campaign Chief Created an Online Haven for White Nationalists," *Mother Jones,* Aug. 22, 2016. For numerous examples of white supremacist enthusiasm for Trump, see Richard Cohen, "Welcome to Donald Trump's America," SPLC Report, Summer 2017; Ryan Lenz et al., "100 Days in Trump's America," Southern Poverty Law Center, 2017. Heimbach trial: "Will Trump have to testify on rally attacks?" *DB*, April 19, 2017. Heimbach quotations: Michel, "Beyond Trump and Putin"; see also Heather Digby Parton, "Trump, the alt-right and the Kremlin," *Salon*, Aug. 17, 2017. Bannon, David Bossie, and Citizens United: Michael Wolff, "Ringside with Steve Bannon at Trump Tower as the President-Elect's Strategist Plots 'An Entirely New Political Movement,'" *Hollywood Reporter,* Nov. 18, 2016. Bannon and Mercers: Matthew Kelly, Kate Goldstein, and Nicholas Confessore, "Robert Mercer, Bannon Patron, Is Leaving Helm of $50 Billion Hedge Fund," *NYT*, Nov. 2, 2017.

235 *Bannon's extreme-Right ideology* Bannon quotation: Owen Matthews, "Alexander Dugin and Steve Bannon's Ideological Ties to Vladimir Putin's Russia," *NW*, April 17, 2017. Bannon's ideology and films: Ronald Radosh, "Steve Bannon, Trump's Top Guy, Told Me He Was 'A Leninist' Who Wants to 'Destroy the State,'" *DB*, Aug. 22, 2016; Jeremy Peters, "Bannon's Views Can be Traced to a Book That Warns, 'Winter Is Coming,'" *NYT*, April 8, 2017; Owen Matthews, "Alexander Dugin and Steve

Bannon's Ideological Ties to Vladimir Putin's Russia," *NW,* April 17, 2017; Christopher Dickey and Asawin Suebsaeng, "Steve Bannon's Dream: A Worldwise Ultra-Right," *DB,* Nov. 13, 2016.

236 *Bannon's films were simplistic* Bannon quotation: Wolff, "Ringside with Steve Bannon." Views: Radosh, "Steve Bannon"; Peters, "Bannon's Views"; Matthews, "Alexander Dugin." Bannon on the "treasonous" behavior of Manafort, Kushner, and Donald Trump Jr.: David Smith, "Trump Tower meeting with Russians 'treasonous,' Bannon says in explosive book," *TG,* Jan. 3, 2018. Protectorate: Greg Miller, Greg Jaffe, and Philip Rucker, "Doubting the intelligence, Trump pursues Putin and leaves a Russian threat unchecked," *WP,* Dec. 14, 2017.

236 *Throughout the campaign* Cadre: Jon Swaine and Luke Harding, "Russia funded Facebook and Twitter investments through Kushner investor," *TG,* Nov. 5, 2017. Deutsche Bank: Harding, *Collusion,* 312–14; Michael Kranish, "Kushner firm's $285 million Deutsche Bank loan came just before Election Day," *WP,* June 25, 2017. "Get along": Andrew Kaczynski, Chris Massie, and Nathan McDermott, "80 Times Trump Talked About Putin," CNN, March 2017.

237 *After his father-in-law* Jo Becker and Matthew Rosenberg, "Kushner Omitted Meeting with Russians on Security Clearance Forms," *NYT,* April 6, 2017; Jon Swaine, "Jared Kushner failed to disclose emails sent to Trump team about WikiLeaks and Russia," *TG,* Nov. 16, 2017; Jason Le Miere, "Jared Kushner's Security Clearance Form Has Unprecedented Level of Mistakes, Says Leading Official," *NW,* Oct. 13, 2017.

237 *In addition to his participation* Veselnitskaia and Agalarov: Harding, *Collusion,* 232. Press release: Amber Phillips, "12 things we can definitely say the Russia investigation has uncovered," *WP,* Dec. 23, 2017. See also the sources at other discussions of this meeting.

237 *During the campaign* Words of praise: Franklin Foer, "Putin's Puppet," *Slate,* July 21, 2016. Burt: Ben Schreckinger and Julia Ioffe, "Lobbyist Advised Trump Campaign While Promoting Russian Pipeline," *Politico,* Oct. 7, 2016; James Miller, "Trump and Russia," *DB,* Nov. 7, 2016. Server: Frank Foer, "Was a Trump Server Communicating with Russia?" *Slate,* Oct. 31, 2016.

238 *As soon as Trump named* Karla Adams, Jonathan Krohn, and Griff Witte, "Professor at center of Russia disclosures," *WP,* Oct. 31, 2017; Ali Watkins, "Mysterious Putin 'niece' has a name," *Politico,* Nov. 9, 2017; Sharon LaFraniere, Mark Mazzetti, and Matt Apuzzo, "How the Russia Inquiry Began," *NYT,* Dec. 30, 2017; Luke Harding and Stephanie Kirchgaessner, "The boss, the boyfriend and the FBI," *TG,* Jan. 18, 2018.

238 *One evening in May* Arrested: Matt Apuzzo and Michael E. Schmidt, "Trump Campaign Advisor Met with Russian," *NYT,* Oct. 30, 2017. Quotation: LaFraniere, Mazzetti, and Apuzzo, "How the Russia Inquiry Began."

238 *A second Trump advisor* Wackadoodle: Stephanie Kirchgaessner et al., "Former Trump Advisor Carter Page Held 'Strong Pro-Kremlin Views,'

Says Ex-Boss," Rosalind S. Helderman, *TG,* April 14, 2017. 2013 documents: Harding, *Collusion,* 45. Clients: "Here's What We Know about Donald Trump and His Ties to Russia," *WP,* July 29, 2016. Owned shares: Foer, "Putin's Puppet."

239 *Page traveled* Senior members: Rosalind S. Helderman, Matt Zapotolsky, and Karoun Demirjian, "Trump adviser sent email describing 'private conversation' with Russian official," *WP,* Nov. 7, 2017. Convention: Natasha Bertrand, "It looks like another Trump advisor has significantly changed his story about the GOP's dramatic shift on Ukraine," *BI,* March 3, 2017.

239 *A third foreign policy advisor* Foreign connections: Michael Kranish, Tom Hamburger, and Carol D. Leonnig, "Michael Flynn's role in Mideast nuclear project could compound legal issues," *WP,* Nov. 27, 2017. Flynn's tweets: Ben Collins and Kevin Poulsen, "Michael Flynn Followed Russian Troll Accounts, Pushed Their Messages in Days Before Election," *DB,* Nov. 1, 2017; Michael Flynn, tweets, Nov. 2 and 4, 2016.

239 *In the fog of mental confusion* Flynn at gala dinner: Greg Miller, "Trump's pick for national security adviser brings experience and controversy," *WP,* Nov. 17, 2016. GRU, Misha, RT gala: Harding, *Collusion,* 116, 121, 126. Tweets: see previous note; also see Bryan Bender and Andrew Hanna, "Flynn under fire," *Politico,* Dec. 5, 2016.

240 *On December 29, 2016* McFarland quotation and generally: Michael S. Schmidt, Sharon LaFraniere, and Scott Shane, "Emails Dispute White House Claims That Flynn Acted Independently on Russia," *NYT,* Dec. 2, 2017.

240 *Barack Obama personally* Warnings from Obama and Yates: Harding, *Collusion,* 130, 133. Trump fires Yates: Michael D. Shear, Mark Landler, Matt Apuzzo, and Eric Lichtblau, "Trump Fires Acting Attorney General Who Defied Him," *NYT,* Jan. 30, 2017. Flynn pleads guilty: Michael Shear and Adam Goldman, "Michael Flynn Pleads Guilty to Lying to the F.B.I. and Will Cooperate," *NYT,* Dec. 1, 2017.

241 *In addition to Flynn* Philip Bump, "What Jeff Sessions said about Russia, and when," *WP,* March 2, 2017. Pema Levy and Dan Friedman, "3 Times Jeff Sessions Made False Statements to Congress Under Oath," *Mother Jones,* Nov. 8, 2017.

241 *Trump's secretary of commerce* Bank: "Kak novyi ministr torgovli SShA sviazan s Rossiei," *RBK,* Dec. 6, 2016; James S. Henry, "Wilbur Ross Comes to D.C. with an Unexamined History of Russian Connections," *DCReport,* Feb. 25, 2017; Stephanie Kirchgaessner, "Trump's commerce secretary oversaw Russia deal while at Bank of Cyprus," *TG,* March 23, 2017. Vekselberg: Harding, *Collusion,* 283. Reburial: Eltchaninoff, *Dans la tête de Vladimir Poutine,* 46.

241 *Once named secretary of commerce* Jon Swaine and Luke Harding, "Trump commerce secretary's business links with Putin family laid out in leaked files," *TG,* Nov. 5, 2017; Christina Maza, "Putin's daughter is linked to Wilbur Ross," *NW,* Nov. 28, 2017.

241 *The United States had never* Elaine Lies, "Tillerson says State Depart-

ment spending 'simply not sustainable,'" Reuters, March 17, 2017; Colum Lynch, "Tillerson to Shutter State Department War Crimes Office," *Foreign Policy*, July 17, 2017; Josh Rogan, "State Department considers scrubbing democracy promotion from its mission," *WP*, Aug. 1, 2017.

242 *The weakening of American diplomacy* Aug. 2016: Michael Morell, "I Ran the CIA. Now I'm Endorsing Hillary Clinton," *NYT*, Aug. 5, 2016. Asset: Glenn Carle quotation: Jeff Stein, "Putin's Man in the White House?" *NW*, Dec. 21, 2017. Three experts: Alex Finley, Asha Rangappa, and John Sipher, "Collusion Doesn't Have to Be Criminal to Be an Ongoing Threat," *Just Security*, Dec. 15, 2017. Sanctions: "Sanctioned Russian Spy Official Met with Counterparts in US," *NYT*, Jan. 30, 2018; Julian Borger, "US 'name-and-shame' list of Russian oligarchs binned," *TG*, Jan. 30, 2018; John Hudson, "Trump Administration Admits It Cribbed from *Forbes* Magazine," *BuzzFeed*, Jan. 30, 2018.

242 *Trump himself repeatedly* Matthew Haag, "Preet Bharara Says Trump Tried to Build Relationship With Him Before Firing," *NYT*, June 11, 2017; Harriet Sinclair, "Preet Bharara, Fired By Trump, Says 'Absolutely' Enough Evidence for Obstruction Probe," *NW*, June 11, 2017. Trump used the term "hoax" numerous times; for example: Tweet, Jan. 2018: "total hoax on the American public."

243 *The FBI had been investigating* Allies: Luke Harding, Stephanie Kirchgaessner, and Nick Hopkins, "British spies were first to spot Trump team's links with Russia," *TG*, April 13, 2017. FBI investigates Page: Marshall Cohen and Sam Petulla, "Papadopoulos' guilty plea visualized," *CNN Politics*, Nov. 1, 2017. Comey timelines: Glenn Kessler and Meg Kelly, "Timeline," *WP*, Oct. 20, 2017; Morgan Chalfant, "Timeline," *The Hill*, May 9, 2017.

243 *Even so, the FBI* Pressure: Matt Apuzzo, Maggie Haberman, and Matthew Rosenberg, "Trump Told Russians That Firing 'Nut Job' Comey Eased Pressure From Investigation," *NYT*, May 19, 2017. Israeli double agent: Harding, *Collusion*, 194. Julie Hirschfeld Davis, "Trump Bars U.S. Press, but Not Russia's, at Meeting with Russian Officials," *NYT*, May 10, 2017; Lily Hay Newman, "You Can't Bug the Oval Office (for Long Anyway)," *Wired*, May 11, 2017.

244 *In the aftermath* Puppet: PK, May 10, 2017. Putin on Comey: *Vesti*, May 14, 2017. Mueller firing: Michael E. Schmidt and Maggie Haberman, "Trump Ordered Mueller Fired, *NYT*, Jan. 25, 2018. Trump lying: James Hohmann, "Five Takeaways from Trump's Threatened Effort to Fire Mueller," *WP*, Jan. 26, 2018. Law and order: "FBI urges White House not to release GOP Russia-probe memo," NBC, Jan. 31, 2018.

244 *Russia enabled and sustained* Pomerantsev, *Nothing Is True*, 49.

244 *In important respects* Chava Gourarie, "Chris Arnade on his year embedded with Trump supporters," *Columbia Journalism Review*, Nov. 15, 2016; Timothy Snyder, "In the Land of No News," *NYR*, Oct. 27, 2011. Layoffs: Mark Jurkowitz, "The Losses in Legacy," Pew Research Center, March 26, 2014.

245 *It was an American* Moonves: James Williams, "The Clickbait Candidate," *Quillette*, Oct. 3, 2016. Twitter accounts: Steven Levitsky and Daniel Ziblatt, *How Democracies Die* (New York: Crown, 2018), 58. On spectacle, see Peter Pomerantsev, "Inside the Kremlin's hall of mirrors," *TG*, April 9, 2015.

245 *Unlike Russians* Alice Marwick and Rebecca Lewis, "Media Manipulation and Disinformation Online," Data & Society Research Institite, 2017, 42–43, sic passim. Tamsin Shaw, "Invisible Manipulators of Your Mind," *NYR*, April 20, 2017; Paul Lewis, "Our minds can be hijacked," *TG*, Oct. 6, 2017. 44% figure: Pew Research Center, cited in Olivia Solon, "Facebook's Failure," *TG*, Nov. 10, 2016. For a profound description of the undoing of the psychological preconditions to democratic politics, see Schlögel, *Entscheidung in Kiew*, 17–22.

246 *Though internet platforms* Facebook products: Elizabeth Dwoskin, Caitlin Dewey, and Craig Timberg, "Why Facebook and Google are struggling to purge fake news," *WP*, Nov. 15, 2016. 56 million: Craig Timberg, "Russian propaganda effort helped spread 'fake news' during election, experts say," *WP*, Nov. 24, 2016. Russians promote Fox and Breitbart: Eisentraut, "Russia Pulling Strings."

246 *The "pizzagate"* Marc Fisher, John Woodrow Cox, and Peter Hermann, "Pizzagate: From rumor, to hashtag, to gunfire in D.C.," *WP*, Dec. 6, 2016; Ben Popken, "Russian trolls pushed graphic, racist tweets to American voters," NBC, Nov. 30, 2017; Mary Papenfuss, "Russian Trolls Linked Clinton to 'Satanic Ritual,'" *HP*, Dec. 1, 2016.

247 *Russian platforms served* Ben Collins, "WikiLeaks Plays Doctor," *DB*, Aug. 25, 2016.

247 *Russians exploited* Casey Michel, "How the Russians pretended to be Texans," *WP*, Oct. 17, 2017; Ryan Grenoble, "Here are some of the ads Russia paid to promote on Facebook," *HP*, Nov. 1, 2017. Further on secession: "Is Russia Behind a Secession Effort in California?" *The Atlantic*, March 1, 2017. The United Kingdom, France, and the European Union were subjects of chapter 3. On Catalonia: David Alandete, "Putin encourages independence movement," *El Pais*, Oct. 26, 2017.

248 *Americans trusted Russians* TEN_GOP and Obama: "Russia Twitter Trolls rushed to deflect Trump bad news," AP, Nov. 9, 2017. Conway retweeting: Denise Clifton, "Putin's Pro-Trump Trolls," *Mother Jones*, Oct. 31, 2017. Pasobiec and generally: Kevin Collier, "Twitter Was Warned Repeatedly," *BuzzFeed*, Oct. 18, 2017. "Love you back": Ryan Lenz et al., "100 Days in Trump's America," Southern Poverty Law Center, 2017. Flynn: Collins and Poulsen, "Michael Flynn Followed Russian Troll Accounts."

250 *The rule of law* Trump: Speech in Miami, Sept. 16, 2016. On Butina: "The Kremlin and the GOP Have a New Friend—and Boy Does She Love Guns," *DB*, Feb. 23, 2017. Specific Russian ads and memes such as "American Gunslinger" are discussed above and below.

250 *Meanwhile, Russian authorities* Rosalind S. Helderman and Tom Hamburger, "Guns and religion," *WP*, April 30, 2017. Nicholas Fandos, "Op-

erative Offered Trump Campaign 'Kremlin Connection,'" *NYT,* Dec. 3, 2017.

251 *In February 2016* Butina to Torshin: Matt Apuzzo, Matthew Rosenberg, and Adam Goldman, "Top Russian Official Tried to Broker 'Backdoor' Meeting Between Trump and Putin," *NYT,* Nov. 18, 2017; also see Tim Mak, "Top Trump Ally Met with Putin's Deputy in Moscow," *DB,* March 2017. Trump Jr. and Torshin: "Trump Jr. met with man with close ties to Kremlin," CBS, Nov. 20, 2017. NRA and *NYT:* Amanda Holpuch, "'We're coming for you,'" *TG,* Aug. 5, 2017. Torshin has denied the charges of criminal money laundering. Paramilitaries: Anton Shekhovtsov, "Slovak Far-Right Allies of Putin's Regime," *TI,* Feb. 8, 2016; Petra Vejvodová, Jakub Janda, and Veronika Víchová, *The Russian Connections of Far-Right and Paramilitary Organizations in the Czech Republic* (Budapest: Political Capital, 2017); Attila Juhász, Lóránt Györi, Edit Zgut, and András Dezsö, *The Activity of Pro-Russian Extremist Groups in Hungary* (Budapest: Political Capital, 2017).

253 *In 2013, the Supreme Court* Carol Anderson, *White Rage* (New York, London: Bloomsbury, 2017), 151, 163; Zachary Roth, "The Real Voting Problem in the 2016 Election," *Politico,* Oct. 24, 2016. See also Levitsky and Ziblatt, *How Democracies Die,* 183.

253 *In the election of 2016* Anderson, *White Rage,* 163, 165, 168.

254 *American race relations* Ryan C. Brooks, "How Russians Attempted to Use Instagram to Influence Native Americans," *BuzzFeed,* Oct. 23, 2017; Ryan Grenoble, "Here are some of the ads Russia paid to promote on Facebook," *HP,* Nov. 1, 2017; Cecilia Kang, "Russia-Financed Ad Linked Clinton and Satan," *NYT,* Nov. 2, 2017; Ben Collins, Gideon Resnick, and Spencer Ackerman, "Russia Recruited YouTubers," *DB,* Oct. 8, 2017; April Glaser, "Russian Trolls Are Still Co-Opting Black Organizers' Events," *Technology,* Nov. 7, 2017.

254 *Barack Obama's race* Deputy: Elena Chinkova, "Rodnina 'pokazala' Obame banan," *KP,* Sept. 14, 2013. Birthday: the photographs and commentary are available at the students' VKontakte page, vk.com/mskstud?w=wall-73663964_66. Grocery store: Vesti.ru, Dec. 10, 2015, 2698780. Car wash: Amur.info, May 25, 2016, 111458; LifeNews: Life.ru, Dec. 30, 2016, 954218.

254 *Race was on the Russian mind* Adam Entous, "House majority leader to colleagues in 2016: 'I think Putin pays' Trump," *WP,* May 17, 2017. The importance of conventions and customs is a major thesis of Levitsky and Ziblatt, *How Democracies Die.* Quotation: *Vesti,* Feb. 20, 2016, 2777956.

255 *In June 2016* In fairness, Senator Lindsey Graham did say in May 2017, "When one party is attacked, all of us should feel an attack." This was not a view that was widely expressed; and by then it was too late. Camila Domonoske, "Sally Yates Testifies: 'We Believed Gen. Flynn Was Compromised,'" NPR, May 8, 2017.

255 *As Republicans realized* McConnell: Adam Entous, Ellen Nakashima, and Greg Miller, "Secret CIA assessment says Russia was trying to help

Trump win White House," *WP*, Dec. 9, 2016; Greg Miller, Ellen Na-kashima, and Adam Entous, "Obama's secret struggle to punish Russia," *WP*, June 23, 2017. Quotation: "Background to 'Assessing Russian Activities and Intentions in Recent US Elections': The Analytic Process and Cyber Incident Attribution," Director of National Intelligence (DNI), Jan. 6, 2017.

256 *At the crucial moment* This argument about race and Russia was made by Anderson, *White Rage*, 163; as well as by Ta-Nehisi Coates, "The First White President," *The Atlantic*, Oct. 2017, 74–87. Quotation: Aaron Blake, "'I feel like we sort of choked,'" *WP*, June 23, 2017.

256 *To be sure, a number* Rubio: Sparrow, "From Maidan to Moscow," 339. Kasich: Caitlin Yilek, "Kasich campaign launches 'Trump-Putin 2016' website," *The Hill*, Dec. 19, 2015.

257 *The road to unfreedom* On inequality globally, see Paul Collier, *The Bottom Billion* (Oxford, UK: Oxford UP, 2007). Donald Trump, announcement of candidacy, June 15, 2015: "Sadly, the American dream is dead."

257 *It is easy to see Trotsky*, 2017, dir. Aleksandr Kott and Konstantyn Statskii, debate between Trotsky and Ilyin in episode 8, at 26:20–29.40.

258 *In 2016, Russia* Figures from Anastasiya Novatorskaya, "Economic Inequality in the United States and Russia, 1989–2012," 2017; see also (89% and 76%) Credit Suisse, "Global Wealth Report 2016." Friends: Anders Åslund, "Russia's Crony Capitalism," *Zeszyty mBank*, no. 128, 2017. Cellist: Luke Harding, "Revealed: the $2bn offshore trail that leads to Vladimir Putin," *TG*, April 3, 2006.

258 *The case of the billionaire cellist* $7 trillion: Oxfam Briefing Paper, Jan. 18, 2016. $21 trillion: Interview with James Henry, "World's Super-Rich Hide $21 Trillion Offshore," *RFE/RL*, July 31, 2016.

259 *In June 2016* Anders Åslund, "Putin's greatest weakness may be located on US shores," *The Hill*, Oct. 17, 2017; Harding, *Collusion*, 244; Anne Applebaum, "The ugly way Trump's rise and Putin's are connected," *WP*, July 25, 2017. On the meeting: Sharon LaFraniere and Andrew E. Kramer, "Talking Points Brought to Trump Tower Meeting Were Shared with Kremlin," *NYT*, Oct. 27, 2017.

259 *Russians used shell companies* Unger, "Trump's Russian Laundromat." Trump quotations: Tweet, Jan. 6, 2018. In London, a thief talked his way into the houses of the wealthy using a Russian accent. Pomerantsev, *Nothing Is True*, 219.

260 *The American politics* See Tony Judt and Timothy Snyder, *Thinking the Twentieth Century* (New York: Penguin, 2012).

260 *The United States had the resources* For statistics, and on the relationship between deunionization and inequality, see Bruce Western and Jake Rosenfeld, "Unions, Norms, and the Rise in U.S. Wage Inequality," *American Sociological Review*, vol. 76, no. 4, 2011, 513–37. Their estimate is that deunionization accounts for between one-fifth and one-third of the increase in inequality. Taxes: Thomas Piketty, Emmanuel Saez, and Gabriel Zucman, *Distributional Accounts: Methods and Estimates for the*

*United States* (Cambridge, Mass.: National Bureau of Economic Research, 2016), 28.

261 *In the era of inevitability* Figures in this paragraph from Piketty, Saez, Zucman, "Distributional Accounts," 1, 17, 19, unless otherwise noted. 2016 39%: Ben Casselman, "Wealth Grew Broadly Over Three Years, but Inequality Also Widened," *NYT,* Sept. 28, 2017. For 7% to 22%, and 220 to 1,120: Emmanuel Saez and Gabriel Zucman, "Wealth Inequality in the United States Since 1913: Evidence from Capitalized Income Tax Data," National Bureau of Economic Research, Working Paper 20265, Oct. 2014, 1, 23.

262 *For many Americans* Lost time: Katznelson, *Fear Itself,* 12. See also Studs Terkel, *Hard Times* (New York: Pantheon Books, 1970). Expectations of generations: Raj Chetty et al., "The fading American dream," *Science,* vol. 356, April 28, 2017. One-third decrease: Mark Muro, "Manufacturing jobs aren't coming back," *MIT Technology Review,* Nov. 18, 2016. Student debt: Casselman, "Wealth Grew Broadly Over Three Years, but Inequality Also Widened."

262 *Inequality means* Exposure to inequality: Benjamin Newman, Christopher Johnston, and Patrick Lown, "False Consciousness or Class Awareness?" *American Journal of Political Science,* vol. 59, no. 2, 326–40. The increasing economic value of education: "The Rising Cost of Not Going to College," Pew Research Center, Feb. 11, 2014. Life with parents: Rebecca Beyer, "This is not your parents' economy," *Stanford,* July–Aug. 2017, 46. Children: Melissa Schettini Kearney, "Income Inequality in the United States," testimony before the Joint Economic Committee of the U.S. Congress, Jan. 16, 2014. San Francisco: Rebecca Solnit, "Death by Gentrification," in John Freeman, ed., *Tales of Two Americas: Stories of Inequality in a Divided Nation* (New York: Penguin, 2017).

263 *As Warren Buffett put it* Buffett quotation: Mark Stelzner, *Economic Inequality and Policy Control in the United States* (New York: Palgrave Macmillan, 2015), 3. On health and voting, see the next note.

263 *The factor that most strongly* County-level health crisis and Trump vote: J. Wasfy et al., "County community health associations of net voting shift in the 2016 U.S. presidential election," *PLoS ONE,* vol. 12, no. 10, 2017; Shannon Monnat, "Deaths of Despair and Support for Trump in the 2016 Presidential Election," Research Brief, 2016; also see "The Presidential Election: Illness as Indicator," *The Economist,* Nov. 19, 2016. Inequality and health crisis: John Lynch et al., "Is Inequality a Determinant of Population Health?" *The Milbank Quarterly,* vol. 82, no. 1, 2004, 62, 81, sic passim. Farmer suicide: Debbie Weingarten, "Why are America's farmers killing themselves in record numbers?" *TG,* Dec. 6, 2017. About twenty American veterans committed suicide each day in 2014: "Suicide Among Veterans and Other Americans," U.S. Department of Veteran Affairs, Aug. 3, 2016, 4.

263 *A spectacular consequence* Sam Quinones, *Dreamland: The True Tale of America's Opiate Epidemic* (London: Bloomsbury Press, 2016), 87, 97, 125,

126, 133, 327. See generally Nora A. Volkow and A. Thomas McLellan, "Opioid Abuse in Chronic Pain: Misconceptions and Mitigation Strategies," *New England Journal of Medicine*, vol. 374, March 31, 2016.

264 *In the late 1990s* Quinones, *Dreamland*, 134, 147, 190, 193, 268, 276. See also Sabrina Tavernise, "Ohio County Losing Its Young to Painkillers' Grip," *NYT*, April 19, 2011. On another pattern that needs further study: Jan Hoffman, "In Opioid Battle, Cherokee Look to Tribal Court," *NYT*, Dec. 17, 2017.

264 *In Russia and in Ukraine* On the idea of zombies, see Shore, *Ukrainian Nights*.

265 *The opioid plague* Anne Case and Angus Deaton, "Rising morbidity and mortality in midlife among white non-Hispanic Americans in the 21st century," *PNAS*, vol. 112, no. 49, Dec. 8, 2015. See also Case and Deaton, "Mortality and morbidity in the 21st century," Brookings Paper, March 17, 2017, pain medication at 32. Life expectancy in 2015 and 2016, figure of 63,600, and tripling of death rate: Kim Palmer, "Life expectancy is down for a second year," *USA Today*, Dec. 21, 2017. Primary vote: Jeff Guo, "Death predicts whether people vote for Donald Trump," *WP*, March 3, 2016.

265 *Anyone who suffers* Volkow and McLellan, "Opioid Abuse in Chronic Pain," 1257; Quinones, *Dreamland*, 293. David Foster Wallace's novel *Infinite Jest*, published in 1996, looked like prophecy two decades later.

265 *Americans were prepared* Scioto and Coös Counties: Monnat, "Deaths of Despair." Ohio and Pennsylvania counties: Kathlyn Fydl, "The Oxy Electorate," *Medium*, Nov. 16, 2016; Harrison Jacobs, "The revenge of the 'Oxy electorate' helped fuel Trump's election upset," *BI*, Nov. 23, 2016. Mingo County: Lindsay Bever, "A town of 3,200 was flooded with nearly 21 million pain pills," *WP*, Jan. 31, 2018. See also Sam Quinones, "Donald Trump and Opiates in America," *Medium*, Nov. 21, 2016.

266 *The politics of eternity triumphs* 91: Fact Checker, *WP*, Oct. 10, 2017. 298: Fact Checker, *WP*, Nov. 14, 2017. For a comparison with Obama and Bush, see David Leonhardt, "Trump's Lies vs. Obama's," *NYT*, Dec. 17, 2017. Half-hour: Fact Checker, *NYT*, Dec. 29, 2017. See also the compendium published by the *Los Angeles Times* under the title *Our Dishonest President*.

267 *Many Americans did not see* Enemy: Michael M. Grynbaum, "Trump Calls the News Media the 'Enemy of the American People,'" *NYT*, Feb. 17, 2017. "Fake news": "Trump, in New TV Ad, Declares First 100 Days a Success," *NYT*, May 1, 2017; Donald Trump, Tweet, Jan. 6, 2018: "the Fake News Mainstream Media". Cf "The Kremlin's Fake Fake-News Debunker," *RFE/RL*, Feb. 22, 2017.

267 *In the Russian model* See Matthew Gentzkow, "Polarization in 2016," Stanford University, 2016.

267 *The politics of eternity tempts* 1930s as ideal: Wolff, "Ringside with Steve Bannon"; Timothy Snyder, "Trump Is Ushering In a Dark New Conservatism," *TG*, July 15, 2017. 1929 and 0.1%: Saez and Zucman, "Wealth

Inequality," 3. Cf Robbie J. Taylor, Cassandra G. Burton-Wood, and Maryanne Garry, "America was Great When Nationally Relevant Events Occurred and When Americans Were Young," *Journal of Applied Memory and Cognition*, vol. 30, 2017. Such an alternative reality was portrayed in Philip Roth's novel *The Plot Against America*.

268 *The slogan of Trump's campaign* Using a different term ("anti-history"), Jill Lepore makes a similar argument about the Tea Party: *The Whites of Their Eyes* (Princeton: Princeton UP, 2010), 5, 8, 15, 64, 125. Trump on America First: Speech in Miami, Sept. 16, 2016: "America first, folks. America first. America. Right, America first. America first." It was also the theme of his inaugural address. See Frank Rich, "Trump's Appeasers," *New York*, Nov. 1, 2016.

268 *In Trump's politics of eternity* See Timothy Snyder, "The White House Forgets the Holocaust (Again)," *TG*, April 11, 2017. Navaho: Felicia Fonseca and Laurie Kellman, "Trump's 'Pocahontas' jab stuns families of Navajo war vets," AP, Nov. 28, 2017.

268 *Like his Russian patrons* Eunuch: Kiselev, "Vesti Nedeli," Rossiia Odin, Nov. 20, 2016. Cuckservative: Dana Schwarts, "Why Angry White Men Love Calling People 'Cucks,'" *Gentleman's Quarterly*, Aug. 1, 2016. Birtherism: Jeff Greenfield, "Donald Trump's Birther Strategy," *Politico*, July 22, 2015.

269 *In an American eternity* "Trump on Civil War," *NYT*, May 1, 2017; Philip Bump, "Historians respond to John F. Kelly's Civil War remarks," *WP*, Oct. 31, 2017. Slavery was a subject of compromise throughout the early history of the United States, from the agreement to count Africans as three-fifths of a person for the purposes of reckoning population, to the difficult and eventually unsustainable compromises regarding the addition of slave and free states to the Union in the nineteenth century. Getting one's own history wrong is part of the politics of eternity. On symbols: Sara Bloomfield, "White supremacists are openly using Nazi symbols," *WP*, Aug. 22, 2017.

269 *To proclaim "America First"* Rosie Gray, "Trump Defends White-Nationalist Protestors: 'Some Very Fine People on Both Sides,'" *WP*, Aug. 15, 2017. W. E. B. Du Bois, *Black Reconstruction: An Essay Toward a History of the Part Which Black Folk Played in the Attempt to Reconstruct Democracy in America, 1860–1880* (New York: Harcourt, Brace and Company, 1935), at 241; see also 285. Will Rogers, *The Autobiography of Will Rogers*, ed. Donald Day (New York: Lancet, 1963), 281. Du Bois was African American, and Rogers identified as Cherokee.

270 *An American politics of eternity* Patrick Condon, "Urban-Rural Split in Minnesota," *Minnesota Star-Tribune*, Jan. 25, 2015; "Rural Divide" (Rural and Small-Town America Poll), June 17, 2017; Nathan Kelly and Peter Enns, "Inequality and the Dynamics of Public Opinion," *American Journal of Political Science*, vol. 54, no. 4, 2010, 867. In one poll, 45% of Trump voters said that whites suffer "a lot of discrimination" in the U.S., whereas only 22% affirmed the same for blacks. In another poll, 44% of Trump

voters said that whites were losing out to blacks and Hispanics, with 16% affirming the opposite. Respectively: Huffington Post/YouGov Poll reported in *HP*, Nov. 21, 2016; Washington Post/Kaiser Family Foundation Poll reported in *WP*, Aug. 2, 2016.

271 *An eternity politician defines foes* Examples of violence are from Richard Cohen, "Welcome to Donald Trump's America," SPLC Report, Summer 2017; Ryan Lenz et al., "100 Days in Trump's America," Southern Poverty Law Center, 2017. On schools, see Christina Wilkie, "'The Trump Effect': Hatred, Fear and Bullying on the Rise in Schools," *HP*, April 13, 2016; Dan Barry and John Eligon, "A Rallying Cry or a Racial Taunt," *NYT*, Dec. 17, 2017. Hurricane response: Ron Nixon and Matt Stevens, "Harvey, Irma, Maria: Trump Administration's Response Compared," *NYT*, Sept. 27, 2017. On the denunciation program: Timothy Snyder, "The VOICE program enables citizens to denounce," *Boston Globe*, May 6, 2017. Paid protestors: "Trump Lashes Out at Protestors," *DB*, April 16, 2017. Holocaust: Snyder, "White House forgets." "Son of a bitch": Aric Jenkins, "Read President Trump's NFL Speech on National Anthem Protests," *Time*, Sept. 23, 2017. See Victor Klemperer, *The Language of the Third Reich*, trans. Martin Brady (London: Continuum, 2006).

271 *Insofar as the American politics* Michael I. Norton and Samuel R. Sommers, "Whites See Racism as a Zero-Sum Game That They Are Now Losing," *Perspectives on Psychological Science*, vol. 6, no. 215, 2011; Kelly and Enns, "Inequality and the Dynamics of Public Opinion"; Victor Tan Chen, "Getting Ahead by Hard Work," July 18, 2015. When asked about health insurance on May 24, 2017, the congressional candidate Greg Gianforte physically attacked the reporter. This was a revealing move: the point is *pain*. Once politicians believe that their job is its creation and redistribution, to speak about health becomes a provocation.

272 *Trump was called a "populist"* Ed Pilkington, "Trump turning US into 'world champion of extreme inequality,' UN envoy warns," *TG*, Dec. 15, 2017. 13 million: Sy Mukherjee, "The GOP Tax Bill Repeals Obamacare's Individual Mandate," *Fortune*, Dec. 20, 2017. Trump quotation: "Excerpts from Trump's Interview with the *Times*," *NYT*, Dec. 28, 2017.

272 *On one level* See Katznelson, *Fear Itself*, 33, sic passim. Cf Zygmunt Bauman, *Liquid Modernity* (London: Polity, 2000): "the dearth of workable solutions at their disposal needs to be compensated for by imaginary ones." Of course, some workable solutions are available to governments if not to individuals; it is the task of political racism to make them seem not so, and the task of political fiction to prevent the question of workability from even arising. For specific proposals for a more representative democracy, see Martin Gilens, *Affluence and Influence* (Princeton: Princeton UP, 2012), chapter 8. For specific proposals to reduce inequality, see World Inequality Report, 2017, wir2018.wid.world.

273 *Moscow won* This argument about negative-sum games was made by Volodomyr Yermolenko, "Russia, zoopolitics, and information bombs," *Euromaidan Press*, May 26, 2015.

274 *Such a turn away* Firsts: Levitsky and Ziblatt, *How Democracies Die*, 61–64. The two instances when Trump suggested Clinton should be shot: Wilmington, North Carolina, Aug. 9, 2016: "If she gets to pick her judges, nothing you can do, folks. Although the Second Amendment people, maybe there is." Miami, Sept. 16, 2016: "I think that her bodyguards should drop all of their weapons. They should disarm them, right? I think they should disarm them immediately. What do you think? Yes? Yeah. Take their guns away. She doesn't want guns. Take their . . . Let's see what happens to her." Dictators: "Trump's 'Very Friendly' Talks with Duterte," *NYT*, April 30, 2017; Lauren Gambino, "Trump congratulates Erdoğan," *TG*, April 18, 2017. Trump refferred to President Xi of China as "a friend of mine": "Excerpts from Trump's Interview with the *Times*," *NYT*, Dec. 28, 2017. Dead souls: PK, Nov. 1, 2016.

274 *The electoral logic* The voter suppression commission operated for a year within the White House, and then was transferred to the Department of Homeland Security in order to dodge legal challenges. Michael Tackett and Michael Wines, "Trump Disbands Commission on Voter Fraud," *NYT*, Jan. 3, 2018. "Major event": Eric Levitz, "The President Seems to Think a Second 9/11 Would Have Its Upsides," *NY*, Jan. 30, 2018; Yamiche Alcindor, "Trump says it will be hard to unify the country without a 'major event,'" PBS, Jan. 30, 2018. See also Mark Edele and Michael Geyer, "States of Exception," in Michael Geyer and Sheila Fitzpatrick, eds., *Beyond Totalitarianism* (Cambridge, UK: Cambridge UP, 2009), 345–95.

275 *The temptation Russia offered* I focus here on the immediate risks for the United States. On the possibility of a global return to mass killing, see the conclusion of Snyder, *Black Earth*.

# INDEX

Page numbers in *italics* refer to illustrations.

## ABOUT THE AUTHOR

Timothy Snyder is the Richard C. Levin Professor of History at Yale University and a permanent fellow of the Institute for Human Sciences in Vienna. He is the author of a number of works of history, such as *Bloodlands* and *Black Earth*. His most recent book was the political pamphlet *On Tyranny: Twenty Lessons from the Twentieth Century*. He lives in New Haven, Connecticut.